# KEPLER

# KEPLER

## The Biography

Edward Griffiths

PELHAM BOOKS

PELHAM BOOKS

Published by the Penguin Group
27 Wrights Lane, London W8 5TZ, England
Viking Penguin, a division of Penguin Books USA Inc, 375 Hudson Street, New York, New York
10014, USA
Penguin Books Australia Ltd, Ringwood, Victoria, Australia
Penguin Books Canada Ltd, 10 Alcorn Avenue, Toronto, Ontario, Canada M4V 3B2
Penguin Books (NZ) Ltd, 182-190 Wairau Road, Auckland 10, New Zealand
Penguin Books, Amethyst Street, Theta Ext 1, Johannesburg

Penguin Books Ltd, Registered Offices: Harmondsworth, Middlesex, England

First published in 1994

Copyright © Edward Griffiths 1994

The moral right of the author has been asserted.

ISBN 0 720 72045 1

Typeset by Iskova Image Setting
Reproduction by Dando & Van Wyk, Johannesburg
Printed and bound by CTP Book Printers, Cape
Cover design by Hadaway Illustration & Design
Front cover photograph: Shaun Botterill, Allsport
Back cover photograph: Sports Photo Library

*This book is dedicated to everyone who works and dreams
within the development scheme of the
United Cricket Board of South Africa,
particularly in Mamelodi, because it proves that,
if you are dedicated and brave,
anything is possible*

# Contents

# Preface

Nobody ever said he had to be fun. Where did he sign a contract that stipulated he had to exchange witticisms with the journalists, banter with the officials or lead a swashbuckling chorus of Three Men Went To Mow A Meadow on the team bus?

Nowhere. That's where.

But it never stops. The incessant droning about how he never lightens up (he does), about how he never grins (he does, often), about how he is just too deadly dour (he isn't).

Kepler Wessels doesn't care. That's just the way he is. Take him or leave him. This is professional cricket, and in professional cricket there's no room for hand-wringing. 'I train hard and I play hard,' he says. 'I don't give up and I do my best to win. The rest doesn't really matter. I may look at a newspaper now and then, but, you know, I've got other things to worry about.'

Sum up his career in 21 words? Here goes... Confronted by innumerable obstacles, he has hunted down his ambitions with a kind of resolve that most men can scarcely imagine.

He faced the obstacle of race because he was an Afrikaner in a game dominated by English speakers, but he prevailed by training hour after hour, day after day, decade after decade.

He faced the obstacle of South Africa's political isolation, but he prevailed by ripping up the roots of his life, settling in Australia and playing 24 Tests for that country.

He faced the obstacle of being targeted by the West Indian attack as a Springbok in Australian clothing, but he did not yield and fought back to score centuries against them.

He faced the obstacle of being hounded out of Australia when he was falsely accused of helping to organise a rebel tour to South Africa, but he regrouped by building a new life in Port Elizabeth and leading Eastern Province to unprecedented success.

He faced the obstacle of being told he was unwelcome in the Springbok team of 1990, but he overcame resentment by proving himself the most reliable opening batsman in the country.

He faced the obstacle of assuming the national captaincy amid public uproar over the dismissal of Clive Rice, but he took a young team to the World Cup semi-finals and to Test victories over India, Sri Lanka and Australia, leading with courage and guts.

Throughout, he has endured as much criticism as praise but in times and places when lesser men would have walked away, Wessels has stood his ground, gutsed it out ... and prevailed.

The game of cricket has been played by many batsmen with more natural talent, by many who have provided greater excitement and by many with more flair, but by very few as brave.

Why spend a year writing the biography of such a capable but unflamboyant cricketer? Because, through the story of his career, Wessels proves an eternal truth: that no matter how dark the night, no matter how great the obstacle, guts can carry you through.

Even if you don't tell jokes.

* * * * *

The writing of this biography would not have been possible without the kind assistance of many people and particular gratitude is due to the following: Ali Bacher, Allsport, John Barclay, Eddie Barlow, Allan Border, Shaun Botterill, Naas Botha, Colin Bryden, Mike Buss, David Callaghan, Mel Channer, Greg Chappell, Ian Chappell, Trevor Chesterfield, Danie Coetzer, Hansie Cronje, Daryll Cullinan, Gerald de Kock, Roger Ellis, Anton Ferreira, Bruce Francis, Tony Greig, Anne Griffiths, Kotie Grové, Rodney Hartmann, Ian Hawkey, Guy Hawthorne, Mike Haysman, Michael Holding, Kim Hughes, Conrad Hunte, Ray Jennings, Alan Jordaan, Peter Kirsten, Adrian Kuiper, Ashley Lazarus, Garth le Roux, Brian Levine, Clive Lloyd, Krish Mackerdhuj, Nicholas Maphopha, Ray McCauley, Rod McCurdy, Ephraim Mokonyama, Rob Moore, Robbie Muzzell, Vincent Naidoo, Mykel Nicolaou, Neville Oliver, Tertius Pickard, Roy Pienaar, Peter Pollock, Mike Procter, Trevor Quirk, David Richardson, Jeremy Ritchens, Peter Robinson, Jan Roos, MCC Library, Mark Rushmere, Gavin Schmidt, Richard Snell, Reg Stewart, Eric Sturgess, the (SA) *Sunday Times,* Sussex CCC, Vintcent van der Bijl, Johan Volsteedt, Louis Vorster, Vivian Ward, Kepler Wessels, Sally Wessels, Tewie Wessels, Wessel Wessels, Raymond White, Ray Williams, Alan Wilkins.

With several exceptions, the photographs are reproduced courtesy of the Allsport/SASI agency, to whom I am grateful. The front cover photograph, which comes dangerously close to telling the whole story, was taken in the Caribbean by Shaun Botterill.

I am also indebted to Andrew Samson for his statistics, to Alison Lowry and Pam Thornley of Penguin South Africa for their diligence, and finally to my wife, Bridget, who has had to share our first year of marriage with the writing of this book.

Edward Griffiths
Johannesburg
February, 1994

# 1

# Creation of an Iron Resolve

A small Afrikaans boy sits at his bedroom window, waiting, tense, focused. His eyes burn with a chilling intensity, his hair is cut in an unerringly straight fringe. It is Sunday, God's day, a quiet day. So he sits in his room, and waits, and stares.

Throughout the previous week, just like every other week, he had not sat still at all. He had charged perpetually around the neighbourhood with his friends, devising games, competing, eyes always aflame, forever looking for some opportunity to play, and to win.

He was, of course, just one among many thousands of young Afrikaners running, chasing and laughing the length and breadth of South Africa. Barefoot from dawn to dusk, invariably spike-haired, cuts and bruises at every joint, resourceful, they were the children of a unique and peculiar African tribe.

In the determination and zeal spread across almost every face, there was a spirit not found in the diffident approach of many young Englishmen, nor in the diverse athleticism of most developing Australians. It was a spirit which had manifested itself most obviously in the Afrikaner's struggle to survive ever since his ancestors fled Europe during the 17th and 18th centuries. It was the spirit that had transformed acres of wild bush into prosperous farms, that had developed the technology to mine precious metals from the depths of their land and that was prepared to defy, for better or for worse, a hostile world.

This tribal resolve, for that is what it was, had also been the source of sporting performances far beyond what might have been expected from only three million tribal members. In boxing rings and athletics stadiums, Afrikaans men and women dug deep and, through guts alone, won when others might have lost. Above all, most crucial to their pride, they produced one of the world's finest rugby union teams. As the global community padlocked the chains of isolation, the players wearing

*1*

the green and gold jerseys grew to represent Afrikanerdom at large: 'the best', no matter what the world said or did. The team became the tribal totems, the personification of glory for every lad chasing around town, the idols who had realised every boy's dream: to be a Springbok.

So the boy sat at his bedroom window. Longed-for rains had swept over the arid Orange Free State plains only a few days before, miraculously bringing fresh life to the verdant suburbs of Bloemfontein. It was early September, 1963. The celebration of his sixth birthday was imminent but, for now, the boy was preoccupied by the fact that his 13-year-old sister, Marietta, was expecting a male visitor. So he sat at his window, patiently. He didn't want to miss the young man as he walked up towards the house.

Johan Volsteedt was nervous. The son of A.K. Volsteedt, the much revered headmaster of Grey College, he had noticed Marietta Wessels at the Oranje High School she attended and had arranged this meeting according to the established rules. Boys may visit girls for an hour, maybe two, on Sunday afternoons. This was his moment and, shortly, he was striding up the drive.

'What sport do you play?'

The question, fired out from a window adjacent to the drive, startled him. Volsteedt, dressed formally in shirt and tie, fresh from church, turned to find the five-year-old boy Marietta had warned him about.

'Hello, Kepler. Actually, I'm playing cricket at the moment. Do you know anything about it? I don't think you do.'

By evening, a frost had settled over the entire house. Marietta was not talking to Kepler, and Kepler was too intrigued to worry. The date had not worked out as anyone intended. What should have been a nerve-racked conversation between Volsteedt and Marietta had materialised as an impromptu introduction to cricket for Kepler.

The five-year-old had virtually dragged Volsteedt into the garden and demanded to be shown how batsmen stood, how bowlers ran up and how games were won and lost. By the time the young suitor returned to visit Marietta the following Sunday, Kepler had found himself an old cricket bat and a pair of pads. His nagging cry of 'show me' had become 'bowl to me'. It would not change for 30 years.

Volsteedt was happy to oblige, even if, as the cricketing Sundays went by, it meant his friendship with Marietta hardly advanced past saying hello. She was not bitter. Some Sundays she was even persuaded to field while Volsteedt bowled to her younger brother.

Tewie Wessels surveyed his children's antics with pleasure. He knew other young men would soon be knocking on Marietta's door, and he had decided not to fight the wilful determination that his second son had begun to demonstrate. His elder boy, Wessel, had shown talent but less of the focused, one-track obsession. This was a dubious quality. It would, Tewie suspected, lead to a life of strife, perhaps a lonely existence in some ways, but that was the boy's nature and it was not going to be opposed.

His wife, Marguerite, had already noticed tell-tale signs. She had looked on in wonder as Kepler, playing a game where different shaped wooden blocks had to be fitted into appropriate slots, would fight to hammer a square block into a round hole. 'That boy,' she told her husband with a smile, 'will either be prime minister or he'll end up in jail.'

Either way, the boy would not be restrained. If he wanted to attend swimming practice at six o'clock in the morning, then one of his parents would get up and drive him to the pool. Neither Tewie nor his wife had known all the benefits of a close family as a child and it was their highest priority that these should be provided to their offspring. Both their mothers had died young and both their fathers had remarried. As step-brothers and step-sisters appeared, difficult times followed. It was an unforgiving era in many different respects, yet each had found their own way to the University of Pretoria and, once there, each had been pleased to meet someone from a similar background with similar experience.

Tewie, christened Mattheus Hendricus Wessels, had grown up on a farm near the town of Ventersburg, deep in the Free State, and attended school at Boshof. His ancestors had arrived in Africa from northern Germany almost three hundred years previously, long before Europeans settled in the Americas or Australia. Life on the land was hard, sometimes brutal, because rain did not fall on South Africa with the frequency or force that it did over lands to the north. Free State farmers planted maize four to a metre, while their counterparts further north in Rhodesia and the Congo, later to become Zimbabwe, Zambia and Zaire, sowed the staple food at eight or nine to the metre. Yet on the dry, brown, flat lands of the Free State, stretching away to clear horizons in every direction, there was a worthwhile life to be lived, and Tewie had lived it. As he grew older, however, his ambition turned away from the soil towards medicine.

Marguerite had grown up as a Vercueil, descending from French Huguenots who sailed to Africa seeking refuge from religious persecution in Catholic France. Her family lived in the town of

Middelburg, east of Johannesburg, and at the age of 18 she was admitted to the University of Pretoria. There she found Tewie Wessels, a tall, upstanding fullback playing in the University's first rugby XV. From those sepia days, each would become the most important anchor in the other's life.

Once Tewie had qualified in medicine, he joined a general practice in Krugersdorp, a dormitory town west of Johannesburg, but he soon sought a new opportunity in private medicine. He had agreed to a transfer to Klerksdorp when an old friend, who had established himself at a hospital in Bloemfontein, called. He wanted Tewie to join him as a specialist surgeon. It was perfect. Late in 1956, Tewie and Marguerite packed their worldly goods and moved to the Free State capital with their daughter, Marietta, and son, Wessel.

The following year their third child was born, a son, on September 14th, 1957. According to the tradition of Afrikaans families, the eldest son was named after his paternal grandfather. Thus Tewie's first son had been called Wessel Wessels. And the second son would take his Christian names from his maternal grandfather. Soon after the birth, Tewie duly telephoned his father-in-law in Middelburg and respectfully informed him that the infant would be called Petrus Christoffel.

'Well,' replied the old man, 'there is something else.' And he went on to tell of his own son who had been born with all the talents, sporting, wit and musical, but who had tragically died of pneumonia at the age of 11. He went on: 'He was also born on September 14th, and he was called Kepler. It's an old name in my wife's family, one that has been used by men as well as women, but I would be very pleased if you could let my son's memory live on in your own boy. Would that be all right?'

It was. The child was named Kepler Christoffel Wessels and soon afterwards was christened into the Dutch Reformed Church, as almost every Afrikaans child would be. The tribe had, after all, made a covenant with God. That had been sealed at the Battle of Blood River in 1838 when 300 Afrikaners, surrounded by thousands of warring Zulus on a plain in mid-Natal, had pledged their Maker that, if He gave them victory the next day, they would worship Him for ever. The following morning the air was thick with assegais, but the Zulus were repelled by the rifle-bearing Boers and the covenant was established. The day, December 16th, became a day of thanksgiving in the Afrikaner calendar.

The family faithfully attended church every Sunday and, from a young age, Kepler would eagerly take part in Bible study classes each

Friday evening with a group of friends that included Ian Palmer, who would eventually make his career as a professional golfer winning titles on the European tour. This adherence to a moral code dominated every aspect of life: from the suits and starched collars worn to church, from dresses worn below the knee, to a communal disregard for any who slipped below acceptable standards. Strict discipline was everywhere. There was a way of doing things, and a way of not doing things.

As their congregations sat in pews on a Sunday morning, all dressed to the nines, quiet and courteous, the more enlightened ministers would preach: 'Lekker op 'n Sondag!' ('So nice on a Sunday') and go on to demand whether the same standards of behaviour were applied to every other day of the week. The fact that Afrikaners, in general, regularly cited such lofty moral standards did not always mean that, in general, they lived up to them.

Most obviously contrary to basic Christian principle, they had voted in overwhelming numbers for the system of government that the world grew to loathe as 'apartheid'. In the city of Bloemfontein during the 1960s, there would have been very few voices raised against the concept that black people should live in ramshackle townships several miles away from comfortable white suburbs, or that white lives should be insulated from black lives. At the time, there was absolutely no question of playing sport against a black person, much less of sitting next to a black person in church on Sunday.

But children brought up within this blatantly racist world could hardly be blamed. Much like the animal born in a zoo, they knew nothing else; and the simple fact is that, fearing they would be overwhelmed, most Afrikaners saw apartheid as the system offering the greatest chance of survival to a group of puritan Europeans, trapped by the rising tides of history and stranded in a restless African sea. They would be proved misguided, and millions would suffer as a result, but that was the consensus at the time.

There was, however, nothing dubious about the Afrikaner's capacity to work hard, nor about the absolute commitment to family. These were common traits in the tribe and both were set in Kepler Wessels at a young age.

His ability to work harder and longer than most of his team-mates wherever he played would become legendary. Just as his forefathers had risen at dawn and tilled the Free State soil until dusk without any complaint, revelling in the pleasure of applying themselves to the job and then resting in the satisfaction of a task well done, so he would apply himself to his sport.

Equally, his sense of family never faltered. Circumstances might take him far from his parents, brother and sister, but never so far that he allowed the basic unit to fracture. In the early days, his elder brother Wessel was his role model. When Wessel went to play rugby at Grey College, Kepler would follow and watch from the stand, dressed in exactly the same strip as his brother was wearing that day. They would often play together in the garden but the six-year age difference meant they were hardly cast as rivals. Tewie was delighted that sport would play a central role in his sons' lives because, in a rugby career that took him to every position on the field except hooker and scrumhalf, he had learnt the value of team spirit in a man's life.

Tewie retired as a player in 1961, to protect his surgeon's hands, but he subsequently committed himself to refereeing the game. As he rose through the ranks of the Free State referees society, eventually becoming its chairman, rugby continued to fire the spirit of his family. Most Saturdays, he would take his boys to watch a match at the Free State stadium, a scaffolding bowl with a 50 000 capacity that had long since become feared by the British Lions and All Blacks alike. By July the grass would usually have turned a scorched brown and the rugby would always be hard, fast and physical.

The Free State side were accustomed to running the ball from all over the field, and to tackle until their opponents dropped. Their supporters, pound for pound probably the heaviest rugby spectators in the world, used to gather from all over the province and, sustained by large quantities of biltong, naartjies and brandy, would roar on the team wearing white jerseys with orange collars. It was a proud tradition, and the Wessels family was a part of it all.

Kepler would watch the game from the very front of the stand, almost on the touchline, enjoying distinction among his friends by virtue of the fact that his family knew Joggie Jansen, the celebrated crash-tackling Free State centre who would represent South Africa against New Zealand in 1970. Jansen had been his babysitter. Then, after the game, his father would pull on his referees society blazer and take his place at the cocktail party for players, officials and the media. Kepler would wait outside, just another fresh-faced *laaitjie,* bright eyes, easy grin, square fringe, straining to spot his heroes as they came and went. Some weekends Tewie would pack the car and drive his sons to watch South Africa play Test matches at the great stadiums in the Transvaal, the cavernous Ellis Park in Johannesburg and Loftus Versfeld in Pretoria. *Op die Bokke!* They seemed perfect, carefree days.

Tewie Wessels eventually became a Currie Cup referee, handling top matches between the leading provinces; as such, he became the target of abuse from spectators who disagreed with his decisions. Fans sitting near the front of the main stand, however, learnt to keep their opinions to themselves because if they did complain about the referee, they knew the referee's younger son would turn from his seat and shout back at them. Tewie reached the peak of his career in July 1970, refereeing the game between the All Blacks and Natal at King's Park in Durban, and retired soon afterwards, believing younger men should have the opportunity to referee provincial matches in Bloemfontein.

But his contribution to the game did not end there. As a close associate of A.K. Volsteedt, the former headmaster of Grey College who took over as president of the Free State rugby union, he became vice-president of the OFSRU and, for several years, attended the SA rugby board's annual general meetings at Newlands in Cape Town. These marathon occasions, where the executive committee sat around a half-moon shaped table peering down the hall at the rows of desks accommodating the provincial delegates, were presided over by Dr Danie Craven, the SARB president from 1956 until 1993, and Tewie Wessels became a popular and respected delegate.

Reg Stewart, one of Rhodesia's representatives on the Board for many seasons, recalls Wessels as a convivial volunteer who would happily leap over the bar to assist Alex Kellermann, the SARB manager, in dispensing hard-earned beverages to his colleagues. The Free State vice-president relished the rugby union life, the friends, the loyalty, all of it.

His sons played the game with vigour. Wessel moved through the ranks at Grey College, on to the Rand Afrikaans University side in Johannesburg and then into the Transvaal under-20 side, emerging as a highly talented flyhalf, but his career was cut short by a spinal injury. Wessel was married in 1976 and embarked upon a highly successful career in business, first with Toyota, then with Volkskas Bank and subsequently with the Saambou building society.

As soon as he was old enough, Kepler joined the rugby fray at Grey. By April 1970 he was playing fullback for the Free State primary schools team, running free in matches arranged as early curtain-raisers, kick-off 11.15 a.m., to entertain the crowds gathering for Currie Cup matches starting at 3.30 p.m.; and he enjoyed himself to such an extent that, decades later, he would still recall every result of that barefoot campaign.

The happy band first drew 3-3 with Griqualand West in Kimberley, then defeated Transvaal 20-3. In the next match against Northern Transvaal, the scores were level with two minutes remaining when Wessels' opposite number at fullback, a thin and scraggy boy, broke through the Free State defence and sprinted towards the try-line. Remarkably, the boy then stopped still in his tracks and, instead of running on to score the try, kicked a drop goal from ten metres out. Northerns won by three points. The 12-year-old's name was Naas Botha. Free State's season ended with wins over Eastern Transvaal and Northern Free State, but Wessels would not need his rugby boots for much longer. His winter afternoons would shortly be filled by tennis.

Very soon, sport was everything. His mother, a teacher by profession and a worrier by nature, was concerned that such a one-track mind would leave her son unqualified to do anything else when he was older. Day after day, she would implore him to finish his homework when he only wanted to practise and play. It was due to her that, somehow, he did enough. Just.

When she became a mother, Marguerite Wessels had relinquished her teaching and taken up a brand new career: driving her children to and from the sporting venues of Bloemfontein to their next training session or match. Without fail, she was there when they needed her, dropping them off, waiting patiently in the car for them to finish, asking them how it had gone, taking them home, feeding them, patching them up. Such quiet, undemanding parental care too often goes unnoticed but, without it, eager and talented boys would not grow into great sportsmen, admired by millions.

Her first shift usually began at 5.30 a.m., hauling herself out of bed to find Kepler already waiting in the hall, his swimming trunks and towel packed in a bag, all raring to go. He was among the leading schoolboy swimmers in the province and had been included in a training squad for the top performers from all age-groups. They would start their dawn session by swimming 20 lengths of the 50-metre pool at the Oranje High School, and the nine-year-old would strive to keep pace with his elders. Before too long, he set Free State junior records in backstroke and breaststroke, but he was pushed too far, too fast.

In 1966 his kidneys became dangerously inflamed and he fell seriously ill with nephritis. His father recognised the symptoms, and the boy was rushed to hospital amid fears that he would not survive. Within six weeks, Kepler had recovered sufficiently to return home but, Tewie decided, that was the end of his son's swimming career. He was no longer prepared to see the boy driven off before dawn and then to be left shivering by the pool after a tough practice. Another sport would have to be found. What about cricket?

Tewie had never played the game which was then regarded by most Afrikaners as the Englishman's preserve, but his attention was attracted by the success of the South African team during the 1960s. Galvanised by the brash, new, winning approach of Eddie Barlow and inspired by the Pollock brothers and others, the cricketing Springboks had defeated both England and Australia. Once the gentle mice of international cricket, they were starting to bare some tiger teeth, and the interest of the Wessels family, as of many South African families, was stirred. The SABC radio commentaries from faraway Test venues like Lord's and the Sydney Cricket Ground became massively popular listening.

Kepler had taken an interest in the game ever since Johan Volsteedt had visited his sister all those Sunday afternoons ago, but his opportunities to play had been restricted to impromptu games with his friends or, more often, the solitary practice he devised for himself: putting an old cricket ball in a rugby sock, hanging it from a low branch and playing strokes at it, over and over again. Such an activity might have seemed repetitive to some, but not to the boy who loved the feeling of a bat in his hand. His father was aware how much Kepler enjoyed batting because when he returned home after an arduous day in the operating theatre, he would often find the boy perched on the gatepost at the end of the drive and the pleading would start. 'Please throw the ball at me, Pa.' Pa did, hour after hour, day after day.

With swimming ruled out, Tewie Wessels sought the master in charge of cricket at Grey College to ask if his son could play some sort of role at the net practices, even if the rules did stipulate that he was still too young. The master was happy to oblige. Kepler was delighted and the decision also pleased the newly appointed captain of the school first team, Johan Volsteedt. Cricket would become the focus of Kepler's summer energies.

From March until September, he threw himself whole-heartedly into tennis. Initially this took the form of tennisette, a junior version of the game played on a half-size court with small rackets. Kepler would string a makeshift net between the trees on either side of the drive at home and challenge his brother or father. Hard though they tried, they could not beat him. Kepler had mastered all the angles. It swiftly became clear that his exceptional natural sporting talent would make him an exceptional tennis player as well.

Hours of practice at the Ramblers club courts, where he was guided by experienced coaches like Jackie du Toit, armed him with a strong serve, a solid volley and a double-handed backhand, and he relished the contest. Already so serious about the game that defeat left him in tears and bad-tempered for some time afterwards, he thrived. Like much else later in life, tennis became an obsession. Where his swimming training had started at six in the morning, his tennis would now begin at four o'clock in the morning. He knew only one path to success: work harder than anyone else, work longer than anyone else, never give in, never be distracted, always strive.

Wessels won so frequently that he was propelled on to a nationwide circuit of tournaments for teenagers. Travelling around the country, he was actively encouraged by his father who arranged for him to visit Johannesburg regularly to be trained by the well-known coach, Lou Sylvester. Tewie Wessels did not force sport on his sons. He simply wanted to give the boys every opportunity to do what they wanted, whether that involved paying train fares to the Transvaal or giving them a lift at five o'clock in the morning. He was not so much the motivator, merely a facilitator. Tewie had seen for himself the damage done by well-meaning but overbearing Afrikaans fathers on devoted sons.

At Lou Sylvester's courts, the boy practised as hard as any professional, and he loved every minute of it. He would later reflect that Sylvester had been the first person to show him the value of a truly professional coach but it might also be said that such serious, full-time coaching for a 14-year-old boy effectively marked the end of a period when Wessels could still have reaped some 'who wins, who cares' pleasure from his sport.

On reflection, perhaps such a period never existed. To Wessels, sport was never just a game. It was always a serious challenge.

Established as a schoolboy star, earning write-ups in the Bloemfontein newspapers, Wessels' early tennis career was all the more remarkable for the fact that, because of his equal commitment to cricket, his season could only start in March by which time his rivals had already been on court for several months. Despite this, by 1973 he was ranked as the No.1 under-16 player in South Africa. A scholarship offer from America soon followed.

It arrived in December 1973 from the University of Houston and it offered him $25 000 over four years, an astonishing amount of money to a 16-year-old in Bloemfontein. There were many who assumed Wessels would seize the chance, give up cricket and start devoting all his energy and time to tennis. Eric Sturgess, the celebrated South African tennis player who worked with Wessels as part of an elite national squad, recalled: 'You never know how a young player will develop. For each one who makes it to the top, thousands don't. Having said that, at that age, Kepler was certainly good enough.'

The final choice between cricket and tennis approached, but Wessels stalled for as long as possible. By late March 1974 he had begun to compete in senior tournaments and, as a 16-year-old playing against adults, he started to lose more regularly. He hated it. Such a fierce competitor could not abide this period of adjustment, simply could not accept it. He became more frustrated as the weeks went by, more intense, more tortured and more concerned. He finally snapped during the Griqualand West Open in Kimberley.

Playing the capable Cyril Rudman, he won the first set at a stroll and led in the second but his game proceeded to fall apart to such an alarming degree that his father, watching at courtside, believed he was deliberately trying to lose the match. Rudman levelled the match at one set all and cruised through to win the third set 6-1. Wessels was enraged. He stormed off court, straight past his speechless father and emerged from the dressing rooms not long afterwards brandishing his racket. All the strings had been cut. He had found a pair of scissors in the changing room and slashed wildly at the racket head. That was it. He had made up his mind. He would stop playing tennis.

His final decision had not been rational nor was it made after careful thought. It was a raging impulse. Aaaaargh! That was that. No more tennis. Such an impassioned and hot-blooded decision-making process, based on the emotional explosion of pent-up intensity, would become familiar in years to come.

That was that. He would concentrate on cricket. Houston University was informed of his decision. No one can know what might have been but one parallel can be usefully drawn. Wessels' main rival in the junior tournaments was Johan Kriek. In all the matches they played, honours were generally even. Neither won easily. When Kriek received an offer from an American university, he accepted it and worked his way to a place in the world's top ten, winning considerably greater riches than anyone ever earned playing cricket.

Wessels never allowed himself to look back and wonder if only... In time to come, he would occasionally take money off cricketing team-mates who were unaware of his prowess on the tennis court and, many years later, he would help out some friends by playing, and winning, first league tennis in Port Elizabeth. But, essentially, that was that. *Tot siens,* tennis.

Cricket would be his life. His life would be cricket. His first serious contact with the game had been made within the powerful sporting tradition at Grey College, Bloemfontein. The day he first pulled on the school uniform, he strode up the tree-lined avenues ready to learn, work hard and succeed. He had been nurtured according to all the central tenets of Afrikanerdom. Deep within his soul, his background had created an iron resolve.

# 2

## Grey College

E ven the bus seemed to sigh with relief as it veered off the N1 highway at the Zastron off-ramp and headed towards the heart of Bloemfontein. The drive had been long but the Queen's College cricket team were in high spirits, full of expectation. They passed through lush, tree-filled suburbs. Nearly there. Finally, they turned up the broad, distinguished drive and the familiar old buildings appeared before them. This was Grey College, the pride of the Orange Free State, their opponents the next day.

Queen's had not lost to Grey since 1957. They shouldn't. As an established English-speaking school from the Eastern Cape, they ought comfortably to defeat their Afrikaans rivals in Bloemfontein. Rugby might be a different matter, but cricket? It shouldn't be. It was a question of pedigree and the Queen's boys carried the distinctive air of inherited superiority as they clambered from their bus. Grey were good but they were still 'a bunch of Dutchmen'.

Whatever they were, the Dutchmen were motivated. They had put together a run of 17 consecutive victories and this was their final match of the season. Months before, the Grey first XI captain, Kepler Wessels, had circled the date in his diary: October 11th, 1975 — Queen's College at home. It would be his last match before matriculation, his last with Johan Volsteedt, master in charge of cricket, the man who had introduced him to the game so many years before. After all the hours of monotonous practice, all the planning, all the effort and all the time, it came down to this one remaining challenge.

On the Friday evening, Volsteedt summoned his boys to a team meeting and solemnly reminded them that Grey had not beaten Queen's since Ewie Cronje was captain 18 years before. He recalled their frustration when the corresponding fixture in 1974 had been rained off and he concluded by declaring they were the finest cricket XI ever to represent Grey College. Tomorrow, he said, his voice starting to crack, was the day when they had to prove it. His audience, already competitive by nature, began to sizzle with resolve.

For once, the Grey cricket team bore some resemblance to the Grey rugby team, no longer the poor cousin. Through all the college's history, rugby had ruled. It was the first XV who paraded before the entire school on the eve of major matches, amid the hullabaloo of songs and back-slapping exhortations. Grey's soul belonged to rugby. But this day in 1975, cricket glimpsed a little glory.

As the school clock ticked on towards noon, small groups of boys started to saunter down towards the first team cricket oval. Word had spread. Everyone knew about Queen's College, about the record which needed to be put right and everyone knew Kepler Wessels, the boy who had earned a reputation as one of the finest schoolboy batsmen in all South Africa.

Queen's won the toss, decided to bat and very soon assumed command. The Grey bowlers, maybe unnerved by the sight of a large crowd, panicked, charging in as though their life depended on every delivery. Line and length was lost. Wessels, a desperate frown creeping across his forehead, fretted and cussed at mid-off, tried to focus his bowlers but to no avail. The horse had bolted and the scoreboard assumed a momentum all its own. Ivor Foulkes scored 128 in what became a rollicking Queen's College run riot.

Volsteedt was umpiring, barely surviving the sports master's night-mare of watching his team fall apart and being unable to do anything about it. When Queen's reached 226 for four at the end of their 50 overs, Volsteedt languished in a pool of despair. His team slithered off the field to their orange drinks, and reaped a whirlwind. 'OK, we can't win but let's not lose it,' Volsteedt told them, failing to disguise his disappointment. 'Let's get the draw and at least we'll have been unbeaten this season. It's the best we can hope for now. Let's just concentrate and try to bat through.'

With that, Volsteedt headed back towards the square, expecting the worst. His captain felt otherwise. As the players began to disperse, he snapped them back together. 'I know we can win this game,' Wessels barked. 'And we will win it. We'll win it for him.' The young captain pointed at the departing figure of his coach. Turning to the opening batsmen, he continued: 'All I want from you is 30 or 40 runs on the board. It doesn't matter how long it takes but we need that base. Then, I'll come in.'

The young man chiding his team cut an impressive figure. Now strong and evidently confident, this was the boy who had given up a blooming tennis career for his cricket and was now playing for Free State, installed at provincial level. He had even been to England and scored runs for the Sussex second XI. He was richly talented and darkly determined. Queen's were a powerful side but, he told himself, they would not spoil his glorious farewell to Grey. He would not leave school on a losing note. He would not, he would not ... his head began to throb with the intensity of the moment.

So far as Queen's College were concerned, their old dominance over Grey was already getting older. They courteously applauded the Grey openers to the crease and were not too perturbed as the score ebbed on towards 43 before the first wicket fell. That brought a rustle among boys now spread liberally around the boundary. This was it, they muttered, Grey's only chance. Wessels strode to the crease, pausing only to tap the square leg umpire on the back of the leg with his bat: 'Watch this, Meneer Volsteedt. We'll win.'

As Wessels took guard, the Queen's fielders adjusted their positions for the left-hander. They tightened too. The stakes had been raised. The first ball was welcoming, a sweet half-volley outside off-stump and Wessels embraced it, crashing a cover drive to the boundary. Amid cheers from all directions, he turned and grinned at the square leg umpire. You see.

Nearly two hours later, at 5.20 p.m. precisely, Volsteedt bowed his head and wiped the moisture away from his eyes. Bedlam had broken out all around him. For the first time in Grey's history, the captain of the cricket team was being carried off the oval. The sport to which he had dedicated himself was briefly bursting from rugby's shadow and everywhere he looked, smiles beamed. Grey had won, scoring 227 for three ... K.C. Wessels 130 not out.

The boy had played one of the great innings of his life. In 110 minutes, he had faced 96 deliveries, striking no fewer than 24 of them to the boundary. At one stage the Queen's captain, no fool, dispatched five fielders to patrol the picket fence between third man and extra cover, and instructed his bowlers to bowl outside the off-stump. No matter. Wessels repeatedly pierced the field. He had proved magnificently, even eerily, talented.

His heroics earned golden opinions from all directions, but no praise was valued more than that of Mr A.K. Volsteedt, the former headmaster, who sat and watched every ball. Seriously ill, the revered old man had been unable to see the scoreboard from where he sat and had had to ask younger teachers to keep him informed of progress but, amid all the delirium, he simply said it was the finest schoolboy innings he had ever seen.

The image to endure occurred when Grey were nearing their unlikely victory with Wessels in full flight. Toetie Marais, who had just arrived at the crease, was standing at the non-striker's end when he turned towards the umpire, Johan Volsteedt, and said: 'Meneer, I think we're going to win.' As he spoke, tears began to stream down his cheeks. Volsteedt gulped.

Cricket at Grey would know few days of such warm wonder and high emotion. Even Wessels would know few better.

He had first enrolled at the junior school eleven years before, as a small seven-year-old who just couldn't wait to play all the organised sport he had watched his brother enjoy over the years. For Wessels, Grey would be a great adventure. He would relish the school for its robust approach, its shared pride and, above all, for the importance it attached to sport. If ever the boy matched the school, it was Wessels at Grey.

Founded by Sir George Grey, a former governor of Cape Colony, the school counted itself among the elite of South Africa, forever striving, it declared, to produce 'young men who will serve the country'. It distinguished itself from its rivals because it was bilingual. 'The guiding principle of the College,' an early publication announced, 'is a real unison of the two white races, where each could use its own language and respect its own traditions, and yet share a common transcending loyalty to Grey College.'

There was no mention of the other, non-white races living in the same country but their time would come. When young Wessels joined 800 fellow pupils at assembly in the Reunie Hall, the world was still white and black. 'We were indoctrinated,' he would reflect. 'We were just brought up to believe that we were right and the rest of the world was wrong. I don't remember anyone even discussing the political situation. Everyone seemed to agree.'

It was also commonly accepted, frequently yelled, that Grey was the finest sporting school in the country and the measure of its greatness was the number of Springbok blazers, jerseys and caps displayed on the walls of the Reunie Hall. It had become a tradition, another one, that an Old Grey who grew up to represent his country at rugby would present the jersey he wore on his début to the school, back to the Reunie Hall where he had once stood and dreamed, and there it would be displayed.

By 1964, when young Wessels first peered up at the hallowed walls of green and gold, Grey had produced 47 Springboks across all the codes. This success was explained firstly by the prominence of sport within the curriculum, secondly by the dedication of Grey teachers who were willing to coach the teams in their spare and often unpaid time, and thirdly by the fact that the school owned such magnificent facilities, acres of fields.

As a result, a conveyor belt began to carry strong, young sportsmen from Grey into the Free State provincial sides for athletics, swimming, cricket and, most vital, rugby. The best of these went on to represent South Africa. It was no surprise that Grey excelled at sport. How could it have been otherwise when so little was left to chance? Luck didn't come into it.

Wessels' rapt enthusiasm was evident every day he made the trip from his home in Innes Avenue to the school. However, much to his mother's disappointment, this zeal did not extend past the sports fields and into the classroom. All learning seemed such bread and dripping when compared with sport (at least, all except the derring-do history of the Boer War he had heard at his grandfather's knee as far back as he could remember). Wessels set out on a low-key academic course of settling into the lower grade forms, sitting towards the back of the class, enjoying himself on the periphery of, but not quite among, the hooligans, and generally doing just enough to get by.

In sport, of course, he knew no such thing as enough. From an early age, the boy had shown an unusual capacity to commit himself to an arduous training schedule and, as his 11th and 12th birthdays came and went, his enthusiasm for cricket began to grow. His thirst would not be quenched.

'We always knew who wanted us when the telephone rang at 7 a.m. on a winter's morning,' recalls Johan Volsteedt, who returned to the school as a teacher soon after leaving as a pupil. 'It was Kepler wanting me to meet him at the school and throw to him.'

To his wife's despair, Volsteedt would agree and, even in the morning chill of August, would faithfully appear at the Grey nets dressed in overcoat, gloves and balaclava, carrying a bucket of balls. Wessels, of course, would be waiting for him, all padded up. And if it wasn't Volsteedt, it would be his father or brother or a friend. Anyone to throw, so he could bat.

Cricket became his obsession. That was the key. It is often proclaimed that leading sportsmen are born, not made. Their brilliance is dismissed as an accident of birth, more outrageous fortune than anything else. Such views are exposed as nonsense by Wessels' experience. Of course he was created with a natural sporting talent but so were many others. The reason he emerged to be more successful than most is that he was prepared to work harder than most. The seeds of glory lie not in the genes. They grow in sweat.

The law of 'pain for gain' is proven through the formative years of almost every major sporting career: hours of practice, neglected studies, more hours of practice, schoolboy heroics, more practice. With few exceptions, only an extraordinary commitment leads to an extraordinary career.

As a teenager, Wessels was prepared to pay the price to be the best. He had no interest in, nor time for, the ordinary round of parties and frolicking. As he grew older, he would turn away the customary pleasures of alcohol and tobacco and, more often than not, be in bed asleep by nine o'clock. He had to be because training started at six the next morning.

Necessarily, he became content in his own company. His elder brother left home when Kepler was 13, and, whilst there were always friends in the area, he was happy with his own thoughts. Even when the family drove to Plettenberg Bay on holiday, Kepler was usually to be found fishing on his own. His brother would seek out the high life of Jo'burg-by-the-sea, but Kepler would fish.

This boyhood, dominated by sport to the exclusion of almost everything else, had its own compensations in a pattern of success. When Wessels scored his first century at the age of nine, he was catapulted into the Free State under-13 side and on towards the Primary Schools cricket weeks arranged for keen, courteous boys wearing pristine white shirts and shorts. During one such festival, at Springs in 1969, he followed scores of 80, 80 and 88 with 121. His name began to stand out. Blue-blazered teachers presiding over the event took notice of Kepler Wessels, as much for the fact that he was an Afrikaner as for his talent. By the end of the 1969 season, the prodigy from Grey had played nine innings for the school. His batting average was 259.59.

Such statistics brought respect among his peers, and served to further fire his commitment. Cricket, it was obvious to everyone, most importantly himself, was what he was good at. As he passed into the senior school, his status grew. He began to live for Saturdays, relishing both the Friday night train trips when Grey travelled to play schools in and around Johannesburg and also the home games when his parents could watch.

When factors such as the weather proved beyond his control, he would become enraged. One Friday morning, the rain fell so heavily in Bloemfontein that the Grey cricket field was soon flooded. Johan Volsteedt had no option but to telephone Roosevelt High School in Johannesburg and tell them not to travel to Bloemfontein because no play would be possible the next day.

Later that evening Wessels, upon hearing the game had been cancelled, was livid. 'How can you do that?' he raged at Volsteedt. 'You don't know what the weather will be like tomorrow. It might be sunny and warm. How do you know? It might dry out.' Volsteedt tried to explain but it was no use. Wessels subsequently refused to speak to him for a fortnight.

In tandem, the coach and leading player launched a boom era for cricket at Grey. They constructed the school's first turf nets and expanded the fixture list from eight matches a year to almost 20. More than 15 years later, Grey College would be recognised as one of the strongest cricketing schools in South Africa, and the totem of that period, Hansie Cronje, would happily acknowledge the pioneering achievement of Volsteedt and Wessels.

Wessels was selected for the school first team at the age of 14 and, once established in the routine of amassing runs against rival schools, he raised his sights to the next rung on the ladder: the Nuffield Week, an annual festival for provincial teams drawn from the high schools, at the end of which a South African Schools side would be selected. Being selected for this team became his absolute goal from 1972 until 1976.

In the event, Wessels was selected to represent Free State no fewer than five times at the Nuffield Week, falling one short of Hylton Ackerman's record six appearances. He played for SA Schools in 1973 and 1975, and captained the side in 1976. By any standards this was an outstanding schoolboy career although, inevitably, it was not without controversy.

The 15-year-old from Bloemfontein made his Nuffield début at the Wanderers stadium, the Test venue, during the 1972 week in Johannesburg. That experience, coupled with the ceremony where he received his cap, proved an inspiration to work harder. Yet again, the South African policy of promoting schoolboy sport, playing matches in major stadiums and ensuring widespread media coverage, had succeeded in firing the flames of ambition in a young mind.

That was the positive side of a rigorous system. The other dimension was the intense pressure it placed on boys to make the side. Wessels literally lay awake at night for weeks worrying if he would succeed. Sometimes when he was out, he would sadly, silently remove his pads and slink off to weep behind the sightscreen, unable to accept failure. Team-mates remember him and his father praying before matches. It all mattered so much.

As the rivalry among schools to get the most boys into the South African Schools side increased, so the process assumed ugly, manipulative proportions. Teachers-turned-selectors were accused of bias in favour of boys from their own schools, frequently with good reason. It became the annual refrain: the best South African Schools cricket side never gets picked.

Amid the pressure, some boys cracked. Others, like Wessels, thrived.

When he travelled to Cape Town for the 1973 Nuffield Week, Wessels was averaging 187.00 after 11 innings for Grey College. In fine form, he scored two centuries during the week and duly became the second youngest player ever to be selected for the South African Schools team. He was aged only 15 years and 113 days, but was broad and tall for his age, almost chubby. His team-mates included a hard-hitting youngster from Cape Town called Allan Lamb, and a bright young wicketkeeper from Johannesburg named Ray Jennings. The 12th man was also from Cape Town. His name was Peter Kirsten.

The following year, Wessels suffered one of the unexplained decisions characteristic of schools sport. In a Free State side which struggled all week, he batted under constant pressure, but produced scores of 51 not out, 71, 12, 63 and an unbeaten 58, earning praise from many quarters, but disaster struck. He was left out of the South African Schools side. Wessels was shocked, Free State cricket was outraged. So seriously, so personally did the boy take the affront, the wound would still be felt years later.

Sidney Burke, a former Springbok seam bowler, convener of the Nuffield selectors, let it be known that he thought Wessels scored too slowly and that an incorrect backlift meant he was weak on the off-side. The team as selected was due to play against the Northern Transvaal provincial side the following day and, towards the end of the function where the side had been announced, the Northerns captain happened to notice the devastated young Free Stater standing alone in the corner. 'You must take the knocks,' Alan Jordaan told Wessels. 'It's how you accept the knocks that is the key to your career.'

Wessels was cheered by the advice. Seventeen years later, when the two men were appointed captain and manager of the South African side at the World Cup, Jordaan's essential message would be the same.

Putting his life back together again, Wessels found a rock to lean on in the form of an admired Springbok cricketer who had come to Bloemfontein during the twilight of his career. Colin Bland, one of South Africa's finest fielders, was captaining Free State and coaching three afternoons a week at the Grey nets. Introverted by nature, he saw in the young Wessels a kind of application that made him eager to spend more time with the boy.

Wessels recalls most of the Grey team were scared of Bland but he suffered no such inhibitions and reaped the benefit as his first professional cricket coach drummed home the importance of physical fitness and, secondly, that nets were a waste of time unless they were organised with a clear goal in mind. For batsmen, that meant grooving one stroke at a time. Nets were not just a slog because it didn't matter if you were out or not. Bland relentlessly impressed on Wessels that the only good nets were serious nets.

Seeing the schoolboy's disappointment at being left out of the South African Schools side, Bland decided the time was ripe to unleash the talented youngster on first class cricket. Within a fortnight, the 16-year-old was named in the Orange Free State provincial side to play a Bowl match against Northern Transvaal at the Ramblers, Bloemfontein.

On January 25th, 1974, the schoolboy strode out to bat at No.9 with his side urgently requiring 55 runs to secure another batting point. When he reached the crease, he settled to find Trevor Quirk keeping wicket and Jackie Botha, a fast bowler who had toured England with the Springboks in 1965, waiting optimistically at the end of his run-up. There was no escape. Suddenly, this was the real thing.

The first ball passed harmlessly wide outside the off-stump. The second ball pitched short and reared up into Wessels' face. He hesitated, ducked, but was struck above the left ear. He fell to the ground. The fielders hurried round and saw traces of blood around a reddening mark. Someone said the boy should go off but he insisted he was fine. He batted on and Free State safely secured the bonus point. Wessels finished with 32. Not out.

He had earned instant respect. In the following match against Transvaal B, the last provincial game of the season, he was moved up to No.7 in the batting order and, from there, scored a slow 66. 'I wasn't strong enough to hit the ball,' he lamented to his father, going home in the car afterwards. Later in the same match, Wessels broke his nose when, diving to field at cover, the ball bounced into his face. But he didn't flinch. It wasn't his style.

The schoolboy continued to thrive among adults, establishing himself in the Free State side for the next two seasons, learning the ropes from team-mates like Bland, Mike Buss, a Sussex county professional who also coached at Grey, Fred Titmus, the former England spinner, and Rupert Hanley. Wessels looked and learnt but rarely spoke. Team-mates remember him sitting silent in the dressing room, wrapped up in his own challenge but, as Johan Volsteedt points out, it would have been unreasonable to expect anything else.

'This frame of mind was forced on him by circumstances,' Volsteedt says. 'If you're in Standard 1 and you are playing in a team of Standard 5 boys, if you're in Standard 6 and you're playing with Matric boys, if you're in Standard 8 when you play in the Free State senior side, then you're not going to shout the odds. Kepler was always playing in the same team as guys much older than he was, and that forced him to become a loner. He could hardly go to the bar with the Free State players when he was 16 years old.'

Wessels' performance in a successful side left little room for complaint. He led the province's batting averages in 1974/75 with 54.50, and finished as runner-up the next season with 42.62. Some sensed he had already begun to rate his performance according to these figures but it would be unjust to say he was a slave to his average, even if he was forever aware of what it was. Through his career, through all the tribulations, it would become his personal feedback system, the cast-iron evidence that, whatever the critics said, whatever anyone said, he was doing OK. It was in the book.

His summers were becoming crowded by Grey College matches, club fixtures, first with Ramblers and then with Schoeman Park, and provincial games as well. Yet his outstanding challenge, his paramount goal, was still to play so well at the Nuffield Week that even the most blinkered selectors would have to include him in the South African Schools team.

After his omission in 1974, Wessels worked himself into such a nervous state before the 1975 Nuffield Week in Kimberley that he could hardly hold his bat. With four of the Free State side's five matches complete, he had a top score of only 34. Depression set in. Nothing, he told Volsteedt, would go right. In Free State's final fixture, Wessels threw caution to the wind and scored 149. Complete relief. He was included in the team.

A more relaxed approach at his fifth and final Nuffield Week in January 1976 enabled him to produce a run-scoring extravaganza unmatched by any other schoolboy of the era. The sheer weight of statistics appears daunting but they tell the story: 80 out of Free State's 121 against Western Province B, 61 from 152 in the game with Griqualand West, 109 out of 160 versus Eastern Province, 22 from 67 against WP, and 144 out of 208 in the final match with Border. His total of 416 runs in the week was a new record and he was named captain of the South African Schools XI to play Western Province in Cape Town.

Two young South Africans who played in Wessels' excited side that day at Newlands matured during the era when the old mother country happily trawled her isolated former colony for talent. Catching that wave, Neal Radford and Chris Smith would earn official Test caps for England.

As the national schools captain, Wessels left Grey College on a triumphant note. He matriculated safely, and left behind a legend of sporting prowess that would be told and retold to and by future pupils. He did not seek such renown. For him, it was enough to know the hard work had paid off. Even at his tender age, all his greatest pleasure came from within.

He had decided to continue his career and studies, in that order, at the University of Stellenbosch. He saw no future in Bloemfontein because Free State were not playing Currie Cup A section cricket, and the idea of moving to Port Elizabeth had been mooted but that died when the University of Port Elizabeth were slow to show interest. Ultimately, Wessels was attracted to Stellenbosch by the prospect of being directed by Eddie Barlow, bespectacled, eager and widely regarded as the most dynamic cricketer in South Africa.

He would move into a different world but, wherever he went, Wessels would not forget the debt he owed to Grey College, the school that had welcomed him as a boy, offered every opportunity, and then sent him out on the brink of a fine career. Most of the man he became, Grey had made him.

On Tuesday, February 23rd, 1993, the wheel came full circle. It was proclaimed that Grey College would close early, at 10.30 a.m., so the boys could go and watch South Africa play the West Indies in a one-day international at Springbok Park, barely ten minutes' walk away. The South African captain that day was Kepler Wessels and the headmaster who decided Grey would close, not for a major rugby match but to watch cricket, was Johan Volsteedt.

# 3

# The Making of a Pro

---

T he animated confidence with which Western Province approached the 1976/77 season was founded in much more than the go-go-go captaincy of Eddie Barlow. The excitement wafting around cricket circles in Cape Town was also generated by the prospect of fielding a glamorous batting order: Barlow, Ackerman, Bruyns, Kirsten, Wessels, Lamb.

Hopes were high when spring brought green life to the trees surrounding Newlands and few of the bumper crowds were disappointed as a golden summer ran its course. The old ground purred with pleasure as the runs flowed.

Peter Kirsten, aged 21 . . . Allan Lamb, aged 22 . . . Kepler Wessels, only 19: most Test teams would have celebrated such a coming-together of blossoming talent but for a provincial side it was uncanny to draft three such outstanding young batsmen in the same season. Supported by the battle-wise, but not weary, experience of Barlow, André Bruyns and Hylton Ackerman, the young triumvirate batted with all the flair of unchained youth. Each had his own strengths and his own personality but each would become a giant of the game.

Kirsten dazzled above all. Small, always apparently agitated but so richly talented, he embarked upon a scoring streak of monumental proportions. It began with centuries in each innings against Eastern Province and continued with another hundred for South African Universities against Free State. In his next match, against Transvaal at the Wanderers, Kirsten hammered a peerless 165 in the first innings but his sequence of three-figure scores ended when he was dismissed for 22 during a second innings run chase.

He was not finished. In Province's following game, he crashed 111 off Natal at Kingsmead, did not bat in the second innings and then returned to Cape Town for the New Year's fixture against Transvaal. On and on, he burrowed away in the richest seam of form he would ever know. When he passed one hundred for the sixth time in seven innings,

Ackerman, his partner at the crease, walked from the non-striker's end, knelt down in the middle of the pitch and began to bow towards Kirsten. Newlands lapped up the theatre.

Only three players had scored six successive centuries in first class cricket (Mike Procter was one) and three others had previously scored six out of seven. By the end of the season, Kirsten had accumulated 967 runs in the Currie Cup and led the national batting averages with 74.38. Already celebrated as a gifted flyhalf who represented the Quagga-Barbarians against the British Lions at Ellis Park in 1974 (a knee injury forced him to quit rugby soon afterwards), Kirsten had established himself at the very pinnacle of South African cricket. There he would remain for the next 17 seasons.

Allan Lamb, the stocky butcher of a batsman with a technique developed on instinct, had simply taken guard and smacked the ball for as long as anyone could remember. Recruited directly from Wynberg Boys' High School, he made his Province début in 1973 and initially struggled but the 1976/77 season would become the launchpad for a distinguished career.

He scored his maiden first class century against Rhodesia in Bulawayo and his mischievous, winning grin became as familiar a sight around South Africa as it would become all around the cricketing globe. Emboldened by his Currie Cup average of 51.80, Lamb left to play minor league cricket in England during 1977 and the next year he joined Northamptonshire. There, he started his four-year qualification period after which he was eligible to play for England. The rest is history, hard-hitting, fun-packed, chunky history.

Wessels was not hard-hitting, was less fun-packed and not at all chunky. In fact, the youngest of the celebrated trio was barely out of school; he was also unsure and untried in A Section cricket. His reputation was founded on three consistent seasons with Free State in the Bowl and two admired innings against an International Wanderers side the previous season, in March 1976.

Richie Benaud, the former Australian spinner, had brought a touring squad to South Africa which was captained by Ian Chappell and included most of the Australian bowling attack fresh from a series victory over the West Indies. The threat posed by Dennis Lillee, Gary Gilmour and Ashley Mallett, supported by the English slow bowlers Derek Underwood and Phil Edmonds, represented the sternest test so far in Wessels' young career; yet, chosen to play the visitors both in Pretoria and in Port Elizabeth, he emerged with scores of 56 and an unbeaten 88 out of 182. Chappell, at the peak of his powers, made a mental note: 'I remember thinking that this was an exceptionally gutsy young man,' the Australian captain says. 'Gary (Gilmour) was giving him some problems in Pretoria but Kepler kept padding up to him. I recall Gary getting a bit upset and then shouting down the wicket, "Why don't you oil your pad instead of your bat, mate?" but Kepler didn't seem to worry much.'

A prolific 1976 season with the Sussex 2nd XI in England further boosted Wessels' confidence and, when he arrived at the Newlands nets in September 1976, he felt sure of success. Bruyns, one of the more experienced players, vividly recalls Wessels' entrance: 'We looked at him and you could see straight away that he was incredibly dedicated but it was also pretty obvious that he wasn't going to take an attack apart in the way that someone like Kirsten or Lamb could. He was a different type of batsman.'

For the first time in his career, Wessels struggled to make runs. The Cape Press had heralded him as the new opening partner for Barlow but a succession of low scores took him deeper and deeper into the dark and dank mental dumps reserved for talented batsmen who just cannot understand what's going wrong. Why, he wondered, do fielders never drop a chance when he's batting? Why, he asked the shadows skipping across his bedroom ceiling, do other batsmen play, miss and survive when he can only play and be caught behind?

There were no answers, yet Wessels found a balm for his sorrows in the down-to-earth counsel of Barlow: 'Listen chum,' the captain told his novice, 'you're never going to beat this game. You never will. If you go out to bat ten times and you crack it six times, you'll be among the top three batsmen in the world but you will still have failed four times. Failure is just part of batting. So don't fear it every time you go out. Just accept it, calm down, stop panicking and play your natural game.'

Wessels rediscovered some sort of form with scores of 22 and 71 in the match against Transvaal and then flowered in scoring his maiden first class century, a sterling 136, against Rhodesia at Newlands. It was January 7th, 1977. Together with Lamb, he added 122 runs in just 89 minutes and returned to the dressing room, exhausted. The telephone rang. 'Kepler, it's for you.' It was his father, Tewie, calling to congratulate him.

Thereafter Wessels settled. As he found his groove, batting started to seem not quite so impossible and, scoring 511 runs in the season, he salvaged a respectable average of 36.50. At the very least, he had held his ground with Kirsten and Lamb. Each of the trio had affirmed his potential.

To do what? Here were three talented young batsmen striving and thriving but for what? Had they been born Australian or English, they would have sweated to play Test cricket and earn an excellent living around the world, but they were South African, these were the 1970s and there seemed nothing to play for. At the age of 19, Wessels looked around and realised he might have reached the highest level of cricket available to him. At the age of 19, his career seemed stillborn. He was all padded up with nowhere to go.

South Africa had been expelled from world cricket, as it had from almost every international sporting, political, economic and cultural organisation, because the global community objected to the system of apartheid. The laws which forbade black people to vote, live, drink, learn, swim, travel, sleep or even play cricket with white people had resulted in complete isolation. But, of all the sanctions imposed on South Africa, there is no doubt that the sporting boycott hit hardest at the morale of white South Africans.

While many businessmen sustained contact, it was, for instance, impossible to look past the fact that one of the strongest Springbok cricket teams ever, captained by Ali Bacher, featuring such talents as Barry Richards, Graeme and Peter Pollock, Mike Procter and Barlow, a source of great pride to whites, had been effectively enchained, banned and abolished. They simply played no more. The message of global enmity struck home to a degree that, whatever the price of petrol, something like the oil embargo never could.

The first clatter of chains was self-inflicted when prime minister John Vorster rejected an MCC touring squad that included Basil D'Oliveira, a Cape coloured, as 'the team of the anti-apartheid movement'. There was still time for Bacher's brilliant side to thrash a mediocre Australian touring squad in 1969/70 but the Springbok tour of England, scheduled for 1970, was cancelled when it became clear that some fields would have to be secured with barbed wire on the boundary. The light died with the last minute cancellation of a tour to Australia in 1971. Vintcent van der Bijl, a towering fast bowler, was one of the excited young men selected to make his début on that tour, one of those who so nearly played Test cricket but never would.

'There was a general understanding,' Van der Bijl recalls, 'among many players that not enough had been done to make cricket a truly non-racial sport, and that mood was demonstrated when some of the leading players walked off the field at Newlands in 1971. That protest seems minor but it must be seen in the context of the time. It was a courageous thing to do.'

The celebrated walk-off made little difference, neither did the selection of certain non-whites in various representative sides, nor did the election of Indians and Coloureds to administrative posts. Even if one accepts Ali Bacher's later assertion that 95 per cent of provincial cricketers did not support apartheid (a significant figure because the same could never have been said of those who played and followed rugby), it was inconceivable that cricket, however liberal, English-speaking and 'nothing to do with the Nats' it might have been, would not be sucked into the gurgling drain of isolation.

Perhaps the Springboks could have beaten any opposition on the field but they were no match for the politicians, at home or abroad.

Cricket's isolation was soon total, made more frustrating because the South African Rugby Board, insulated from political reality because its sport was not played by non-white countries, kept hosting full international tours: England in 1972, the British Lions in 1974, France in 1975, and the All Blacks in 1976. A generation of cricketers was lost in the darkness and a sad list of names, celebrated in South Africa but anonymous in the annals of Test history, began to grow: Van der Bijl, Garth le Roux, Kenny McEwan, Henry Fotheringham, Clive Rice, Alan Kourie, Ray Jennings and others. They were the unlucky ones, even if many millions endured far greater suffering under apartheid.

The international boycott induced a steady decline in public interest and a fall in playing standards. Private tours were arranged but visits by teams such as Derrick Robins XIs and International Wanderers served only to reveal the extent of decay. In 1970, South Africa could have beaten almost anyone. By 1976, a virtual national side was struggling to defeat makeshift opposition. Season by season, motivation and hunger melted away.

Amid the gloom, an emerging young batsman breaking into Currie Cup cricket might have disappeared in the pool of lethargy. Wessels was lucky. Eddie Barlow might have been created as the natural cure for lethargy. At club level with Stellenbosch and at provincial level with Western Province, Barlow raged against the effects of isolation.

The feisty all-rounder had established himself as a player of genuine Test class before the lights were switched off, putting both a double century and a Test hat-trick into the record books. As the boycott took hold, he committed himself to the cause of Western Province cricket.

Barlow arrived at Newlands in 1969 to find Western Province floundering in the basement of the B section. He dressed them down, worked them up and led the side to promotion the next season. In 1971, they actually shared the Currie Cup title with their old northern rivals, Transvaal. The side was transformed under Barlow's leadership. Daring declarations, spectacular fielding, spinners hurled into the fray, sheer gutsy and aggressive cricket became the norm. There was a buzz around Newlands, the buzz of 'Bunter' in his prime.

Province challenged throughout the 1970s, reaching five of the first seven Gillette Cup finals and winning three. By 1976, the mood was set and Wessels relished it: 'Barlow led from the front and he encouraged you to believe in yourself. He was also one of the first captains to realise cricket had gone beyond an era when gentlemen strolled around the field. Physical fitness was very important to him and he demanded high standards.'

The 1976/77 season at Newlands hinged on the traditional New Year fixture against Transvaal. The winners of that match would, it seemed, go on to win the Currie Cup. Three days of intense competition ebbed and flowed to a famous conclusion. With one ball left, Transvaal needed one more wicket, Western Province required four more runs. The shadow of Table Mountain had started to creep across the famous field, evening was setting in.

Clive Rice was the bowler, Rob Drummond was the batsman. Rice began his run-up, accelerated into the crease and shattered the stumps. Begob and glory be. Transvaal had won, Western Province were gone. The Newlands trophy cabinet remained empty but the season was judged a success because, contrary to the national trend, attendances increased. The people had come and the people had been richly entertained. It had been a lot of fun.

His early form apart, Wessels had contributed in full on the field but was content simply to observe, rather than join, his team-mates in their adventures after the close of play. Generally unseen and unheard, he would sit quietly in the dressing room and go his own way. Often alone.

Of course he was only 19, and a raw 19 at that. Perhaps it was natural for him to appear detached but Wessels had already played three years of provincial cricket. It almost seemed as though he was motivated by setting himself apart from the crowd. Kepler against the rest. They're all after me but I'll come out on top, I'll show them what I can do. Perhaps this was the source of his great inner strength. The most obvious factor that set him apart was that he spoke Afrikaans and the vast majority of his team-mates spoke English.

'Most of them thought I was a stupid Dutchman from the Free State,' he recalls. 'They can say what they like now but that's how it was. There is no doubt that Afrikaans-speaking guys were not regarded that highly. Cricket was an English-speaking game from top to bottom.'

At the end of a hard day's play between Free State and Natal, Wessels had been introduced to Mike Procter, the celebrated Springbok all-rounder. The boy had been excited. Procter had been disinterested, and turned away. Wessels felt belittled and humiliated by what he perceived as a snub.

Another time, heading back to the pavilion after being dismissed against Natal, Wessels noticed Van der Bijl in fits of laughter with Procter. It was as if they were ridiculing the introverted young *boertjie*. Wessels glared and promised himself that he would have the last laugh. For seasons afterwards, he would take particular pleasure in scoring runs off Procter and Van der Bijl. Maybe he did over-react to a very minor incident, maybe he was uptight. Wessels accepts that, but this was his source of motivation.

Van der Bijl recalls the incidents within the context of the usual banter between cricketers: 'You might tease a guy about his accent or his red hair or that he's tall or overweight but it was part of the whole thing. Perhaps Kepler misjudged it. I'm sure that no one was anti-Kepler at all. He was a fine player although I wouldn't say he was among our leading batsmen at that stage. He was workmanlike, an eight-to-fiver, you could say.'

The second issue which set Wessels apart from the average South African cricketer of the era was alcohol. Most of them drank it. He didn't and he would not drink it, not even to make them like him. Within a Western Province team which Bruyns recalls as 'fairly debauched', Wessels' attitude left him open to jibes from members of the party crew, such as Peter Swart.

'Why don't you have a proper drink, Kepler?' Swart asked after Wessels had ordered a lemonade on one occasion. Tempers flared. Wessels lunged across the bar and had to be physically restrained. He would not stand back. He would not be mocked. Lamb, meanwhile, called in another beer.

From the outset, Wessels and Lamb had little in common. By temperament and basic approach, it is hard to imagine two more contrasting men. One smiled as a rule, the other scowled as a rule. The one relished life beyond the limits, the other saw greater value in living within the limits. There is little doubt that one had more fun during his cricket career but there is equally little question that the other enjoyed significantly greater success.

As captain, Barlow was aware of Wessels' detached status. 'Kepler wasn't a bad bloke in any way,' he recalls. 'He just used to give off this vibe the whole time. I spoke to him a lot. His problem was that it took a lot for him to trust someone or to say I'll listen to that guy. That made him suspicious of everyone. He was almost a recluse, and I'm afraid the fact is that one has to take one's place in this world. The world is not going to change for you. You integrate with your circumstances. Kepler had to accept that.'

He did, it was clear, get on well with his captain. Barlow showed none of the smarmy, superior airs which Wessels so resented. 'I think I was the sort of *rof ou* whom he could respond to,' Barlow recalls, 'and I admired him in many ways. He wasn't flamboyant but he was a grafter and he worked hard. That is a trait in the Afrikaans-speaking cricketer. He listens to what he's told and does it. Many English-speaking cricketers think they know better because their dad did something at Wanderers or Wynberg.'

In many ways, Wessels might have felt more at home attending his lectures in physical education at the Afrikaans-speaking University of Stellenbosch than he did in the Newlands dressing room. Set in the lap of the mountains some 60 kilometres north-east of Cape Town, surrounded by idyllic vineyards clinging to the craggy slopes, Stellenbosch was long established as a very special place to learn and an awe-inspiring place to play sport.

The Wilgenhof hall of residence *(koshuis)* had a reputation for producing leading sportsmen. Dr Danie Craven was the tutor *(huisvader)*. Wessels, already known to Dr Craven through his father Tewie, was admitted to Wilgenhof in the footsteps of Springbok rugby captain Morné du Plessis et cetera.

Soon after arrival, however, Wessels and other first year students were confronted by the type of robust initiation ceremony which had become accepted practice at many Afrikaans-orientated institutions, including most provincial rugby teams and universities. Man or mouse? Or fool?

The Springbok rugby team, for example, traditionally gathered during the evening after a Test match to initiate those young men who had made their début that afternoon. At this private ritual, the players would in turn be told to stand on a chair, swallow several cans of beer, then turn around and bend over. Their team-mates, dressed in green and gold blazers, would pass by slapping the exposed buttocks with as much strength as they could muster. It was not rare for slender three-quarters to break down in tears.

At Wilgenhof, the initiates would be told to crawl between the spread legs of some 40 *koshuis* members, all of whom would happily slap away. The temptation was to crawl as fast as possible over the wooden floorboards but this usually resulted in grotesquely grazed knees. When it came to his turn, Wessels scraped large areas of skin from both knees. The wounds turned septic, he spent several days in hospital, and wearing batting pads was agony for weeks. But at least he was now a fully fledged member of the Wilgenhof.

The compensation for this pain was usually three fine years of camaraderie and hearty slapping of other first year students as they lacerated their knees but Wessels studied at Stellenbosch for only one year. It had become clear that he could not fulfil the demands of his course and spend six months of the year playing county cricket in England. He would have to choose between studies and cricket. That had never been a serious problem for Wessels. Urged by his mother to secure a qualification, he did, however, sign on for a correspondence course in communications at the University of South Africa, which, in fairness, he did complete. In April 1977, however, he bade a wan farewell to Stellenbosch, flew to England and promptly landed in the Sussex team.

The county circuit had become recognised as a refuge for frustrated South African cricketers who were determined that somehow, despite isolation, they would make an impact on international cricket. They approached the shires with a mission: to show the world what they were missing. Through the dark years South African sport, in general, laboured under the impression that the rest of the planet was heartbroken by the Springboks' absence. With few exceptions, the harsh reality was 'out of sight, out of mind'.

County cricket, like most major golf and tennis tournaments, represented a small window out of jail through which the imprisoned gorilla of South African sport could escape and beat its chest. A South African century at, say, Hove, like a tournament victory by Gary Player or Kevin Curren, would be triumphantly reported by the morsel-hunting media back home.

For their part, the counties soon developed a taste for the South Africans because, since they were never away on Test duty, they faithfully returned year after year with the result that several formed long and successful associations with their county club. In virtually every case, the South Africans performed exceptionally well. This was their Test arena, and they solemnly vented their pent-up frustration at the top of the county averages.

At various stages through two decades of isolation, almost every county had a Bok. Rice ran Nottinghamshire, and Procter's heroics at Gloucestershire were such that the team was renamed Procter-shire by the Bristol crowd. Others earned great popularity: Kenny McEwan at Essex; Barry Richards and, latterly, the Smith brothers, Chris and Robin, with Hampshire; Lamb at Northamptonshire; Barlow and later Kirsten at Derbyshire; Garth le Roux at Sussex; Rodney Ontong at Glamorgan; Anton Ferreira with Warwickshire; Neal Radford at Worcestershire; Roy Pienaar, for three seasons at Kent; and Vintcent van der Bijl, who shone in a brief, championship-winning spell with Middlesex.

Some decided to stay and become eligible to play Test cricket for England: Lamb, Chris Smith, Robin Smith and Radford all succeeded. In normal times all would have tried to represent South Africa.

Wessels, too, saw not the slightest glimmer of hope that he would ever be able to play Test cricket for South Africa, not the slightest chink of light. If he were to fulfil his potential by playing against the best players in the world, he knew he would have to play county cricket in England.

Fine, he would go. Whatever it takes.

His initial contact was with Mike Buss, a journeyman English professional with Sussex who spent his winters coaching and playing in Bloemfontein. He had been impressed by young Wessels and, in September 1975, invited the 18-year-old to spend three weeks playing in the Sussex second XI.

Tewie and Marguerite Wessels as parents were naturally wary of sending their son around the world but, since they were planning an overseas holiday, they decided it could coincide with Kepler's period at Sussex. They would take Wessel, their elder son, and make a trip of it. Tewie paid all the family's airfares. Kepler recognised the sacrifice. He would not let his father down.

The boy scored freely for the second XI and earned himself a role in the plans of the county captain, Tony Greig. Sussex had finished last in the 1975 championship and Greig's strategy for recovery was to sign two young overseas batsmen who would have to play in the second XI during 1976, and thus become eligible for the county side the following season.

He selected Wessels and a talented Pakistani from Karachi called Javed Miandad.

That qualifying season in 1976 would unfold as Wessels' most enjoyable in England. The sun shone relentlessly in the driest summer for 200 years and he proved far too capable for most second XI attacks, crashing more than 2 000 runs at an average of 79.83. His harvest included the title of 'Player of the Year' in the second XI league, two double centuries and a mention in *Wisden:* 'A thoughtful young man, Wessels possesses rare powers of concentration,' wrote the hardy annual. That summed it up. He had no time for anything else in England, no sightseeing, no travel.

When the touring West Indians arrived to play Sussex, Wessels was granted his chance. Still only 19, he was striding out to face a pace attack comprising Wayne Daniel, Bernard Julien and Vanburn Holder. This was it. Wessels tucked in his chin, kept his head down and gutsed it out. Opening the Sussex innings, he took his guard with 40 minutes of the first day's play remaining and, against all expectation, struck out. He dispatched Daniel's very first delivery to the cover point boundary but was dismissed that evening. The scoreboard read 36 for one. He had hammered a crazy 30, including five boundaries.

More calm in the second innings, he scored 55 not out to secure a draw. Ted Dexter, the former England captain, praised the young batsman for playing straight with the full face of the bat, and Wessels felt he had made it. He was exhilarated to have scored runs against the West Indians. Eight months before, he had been playing against Queen's College for Grey.

A three-year contract with Sussex followed and, in April 1977, Wessels arrived at Hove to start his first full season of county cricket. He was still only 19. Everything had happened so quickly. As the season ran its course, he became better acquainted with Greig, a complex, extraordinary personality who would play a crucial role in the direction of Wessels' career.

Greig, tall, fair and freckled, was born in South Africa and educated at Queen's College but he had risen to the summit of the game in his first adopted country, becoming the captain of England. He would later settle in Australia, his second adopted country. Strong and hard on the field, he was acknowledged as a highly competitive cricketer. Wessels admired him greatly for that and was delighted to be joining him at Sussex.

However, there was not much that was straightforward about Greig off the field and Wessels soon began to gaze at his captain with increasing wonder. Greig appeared mildly eccentric. What sort of man was this who yelled at his fielders when they erred, who drank tea all day, who drove his car like a chariot?

Wessels squinted; and yet, he did what he was told, because Greig ruled Sussex and it was only through Greig that he was there at all. He respected his captain as a cricketer but that was all. The two men might have shared a South African past but it counted for nothing. Greig recalls: 'I never got close to him. I am not sure anyone did. He was just another player in the side. In any case I had a totally different background, with him at Grey College and me at Queen's College, and I also had a different temperament. We had very little in common. He was more like Boycott, the type of guy who doesn't want friends. I don't think he needs to get close to people.'

Greig aside, Wessels soon established himself as a widely respected and well-liked member of the side. He accepted his team-mates for who they were and proved, as ever, a thoroughly disciplined and consistent performer. Perhaps he didn't know the latest jokes and perhaps he was not to be found crawling under a table in the small hours of the morning, but he played his part and became a popular overseas professional with the Sussex public.

Privately, he was dismayed by what he saw as a lack of professionalism in most aspects of the county game. Few players were physically fit, few wanted to be, and the numbing treadmill routine of playing cricket six days a week began to take its toll. Batsmen were not distraught by failure because they knew they would get another chance the next day, and bowlers assumed the explosive nature of an accountant going to work at nine o'clock every morning. Wessels found the average English professional cricketer too cynical, too negative, too laid-back and too sloppy to be respected. Even at the age of 19, this was not the serious young man's idea of being a genuine professional cricketer.

Saying nothing in public, he put his head down again and concentrated on scoring runs. When Sussex won three of their first four Championship matches in 1977, it seemed the county had turned the corner. In the next game, versus Kent at Tunbridge Wells, on a viciously drying pitch against the spinner's wiles of Derek Underwood, Wessels scored a brilliant 138 not out in the Sussex total of 240 for nine. Greig was happy to stand and applaud.

'Look, Kepler was a superb batsman,' Greig recalls, 'but you have to be careful about being too glowing in making an assessment. I don't talk about him in the same breath as Graeme Pollock but, as a youngster,

Kepler was one of the most naturally gifted players. He was orthodox and uncomplicated, and I say that because he eventually became very complex.'

The significance of Wessels' century against Kent went far beyond setting up a fourth championship win for Sussex because, at the same time, Greig was secretly recruiting players to join Kerry Packer's World Series Cricket circus, scheduled to start in Australia later that year. Packer, a tycoon who owned the Channel Nine television network, wanted the rights to broadcast Test cricket in Australia. He couldn't get them, so he decided to sign up all the world's best players, pay them far more than they earned in Test cricket and then launch his own tournament. Greig acted as his agent in England.

These startling developments were no more than rumours around the county game in general as the 1977 season gathered pace but they were well known in the Sussex dressing room because Greig could keep little news to himself. Just like the discussions of the England selectors when he was captain, Packer's plans became part and parcel of the dressing room banter. Wessels had listened intently, ever alert to an opportunity which might enable him to advance his career. That came when, following his performance against Kent, Greig casually asked if Wessels might consider joining Packer's brigade.

'Yes,' Wessels replied. Instantly. The only problem, he explained, was that he was committed to fulfilling his one-year national service in the South African Defence Force from July 1977 until June 1978. This meant he would only be available to join World Series Cricket for its second season, 1978/79. Greig agreed. He needed an opening batsman, and a verbal deal was done.

Packer's brilliant raid on international cricket was confirmed when Greig called a Press conference during Sussex's rain-affected match with Lancashire at Hove. Amidst the outrage, court cases and excitement that followed, Packer emerged from a crisis meeting at Lord's to tell the world 'there's a little bit of the whore in all of us'. He proceeded to prove it, by announcing names of the leading players who had signed his contracts.

Wessels, however, quietly shuffled off the cricketing stage and into the South African Defence Force. When he left England early in August, he was lying third in the county averages and his 20th birthday was still a month away. He had made astonishing progress. Now it would all stop.

Ahhhh-tennnnn-sharrrrrnnnnnnnn! Ja, colonel.

His national service would prove a time of cricketing stagnation, mental frustration and intellectual refrigeration. Only South Africa asked its young sportsmen to give up 12 invaluable months in their athletic prime to march around parade grounds or stand guard at five o'clock in the morning. Yet everyone, no matter how celebrated or talented he was, was expected to serve and prison beckoned for anyone who dodged his patriotic duty.

Wessels received his call-up papers summoning him to Voortrekker-hoogte, near Pretoria. He pleaded for a posting in Cape Town so he might continue to play for Western Province. His plea was refused. The military high brass seemed to delight in publicly proving how they would not bend the rules, not even for a celebrated sportsman. Wessels marched to Pretoria.

His 12 weeks of basic training proved a unique time in Wessels' life, as it was the longest period he spent without touching a cricket bat. There could have been few greater hardships and his barely concealed anger was exacerbated when he tore a knee cartilage playing squash. As a result, he was classified as a G4 soldier, meaning he was unsuitable for strenuous exercise. One of the most dedicated South African sportsmen of the modern era, he was not unsuitable for strenuous exercise, he was obsessed by strenuous exercise. In any event, he was not unhappy to be sent to the sports office and given responsibility for preparing the SADF cricket pitches. It could have been worse.

He was now free to play for Northern Transvaal, the grateful recipients of talented young cricketers summoned to Pretoria by the SADF. Seeking to win the Bowl competition three years in a row, and thus be promoted to the Currie Cup A section, Northerns won the Bowl in 1976/77 and their hopes for a second success were enhanced by the arrival of the famous batsman from Sussex.

In the event, Northerns achieved their goal but Wessels did not live up to their sky-high expectations. He did score 146 against Western Province B but a total of only 217 runs in his nine other Bowl innings represented a depressing loss of form after his success at Hove. He had worked hard, practising each day at the University of Pretoria with Anton Ferreira, a strong young all-rounder. Ferreira, at least, had prospered, taking 35 wickets. 'Kepler was incredibly goal-orientated,' Ferreira recalls. 'He showed fantastic determination that season but I don't think he had much luck.'

The two cricketers also shared a passion for boxing. 'We would play Bowl matches from Friday, Saturday, Monday,' Ferreira, genial and widely nicknamed 'Yogi', recalls. 'On the Sunday, a group of us would go to my father's gym in Vermeulen Street near Pretoria zoo. We would work out, maybe spar a bit. It was all quite light-hearted but Kepler loved it. He got his own key to the gym, so he could go and work on the speedball whenever he wanted.'

Ferreira had earned a healthy reputation as an amateur boxer, once rising far enough to lose a Transvaal junior heavyweight title bout to Gerrie Coetzee, future heavyweight champion of the world, but he eventually concentrated on his cricket and left to play for Warwickshire in England. Wessels was no slouch in the ring either. He never fought competitively but he was rarely able to resist the temptation of an exhibition bout. Throughout his cricket career, he would enthusiastically leap into the ring 'just for fun', although once the first firm punch had been delivered, all sense of fun evaporated.

Through his dispiriting days in Pretoria, Wessels was sustained by the goal of playing World Series Cricket in Australia. He was not able to discuss his plans with anyone outside his family but the challenge ahead was enough to maintain him as the very model of solemn application.

That was not the approach of Trevor Quirk, captain of the Pretoria High School Old Boys club in the Northern Transvaal league and later an SABC TV sports commentator. Wessels played his club cricket for Defence on Saturdays and for Quirk's PHSOB team on Sundays. Once again, his severe professionalism set him apart from other players at the club. It was not a problem. In fact, they admired him for it. But he was set apart. Again.

'I tended to be very chatty on the field,' Quirk recalls. 'Kepler used to field at first slip, I was wicketkeeper and I would always have something to say after every ball, no matter whether it was a club game or a Currie Cup match. It wasn't easy to elicit much reaction from Kepler. He seemed to regard the chat as an intrusion on his concentration.

'He was a professional and I was playing for fun. I never got paid for playing cricket and that showed in my attitude which was to play hard on and off the field. I think he felt we disapproved of him because he was different but that was wrong. Each to his own. He didn't have to drink with us. Kepler seemed very quiet and shy, fairly intense about the game. He didn't want or need time for anything else. That was fine by us.'

Wessels left the SADF in August 1978 and returned to England for the last six weeks of the season with Sussex. He soon wished he hadn't. Out of practice, out of form and out of confidence, he scored 123 runs in eight innings and was promptly dropped into the Sussex second XI.

Greig had left for Australia, Buss had retired, the club suddenly seemed a very different place. As Sussex won the showpiece Gillette Cup final at Lord's, Wessels sat in the stands and watched. At the end of the game, he travelled home, on his own.

To an average cricketer, such a time would have seemed a difficult period. To Wessels, it was catastrophic. No more than a month before he was due to join World Series Cricket, he felt unable to score a run.

Since leaving school, he had not settled. Through circumstances beyond his control, he had represented four different first class teams within the space of 34 months. This blurred kaleidoscope of experience had enabled him to play against many of the world's top players and he was still barely 21. Everything was happening so fast that, at times, he felt like a spinning top, liable at any moment to whirl out of control and finish in ruins.

He had to keep going, had to keep going.

In confused moments, natural insecurity, the sort of self-doubt suffered by every human being, would take over. He had been successful, hadn't he? He had proved himself. He could bat. The runs were in the book. He'd done what was asked, hadn't he? And who was it holding a World Series Cricket contract worth 30 000 Australian dollars in his pocket? Which one of the celebrated trio who had shone so brightly for Western Province in 1976/77? It wasn't Kirsten and it wasn't Lamb. He was doing OK, wasn't he?

After fulfilling his obligations in England, Wessels spent three weeks with his parents in South Africa, a period of tortured introspection. What was happening to his life? What about his career? Stop the world, please, I want to get off. His family became concerned when they saw his demeanour. What, they asked, was he going to do next? He told them he would go to Australia and play for Kerry Packer. They asked what he knew about Packer? Nothing. And about World Series Cricket? Well, the first season had taken place in 1977/78 and there had been a few problems but it seemed all right. What guarantees did he have? A contract, he replied. What was that worth? What did that mean exactly? He was not sure but he did have this phone number in Sydney...

Tewie Wessels was worried. His son was difficult to talk to, impossible to reason with. Tewie finally found a number for the World Series Cricket office in Sydney and telephoned to ask what arrangements had been made for his son. No problem, he was told, Kepler would be met at the airport and everything would be arranged for him. Sure? Yes. All right, he could go.

Two days later, the 21-year-old South African walked into the arrivals hall at Sydney airport. He looked around, looked again. He saw no one waiting to meet him. A new adventure had begun.

He would sink or swim.

# 4

# Packer's Wild Card

W essels looked and looked again. Nobody. Nobody at all. He felt as if he was walking a tightrope to a cricketing promised land but, at this moment, he was starting to wobble. As he searched for a telephone number, he caught sight of the familiar figure striding across the hall. It was Tony Greig.

Thank goodness.

'Hello, Kepler, how are you?'

'Fine. Yourself?'

'Mate, let me introduce you to a couple of people. This is Phil Sullivan, and this is Bruce Francis. Good flight?'

The 21-year-old South African was driven to Francis' home, given a car and told that he had been booked into a downtown hotel. He would be contacted there by Lynton Taylor, an executive with the Packer organisation, who would explain the situation. Great. Wessels grinned. With relief. The tightrope felt a mile wide again. Everything had been organised.

Next morning Taylor strode into the hotel foyer, introduced himself and began: 'OK, Kepler, I think Tony Greig has told you you're going to play for the Waverley club to start with and we'll see how you go. If it looks good, we can talk about how you could fit into the World Series Cricket format. In any case, we'll review the situation at the end of the month.

'And, er, we'll be happy to pay your hotel bills here for a week but after that you had better find yourself somewhere to live ... and I would try to find a job as well. All right, mate.'

Cheers. That was it. Wessels had been under the impression that the contract worth 30 000 Australian dollars in his pocket was his passport into World Series Cricket but now he found himself on trial with a club side and without any immediate means of making a living. He stood in the hotel foyer, dumbfounded and bewildered as the cosmopolitan city bustled around him. Waves of desperation began to wash around his head. This was a disaster. He should have listened to his parents. He started to walk the streets of Sydney, feeling alone and lost. No one to talk to, nowhere to go.

He thought he'd go for a drive and at least have a look around the city. Within an hour, his mood was matched by the weather. A steady drizzle began. He tried to switch on the windscreen wipers. They didn't work. He couldn't see where he was going. This was the lowest of low moments, driving through Sydney, unable to see out of his car, head stuck out the window, drenched, desperately trying not to drive either off the road or into another vehicle.

The following weekend he played his first club game for Waverley. He felt as if he was batting for his life. Uncertain of where he was going to sleep the next week, let alone how he would earn money to buy food, he edged to nine and then wafted at a ball down the leg-side. A faint edge. Out.

If ever Wessels needed a friend, it was now. Up walked Peter Mackenzie, a Waverley player, and conversation began. 'No problem,' said Mackenzie, 'I've got a flat in Woollahara and you can sleep in the back room. It's not five star but it's OK.' The club rallied round. What about a job? There was a friend of a friend who worked for a law firm which was moving offices and they could do with some help. Hold on, let me call. Yeah, they'll take you. The firm is Alan, Alan and Hemsley and they're expecting you on Monday morning.

His spirits soared again. From the first moment, Wessels had felt at ease among Australians. He liked them for being dead straight, for accepting him, for being matish, for being so unlike reserved Englishmen.

By midday on Monday, the young batsman was pushing a supermarket trolley laden with legal papers through the streets of Sydney, dodging traffic and pedestrians. He was being paid 120 dollars per week. 'It's not much,' he had been told, 'but it's all we can afford. Sorry, mate. Take it or leave it.' He took it, working with a couple of guys who were also collecting the dole on the quiet. To them, Wessels was no more than a scraggy bloke with a funny accent. That was fine. They mocked him. He loved it. They liked him.

These were not easy times but Wessels was not going to lie down. His nature was to seize his depression by the scruff of the neck, whirl it around and sweat it out. He would work hard and, when he wasn't working, he would run up and down the hills of Sydney, run until he felt better.

His mood improved to such an extent that he was not completely shattered when Waverley's next match was rained off. He knew he had to make a mark before the end of the month but he was sure his chance would come. In the third match, he scored 123 against Penrith, cutting with such authority that the newspapers began to suggest his name for the New South Wales state side.

The Sydney media were blissfully unaware of his contract with World Series Cricket. They weren't supposed to know anything. That was Packer's plan. If the scheme worked out, events would run like this: promising South African arrives in Sydney, thrives in club cricket and plays himself to the brink of the New South Wales side. Then wham! He is signed up by WSC in another publicity coup. More proof that all the best cricketers play for Packer.

If it didn't work, if Wessels didn't produce his best form for Waverley, it would be a case of sorry mate, find your own way home.

When Wessels scored 137 against the Sydney club side, another remarkable innings under immense pressure, the New South Wales selectors duly blundered into the trap and named him in the state training squad. As they did so, they unwittingly prompted a crucial breakthrough in his career. Packer telephoned: 'Kepler, let's talk. We'll call a Press conference and announce that you have just signed for World Series Cricket. All right? Great. Thanks.'

He had been put on trial and he had passed. Wessels called his parents and nonchalantly informed them that everything was going as planned and, yes, he was going to see Mr Packer tomorrow. No problem.

Ushered into the businessman's office, Wessels remained a token in a power struggle. Greig had always intended that Wessels would play for the World XI but now Packer disagreed. The first leg of World Series Cricket 1978/79, played in New Zealand, had revealed the Australian XI to be in desperate need of a reliable opening batsman. Packer was aware that, if his venture was to draw crowds and succeed, the home team needed to be successful. He suggested that Wessels could solve the problem in the Australian batting order.

Greig emphatically opposed the idea, saying it would be seen as a gimmick but Packer was resolved. He instructed that a meeting should take place between Wessels and Ian Chappell, the WSC Australian captain. The young South African, the omnipotent boss mused, could just be his wild card.

Wessels was thrilled, not because he was going to play for Australia but because he was told his WSC contract would come into force and he would start being paid living expenses. Financial security brought an end to his days of pushing a supermarket trolley. It also meant he had proved the doubters wrong, he was going to play World Series Cricket, he was OK.

Amid the dizzy excitement and fat expenses cheques, Wessels seems hardly to have had time to contemplate the fact that he was breaking away from the land of his birth and of his family, from everything he had known.

Here stood a bold young man ruled by impulse and the simple ambition of playing international cricket. The country where he had been born was banned, so he had decided to seize any chance that came his way. Which team he played for, how much he would be paid, who was happy and who wasn't: such factors made no impression at all on his blazing ambition. Nothing else mattered. He would happily have played for any international side on any terms. Mere fate decreed that it would be Australia with Kerry Packer.

Johan Volsteedt, his friend since childhood, was not at all surprised by the news: 'For a man who was so single-minded about what he wanted to achieve, Kepler had to go. At that stage, there seemed no way South Africa were going to play Test cricket in his lifetime. He had to go.'

To others, the implications of representing another country were far more serious. Wessels' family were profoundly concerned. What would happen, his father wondered, if Kepler didn't make it with the Australians? Then he would have nothing. Would South Africa accept him back? Tewie thought his son was taking a huge gamble but was still supportive. Marguerite Wessels simply prayed everything would turn out for the best.

If the wider implications of his own position did not concern Wessels, he appeared entirely unconcerned about the effects of World Series Cricket on the game at large. These were sensational. An Australian magnate had signed up more than 50 of the world's top cricketers and arranged his own tournament. Packer was angry with 'the establishment' because they had not awarded the rights to televise Test matches in Australia to his Channel Nine network and the leading players were angry with 'the establishment' because they felt underpaid. This combination of discontent led to the Packer revolution.

*The Guardian*, a British newspaper, captured the character of what became a bitter conflict in an editorial on October 2nd, 1978: 'Cricket is a gentlemen's game, run by gentlemen, played by gentlemen and written about by gentlemen. Thus the overwhelming reaction to Kerry Packer, who is not a gentleman, was the kind of spluttering rage you get when lads from the local comprehensive drop bubblegum wrappings in front of the pavilion. How can one have anything to do with chaps who don't know how to behave?'

Michael Davie, writing in *The Observer,* had elaborated on a similar theme a year earlier while Packer was suing the cricket authorities for banning the players who joined him: 'There could be no greater contrast between two groups than between the Authorities and Packer's men. You sense, at once, a different view not only of cricket but of life itself. The Authorities come to court in sober dark suits. The Packer men are a riot of colour: Packer in pale blue with a multi-coloured tie; Richie Benaud, the former Australian captain working for Packer, in a polychromatic costume with crocodile shoes; a Packer partner in primrose yellow; another fellow in orange leather.'

Against this background of schism and chaos, a 21-year-old South African was drafted into a side which purported to represent Australia on nothing more substantial than the spur of the moment. On the one hand, he was lucky because such chicanery would not have been possible in any other era. On the other, he was brave because he had put himself in position to take the chance.

'Good evening, Mr Chappell.'

The personification of Australian cricket sat across the table in the bar of a Sydney hotel. Rough and tough, brave and sometimes rude, Ian Chappell had led Australia through the 1970s and led them from the front, playing hard in every possible sense. Pulling the trigger of such devastating guns as Lillee and Thomson, he had become a giant of the game. Above all, he wanted to win. As captain of the WSC Australian XI, he was not winning against either the West Indies XI or the all-star Rest of the World team.

He felt he needed an opener. Bruce Laird and Ian Davis were struggling to be consistent. Packer had mentioned Wessels and Chappell remembered the name from the International Wanderers tour to South Africa in 1976. So here he sat, with two Packer executives, talking business.

'Do you want to play for Australia?' Chappell asked.

'Yes,' replied Wessels.

'Are you going to live here?'

'Yes, I want to stay here. I like the place and I enjoy the people. But most of all I want to play cricket.'

That was good enough for Chappell. As the evening ran its course, he warmed to the sober young South African. There was a mutual understanding and that was enough. Wessels recalls his first impression of Chappell was that here was a man for whom others would run through a wall. Chappell looks back and says he recognised in Wessels the sort of fighting spirit he admired. They were going to get along. The Packer men nodded. It's a deal.

News that Wessels would join the Australian squad in Perth was not greeted with unanimous applause among his future team-mates, notably the upper order batsmen. So Chappell called a meeting. 'Wessels is coming to play with us,' he said. 'If you don't like it, score more runs than him.'

Most of the mumbling, at least that which was audible, had stopped by the time Wessels checked in at Perth's Sheraton hotel, suddenly finding himself among such legends as Dennis Lillee, Rod Marsh and the Chappell brothers. At squad training that afternoon, Wessels was unable to disguise his nerves but he need not have worried. The Australians soon appreciated his thorough attitude to nets and acknowledged him as a cricketer who deserved to be taken seriously. In the changing room afterwards, Marsh christened the newcomer 'Chopper'. That would be his nickname. It stuck.

The following day, Wessels was taken aside and told he would play a couple of matches for the Cavaliers, a second-string WSC World XI, to help him find his feet before being drafted into the Australian side. His destination was Kalgoorlie, outside Perth. There he found that the Cavaliers were led by a familiar figure, Eddie Barlow. The all-rounder congratulated Wessels on joining up with the Australian squad. 'As South Africans, we had to take what we could get,' Barlow recalls. 'We didn't have much to lose because we were already banned anyway. I completely understood Kepler's position.'

On November 24th, 1978, the Cavaliers team batted first against the WSC West Indian side. Wessels opened the innings and found himself under bombardment from Andy Roberts and Joel Garner. Before long, a short delivery from Roberts thudded into his wiry frame. Chappell, who had driven to Kalgoorlie to watch his new acquisition, thought ribs must have been broken but Wessels waved away the physiotherapist. Only two overs later, another short ball slammed into his chest. Wessels crumpled and was led off the field. Chappell pushed his way through the milling crowds to the Cavaliers dressing room.

'You all right, mate?' he asked.

'Yeah, I'm fine. I don't know why I had to come off.'

Bandaged around the chest, Wessels resumed his innings and finished with 54 out of his team's 224 for six. Chappell had seen enough. He left the ground happy and convinced that 'Chopper' had got what it takes.

Barlow's side returned to action two days later, playing the Rest of the World XI at Bunbury. Wessels thrived again, scoring 50 in a total of 181 on a sub-standard pitch even though the Rest of the World won when Mike Procter, another South African relishing the top-class competition, struck a straight boundary off the last ball to finish unbeaten on 88.

Two half-centuries in two innings had confirmed Wessels' potential and he travelled back to Sydney with the Australian team. The next stop in the garish extravaganza of smash-bang action would be a 'clash' between the Australians and the West Indians, the first major match under floodlights at the Sydney Cricket Ground. The six pylons, monuments to the revolution, became known as Packer's cigars and 44 638 people watched history in the making.

Wessels was entranced by the dramatic atmosphere of the old ground in its new clothing, hardly minding that he was left out of the starting XI. World Series Cricket had struggled to draw spectators the previous year but was being saved by the thrill of cricket under lights and the pizzazz of unashamed show business. The players were introduced one by one over the public address system as they sprinted on to the field. The game had become a TV show. Play could not start until the TV advertisements had finished. These income-earners were now regarded as part of the game, part of the business: Greig endorsing cereals and irons, Daniel eating MacDonald's hamburgers, et cetera... all punctuated by the numbing Packer theme song 'Come on, Aussies, come on'.

Cricket, the old game, had been given an American facelift: microphones had been sunk into the wicket to broadcast the thump of bat on ball; a 42-inch zoom lens showed the sweat and tension on the players' faces; golf buggies took the drinks out to the middle more quickly; the batsmen were interviewed. There was no limit to the ideas of the men in canary yellow.

On the field, the Australians dismissed the West Indians for 128 and ended up winning by five wickets. This success was followed the next night by victory over the World XI. Still Wessels was kept back, given time to watch and become accustomed to the sights and sounds of his new surroundings.

Chappell finally decided he was ready. The name WESSELS was published at the top of the WSC Australian team to play a one-day match against a World XI, spearheaded by four South Africans, Rice, Richards, Le Roux and Procter, in Sydney. Wessels sat in the dressing room, more nervous than ever. Lillee, big, rough, great, kind-hearted, wished him luck.

Wessels scored 20 and was satisfied. He had provided the start Chappell was looking for. He made 21 in the next game, then hit 92 versus the Cavaliers. Early in that innings he had been struck by yet another rising delivery but, of course, he had batted on. The Australians were scheduled to play the Rest of the World the next day. Chappell asked Wessels if he was available. Yes I am, said Wessels. That's the spirit, thought Chappell. The exchange might have been plucked from a 1950s Boy's Own magazine but that was its nature. The young man had to do what the young man had to do and, amid the frantic blur of non-stop one-day internationals, he slotted into the Australian side with amazing ease.

He could hardly believe the pace of events. A Supertest against the Rest of the World to be played over five days and evenings under floodlights at VFL Park in Melbourne beckoned. Wessels let his eyes run over the opposition team sheet and was exhilarated to be playing in such company: Barry Richards, Dennis Amiss, Majiid Khan, Zaheer Abbas, Javed Miandad, Asif Iqbal, Procter, Imran Khan, Allan Knott, Clive Rice and Garth le Roux. Greig, ironically, had been dropped following a run of indifferent form.

The match was dominated by the pitch, a strip grown in a special concrete box. Such preparation was necessary because several of the Packer matches were played in football grounds and, on these occasions, a cricket pitch literally had to be carried into the stadium. The result was a surface taken from a fast bowler's wildest dreams. Barry Richards, ever laconic, was reported to have joked that World Series Cricket would soon be played only by fast bowlers and batsmen in armour. No fielders would be necessary because the batsmen would be unable to run in their protective clothing.

Lillee wasn't complaining when he took four for 51 and the Rest of the World were bowled out for 175. That left Wessels the unusual task of launching his first 'Test' innings shortly before nine o'clock at night.

To his great frustration, he was dismissed in distressingly familiar fashion: playing at yet another fine Procter outswinger to be caught at gully. He had scored eight and the Australian XI were ruthlessly skittled for 150.

Rice was bowling as fast as at any stage of his career and seized four wickets. 'Kepler looked in good form,' he recalls. 'He had a limited range of strokes and he didn't give much away. His discipline was fantastic but we generally thought we had a chance swinging the ball away from him. Proccie was bowling brilliant outswingers at the time.'

Ultimately the WSC Australians were left to score 292 for victory, a task which always seemed beyond them on such a lively pitch. They were bowled out for 190 with only four batsmen reaching double figures: Ian Chappell scored 11, Greg Chappell 81, Marsh 17 and Wessels a defiant 46 before being deceived by Underwood. Even in defeat, Wessels had performed well. He had enjoyed batting with Ian Chappell, watching in awe as his captain launched a volley of amazing abuse at the bowlers and fielders, notably Javed Miandad at short leg, simply to divert the bowlers from the youngster at the other end.

Any contentment, however, was swept away when Packer himself burst into the changing room. Looking directly at Wessels, the boss stormed: 'We don't import people to score 40s. Get your arse into gear.'

Wessels was dumb-struck. Chappell said nothing.

He was playing well, wasn't he? Look at the averages. There he was, over 40. What was wrong with that? The Australian side, playing under the burden of Packer's commercial necessity, regained some prestige by defeating the Rest of the World team in a one-day match. Greg Chappell, all classical elegance, top-scored with 62, Wessels made 58 and Ian Chappell struck 40. This was precisely the sort of company Wessels had longed to keep. It was hard, demanding, serious cricket, and his team-mates really were his mates.

The contest was intense. In the next Supertest, against the West Indians, Wessels found himself facing Roberts, Croft, Garner and King. When a bouncer from Croft struck him on the back of the head, he seemed to stagger. A gasp of unease spread through the crowd but he stayed on his feet. This was it, the heat of the battle. Would he give in? Never. The bump on his head began to throb but he gritted his teeth and was soon cutting Roberts defiantly to the cover point boundary. He moved his score along to 66.

Croft rumbled in again. The ball was short of a length, cut back at the left-handed Wessels and thudded into his groin. His abdomen seemed to explode in agony. He fell to the pitch and fainted. A doctor raced on to the field and brought him round. He suggested Wessels leave the field. No. There was only 20 minutes until the dinner break. He would guts it out till then. He was in a new country and he was going to prove himself. He would not yield.

Wessels recuperated during the interval and promptly resumed his innings. Back at the crease, he resolutely reached his century. Mission accomplished. He was finally dismissed for 126. When Packer arrived in the dressing room soon after stumps, Chappell was waiting. 'So Kerry, is that the sort of innings we expect from an import?' Wessels grinned, all teeth. Again and again, Wessels had shown astonishing levels of commitment and courage.

The Supertest final between the Australians and the Rest of the World was dominated by South Africans but not the one playing for Australia. Greig had fired some pre-match quotes into the headlines and they seemed to be borne out when the Australian XI were dismissed for 147. Wessels was caught by Richards at slip off the bowling of Procter (who else?) for 27. Ten Australian wickets had been shared between Rice, who took two, Procter, three, and Le Roux, at the peak of his form, who claimed five for 57.

Lillee struck back but the Rest of the World scrambled to 168 and then dismissed the Australians for 219. Wessels went cheaply, removed by Procter, again. The Rest of the World were left 224 to win and Barry Richards turned the task into a jaunt. The genius opener scored an unbeaten 101 and, with Procter adding a half-century, victory was secured at a stroll by five wickets. 'It was tough cricket,' Procter recalls. 'It was hard to believe the things that were said in the middle.' The Springboks in exile had excelled beyond anyone's expectation: Le Roux was Man of the Series, Rice was the runner-up.

The culmination of the seemingly eternal one-day series was a best-of-five final between the Australian XI and the West Indians. Wessels retained his place but felt he was in need of runs. Chappell laid down what he wanted from his opening batsman: 'Bat the full 50 overs, Chopper. In one-day cricket, you need a platform and I want you to build it for us.'

In the first match of the final, Wessels followed Chappell's instructions and scored an unbeaten 136 out of the Australian total of 208. He had struck 16 boundaries and a six in one of the superb, free-flowing one-day innings which would punctuate his career. Clive

Lloyd's West Indian side managed only 169 for nine in reply, and the Australians were one-up.

Wessels' confidence soared. 'It was an incredible thrill,' he recalls. 'Everything was going well. I was really into the whole thing. I was psyched out of my brain.' He was seeing the ball early, he was happy within the team, and he was thriving against the most admired bowling attack in the world. In the next match, he top-scored with 40 but was run out by a diving Viv Richards. The West Indians won the match and levelled the series 1-1.

He would not be contained. The West Indians won the third match as well but Wessels had thrived again, scoring 70 from 90 balls. For the first time in his professional career, Wessels felt completely at home in his team's dressing room. He was mercilessly teased, about his way of dressing, his accent, and he enjoyed it. Senior players like Lillee and the Chappells clearly accepted him and he responded to their positive vibes by relaxing. He was even to be seen sipping on a can of beer after a successful day's play.

The influence of Ian Chappell was absolutely crucial to his development, both as a player and as a member of the team. Wessels whole-heartedly pledged himself to his captain: 'In Ian Chappell, I found everything I was looking for. He was somebody I could look up to because he gave everything on the field, for his team, for his country, the whole thing. I just used to watch and follow. He lived everything at full pace. There were some great arguments in that dressing room and some great laughs. Everything was built around guts and respect and winning. I learnt so much so quickly.'

Chappell used to say he wanted people who would stick it out 'in the trenches' and he could hardly have found a more determined infantryman than Wessels. After all the rough edges of the past, at Western Province, Sussex and Northern Transvaal, Chappell seemed to be the answer: Chappell, who would tell his players privately if he thought they were wrong but who would never fail to defend them in public; Chappell, who was dead straight with everyone from the cleaner in the changing room to Kerry Packer; Chappell, who was prepared to gamble on the field but only when the opposition had absolutely no chance of winning. Chappell soon became, and would remain, an idol.

With the West Indians leading 2-1, the fourth leg of the WSC one-day final ended in chaos and called into question the credibility of the entire series. Chasing 241 to win, the West Indians seemed to be coasting to victory but it soon became clear that the Australians would not finish bowling their 50 overs by the scheduled end of the match at 10.30 p.m., in which case the result would have to be determined by the runrate at that time.

As the likelihood of such an unsatisfactory conclusion grew, Packer called Andrew Caro, the WSC managing director, and said he wanted an extra quarter of an hour to be played. Caro was unwilling to run on to the field and deliver the message himself so he delegated the task to the Australian 12th man who passed the instruction to Chappell, but not to either of the umpires or to Lloyd. The West Indian captain was batting at the time.

When 10.30 p.m. arrived, the umpires and batsmen left the field, believing the West Indies had won on a faster scoring rate but the Australians were left standing around the field, bemused and bewildered. Packer later apologised to Chappell's side for the confusion and offered them a share of the $35 000 prize money as compensation. Chappell refused, saying the money was not the issue. He said his side had simply wanted to win. 'Dear Kerry,' Caro was reported as saying afterwards. 'He just can't emotionally keep out of it.'

The shambles prompted a crisis of confidence. To many, the Supertests had not been super at all. They were scarcely noticed beyond Australia and viewed with suspicion by the majority of cricket followers worldwide. How could the players be motivated? Were results fixed by the organisers? Now, the one-day rules appeared to be made up as they went along. The sheer closed nature of an organisation in which every player and official was employed by one powerful man used to getting his own way, bred widespread suspicion.

There is, none the less, no reason to doubt that the players were trying nor that the standard of play was of international quality. Greg Chappell, for one, is adamant. 'World Series Cricket was certainly the toughest form of cricket I ever played,' he recalls. 'It was competitive because of the situation. When the establishment threatened bans, it motivated the players to pull together and prove it was all worth while. There was a spirit among the teams that we were in this together and we had to make it work.'

The WSC teams' shared opposition, as such, was the Ashes series which was being played concurrently. Graham Yallop had been given the task of leading a necessarily young Australian side against England and their inevitable defeat earned them the unkind nickname of 'lambs to the slaughter'. The Ashes suffered in comparison with the show business and there was discussion as to whether the old urn should be contested at all. One correspondent of *The Guardian* newspaper went so far as to suggest the official series should be 'played for a specific set of Ashes — preferably Kerry Packer's.'

History, however, would judge World Series Cricket more kindly. As Barlow points out, 'It took a man who knew nothing about cricket to show everyone how the game must adapt to survive in a modern environment.' By dragging the noble game of empire into the realm of entertainment, a place it had to go if it was to hold its ground as a popular pastime with mass appeal, Packer ultimately did cricket a considerable service. In the age of videos, computer arcades, skateboarding and fast food, the traditionalists had no choice but to compromise; as P.W. Botha might have said, to 'adapt or die'.

Packer should also be credited with the introduction of a variety of major technical advances which have since become widely accepted: batsmen's helmets were first worn in World Series Cricket and, notwithstanding the groans of the 'the-older-we-get, the-better-we-were' army, these have provided life-saving protection on many occasions; coloured clothing and floodlights have transformed the image of the game from something staid and stagnant into something upbeat and exciting, and millions have clicked the turnstiles as a result; the oval marked on the turf 30 metres from the pitch inside which at least four fielders must always stand further refined the one-day game.

Above all, World Series Cricket ensured that the world's leading players were better paid for their efforts and their skills. Once taken for granted by inadequate administrators, the players had flexed their muscles and began to be treated with appropriate respect. Top international rugby players, by contrast, would continue to flounder beneath the yoke of blazered officials. In effect, cricket advanced very quickly. Two decades worth of progress and innovation was achieved within the space of two dramatic, and perhaps traumatic, years. With the benefit of hindsight, revolution prompted evolution.

Wessels, for his part, casts a fond eye back to his season with Packer and regards it as a golden period in his career. Against the odds, he had seized a fleeting chance and established himself as an international player. Incredibly, he emerged from the Australian leg of the 1978/79 WSC season as the leading run-scorer in all matches. His Supertest average was 41.57.

When the circus moved on to the West Indies for a third leg, however, the new Australian opening batsman was forced to stay behind because he still held a South African passport and would not be granted visas for the Caribbean. He had wanted to see his team-mates off at Sydney airport but decided instead to stay at home. 'I was quite emotional about the whole thing,' he recalls. 'I really felt as though I belonged.' Instead, he sent a message wishing them well. For once, his emotions had got the better of him.

The fun, however, would end. During 1979, Packer was granted the TV rights he had been seeking all along and a settlement was agreed with the Australian Cricket Board. World Series Cricket was disbanded. Wessels was disappointed to learn of the truce because he had been keenly looking forward to a second year with Packer. He wondered whether his WSC adventure would turn out to have been his one glimpse of paradise? What would happen now? Nobody knew. He assumed the uncertain status of a nomadic cricketer seeking a home.

If Wessels looks back on cricket's revolution with special affection, it should also be pointed out that he claimed from World Series Cricket a prize more valuable than anything he ever earned with his bat.

Sally Denning, born and bred in Sydney, happy, positive, an extrovert by nature, worked in the public relations department of the World Series Cricket organisation. Towards the end of 1978, she was asked to arrange photographs of the players to be published in a brochure for the Supertest series. One quiet afternoon in the office, she was sorting through the pictures. 'Oh, he looks quite nice,' she said aloud, gazing at the photograph of someone she had never heard of: dark, square jaw, eyes aflame.

Not long afterwards, Sally Denning met Kepler Wessels at a promotional function. They talked, and talked, and ended up sitting in the car. Well, I was wondering if maybe. Er, yeah, fine. Tomorrow? Yes, fine, that's great. About seven? All right. Thumbs up. They started seeing each other on a regular basis, stepping out, staying in, laughing and relaxing, enjoying each other's company. Her easy nature seemed to be the perfect antidote to his intense temperament. 'Come on, Kepler, lighten up.' Day by day, he did.

But the relationship seemed likely to end with World Series Cricket. Wessels was under contract to play for Sussex and that appeared to be that, at least until the next WSC season, if there was one. OK, well, er, yeah, it's been great. Well, bye then. Please write.

On his way back to England, Wessels spent three weeks with his parents in George, a coastal town on the southern coast of South Africa. There was much to tell and tales of Packer filled the evenings. His arrival did, however, prompt a smattering of criticism in the media.

Rice, Procter and Le Roux were hailed for their performances in Australia but Wessels was viewed in a different light because he had defected, hadn't he? Quietly, his entry was dropped from the Who's Who section of the South African Cricket Annual.

Former team-mates, at least, better understood his position. Anton Ferreira was one who saw Wessels during his brief visit. 'I asked him how he survived against that West Indian pace attack,' Ferreira recalls. 'We still saw him as so young. He was only 21 and, to us, it seemed like he'd done it all. He just said that he put on a full visor and thighpad, and always tried to get forward. If it hit him, it hit him, but he never gave up. I marvelled at him. He backed himself against the best attack in the world. He just did it. He was so strong. My dad said he would have made a bloody good fighter because he'd never throw in the towel. It's not how many times you fall down that matters, it's how many times you get up. That seemed to be his motto.'

Wessels enjoyed seeing his parents. Throughout his years in Australia, he would faithfully return home every year. But his thoughts kept drifting back to the World Series Cricket office in Sydney. How was Sally? Was this love, he wondered? Sad letters hurried this way, and that. It began to irritate him. A week passed, another week passed. Soon he had had enough.

One evening in George, he made up his mind. Impulse raged through him once again. He seized the telephone and started to dial.

'Good morning, WSC, how can I help?'

'Sally Denning, please.'

'Certainly, sir.' He tapped his fingers. This was it.

'Hello.'

'Hello, Sally. This is ridiculous. Why don't you get on a plane and come to South Africa? I need you here. And then I want you to come with me to Sussex as well. And, er, why don't you marry me as well?'

'I'm on my way and, yes, I will.'

Ron and Lorraine Denning, Sally's parents, had met Kepler and liked him without reservation but they had not expected this. Sally had told them she wanted to be with him and that she and Kepler planned to be married in Sydney later that year, perhaps October. Her flight from Sydney to Johannesburg was delayed, so she finally staggered into Jan Smuts airport at three o'clock in the morning. Wessels was waiting and the couple flew on to George.

The following week they flew to England. October suddenly began to feel a long time away. What's the point in waiting? Let's make it July.

Two overseas telephone calls, one to George and the other to Sydney, informed the respective parents that Kepler and Sally would be married on July 21st, 1979, at St Wilfreds church, Bognor Regis. That was fine. The Wessels and Denning parents booked their air tickets and travelled to Sussex for the celebration.

Dawie de Villiers, the former Springbok scrumhalf and then South African ambassador in London, provided an Afrikaans blessing at the service and Jerry Groome, a former Sussex cricketer, acted as Wessels' best man. Some county team-mates were invited, some were not. Some were upset. 'We should have asked all of them,' Sally recalls, 'but we didn't think it through.' It hardly mattered. By this time, greater problems with Sussex were starting to fester. With Sally at his side, at least Wessels found them easier to bear.

The seed of his discontent was rooted in the county's inexplicable policy regarding overseas players. The rules stated that only two non-English players could be included in the team but Sussex persistently signed up three or even four. The result was recrimination and anger.

Greig had introduced the scheme. 'We wanted to put pressure on the guys to perform,' he recalls. 'We wanted to keep them sharp and I also thought it might be good for them to have a rest now and again. In any case, if they were not playing well we could send them off to the leagues. I think it was a sound scheme and it would have worked but we had a few guys around with reasonably large egos. That was the problem in the end.'

What Greig envisaged in theory did not materialise in practice. Apart from overloading the club's salary bill, the policy made no cricketing sense. Discontent had simmered during 1978 but it began to boil when Wessels returned to Hove in 1979. A situation had developed where Imran Khan, Javed Miandad and Wessels were competing for two places. Suddenly, one Test-class player had to be left out of the side, sitting on the sidelines, costing the county money and effectively wasting his time. A solution evolved: Imran played in all matches, Wessels played only the first class Championship fixtures and Miandad would be included in the side only for the one-day games.

This was, of course, no solution. Miandad and Wessels grew frustrated and the tension began to affect team morale. The explosion occurred during a match against Glamorgan at Eastbourne. In the red corner, Kepler Wessels, wiry, tough and determined, from South Africa. In the blue corner, Imran Khan, aristocratic, lordly, arrogant and talented, from Pakistan.

Wessels recalls: 'I was actually getting on quite well with Imran at the time. The previous season I felt he was pushing for Javed to play because they were both from Pakistan but I earned his respect during World Series Cricket and at the start of 1979 I felt he was more supportive. At any rate, Glamorgan batted first and Imran opened the bowling. In the second over, he appealed for a catch to the wicketkeeper down the leg-side but the rest of us kept quiet. We could see it had come off the batsman's arm.'

Imran was livid because neither John Barclay at first slip nor Wessels at second slip had joined in. At the end of the over, the fast bowler delivered a torrent of abuse at his team-mates. Barclay brushed it off but Wessels reacted in spectacular fashion, striding across to Imran and challenging him to 'sort it out' there and then in the middle of the pitch. The umpire stepped in to separate the cricketers who wanted to be boxers.

At the end of the day's play, Wessels still seethed and waited for Imran outside the pavilion to resolve the dispute once and for all. Arnold Long, the county captain, was on hand to prevent a physical confrontation. 'It wasn't Imran's fault,' Wessels recalls. 'The whole situation was getting to me and I just let everything go. Everything was a mess. I don't know what the county was trying to achieve. There seemed to be no plan, just this unpleasant atmosphere the whole time. I think it had an effect on everyone.'

Wessels reacted by starting to distance himself from team affairs, say very little in team meetings and simply concentrate on scoring more runs than ever just to show 'them' how foolish they were to leave him out of the one-day side. If they picked him, fine. If they didn't, it was their problem.

His fight was with the officials and the policy, not the players or the supporters. He was still enjoying the Sussex people, he was even slowly coming to terms with the English weather, but he could not be entirely happy when he was only playing in half the matches. He began to withdraw, preferring to sit in the car with Sally than with his team-mates in the pavilion. He would drive to away matches not with other players but with Sally.

That summer she supported him all the way, content to visit castles or country houses in her spare time and prepared to tolerate the ups and downs of a dogged young man not enjoying his cricket. 'Some nights,' Sally remembers, 'Kepler would behave like a complete maniac. I would suddenly wake up to find him pacing up and down the room. It was crazy.'

Despite the strife, Wessels scored 1 619 runs for Sussex in 1979 at an average of 55.82. He had been by far their most productive batsman, scoring no fewer than six championship centuries, three at Hove. In response, Sussex left him out of their one-day side. Asked whether this was right, Tony Buss, the county coach at the time, says he can't remember.

The team finished fourth in the Championship but Miandad, for one, had had enough. He left to play for Glamorgan. If Wessels thought this marked the end of the problems, he was wrong. Sussex promptly signed Garth le Roux as yet another overseas player. Exactly the same tensions would dog the county in 1980. Three stars into two places simply would not go.

Le Roux recalls: 'The arrangement seemed to be that I would play on the green wickets that did a bit and Kepler would play on the flatties. That suited me as a fast bowler because I could stay fresh but I don't think Kepler was very happy about it. He wanted to play the whole time.'

Once again in and out of the team, Wessels calmly resolved to let his bat demonstrate the idiocy of the situation. He began the season with innings of 96 and 76 against Leicestershire and, batting at No.3, continued in similar vein until a ball from Daniel struck him on the hand during a Benson and Hedges Cup quarter-final against Middlesex at Lord's.

The X-rays revealed a broken bone. Wessels would not play for six weeks. 'Oh well,' Tony Buss, ever insensitive, remarked. 'That solves our selection problems for a while.' Wessels seethed. He loathed the dry cynicism and longed for the straight, to-your-face honesty of Australians.

Returning to fitness after a holiday in France (where he found no nets for practice), Wessels replaced the injured Le Roux in the team to play Northants and, after scoring 97, was retained for the next match, against Nottinghamshire at Eastbourne. The visitors failed to master a green pitch and were dismissed for 155 by tea but Wessels had more success, reaching 76 by stumps and batting through to be 197 not out when rain stopped play on the third afternoon. In sight of his maiden first class double century, Wessels arrived at the ground early the next morning to discover that Sussex had declared. He seethed again. Ian Chappell would never have done that. There was nothing in the game anyway. What difference would a couple more overs before declaring have meant? What, he asked Sally again and again, are we doing here?

Wessels' situation was fast deteriorating. Certain Sussex officials saw him as hard-headed, stubborn, a negative influence and a selfish batsman more concerned with his average than the team. The overnight declaration would have been viewed with sniggering amusement in some quarters.

The team was due to play a Gillette Cup semi-final against Middlesex at Hove soon afterwards and, with Le Roux recovered, Wessels was told he had been dropped from the side. Sad and demoralised, he arrived to watch the game an hour and a half after play had begun.

'I've got an urgent message for you, Mr Wessels,' the gateman told him. 'Mr Buss wants to see you immediately in his office.'

The manager started shouting, telling the player that it was a condition of his contract that he turned up for every game and that, if he'd been on time that morning, he would have played. Wessels left Buss enraged and saw Sussex subside to a humiliating defeat. What had gone wrong? Why was he, who had been regarded so positively by every other state or provincial side that he had ever represented, suddenly viewed as being so difficult?

The answer was clear. The Sussex policy of hiring three overseas players to fill two positions had placed Wessels in an intolerable position and it was his nature to say so. The pity was that his sound relations with most players and spectators at the club should have been tainted by problems with a small group of intransigent and unsympathetic officials.

It had become clear that the 1980 season would be his last with Sussex but Wessels would not go quietly. Selected for the home match against Middlesex, he was motivated by the challenge of facing his old rival, Vintcent van der Bijl. The South African fast bowler was nearing the end of a hugely successful season with Middlesex and his team required one more victory to take the championship title. Sussex, and Wessels, were expected to roll over.

When they were dismissed for 172 in reply to Middlesex's 360 for four, it seemed likely. Van der Bijl had taken six for 42 and sensed triumph in the air as Sussex followed on. Wessels opened the second innings and was soon struck by a bouncer from Wayne Daniel. As he regained his composure, he thought he heard a sarcastic remark from Van der Bijl's direction at fine leg. The jaw went out, the head went down and he became grimly resolved to show 'them' once again.

Wessels scored 254, a mammoth effort, and the match was drawn. In his autobiography, Gatting recalls the performance as 'one of the most defiant innings I have ever seen'. Van der Bijl agrees, acknowledging 'a phenomenal performance'. He and Middlesex were not long denied, clinching the title the following week by defeating Glamorgan in Cardiff.

The double century proved Wessels' parting shot at Sussex. Barclay, one of the more sympathetic figures on the staff, had been appointed captain for the 1981 season and, at an appropriate moment, this decent man took Wessels to one side and explained his intention was to use the two quick bowlers, Imran and Le Roux, all season. He was sorry but those were his plans.

'It had become a ridiculous situation,' Barclay recalls. 'It seemed so wrong to have three top-rate players on your books when you could only play two. It was unsettling and it was financially stupid. I decided we should have two. Kepler seemed relieved to be released from the ordeal.

'I was sorry to lose Kepler. He had played supremely well that summer, scoring a volume of runs. It's true that he was never one of the boys but he was quiet and rather removed from the madding crowd. So far as I was aware, everyone had respect both for him and his high principles.'

Wessels was relieved but also disappointed. He had played the greater part of six seasons with the county. It had been a long association with many proud achievements which, unfortunately, ended on a sour note.

'I knew I had played county cricket for long enough,' he recalls. 'I think it can be a very useful experience for South African cricketers because it exposes you to very different conditions. The danger is that, if you stay in England too long, you can pick up bad habits.'

Sussex had finished fourth in the championship again and the fact that Imran and Le Roux took the first two places in the bowling averages indicated Barclay's decision was correct. But Wessels' performance had not been too bad either: he finished third in the batting averages with 65.08. Two familiar names were ahead of him on the list: Lamb and Kirsten. The emerging triumvirate from Western Province in 1976/77 were extending their realms.

In September 1980, Kepler and Sally Wessels left Sussex and returned to Australia. That was, it had become clear, where his future lay.

# 5

# Ons vir jou, Australia

---

The switchboard operator at the Clarendon Hotel in Bognor Regis, Sussex, was having to deal with an unusual request. She had been all set for tea on a quiet Wednesday afternoon when the gentleman in Room 8 asked to make a collect call to Sydney, Australia and she wasn't sure of the code. She searched, found it and spoke the numbers aloud as she dialled. Soon, it was ringing.

'Hello.'

'Hello, this is Bognor. Is that Australia?' she asked.

'Yes this is Australia,' a voice yawned. 'Do you know what time it is, lady? It's nearly three in the morning.'

'Oh, I am sorry. I have a Mr Wessels on the line wanting to speak to a Mr Packer. Will you accept the charges?'

'Er, yes, all right.'

'Thank you. You may talk now.' With that, she replaced the receiver and settled back with her tea and shortbread.

There followed a shouting match across the oceans. At one end, paying for the call which had roused him, was Kerry Packer, one of the richest men in Australia; at the other end was Kepler Wessels, a professional cricketer not completely aware of the time difference between Bognor and Sydney.

The issue was simple. After the disbandment of World Series Cricket, Wessels had been told by the WSC office that he was a free agent, at liberty to play for whichever state he wanted in official domestic cricket. He dispatched letters to Rod Marsh in Western Australia, Ian Chappell in South Australia and to Greg Chappell in Queensland. When the replies came in, Queensland seemed the most keen. A contract was drawn up and Wessels' signature crawled along the dotted line. He was delighted to join Greg Chappell.

As a matter of courtesy, Wessels informed the WSC office of his decision. Thank you, Kepler. The following day, the storm broke.

Packer executives were suddenly adamant that he should play for New South Wales, warning Wessels that if he refused he would forfeit the balance of his A$30 000 contract. The player was not bad at being adamant either. He said he was sorry but he was not going to tear up his agreement with Queensland. The row rumbled back and forth until, one quiet afternoon in Bognor, Wessels grew so exasperated he decided he would speak directly to Packer to explain his situation. Greg Chappell had told him to 'get on the front foot' with the boss. So he did, there and then; and he reckoned Packer could afford the call, as well.

'Wessels, you better understand that I own you and you will play for New South Wales. Have you got that?'

'No, you don't own me and no, I will not play for New South Wales. I just want you to see it from . . . hello, hello?'

Packer, angered by such impertinence, had hung up. Wessels, sitting with his wife in Room 8, wondered if he had gone too far but he was determined to play for Queensland. Firstly, he was attracted by Chappell; secondly, he was told it would be harder to get into the New South Wales side. Sally gamely accepted Brisbane would benefit his cricket, even if her own friends and family lived in Sydney. Fifteen minutes later, the telephone in Room 8 was ringing again.

'Hello.' Wessels answered.

'Hello Kepler, it's Tony Greig speaking. You've really upset Kerry now. What's the matter with you?'

Once again the inter-continental telephone lines turned blue as the conversation deteriorated from explanation to abuse, but Greig was no more successful than Packer had been. The more anyone threatened Wessels, the more resolved he became. That was it. He would play for Queensland. That evening the Wessels family counted the cost of their decision. The agreement had been that WSC would pay contracted players the difference between what they earned from their State side during the 1979/80 season and the A$30 000 that would have been paid for another WSC season. In Wessels' case, Queensland had offered him A$25 000 for the season. His resistance had cost A$5 000.

It was worth it. He would not be bullied. His sense of honour was notably laudable because it was likely that the repercussions would extend far beyond a mere financial loss. To upset Kerry Packer on a reverse charge call was not the finest career move an Australian cricketer could make in the late 1970s. Even after the disbanding of his series, Packer remained a highly influential figure within Australian cricket, and an unforgiving adversary.

When Wessels first arrived at the Woollongabba Ground, more regularly known as The Gabba, home of the Queensland Cricket Club, he was not the model of positive thinking. It was October 1979 and he had emerged from an arduous and sometimes unpleasant season with Sussex. Yet there was much to be done. He needed to establish a new home with Sally and also to establish himself within a new team. Everything suddenly seemed rather complicated.

Wessels' first year in Australia had been glamorous and exhilarating, a multi-coloured dream played out in the bright lights of World Series Cricket. His second season would be more mundane. After the wonderful party in 1978/79, the bills began to drop on his doorstep in 1979/80.

World Series Cricket had sent him into such a whirl that he had not fully faced up to the consequences of leaving South Africa. Only now, with more time on his hands, did the magnitude of his decision begin to sink in. At stages, he would feel sickeningly lonely. He would convince himself he had made a terrible decision... and then Sally would haul him back together. Day after day, she stressed the positive. 'Are you going to make this work, or not? Are you going to give in? Heh, lighten up! What's the matter with you?'

Some evenings, he would turn on the television and peer into a cultural canyon. The Australian sense of humour, which had seemed so refreshing in the mouths of the Chappells, Lillee and Marsh, now sounded like a foreign language. In the shopping centre, at the doctor, he struggled to understand what people said to him and, conversely, they were misled by his Afrikaans accent. Nothing in life was easy, everything became a chore.

His three-year contract with Queensland incorporated employment as a public relations officer with Ron McConnell Holdings. The job was a sportsman's position with McConnell effectively filling the role of sponsor but Wessels was eager to learn about business beyond cricket. In 1979/80, however, he was not in an ideal frame of mind for public relations. McConnell would ask Wessels to join him and his clients for a drink at the end of the day and Wessels would pour himself a Coke. He was striking the wrong note.

'I began to feel that people were terribly disappointed in me,' Wessels reflects. 'I had a communication problem with nearly everyone, but some of the people who were hard on me then now have sons aged 22, and they realise that few young men of that age are completely mature in ordinary circumstances, let alone those under the type of pressure I was facing.'

His career with Queensland started with a thud on the head during the state trials. Fielding at short leg, a full-blooded pull struck him above the left ear. Concussed but forever the wounded warrior battling on, Wessels was none the less included in the team for the opening match.

He scored 56 on his début against Victoria, setting the tone for a season when he would bat consistently well and yet fail to convert confident 50s and 60s into centuries. Many batsmen would have been satisfied to have their glass half full with 50 runs but Wessels, of course, saw his as half empty and, as a result, brought more pressure on himself. When Greg Chappell was away from the side on Test duty, Wessels believed he was expected to be the premier batsman. No one said so. He simply assumed it. Some team-mates began to think he created the pressure to motivate himself, others simply gazed in wonder as Wessels sat head in hands in tortured despair after scoring 60-odd.

The tension, nerves and frustration combined to provoke another explosion of the increasingly famous Wessels temper. Bad light had stopped play during a Shield match against New South Wales and Wessels, unbeaten on 57, was strolling off the field when a group of spectators began shouting at him: 'Why don't you bugger off to where you came from, you South African bastard? Go home, Wessels. We don't need you here. Bugger off! Bugg-gger off!'

All fuses blew. Oblivious of the fact that he was still wearing his pads, thighpad and batting gloves, Wessels stormed into the grandstand, clambering over seats to confront the group. 'What's your problem?' he shouted, fingers clenching in his gloves. 'Do you want to make something of it?'

'No, no, we're only joking,' one replied.

'Well, I think you had better go and make your *** jokes somewhere else.' The argument escalated and the hecklers became braver. When there were eight of them, Wessels began to feel a little uneasy. He was wondering why one of them hadn't accepted his invitation to 'sort this out' when he turned to discover Louis Schuller, the tall, thickset Queensland fast bowler, standing full square behind him. 'OK, Chopper, let's leave these idiots,' Schuller suggested, overcoming the temptation to get stuck in. Wessels puffed out his cheeks and sighed. 'Yep, all right, mate.'

The season, made awkward when he struggled to feel accepted and settled, was none the less successful. He continued to score freely, finishing top of the state's batting averages with 36.64. For once, however, the statistics failed to stiffen his resolve. Scoring runs was not his only aim now. His chief goal was to play official Test cricket. That was why he had come to Australia. That was why he was anxious, and awkward ... to play Test cricket.

He knew the rules. The International Cricket Conference regulations stated that a player must reside in his adopted country for at least four years before becoming eligible. What he didn't know was whether the Australian Cricket Board would balk at his South African background. Perhaps they would feel he was too much of a hot potato and steer clear of selecting him.

Well, what did they feel? If they weren't going to pick him, he wanted to know. He was becoming frantic. He sought confirmation of his status from the ACB but never received a definitive answer. Were they unsure? He began to fret. Was this whole adventure a waste of time? Why weren't the ACB being clear? He was slowly but surely driving himself to utter distraction.

Ian Chappell had heard enough. Wessels was seeking his advice and telling how the world was against him, how everything was unfair. 'You're half the problem yourself,' Chappell interrupted. 'Go on with this attitude and you'll get nowhere. Every time you have a problem, you blame everyone else. Stop being so negative. Get on with it and get the thing done.' Wessels was surprised by the outburst, even a little bit hurt. He went home and told Sally what Chappell had said. Sally said she agreed with Chappell. Fair enough.

Returning to Brisbane after the 1980 season in England, Wessels felt more positive. He had accepted Chappell's advice and the conclusion of his ordeal at Sussex had been a relief. It was, he sensed, a chance to make a fresh start. He craved a period of stability after coming a long way very quickly.

This mood of renewal was enhanced in October 1980 when Allan McFarland, the government Minister of Immigration and Ethnic Affairs, officially presented Wessels with his Australian citizenship in a ceremony at the Queensland Cricket Association offices. He still had two years to wait before qualifying for the Test team but it meant he was no longer classified as an overseas player. He was thrilled. He had begun to feel and look (with the standard-issue Australian cricketer's moustache) at home. Allan Border, his Queensland team-mate and now a colleague at Ron McConnell Holdings, attended the ceremony.

Border, 25, the son of a wool merchant, had recently arrived in Brisbane from Sydney on a similar deal to Wessels. McConnell used to say Border couldn't work an iron lung and the young batsman recalls that he and Wessels 'basically did bugger all'. But the two players got along. 'Kepler was very serious about the game and he was totally dedicated,' Border remembers. 'I think he enjoyed the training more than I did but he dragged me along a few times.'

A boyhood love of baseball meant Border hardly played serious cricket until his late teens but he made his Test début following the Packer exodus in 1978 and soon became a widely admired cricketer, not least by Wessels: 'If I had to pick someone to bat for my life, it would be Allan. He's very tough out in the middle. That's his strength. A fantastic temperament.'

Border was another of the straight-talking Australians whom Wessels so enjoyed. When things went wrong, he would be grumpy. If he was criticised, he would brush it aside. He knew how to relax, how to enjoy himself and he knew which quality he valued above all. That was loyalty: the kind you give your mates and your mates give you back. Unconditionally.

An incident during an Australian tour of India, much later in his career, best illustrates the essence of Border to which Wessels felt so drawn. Batting on a stifling hot day in Madras, Border was at the crease with Dean Jones. In brilliant form, Jones was none the less suffering from bouts of chronic nausea and dehydration. After retching not far from the pitch on several occasions, he staggered up to Border, his captain, and said he'd have to retire. Border shrugged and said that suited him because he would prefer to have someone out there with him who had the guts to tough it out.

Jones, chastened, toughed it out, finally adding 210 runs with Border in Australia's highest partnership in Tests versus India. That was guts, the only currency of any value in the macho world of Australian cricket.

'Allan could maybe have trained a bit harder,' Wessels adds. 'He used to go out on a binge, play brilliantly the next day and then come and tell me you didn't have to be a fitness fanatic to do well. I always replied he might get away with it once in a while but it would eventually catch up with him. It was always a joke between us. We were just different.'

Some evenings during the Queensland era, Wessels would drop Sally at the Borders' home — Sally and Jane Border became good friends —

and persuade his team-mate to train with him at the Railway Institute Gym, run by fight veteran Hilton Brookes, in a less salubrious area of the city.

More often he would go to the gym alone, and slip into a different world. The Institute was no top people's push-pose-and-sigh centre. It was a tough and uncompromising place. Some of its customers had been in trouble with the law, others wore an extravagant tattoo on a bulging bicep, a few were down on their luck but almost everyone was cheerful.

It would become a second home to Wessels. Far away from the fuss and fame, he would make his way to the Institute and relax. Work on the speed-ball a bit, maybe even spar a bit, whatever. It didn't matter. His mates were rough but so, in a way, was he. They were his kind, the ones who didn't care how quickly he scored in the first 20 overs. Here, beyond question, he was OK.

'Trevor' was a mate from the Institute. Claiming the longest record of juvenile crime in the state of Queensland, he was tattooed from his neck to his toes and his head was clean shaven. Late one night the telephone rang at the Wessels home. It was Trevor. 'Kepler, I've got a problem...'

'What's wrong, Trev?'

The story unfolded. The son of one of Trevor's friends had been beaten up at school, so Trevor and his friend had set off down the coast to sort things out with the other boy's father. They found him and knocked him around a bit. Everything was going well until Trevor's friend failed to resist the temptation of picking up the TV and video on his way out of the house. Trevor was phoning from the local police cells. He said he needed a character reference. Wessels obliged by telling the police he had met Trevor through boxing and that he was sure he would not do anything wrong. That was being a mate.

Steve Aczel, a former Commonwealth boxing champion, was another regular at the Institute. One Friday Trevor asked Steve if he could borrow 20 dollars. No problem. Steve went away for the weekend and arrived back home on the Sunday evening to find a $20 bill pinned on his table with the message: 'This place is a thief's paradise. Thanks for the loan. Trevor.'

Always something going on, something to laugh about at the Institute. One day a wealthy man came in, worked out and then complained that his yacht had been stolen. Trevor thought he looked a decent guy, so he made a few calls and, two days later, the yacht miraculously reappeared at its berth. Another day, someone walks into the gym. He's no model. 'It's all right, mate,' Trevor says. 'You can take the mask off now. The robbery's over.'

Other times, it was rough. Wessels is minding his own business, taking out his frustrations on the speed-ball when a painter from the docks turns up and has something to say about the cricketer's birthright. They argue and decide to sort it out in the ring. Wessels is pummelled.

'He looked pretty bad afterwards,' Wessels remembers, 'but not as bad as me. He broke my nose.' Aczel, who had watched, decided he should teach his mate a few of the dirtier tricks of the trade so he could look after himself a bit better. As boxing drills played a prominent role in his training schedule, Wessels attended the Institute on a regular basis.

If the language around the gym was not quite the Queen's English, it was no cleaner on the first class cricket fields of Australia as Wessels began the 1980/81 season with Queensland. The 'Maroons', as they were known, had never won the Sheffield Shield but a new optimism was abroad, founded on a team with a bowling attack led by Jeff Thomson, supported by Carl Rackemann, Geoff Dymock and Trevor Hohns, and with a batting order which included Greg Chappell, Allan Border, Greg Ritchie, Martin Kent and Wessels.

They all spoke English, with a twist. Playing against New South Wales in Sydney, Wessels found himself the target of an astonishing verbal assault from the fast bowlers, Lenny Pascoe and Geoff Lawson. Sledging, as the practice was known, played a major role in Australian cricket. It was happily justified as the bowler's legitimate attempt to intimidate the batsman in what was a man's game, and there were no limits as broad, brawny pacemen trawled the deepest and darkest sewers of the language for new forms of abuse. Wessels was a target but he soon learned and became a skilful exponent himself.

Pascoe, broad, dark and smouldering, struck Wessels twice on the forearm and followed up with a volley of 'f's and 'c's but the Queenslander stood firm. After an hour, Pascoe, all but frothing at the mouth, bowled a complete over of bouncers at Wessels. Six in a row. The crowd urged him on, but Wessels swayed out of line and glared back down the wicket. **** you, too.

The first delivery of Pascoe's next over was a beamer directed at Wessels' head. Wessels eased clear again. **** you, again. The scene was becoming comic with Pascoe, Wessels and Lawson all screaming abuse at one another. The umpire, Arthur Watson, pleaded for restraint but to no avail. Amid the crazy cacophony, Wessels was accumulating runs. He finished the day 146 not out and could not resist swearing at

Pascoe again as they walked off the field. Jeff Thomson had thoroughly enjoyed the X-rated entertainment and he executed the *coup de grâce* by sending a saucer of milk across to the New South Wales dressing room with a message: 'To Lenny. You bowl like a pussycat.'

Queensland's challenge fell away, as it often did, during a disappointing Eastern tour (away matches in Adelaide, Hobart and Melbourne) and they finished third on the Shield log but won the McDonalds Cup, the one-day trophy. Wessels finished eighth in the batting averages with 50.88. In his sure and steady way, he had begun to settle down in his adopted country.

The challenge of the Australian winter, his first cricketless spell for seven years, was met by the purchase of The Golden Goose in Adelaide Street, Brisbane. In partnership with his parents-in-law, who had retired and moved to Queensland, Wessels bought the newsagents and made it work. Careful and calm in business, he ensured the venture began to yield a working profit. Each morning, Wessels would rise at five o'clock to set out the newspapers. After his shift behind the counter, he would be free to train in the afternoon.

Life began to find a steady rhythm. At weekends, he and Sally would drive up the coast, or swim, or play tennis. Australia, the young land of opportunity and growth where the sun shone, suited him. He was happy, and as he began to accept the pattern of Australian life, so he enjoyed it. 'It was good to feel part of the world,' he recalls. 'There was a sense of freedom which everyone seemed to take for granted. I loved it.'

The 1981/82 season approached. It would be the last, Wessels knew, before he qualified to represent Australia. David Richards, the chief executive of the Australian Cricket Board, had announced Wessels would be eligible to play Test cricket in September 1982, precisely four years after he had first arrived at Sydney airport. His quest was assuming the proportions of a crusade. He began to run further, train longer, work harder. On and on.

His pre-season form was auspicious. Turning out for the Valleys club, with Border and Gary Moore, a close friend, he appeared commanding and confident. It was going to be a 'big' season. It had to be.

Wessels was not to be disappointed. No more than six Australians had ever scored more than 1 000 runs in a Shield season. He became the seventh, scoring five centuries and an outstanding 220 in Tasmania. All summer long, he batted with purpose and panache. He didn't graft. He stroked and, by autumn, he had earned a place among some highly distinguished names in the history books. The Australians to have scored more than 1 000 runs in a Shield season were Bill Ponsford (1926/27 and 1927/28), Don Bradman (1939/40), Norm O'Neill (1957/58), Barry Richards (1970/71), Greg Chappell (1973/74), David Ogilvie (1977/78), and Kepler Christoffel Wessels in 1981/82.

Queensland, however, won only one of nine Shield fixtures that season. Wessels was named Player of the Year by a panel of umpires but the team had not been in a position to reap the rewards. There was some consolation in a second successive McDonalds Cup triumph but the premier prize eluded the State again and that, rather than the personal success of their dedicated opener, occupied most minds at the Gabba as another campaign drew to a close.

The Australian side toured Pakistan during August 1982 and they struggled. Kim Hughes' side did not win a match and lost all three Tests with the spinner Abdul Qadir taking 22 wickets in the series. As he studied the disappointing scorecards from Pakistan, Wessels could hardly suppress his excitement. The opening batsmen all seemed out of form.

As paradise beckoned, Wessels' nerve began to crack. It was all so close, the realisation of this burning ambition. Surely something would go wrong. It seemed too good to be true. When Hughes returned from Pakistan, he was asked about Wessels' prospects of playing for Australia. 'Well, he'll have to prove himself in domestic cricket first,' Hughes replied. It seemed an inoffensive remark, the sort of comment any captain might have made when quizzed about a player outside his squad but Wessels did not see it that way. The nerves, the pressure overflowed again.

'You see,' he told Sally. 'Hughes doesn't want me in his team. Prove myself? I scored 1 000 runs in the Sheffield Shield season. What more does he want? He doesn't like me because I played for Packer and he thinks I'm in the Chappell camp. They're never going to pick me. It's a disaster.'

Within weeks, the Australian selectors appointed Greg Chappell as captain for the forthcoming series against England. His experience, it was said, would be vital. Wessels calmed down. Maybe it wasn't going to be such a disaster after all.

The tourists' match against Queensland would evidently be crucial to his hopes. After scoring 14 in the first innings, Wessels opened the second innings, feeling as if he was batting for a Test career, nothing less. With 35 minutes left to play on the third evening, he carefully advanced to reach 13 not out by the close. Next morning, his nerves were such that he was hardly able to think straight. He started to talk to himself at the crease. Come on, no panic. Tuck the chin in. Hold the head still. Get in line. Concentrate.

Yet again, he rose to the big occasion. Wessels scored 103, Greg Chappell made 126 and Queensland declared at 435 for five. England were bowled out for 189 and the state had won by 171 runs, their first victory over England for 30 years. Wessels heartily joined in the celebrations. It had been his first taste of Pom-bashing, and it could not have been better timed.

Australia's team for the first Test was due to be announced the following weekend. Queensland were playing in Tasmania and Wessels was hoping for good news. When he scored 65, easily coping with Michael Holding on a green pitch, his expectations grew. On the Sunday morning, Chappell took him aside. Wessels' heart began to leap. Surely, this was the moment. Yes, yes...

'No, Chopper, they haven't picked you,' Chappell said. 'I'm sorry. The selectors told me they had discussed you and they said you're very much in the running. You've just got to keep scoring runs.'

Wessels' roller-coaster spirits dipped again. Would they ever select him? The first Test ended in a draw and neither of the opening batsmen, John Dyson and Graeme Wood, batted well. The speculation gathered pace again. His name was hovering around the headlines as he prepared to face Victoria in Queensland's next Shield match. Just one more big score, he told himself, one big score. His future, his career, his ambition, everything went on the line again. Dropped on 10, Wessels rode his luck to score 86. Was it enough?

It's Sunday evening again. The Australian selectors are meeting to choose their side for the second Test and Wessels is attending a barbecue arranged for the Queensland and Victoria teams at the Gabba. He can hardly eat. Chappell is there too, waiting for a call from the selectors. Brrrrbrrrr Brrrrbrrrr. It's for you, Greg. Wessels watches the upright man leave the table, then he watches him return to his place. He looks at Wessels, smiles, says nothing. They finish the meal. Chappell finally gestures Wessels outside.

He whispers. 'No one else is supposed to know, Chopper, so don't go back and tell everyone, but you're in. You're in the side.'

Wessels' mind, for four years so tortured first by anxiety, then by hope, then by anxiety again, erupted. Of all the South African cricketers who had been led into isolation by the politics of their government, only one man had shown the will and the strength to get up and do something about it, emigrate to a country where he had no ties, wait through the period of qualification and earn a place in the Test team. They had said he was mad but now he had done it. The loneliness, the sadness of leaving his home: it had all paid off. He had won. Just as he had been taught as a young Afrikaner in the Free State, he had not shrunk from the massive task, and he had seen it through.

Not everyone saw his elevation in such triumphal light. Some regarded it as wrong. Several newspapers pointed out that Wood, the player he replaced, was a true blue Australian. Many of the English cricket writers covering the Ashes series joined the haughty derision. Some saw it as an indication of how far the Australians were prepared to stretch the rules to stabilise their upper order, others grandly pontificated about ruptured ethics.

Within the Australian side, Wessels was broadly welcomed. The players, at least, knew how much he wanted to play for Australia and what he had endured to win his place. It helped that five of his team-mates for Australia were also his team-mates at Queensland. Chappell, his captain, ever utterly reliable and supportive in times of need, was unequivocal: 'I only have admiration for the single-minded way that Kepler has worked towards his goal.'

November 26th 1982 dawned overcast, dry. Wessels, only 25 but experienced beyond his years, arrived at the Gabba in Brisbane with his wife. 'Australia vs England, the second Test.'

'Just remember,' Sally told him, 'it's just another game. You've played against these guys before. You know you're good enough.'

Wessels smiled. This was it. Crowds milled outside the ground. 'Good luck, Kepler,' someone shouted as, head down, he made his way to the Main Gate and on towards the Australian changing room. At last.

The team charged with regaining the Ashes, lost in 1977, had started to gather: Wessels, Dyson, Border, Chappell, Hughes, David Hookes, Marsh, Bruce Yardley, Lawson, Rackemann, Thomson. England were ready: Chris Tavare, Graeme Fowler, David Gower, Allan Lamb, Ian Botham, Derek Randall, Geoff Miller, Bob Taylor, Eddie Hemmings, Bob Willis and Norman Cowans.

Chappell won the toss, took one look at the Brisbane pitch he knew so well and asked England to bat. Lawson, who had been hailed by Lillee as 'Australia's fast-bowling king of the 1980s', removed both openers with only 13 runs on the board. Gower settled quickly and soon cut Rackemann for four past point. Facing Lawson, he then glanced at a delivery outside leg-stump. The ball flew high to the right of leg slip.

An instinctive hand thrown out, ten clenched fingers, a dazzling catch. Wessels, wearing his baggy green cap with pride, was submerged beneath a tide of congratulating team-mates. What a start! The scorebook told the happy tale... D.I. Gower ct Wessels b Lawson 18.

England were all out for 220 early on the second morning, Lawson finishing with six for 47. At 11.15 a.m., Wessels and Dyson strode out.

'Do you want the strike?' Dyson, dark and thoughtful, asked as the two batsmen neared the pitch. Willis was preparing to bowl.

'Yep, I don't mind. That's fine,' Wessels replied. Game on. He was soon off the mark with a solid pull for two. This was fun. Pinch yourself. This is Australia versus England. An Ashes test. Wessels breathed deeply.

His team were soon in crisis. Dyson was bowled by Botham, and Border was caught behind. At 11 for two, Chappell arrived at the crease and Wessels went to school. 'Greg was the most complete batsman I've seen,' Wessels declares. 'He came out and played perfectly that day. He wasn't panicked at all. I was happy just to give him the strike and watch him bat.'

Chappell cruised to 53, the total to 94. Then he pushed towards cover and called for a swift single. Wessels froze. It wasn't there. This was all wrong. Chappell was committed to the run, stranded, run out. Wessels was mortified. He blamed himself. 'There was no need,' Chappell affirms. 'It was entirely my fault.' Wessels swallowed hard. The crowd was restless.

Neither Hughes nor Hookes lasted long. At 130 for five, Wessels suddenly found himself cast as the last remaining specialist batsman, the last line of defence. He was comfortable with that. Following the accepted wisdom on the county circuit, the England bowlers were trying to swing the ball away from him but Wessels would not feed the slips this day. Instead he scored heavily in the arc between third man and cover point. His trademark cut may have been more of a chop but it proved impressively effective. Botham, among others, was becoming frustrated. He wanted a word with Lamb.

'You played with this guy in South Africa, didn't you?'

He had.

'Well, why don't you try and upset him a bit? You must know how to wind him up. What about some of those Afrikaans swearwords?'

Lamb duly wheeled out his vocabulary but Wessels hardly batted an eyelid. 'Botham even got me to teach him some of the words,' Lamb recalls, 'so he could try them on Kepler. That didn't work either.'

Wessels continued to prosper, partnered first by Marsh, then by Yardley, all the while edging towards a milestone which even he had never contemplated. Only 12 Australians had previously scored a century on their Test début and the Gabba crowd, his home crowd, began to sense the onset of history. The cheers grew louder and more prolonged with each run. As he reached 90, the Test became his stage and England the supporting cast. Closer, closer.

With 18 minutes left before stumps on the second day, and his score on 97, Wessels settled again. Eddie Hemmings, the spinner from Nottinghamshire, stood at his mark and moved in again. A brave rush of blood. Wessels stepped down the pitch and aimed a majestic drive towards the vacant long-on boundary. The ball pitched, leapt and turned. Wessels played, and missed. The trajectory deceived him ... what tragedy! ... and also beat the wicketkeeper. The ball bounced off Taylor's chest and Wessels scrambled back into his ground.

He had danced with disaster. His heart began to pound. Come on, head down, chin in, concentrate. Hemmings slowly shook his head. Within an instant, he was skipping in again. This delivery was short, drifting to leg. Wessels spun into position and pulled powerfully past the diving Lamb at mid-wicket.

Yes! Bedlam. Spectators ran on the field. Wessels shyly raised his bat to the thunderous Gabba applause. This was the pinnacle. This was the moment that made the struggle seem so worth while. No one could dispute his status. There it was on the scoreboard. K.C. Wessels ... 101 not out.

When he struck the last ball of the day for another boundary, he sent his team to bed at 246 for six. That evening a Press conference was hastily arranged and Wessels ushered in to face the notebooks, but Australia's new hero could hardly utter a coherent word. He was exhausted and sick. Towards the late afternoon, a ringing noise had started in his right ear. He had felt dizzy but, of course, had played on. A doctor told him to go and sleep.

Sally drove. Away from the back-slapping, they were together. Alone. There was no need for words. They both understood the simple significance of what had taken place. Through hard days at Sussex and settling times at Queensland, they had won through. This was triumph: quiet, sweet, perfect triumph.

Back at the house, Wessels called his parents. No, they had not heard the news. Kepler had done it. Would you believe it? A century on his Test début for Australia. Kepler had done it. But they were far away.

He missed them and the pain in his ear was not easing. A local doctor was summoned and, one injection later, Wessels was sleeping soundly with, as Churchill might have said, no need of cheering dreams. Facts were better than dreams.

Next morning Wessels resumed his innings in aggressive fashion. Cowans was cut for successive boundaries as Australia chased a quick and substantial first innings lead. But their wickets continued to fall and, finally, just before the lunch interval, a tiring Wessels was bowled by Willis for 162. His was the last wicket to fall and Australia were 341 all out.

All hail. The opener had batted for seven and a half hours, and only two men had scored more runs on their Test début for Australia: Charles Bannerman, whose 165 was scored in 1877 during the first Test ever played, and A.A. Wilson, who struck 164 against England at Adelaide in 1928. Wessels' heroics had earned a decisive advantage and the Australians never lost it.

Thomson and Lawson claimed five wickets each as England were dismissed for 309 in their second innings. Wessels could not be kept out of the game, holding another fine catch off the full face of Lamb's bat at short leg. Nothing could go wrong. Australia were set the moderate target of 189 to win but there was no complacency in the air because there were enough players around to remember the shame of Headingley in 1981 (when England followed on and, galvanised by Botham at the peak of his form, set Australia a target of 130 to win, and, to their horror, Australia were bowled out for 111). 'Not this time,' Chappell warned his team with a scowl. 'We'll have no messing about this time.'

There was no messing. Wessels was bowled off his gloves for 46 but Hughes and Hookes took Australia to victory by seven wickets. Wessels was named as Man of the Match. Amid all the cheers, the glory was his.

Australia won the third Test at a stroll but England produced a very much stronger challenge in the fourth match of the series at the Melbourne Cricket Ground, a contest thrust into epic history by its conclusion. For three days, it was uncannily even. England all out 284, Australia all out 287, England all out 294, Australia set 292 to win the Test and the Ashes.

From apparent comfort at 171 for four, Cowans tumbled Australia to 218 for nine. With Border and Thomson at the crease, all hope seemed lost. Run by run, scrambled single by scrambled single, classic Border cut by classic Border cut, home side hopes were rekindled. By stumps on the fourth day, the total had been courageously cranked up to 255 for nine.

Still 37 runs short, the last wicket pair walked out to resume their stand the next morning and were astonished to find no fewer than 17 463 spectators in the stands. Every run was mightily roared. He may have been a citizen for only two years but there was no more enthusiastic Australian at the MCG than the one with the Afrikaans name. Amid crackling tension, Wessels began to understand, for the first time in his life, the full meaning of national pride, to see how it floods the senses and invigorates the soul.

Run by run, the Test was going to the wire. With four more runs needed and England still seeking the elusive last wicket, Botham, by basic nature the most Australian of Englishmen, seized the ball and prepared to bowl the 18th over of the morning. The Ashes were slip-sliding away. He bounded in and bowled short outside off-stump. Thomson saw a ball tailor-made for the winning boundary. A swing, an edge, a juggled catch at slip. Thomson was out. England had won. The Test had been watched by 214 861 people over five days.

Disappointed in defeat, Wessels had none the less been exhilarated by the match: 'It just made me feel so positive about the whole thing,' he recalls. 'I kept telling myself that getting into the Test team was not the end of it. I wanted to be a successful Test player. I knew I would have to work harder to keep my place because I wasn't a born-and-bred Australian but I was so keen for the whole thing. It was an incredible feeling.'

In a perfect world, he would have slipped quietly into the Australian team and largely been left alone to establish himself in the side. Wessels, however, has never lived in a perfect world. He remained a hot potato, what journalists recognise as 'a good story'. Like it or not (in fact, he hated it), he remained in the limelight, a captive catalyst for controversy.

Richie Benaud, former Australian captain, shrewd TV commentator and Packer man, is talking to the world of Channel Nine: 'The main problem with Wessels is that he shifts his front leg towards any ball pitched between the leg and middle stumps. It is not much of a movement but it is enough to drag the bat away and leave a gap.' All aboard the bandwagon.

The fatal flaw, went the melody, is on leg-stump. Bowl at his legs and you will soon get his measure. When Willis catapulted his leg-stump out of the turf in the first innings at the MCG, the melody became an aria. When he was bowled off his pads by Cowans in the second innings at the MCG, the aria became a full-scale opera. Here comes the fat lady. Has Wessels been found out?

'It was a problem,' he recalls, 'but not so much in terms of getting me out. Their leg-side attack restricted my scoring for a while but it was just a technical thing I had to look at. It was hardly a crisis.' Ever more resolved, Wessels approached the fifth Test in Sydney determined to scupper the leg theory chatter, to show 'them', the critics, all over again.

Out cheaply in the first innings, he felt the nerves fraying as he walked out to bat for the second time. The first ball was pitched on middle-and-leg and full. Moving neatly into position, he flicked his wrists and, with perfect timing, dispatched the ball to the mid-wicket boundary. Bowl at my legs? You're welcome. England did, and they were. Wessels was harshly judged LBW on 53 but he had made his point. Like all the greatest myths, however, the tale of his leg-stump weakness would live on long after it had been exposed.

Australia comfortably secured the draw in Sydney which was enough to win back the Ashes they had lost in 1977 after Hughes' patient 137 took the match beyond England's reach. Wessels was thrilled to be in a winning side, genuinely thrilled. It was all so new and he had played his part. And yet... and yet... it didn't feel quite right. Slotting into the WSC Australian side had seemed so uncomplicated but this was difficult. Damn it, it was awkward.

He wanted to be Australian but he remained Australia's South African-born opener in print and in thought. He was playing. That was fine. But he wanted to be accepted. That was the problem. He wished he could wash away the stigma, the look in people's eyes. But he couldn't. It was there.

It was certainly there when Malcolm Fraser, the Australian prime minister, had hosted a cocktail party for the Australia and England teams at the Hilton Head hotel on the eve of the Test in Sydney. Fraser, tall, smooth, a politician down to his shiny shoes, had fervently and emotionally campaigned for the total isolation of everything relating to South Africa. Wessels was virtually on red alert as he casually strode into the function.

Wearing his Australian blazer proudly, Wessels was one of seven players ushered into a line to shake the smiling premier's hand. Some of his team-mates, Marsh among them, believed Wessels was preparing to deliver a vigorous defence of South Africa but this was not true. The nervous opener did not plan to rock the boat. He wanted to be treated like one of the crew.

Fraser approached. Wessels braced. One player greeted, two, three . . . as Fraser shook the fourth cricketer's hand, he glared at Wessels, the fifth, and abruptly turned away. Wessels had been snubbed. Speechless, he shook his head sadly. Some team-mates told him not to worry about it, many others looked on and muttered. It had been a humiliating moment.

Wessels swiftly brushed the incident aside but he was clearly shaken: 'I had qualified to play for Australia by all the rules. I had committed myself to the country and never given anything less than my absolute best. I don't know what he was thinking but I don't think it was justified.' One petulant prime minister aside, Wessels was able to reflect on a highly successful series. With an average of 48.25, he had established himself in the side — for Test matches, at least. One-day cricket would be a different matter.

In the days when cricket was cricket, not a prime time television event, the end of the Ashes series would have signalled a jocular round of farewells and a return home. Not in 1982/83. Packer had changed all that. The players were now confronted by a flurry of one-day internationals. World Series Cricket had transformed international cricket's gentle circuit of traditional tours into a dizzy, multi-coloured merry-go-round of androgynous one-day matches. This harsh evolution was justified by the fact that a new breed of fan flocked to the wham-bam entertainment in their thousands. The coffers overflowed. It did not seem to matter that scarcely anyone could remember any of the results a month later. Take out the roast beef, bring in the burgers.

So the New Zealand side was flown in to join Australia and England for a triangular series. Amid the hype, the players prepared for the business end of the summer. They would all try, of course, but they fully understood the unpredictable nature of one-day cricket. On any given day, in any given ground, anyone can defeat anyone. Defeat would never be a crisis.

Chappell, for one, was not sufficiently enthused by the prospect of nine matches in 22 days to retain the captaincy. He handed it back to Hughes but remained available to play. For Wessels, in contrast, the triangular event was still new. He felt in excellent form, and he rared to go.

Australia won their first three matches, with Wessels scoring 79, 18 and 19. It was, he soon realised, a high-pressure form of cricket. The words of Ian Chappell during the Packer series remained in his mind. 'Bat through the whole 50 overs,' the captain had frequently told him. 'You keep one end up for the entire innings and you'll have done your job.'

Unfortunately the selectors did not accept this strategy. From the start, Wessels would be a controversial figure in one-day cricket. He formed his own opinions of establishing a sound base before hitting out and he believed they worked. Many others maintained that he batted far too slowly and put pressure on the batsmen following him to the crease. From his very first limited overs series, the well-worn debate would rage around his head.

Australia prepared to play two consecutive matches against New Zealand. In the first, Wessels watched the fall of three early wickets and dug in to grind out a defiant 58. That was fine, but his side still finished 47 runs short of the target. Was the defeat his fault? Who was to blame? The next day, Australia were set to chase 248. Once again, they lost early wickets. Once again, Wessels dug in. He finished with a creditable 58, but he had batted for fully 38 overs and his side still lost by the margin of 58 runs.

Greig, perched in the Channel Nine commentary box, let rip at the man he had effectively brought to Australia. 'Kepler batted atrociously in one-day cricket,' Greig recalls. 'He went through a period when his temperament was totally against everything that one-day cricket stood for.'

The cannonball came from out of the blue. Wessels had top-scored in both matches against New Zealand. Sorry, mate. He was dropped for the next fixture against England at the Melbourne Cricket Ground. A fortnight before, he had been on top of the world. Now, he was back on the sidelines.

Why? Was it his fault that Australia had lost early wickets? What else was he supposed to do but consolidate? Would he have been dropped if he had got out early as well? Wessels, inevitably, felt hard done by. The terrible fear reared its head again. Perhaps Australia didn't feel he belonged. Travelling with the squad but not playing in the team, unaware of having done anything wrong, still feeling in form, Wessels' spirits plunged. At that stage, his batting average in international one-day cricket was 52.4. Look! He was doing OK. Look at the statistics. But he wasn't OK. He was dropped. Why?

The Australian selectors, persistently over-reacting to the public outcry which followed defeat, became less predictable than the weather and Wessels was treated in confused fashion. Dropped for one match, he was recalled to the side but batted at No.7. Next game, he batted at No.6. He was then dropped again. So was Dennis Lillee. Despite their confused selectors, Australia went on to beat New Zealand in the best-of-three final. Wessels looked on.

No sooner had they been carefully constructed, than the walls seemed to have come crumbling down on his international career. For as long as he could remember, he had stretched every sinew to play official Test cricket. Now, upon achieving that goal, he had discovered not some cricketing wonderland but a more brutal landscape than he had ever imagined, where you are no better than your last innings, where your place is always under threat, from where there is no escape. After two weeks spent chewing old proverbs about heated kitchens and high trees catching the most wind, Wessels recharged his spirits.

He was still in the Australian squad, wasn't he? A short, inaugural tour of Sri Lanka beckoned, followed by the 1983 World Cup in England. Opportunity was everywhere. He would fight on. The struggle would continue.

# 6

# With Kim, Against the World

---

They came from different worlds. One was dark, quiet, pessimistic. The other was fair, emotional, positive. Both were talented and impulsive. Both craved success above all, and both would be wounded by defeat.

Through two turbulent years, from April 1983 until March 1985, they came together under the baggy green cap of Australia and wholeheartedly took on every major cricket-playing nation in the world.

Sometimes they wept in defeat, sometimes they wept in triumph. They argued and fought, mocked and sulked. They began as rivals but the struggle brought them together. They lived each crisis and drama to the full. They didn't always win. They were criticised and ridiculed but they never flinched. Every step of the way, they were brave... brave beyond most men's understanding.

*****

March, 1983 — Kim Hughes is at the crease. Cricket is fun again. He stands, poised, waiting, restless, as ever prepared to swing the bat and to hit the ball. He knows no other tactics. Attack.

The Queensland spinners are bowling. Meat and drink. Western Australia need quick runs. He's in form and it feels great. Hughes is all played in and, as is his habit when life is good, he has started talking to himself, goading himself on. The next delivery is generously flighted. A nimble two-step and a full drive. The ball soars over the boundary at long-off.

'Yes, yes,' Hughes tells himself, cuffing his hips as adrenalin floods his veins. 'Great shot, Kim, great shot. That'd be a six on any ground in the world. Yes, yes. Great shot, Kim.'

His voice is loud enough for the fielders to hear his chatter. Some can hardly believe it. One of the greatest batsmen in the history of

Australian cricket stands at first slip, and laughs. 'For goodness sake, Hughes,' Greg Chappell shouts. 'Don't be a **** all your life.'

Kepler Wessels stands at second slip. He laughs too.

The leading cricketers in Australia are divided. Four seasons after the disbandment of World Series Cricket, the breach has not healed. Resentment and mistrust linger on. It is a classic conflict: like that which rages in most classrooms between the rough boys in the back row and the eager pupil answering all the questions at the front; like that which burns between any band of angry strikers seeking better wages and the man they call 'scab' because he chooses to remain unquestioningly loyal to the employer.

On the one side are the senior professionals, like Chappell, Lillee, Marsh and those who played for Packer because they felt underpaid, and Wessels who had fitted in so well with the disgruntled stars. On the other side is Hughes, the fabled hero who refused to sign for Packer because he wanted to play for Australia, who stood firm with the Australian Cricket Board because, ever since his boyhood, he had dreamed of winning Tests.

The senior pros can scarcely stand the sight of Hughes, the freckled darling of the establishment, wholesome beyond words. For pity's sake, he was even born on Australia Day. Hughes looks at the legends and admires their skill and their achievements but is disappointed by their negative, destructive and invariably dissatisfied approach to the game.

The differences are not always visible, fully-fledged rows are rare and, whatever they think of each other, they still fight the same Test match fight, but there is no trust and there is no affection. It's work.

So Chappell laughs at Hughes, and Wessels laughs too.

Hughes bats on. Why shouldn't he? Since making his début at the age of 21, he has played in 53 consecutive Tests, establishing himself among the finest batsmen in the world. Who doesn't recall his 117 and 84 during the Centenary Test at Lord's in 1980, and an unbeaten century against the West Indies at the MCG the next season? Why should he stand back for Lillee and Chappell, much less for this adopted Australian who stands laughing at second slip?

Hughes led Australia to Pakistan in 1982, Chappell took over as captain to regain the Ashes in 1982/83, then Hughes returned to lead the side through the triangular series against New Zealand and England. Now the pendulum swings again. Hughes withdraws from the short tour to Sri Lanka for personal reasons. Chappell agrees to lead the squad and Wessels is mightily relieved. Far better to be led by your mate, than by your rival...

Sri Lanka beckoned, an inaugural tour scheduled as a warm-up to the 1983 World Cup. Marsh, Thomson and Lawson had, like Hughes, stayed at home but Wessels was not going to miss this for anything. This was touring, the bonus of an international cricketer's life. As he stepped from the plane into the heat of Colombo, wearing his dark green blazer, his mind drifted back to his roots, to his own generation of South African cricketers who sat isolated, seeing no further than the Currie Cup, growing numb on the old circuit... Wanderers, Kingsmead, Newlands, St George's Park, Wanderers...

But this was Asia and Wessels discovered cricket fanaticism on a scale he had never previously imagined. When the Sri Lankans won the first two one-day internationals, the bustling, beautiful island began the celebrations. Concern over the worst drought in 30 years was briefly set aside as newspapers hailed Arjuna Ranatunga as 'the whizz-kid who smashed an exhilarating 55 in only 39 deliveries'. The pitifully waterless paddy-fields baking around the outskirts of Colombo were briefly replaced at the forefront of the public consciousness by 19-year-old Ranatunga, this 'Wizard of Ours'.

This was Asia, and here was poverty. The first one-day international had been played at the Sara stadium, situated in the midst of a squatter camp. As the Australian team bus approached the stadium, wretchedly thin young men and women scurried between the shacks, and young children, squatting in the dust beside the road, played quietly. So many people.

The touring team lost the match but, undisturbed, they approached the solitary Test with conviction. It mattered, and Chappell elected to bat first on a well-grassed pitch. Wessels, who had enjoyed some success on tour to date, discovered his most destructive form. When drinks were taken after an hour of play, Wessels had already scored 37. In the Press box, adjectives such as dour and negative were being tossed into the waste basket. Rousing and resourceful were diligently typed and dispatched. Someone said he was batting like Hughes, and Wessels was pleased with the comparison.

He reached his second Test century with a cavalier leg glance off Asantha de Mel, the off-spinner, and then leaned jauntily on his bat to survey the spectacle as fire crackers were let off around the ground in celebration of a fine innings. He was out soon after tea for 141 but, with David Hookes also scoring a century, Australia were able to declare their innings at 514 for four. Sri Lanka yielded under the resulting pressure. Bowled out for 271 and then 243, they were defeated, effectively humbled, by an innings and 38 runs with more than a day and a half to spare.

Even the downpour which washed out the last two one-day internationals could not dampen Wessels' optimism as the World Cup approached. The West Indies had won the trophy in 1975 and 1979 but the Australians travelled to England in brightly confident mood. They had been drawn to play the West Indians, Zimbabwe and India in a group from which two teams would qualify for the semi-finals. Their first match was against little Zimbabwe at Trent Bridge, an ideal warm-up for the significantly greater challenges ahead.

* * * * *

May, 1983 — A group of Australian cricketers have gathered in the bar of the Waldorf Astoria hotel, on the Strand, London. They talk quietly and drink slowly. Their shoulders are sagging and their smiles are weak because they have been eliminated from the World Cup. The previous day at Chelmsford, they had been beaten by India, bowled out for 129 in only 29 overs.

Morale had plunged. Kepler Wessels was in the bar, depressed. He had been dropped after three matches and, to his utter dismay, was still omitted when only five specialist batsmen were selected for the decisive match against India. He had been warned that when the wheels came off the Australian team, they usually came off in spectacular fashion. So they had, and here they sat, humiliated as also-rans. The squad was booked to fly home the next day. The reception would be tough but at least their nightmare would end.

Suddenly the captain appeared at the entrance to the bar. All heads turned. Kim Hughes was fully kitted out with his official team blazer, tie and slacks but he seemed curiously ill at ease.

'All right, well, I'll see you later,' he said.

'Where are you going?'

'Home.'

'When?'

'Now. I'm on a flight tonight. See you.'

Hughes was gone. The group in the bar were dumb-struck. 'It's obvious why he's left now,' ventured one. 'He just wants to put his side of the story to the ACB before we get back.' Accurate or not, it was

(*left*) 'Take the picture, please. I'm late for practice.' The Wessels family at home in 1968: *left to right,* Marguerite, Kepler, Wessel, Tewie and Marietta.

(*below*) 'One day, your son and I...' Wessels sits second from the right in the front row of a young Grey College tennis squad. It is 1970. Fourth from the right sits the coach, San-Marie Cronje. Her eldest son would be called Hansie ...

'When I grow up, I want to play for South Africa…' The South African Schools team of 1973. Wessels, broad for his age
sits second from the right in the front row next to Ray Jennings. Also in the front row is Allan Lamb, second from the left
and Kevin Verdoorn, third from the left. The twelfth man, second from the right in the back row, is Peter Kirsten.

'Yes, colonel, I'm sorry, really.' Soon after this photograph appeared in the *Sunday Times*, Wessels was hauled before the military top brass and admonished for making a mockery of the SADF uniform. It is Pretoria, 1977 and one frustrating year of national service has just begun.

ıble lieutenants in Packer's army.' Tony Greig (*left*) recruited Wessels from Sussex into World Series Cricket. Eddie ıarlow (*centre*) captained Wessels at Western Province and again at the circus. Garth le Roux (*right*), in his prime, was əted Man of the Series in Australia and would become a team-mate at Sussex.

Chopper, mate, Kerry's not gonna be happy.' The World Series Cricket Australian side wait for the prize-giving after ɔsing the Supertest final to the Rest of the World XI in Sydney, February 4, 1979. Downcast and disappointed are, *from eft to right,* Lenny Pascoe, Rodney Marsh, Bruce Laird, Wessels, David Hookes and Dennis Lillee.

(*above*) Dreams can come true: Wessels scored 162 on his Test début for Australia against England in Brisbane on November 27th, 1982. David Gower stands at silly point and Bob Taylor is the England wicketkeeper as Wessels sweeps.

(*below*) Repeatedly battered by the West Indian fast bowlers, Wessels ultimately earned their respect because he never gave up. Here, in a night match at the Melbourne Cricket Ground, a psyched-up Wessels appeals as Gus Logie is run out.

(*left*) A glance to leg: Wessels, in control in 1985, bats with an arm brace after being struck by Courtney Walsh.

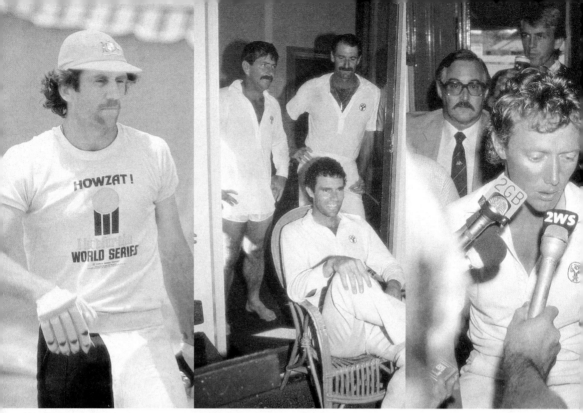

(*above*) 'Everything was based on guts and loyalty. I admired them so much.' Wessels revered the giants of the Australian game. Ian Chappell (*left*) was 'the perfect captain'. Rodney Marsh ('the arch-patriot'), Greg Chappell ('the mc elegant batsman') and Dennis Lillee ('the big heart') (*centre*) pictured during the 1983 series against Pakistan. Kim Hughes (*right*), so many good times, so many hard times…
(*below*) 'One smile in a difficult tour.' Laughing with English players during the fourth Test at Old Trafford in 1985.
*From the left*, David Gower, Ian Botham and Mike Gatting (*rear*), Wessels, Paul Allott and Allan Lamb.

'He never hooks.' On various occasions throughout his career, Wessels has suddenly clicked, releasing an array of strokes so dazzling that his critics have been dumbfounded. In England in 1985 they said he couldn't score on the leg side. Here, he hooks on his way to a century against Somerset.

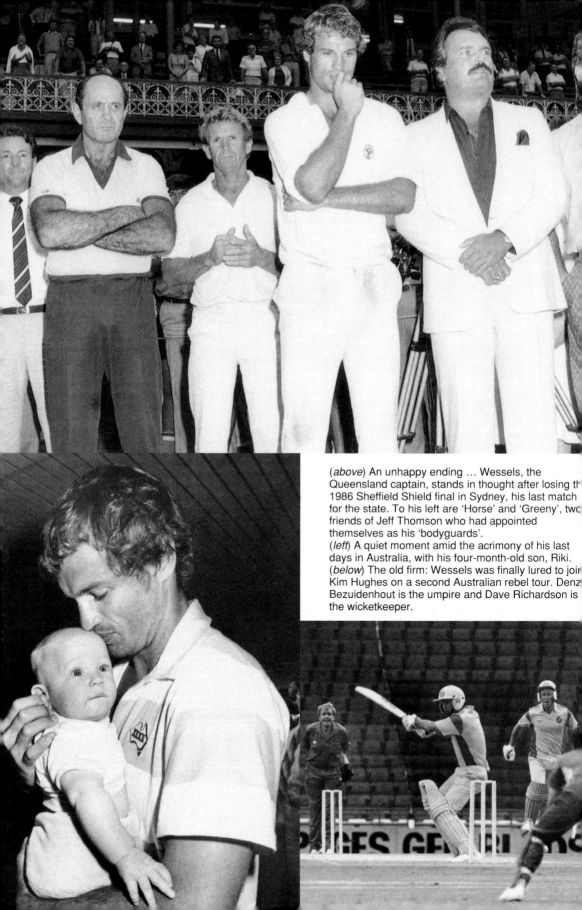

(*above*) An unhappy ending … Wessels, the Queensland captain, stands in thought after losing the 1986 Sheffield Shield final in Sydney, his last match for the state. To his left are 'Horse' and 'Greeny', two friends of Jeff Thomson who had appointed themselves as his 'bodyguards'.

(*left*) A quiet moment amid the acrimony of his last days in Australia, with his four-month-old son, Riki.

(*below*) The old firm: Wessels was finally lured to join Kim Hughes on a second Australian rebel tour. Denzil Bezuidenhout is the umpire and Dave Richardson is the wicketkeeper.

what many of the squad believed. They blamed their captain, he blamed them. They believed he had let them down, he believed they had let him down.

The strong emotions and energies, which all point in the same direction in a happy and successful team, had spun wildly out of control. Hughes was alleged to have said Dennis Lillee was bowling 'like a punch-drunk boxer', and the captain was scarcely awarded appropriate respect.

Whatever the underlying reasons, and neither camp appeared completely innocent, the result was a talented team playing like proverbial drains. They had approached the opening match against 'little' Zimbabwe with swaggering nonchalance, and lost. A ridiculous series of spilled catches enabled the eager part-timers from Africa to score 239 for six from their 60 overs. In pursuit, Wessels scored 70, but Australia's middle order imploded and, although Marsh scored a defiant half-century, the innings struggled to 226 for seven. Even allowing for what Hughes exhaustively explained as the unpredictability of one-day cricket, a major power had been emphatically humiliated.

Australia's second match yielded a more familiar result. The West Indies won by 101 runs at Headingley. Wessels was drowning in despair. Hardly able to move the ball off the square, he had begun to sense the gleaming axe hovering above him once again. While the team returned to form with a huge 162-run victory over India, with Hughes scoring a sprightly 52, Wessels continued to struggle. Out for 1. He was dropped. His World Cup was sadly over... 'Bloody Hughes, I knew he never wanted me in the side anyway.'

'Typical Wessels, I'll let him sulk and stew in his own juice.' The captain had other matters on his mind. With the semi-finals still within reach, Hughes led his side to a return victory over Zimbabwe but even his innings of 69 could not prevent a second defeat against the West Indies. As other results turned out, that didn't matter. Australia would progress if they beat India at Chelmsford. Hughes was confident they would, so confident that he decided to rest himself and give his nagging hamstring injury some extra time to recover for the semi-final. Chasing 247, Australia were bowled out for 129. Hughes sat in the stands, stunned and eliminated.

The Indian team went on to beat England in the semi-final, and the West Indies in the final but their surprising triumph offered little consolation to the Australians on their way home, and less to Wessels.

'So long as Hughes is captain,' he told himself, 'I'll never settle in the Australian side.'

\* \* \* \* \*

October, 1983 — In Brisbane and in Perth, it had been a long, hard winter of reflection, of resolution and of renewal. Hughes, at home in Perth, confirmed as captain for the imminent home series versus Pakistan, was planning to assert his authority and communicate his ambitions and tactics more effectively to his players. In Brisbane, Wessels made certain he was fit for the next campaign. Early in the season, Western Australia played Queensland...

'Kepler, have you got a minute?' It is Hughes, gesturing the Queensland opener to one side. Wessels is surprised.

'Sure. Now?'

'Yeah.'

They sit and talk. The clouds part. The sun breaks through.

Hughes speaks. 'Kepler, you should know that, as far as I'm concerned, you are the number one opener in Australia and we need you in the team to play Pakistan. The only way we're going to be successful is by picking guys with courage. I know you've got it and you've got my support.'

Wessels listens, heart pounding with delight...

Years later, he would recall the discussion as a turning point in his Australian career: 'It was like talking to a different person. Kim's attitude to me seemed to have changed completely. His support immediately made me feel much more positive. Everything changed overnight.'

Hughes had reached a conclusion that he needed to create a nucleus around which his team could develop strength and spirit, and he wanted Wessels in that nucleus. He recalls: 'I started to believe in Kepler because of his strength of character. He had always shown he was a fighter and I felt that if someone showed faith in him, he would respond magnificently.'

Positively believing in each other, Hughes and Wessels looked forward to the series against Pakistan as an opportunity to build confidence and establish their respective positions. Steady, solid, winning performances were required. Their opponents were emerging as a familiar Pakistani blend: massively talented players, bizarre administrators, and an awkward superstar.

Zaheer Abbas, Mohsin Khan, Abdul Qadir were cricketers who deserved better than to learn, only days before the tour, that Air Marshal Nur Khan, chairman of the Pakistani board, had decreed Imran Khan would captain the side. Zaheer had already been appointed to lead the tour with Imran injured, but Imran had declared himself recovered from a stress fracture in his shin. His 'can play-can't play' soap opera blighted the trip. In the event, he didn't play in the first three Tests and was unable to bowl at any stage.

Hughes primed his side to land an early punch in the first Test at the WACA ground in Perth. With Wayne Phillips scoring 159 on his début and Carl Rackemann claiming match analysis of eleven for 118, Pakistan were beaten by an innings and nine runs. The second Test in Brisbane followed a similar pattern with Australia's batsmen thriving. Chappell and Border scored centuries, Hughes made 53 and Pakistan were saved only by the rain.

The World Cup suddenly seemed a long time ago. Hughes was different, less suspicious, more up-front, and his players reacted positively. They were also winning. That helped. Wessels, however, was quiet again. With only 48 runs in three innings, he approached the third Test in Adelaide feeling due a major innings. Hughes reassured him but he cried out for runs.

With seven to his name, Wessels hooked at Sarfraz Nawaz and watched with horror as the ball lobbed gently towards Azeem at fine leg. But the fielder dropped it. All right, he told himself, that's the bit of luck I haven't had all season. Now get your head down and use it.

He survived until lunch, when his barely contained nerves finally took a spectacular toll. Wessels leapt up from his seat at the table and left to vomit in the lavatories. Cleaned up, he resumed his innings and gradually began to thrive, first in partnership with Graham Yallop, and then with his captain. The square boundaries were famously short at the Adelaide Oval and Wessels began to pummel them. Boundary followed boundary. He reached his century off 143 balls, and Hughes bounced down the wicket to shake his hand. His form and confidence were flooding back. His bat began to feel all unmissable middle.

Finally dismissed an hour before the close, Wessels glanced up at the scoreboard and thanked his Maker for the 179 beside his name. He had struck no fewer than 23 boundaries. Hughes felt vindicated.

The Pakistanis fought hard in reply, with Qasim Omar scoring a century after Wessels, at short leg, had called him back when the umpire had adjudged him to be caught, but Hughes consolidated his team's position with a century in the second innings. The Test was drawn, and Hughes was Man of the Match.

Imran's return made little impact. Australia held too many batting guns for Pakistan ever to force a winning position. Hughes, growing in confidence and stature, struck 94 in the first innings of the fourth Test and Australia were never threatened after Yallop's 268 took them to a total of 555. Pakistan held on for the draw and approached the final Test 1-0 down.

Greg Chappell, at ease within the team, had also reached the point of no return. In what he decided would be his 87th and final Test for Australia, the elegant left-hander might have written the script as he produced an immaculate innings of 182, in the process passing Don Bradman's record aggregate of runs for Australia. Chappell ended with 7 110 runs at an average of 53.86. Bradman had scored 6 996 at an average of 99.94, in only 52 Tests.

Australia won the match, with Hughes scoring 76, and clinched the series by two Tests to nil. The captain's world, so barren six months previously, was blooming. His own form was superb and his team had produced a convincing and consistent performance. With Chappell out of the frame, his position was as strong as it had ever been and he used it to protect 'his' players, those to whom he had pledged support at the start of the summer...

'No, no, no. Wessels will play.'

The selector would not be put off. Kim, look at the figures. Apart from his 179, Wessels had scored only 77 runs in his six other innings during the Test series. 'And you know he can't play one-day cricket.'

Hughes bristled. The West Indies had arrived, again, joining Pakistan and Australia in the perennial triangular one-day series, and the captain was coming under pressure. He was irritated.

'Listen, mate,' said Hughes, dead straight. 'You don't know what you're talking about. Kepler hits so many boundaries that he is always going to score enough runs and, even in one-day cricket, you need someone who can anchor the innings. He's the bloke I want in that role. All right?'

Wessels played. Hughes recalls that, for a fortnight or so, he 'spent most of my time defending Kepler'. The selectors wanted him out, Hughes wanted him in. As the series ran its course, Hughes followed his instinct. Put your faith in Wessels, and he won't let you down. The captain did, and the result was a consistent supply of swiftly scored runs.

Tucking into another mind-boggling schedule, in which Australia would play 13 internationals in 27 days, Wessels batted, and batted, and batted. He scored seven against the West Indies on January 11th, then 92, from 122 balls, against Pakistan on January 12th to be Man of the Match.

On and on. Four not out. 27. 86. 60. 7. 4. 61. 50. Beyond the runs, Wessels had also begun to bowl for Australia. Hughes had been watching him in the nets and believed his 'baby seamers' on a length could irritate opposing batsmen. At the MCG on January 21st, Hughes threw Wessels the ball. 'OK, bowl.' More than 80 000 spectators wondered what was going on but the batsman scurried through eight overs for 32 runs. Wessels had done his job, and he started to do so regularly as the series hurtled towards its final stages.

Australia met the West Indies in the best-of-three final and lost the opening game by eight wickets. When Viv Richards stroked a happy 59 in a total of 222 in the second match, the West Indians appeared well placed to take a 2-0 lead but the Australians had not given up.

Hughes joined Wessels at the crease. As a long, eventful season drew to a close, they began to reel in the target: Hughes, all extravagant thrusts of his shoulder blades on his way to a swift 53, and Wessels, all deep concentration, prodded singles and carefully placed drives, on his way to 77. They added 109 and left their team needing 36 runs off 30 balls. The countdown culminated in Rackemann being run out off the last ball. It was a tie.

The West Indians thought the series was theirs but the ACB ruled a third match would be played. Amid acrimony, both Clive Lloyd and Richards discovered 'injuries' and withdrew from the third game but it made no difference. Despite Hughes' fighting 65 off 85 balls, the West Indies won by six runs.

Hughes and his side finished with some honour in defeat and Wessels was named Man of the Series. He was only too pleased to accept the award from Tony Greig, his chief critic in the Channel Nine commentary box.

* * * * *

February 12th, 1984 — Rod Marsh, the legendary wicketkeeper, sings, laughs, drinks and cries. He has announced his retirement from international cricket, so he sits at the centre of an Australian dressing room awash with emotion and nostalgia. If ever a man loved his country . . .

The team had lost the World Series final to the West Indians but, more importantly, they were losing the services of three great cricketers. Dennis Lillee and Greg Chappell had retired after the final Test against Pakistan. Now Marsh was following them to the sidelines.

Matilda waltzed in the Australian dressing room until eleven o'clock that night. Amid an atmosphere heavy with sweat, mateship, exaggerated tales and beer, an era was ending. Beyond his leviathan haul of wicketkeeping records, many established catching the deflected cannonballs of Lillee and Thomson, the swarthy, competitive Marsh had played with his heart. During one Test in England, he had insisted on batting despite a broken toe. 'Are you OK?' asked umpire Harold Bird. 'I will be if we win,' Marsh replied.

Wessels stayed all night. Marsh had been good to him ever since the earliest days with Packer. Hughes stayed a while too. Some observers suggested the departure of three such influential characters would enhance the captain's authority within the squad but Hughes, as ever, was looking forward, not back. He was more concerned by the prospect of leading a weakened Australian side against one of the most powerful teams in history.

Within days, Hughes would take Australia on a five-Test tour of the West Indies, and that series would be followed by another five Tests against the West Indies in Australia at the end of the year.

Ten in a row. It was a prospect filled with foreboding . . . facing this array of superstars who had no conspicuous weakness. Yet neither Hughes nor Wessels shook with fear. They were exhilarated. This was the ultimate challenge their sport could offer, the sternest test. They would stand or fall, but it was far better to fight the fight and lose, than not to fight the fight at all.

Hughes planned his strategy. It was based on courage. He recalls: 'I know everyone has it to some extent but some have it more than others. Talent was not going to be enough on its own. Kepler was an obvious selection because he wasn't scared of the quicks. I rated him among the top three or four batsmen anywhere for handling fast bowling, and that was largely down to guts. That was the only way we were going to survive against the West Indies. Somehow, we would have to hang in there and put pressure on them.'

Clive Lloyd predicted plenty of pressure as well, but in the opposite direction. Tall, loping, powerful, bespectacled, the West Indian captain was at the height of his powers. He had united the disparate, sometimes divided forces of the Caribbean islands into an effective unit in much the same way as Frank Worrell had done before him. He was a born leader, no less.

Forced to support his young siblings, a brother and four sisters, after his father's death, Lloyd had left school and taken a clerical job which paid 16 pounds a week. He skipped adolescence. Leadership potential surfaced at the age of 12. Walking home from school, Lloyd found two boys fighting and imposed a little peace. For his trouble, a ruler was stabbed into his eye and he was left having to wear the thick spectacles which became his trademark.

He made his Test début in 1966 and was handed the captaincy eight years later. Taking control of a mediocre side (it is often overlooked that the West Indies failed to win a single Test series at home between 1965 and 1974), he gradually made it strong, then powerful, then invincible.

Lloyd's method was moulded by the harsh experience of his first major tour as captain. During the summer of 1975/76, his West Indian side was beaten by five Tests to one in Australia. They had been routed by Lillee and Thomson. Fast bowling, Lloyd decided, was the way to go. Then he started to dream a little. Imagine not two fast bowlers, but four. Imagine a relentless barrage of bounce and pace from which there would be no respite.

These plans were nearing completion when the entire West Indian team, then severely underpaid by their Board, signed up with Kerry Packer. There, on the under-prepared pitches of World Series Cricket, the sport glimpsed its future. Batsmen wore helmets and they have not taken them off since...

Now it is 1984 and Lloyd holds an awesome group of pace bowlers straining on the leash. Garner, Marshall and Holding lead as intimidating a battery as has ever been gathered in one team at one time. Supported by Daniel and Davis, they are ready to bounce and blitz the world.

The batting power at Lloyd's disposal oozes flair and genius: Greenidge and Haynes will open, to be followed by Richards and Lloyd himself. Around this quartet of legends, Richie Richardson and Larry Gomes take their places. Adding the talents of Jeff Dujon, the wicketkeeper-batsman, and Roger Harper, the spinner, there stands a team with the potential to destroy any opposition. The sole key to this potential is in Lloyd's safe possession. He has designed and built the machine. Now, majestically, he will drive it.

Assured as the longest-serving captain in Test history (he has led the West Indies in 54 consecutive Tests), Lloyd awaits the arrival of Kim Hughes' Australian team. The Caribbean is preparing a warm welcome.

* * * * *

March 23rd, 1984 — Another day, another net practice. The Australian squad is at work in Port of Spain. Hughes barks instructions. The bowlers pound in and the batsmen get in line. The team is fighting, holding its own against the West Indies. Just. The first two Test matches have been drawn.

Kepler Wessels stands to one side, sullen and downcast. His tour is over. He had struggled through the second Test match with a sore, swollen knee but now could play no more. It was a simple case of wear and tear, a problem which was recurring throughout his career. The tour doctor has told him to fly home for an operation. There was no point battling on. The knife beckoned.

It's a miserable feeling to be withdrawn from the frontline just as the battle is warming up. His flight is four hours away ...

Wessels had begun his first tour of the West Indies so well: scoring a century in the opening match against the Leeward Islands, and then being warmly received in Georgetown. Three years previously, a Test match had been cancelled when the Guyana government objected to the South African connections of Robin Jackman, an English bowler. There was widespread speculation that Wessels would prompt similar protest. Instead, the Afrikaner was welcomed.

In form and at ease, Wessels first encountered the fervour of West Indian supporters at the opening one-day international, played on a turbulent day in Berbice, Guyana. Fourteen thousand people had squeezed into an arena built for half that number. So great was the crowd around the ground that the two teams had to be airlifted into the stadium by army helicopter. The cricket was played to the unbroken rhythm of clanking cans and beer bottles, the scoreboard collapsed under the weight of spectators perched on top, Haynes scored 133 not out and the all-star, hip-hop West Indians won.

The first Test, played at Bourda stadium in Guyana a few days later, had not been so one-sided. The Australian batting did totter at stages but the sort of courage characterised by a tenth wicket stand of 97 between Rod Hogg and Tom Hogan had carried the touring team to a position where they could declare on the fifth morning, setting the West

Indies 323 to win. The target proved beyond them even though Haynes and Greenidge both scored unbeaten centuries. They had both mastered the Australian bowling. The writing was on the wall.

Hughes, forever the optimist, was none the less encouraged. It's not the dog in the fight, it's the fight in the dog. He became grimly determined that his team would stand and battle. In the match against Trinidad and Tobago, however, his nervy resolve extended to comic proportions. When, on the last day, the local captain delayed his declaration so long that the Australians were set an impossible target of 186 runs in just over an hour, Hughes impulsively decided to open the innings himself and clearly demonstrate his anger.

For 26 overs, he and Wayne Phillips blocked half-volleys and patted full tosses back to the bowler. Hughes struck one six and a boundary but did not score a further run. At one stage, Phillips sat down at the non-striker's end. For the last over, he took his pads off and held them under his arm. Hughes was fined A$300 but probably felt it was worth it. The Australians were not winning friends but that was fine. They were more interested in winning.

They did win the second one-day international in Trinidad. After the West Indies had been restricted to 190 for seven in a rain-reduced 37 overs, Wessels launched the Australian innings by hooking Marshall for six in the first over. Back in the pavilion, Hughes was exhilarated. That's the way, Chopper. Attack them. When they go for your jugular, you go for theirs. Australia won by four wickets. Wessels had hit 67 from 92 balls, and was Man of the Match. Stepping forward to collect the award, he was limping badly.

'Are you all right, mate?'

'Sure, no problem, really.'

Wild horses would not have kept Wessels and his swollen knee out of the second Test but there were no heroics. He was dismissed for 4 in the first innings and for 0 in the second, on both occasions by Garner. Australia salvaged a draw by virtue of one man's heroics. Border held the team together with innings of 98 not out and 100 not out. He stood alone, courageously moving into line against the fast bowlers and refusing to roll over.

Wessels, pleased and proud for his friend, could hardly walk away from the Queen's Park Oval when the Test was over. The doctor inspected the knee and said it required an operation. That was it. End of tour. He returned to Australia for surgery.

93

Graeme Wood was flown in to replace Wessels but he fractured a finger during the third Test and the fragile dam of courage which had held during the first two Tests caved in. The West Indies won the third, fourth and fifth Test matches in a torrent of strokeplay and bouncers rearing high at the batsmen's throats. Hughes fought hard. He battled past 20 each time he batted in the last three Tests, and yet his highest score was 29.

The final tour statistics offered harsh confirmation that all the guts in the world could not withstand Lloyd's team ... Garner had taken a record 31 wickets in the series, the West Indies had not lost a single second innings wicket in five Tests and had only once amassed less than 300 in an innings. By contrast, Australia had only once moved past 300 in an innings and, during the third Test at Bridgetown, Barbados, had been dismissed for an awful 97. Border emerged as the top-scorer in five of their 10 innings.

Hughes held his hands up at the end of the series and proclaimed the West Indies as 'the strongest, most professional and disciplined side I've played against'. The West Indians subsequently continued their irresistible rampage through England, where they won all five Test matches.

Their next destination was Australia in November. What could be done to tame the whirlwind? Hughes needed to rebuild morale ...

\* \* \* \* \*

September, 1984 — The Jawaharlal Nehru stadium roars its approval. The batsman, hair soaked in sweat, collects his trophy and raises it towards the stands. Kepler Wessels, of Australia: Man of the Match, the talk of New Delhi. This opening batsman ... where is he from? ... South Africa? ... Oh ...

The Australians had immersed themselves in the knowledgeable, fanatic cricket world of India for the Ranjit Trophy series which comprised five one-day internationals against the previous year's world champions. Hughes saw the trip as an opportunity to rebuild confidence before the home series against the West Indies. So it had turned out. Australia won three of the matches, and rain had claimed the other two.

Wessels could hardly keep his eyes off the towering stands of spectators: vast bowls of concrete spread thick with humanity. Inspired, he scored a brisk 42 in Ahmedabad and 35 not out in Indore. At New Delhi, he and Hughes had added 124 in two hours. Conquering a slow pitch and untroubled by his knee, Wessels stroked 107, and was left clutching his haul of awards.

Lawson had bowled well, Border and Yallop also scored freely and Hughes had led the side with new distinction. 'From the pre-tour training session in Canberra, Kim was on top of the whole situation,' Wessels recalls. 'He was clear and direct with all the players and we were a very happy team. I reckon he captained the side better in India than ever before.'

Australian cricket was smiling once again, playing well and looking good off the field too. The team had won 25 000 rupees in prize money, most of which was subsequently donated towards the building of a new home for crippled children on the outskirts of Ahmedabad.

Ahead of the gently soaring morale, the West Indies lay in wait. When the Australians arrived back home, Clive Lloyd's side had already begun their tour. 'Yes, we can do it,' Hughes urged his players...

* * * * *

November, 1984 — The captain sits, red-faced, harassed, trying in vain to choke back the tears. He is surrounded by notebooks at the ready, cameras flashing in his face, by men wrestling for a better position, a better view. All his hopes, his bustling optimism, all his effort has come to this. Head bowed, he reads his own epitaph as the captain of Australia... to the world.

'The constant criticism, speculation and innuendo by former players and sections of the media over the past four or five years have finally taken their toll,' Hughes reads. Australia have lost the second Test by eight wickets. It is their fifth consecutive Test match defeat.

Kim Hughes resigns as captain. He finishes the statement and leaves the media to chew on their story, finding a way through the scrum and back to the dressing room. Players don't quite know which way to look. Hasn't he shouldered a responsibility they all share? Hughes is shattered. He sits on a bench, alone...

Across the room, Wessels stood and stared. Two years earlier he had been upset when Hughes took over as captain but now he was demoralised: 'I looked across at him and I felt this sense of injustice. He was completely devastated and it wasn't his fault. All the players knew he couldn't be blamed for losing to the West Indies. The media wanted a scapegoat, and it turned out to be Kim. It was a horrible day for everyone.'

If Hughes had been slaughtered in the media, then Wessels had been treated little better. Two sportsmen, both trying their best, were condemned by an inexorable flood of printed vitriol. It didn't seem fair, but it was part of their life in the limelight.

Effort, it was confirmed, had not been enough. Hughes had been confident approaching the first Test and he was thrilled when the tourists were reduced to 104 for five. But then Dujon and Gomes scored centuries, taking the first innings total to 416 and the pressure was again on Australia. They buckled. All out for 76. Wessels, one of only three batsmen to reach double figures, had batted for an hour, just trying to survive, but scored only 13. Following on, Australia eked out 228 and were defeated by an innings and 112 runs.

Wessels, like his team-mates, was struggling. He had played four innings against the West Indians, two for Queensland, and scored a total of 20 runs. He had been dismissed by Joel Garner three times, on each occasion edging a rising delivery slanted across him. Twice he had been dismissed for 0 in the opening over of the innings. That should not happen. A crisis was developing.

Garner was the Bogeyman: 6 feet 8 inches tall, able to find excessive bounce in any pitch, in his prime. Coached by former Test fast bowlers Wes Hall and Charlie Griffith in Barbados, Garner did not make his first class début until he was 23 yet he soon became consistently threatening. Nicknamed 'Big Bird' after the character in Sesame Street, he had suffered both shoulder and knee injuries but was now recovered. So gentle and genial that John Arlott, the English cricket doyen, once said he had 'a smile like a slice of melon', Garner appeared to have Wessels neatly wrapped up. With a bow.

'Wessels is a broken man,' a Sydney newspaper sniped as the second Test approached. He was certainly a worried man, seeking some kind of solution to the problem which threatened his career. Walking along a street in Brisbane, on the eve of the Test, Wessels was startled by the shouts of a truck driver. It was Trevor from the Railway Institute gym.

'I see you're getting a bit of strife in the papers,' Trevor shouted, frantically winding down his window.

'Yeah, well, a bit,' Wessels replied.

'Do you want me to do anything about it? I mean, you know, make a couple of visits to a couple of people.'

'No, I thought about it, but no. You'll get into trouble.'

'Really mate, I will. It'd be no problem.'

'No thanks.'

'All right. Anyway, I'll see you at the gym.'

Garner would have to be faced alone. Wessels knew that. One on one. Garner with the ball, Wessels with the bat. No draws. One winner, one loser. It was better than boxing. His spirits boosted by a brilliant Shield 144 against South Australia, Wessels strode out to open the Australian innings in the second Test at the Gabba. Before his home crowd, he could not fail.

Head down, chin in, concentrate. Wessels took his guard and steadied as Garner loped into action. Three balls passed through to Dujon, the fourth was stabbed to cover, the fifth was also let by. Garner moved in to bowl the last delivery of the first over. Wessels shouldered arms... and was bowled. A moment of unearthly silence. Aghast, Wessels turned to look down on shattered stumps. He headed back to the pavilion amid a murmuring knell.

GOODBYE KEPLER, BIG BIRD'S BUNNY AGAIN. The following day's Brisbane newspapers reported the end of Wessels' Test career. They also featured a cartoon which depicted him as a rabbit clutching a bat and wearing a plaster. The second innings was still to come. One last chance.

Australia finished with 175 in the first innings and the West Indians replied with 424. As Wessels strapped on his pads, his side faced another huge defeat. He felt no pressure. Everybody expected him to be dropped for the next Test, so he resolved to strike out. If he was going to go down, he would go down with all guns blazing.

He would swing the bat at any delivery remotely off line. His innings in the first Test, when he scored 13 in an hour, had shown there was no point just trying to survive, waiting to get out. In boxing terms, he was ready to stand toe to toe and to slug it out. Striding out to bat, he suddenly felt calm. Joel's Bunny showed his teeth.

Garner loped in but strayed down the leg-side. Wessels moved into position and glanced to fine leg for two. The Gabba grandstand roared, part irony and part relief. Garner had returned to his mark. This time, he bowled fractionally short, outside the off-stump. Wessels rocked back on to his heel and crashed the ball off sweet, sweet middle to the square boundary. Cover point had not moved. The Gabba roared again. Attack. Attack.

Hook. Cut. Drive. Head still, chin tucked in. After 90 minutes' play, the Australian openers, Wessels and Dyson, had taken the score to 88 without loss. K.C. Wessels... 61 not out. Aiming past cover point again, he was finally caught off Walsh. His effort did not save the match because Australia were dismissed for 271 and still lost the Test by eight wickets, and it could not save his captain, and friend, who resigned shortly afterwards. It did, however, retain his place in the side.

* * * * *

November, 1984 — Another captain, another Test. Allan Border stands in the Australian dressing room at the Adelaide Oval, speaking only minutes before the third Test is due to start. The West Indies have won the toss, and will bat... 'We must stop them getting a flyer,' Border says. 'That means the bowlers have got to keep tight and the fielding has got to be...'

His words abruptly fade out. His tightly focused eyes catch sight of a man standing at the back of the room, small, quiet and listening intently. It is Don Bradman. Border, asked to lead a side in crisis, gulps.

'... sharp,' he says finally. 'The fielding must be sharp. Let's get out there.' Then he looks back at the legend of Australian cricket and Bradman sort of smiles and nods. Past and present, in it together...

The Test marked the centenary of Test cricket in Adelaide and 22 former international captains watched as the West Indies amassed 356 in their first innings. Lawson, a qualified optometrist by profession, heroically epitomised the new spirit of a new era under the new captain, claiming eight for 112, yet when Australia began their reply, the pressure returned.

'Kepler, I want you to bat at No.3,' Border said.

'No problem.'

Wood and Dyson opened but the latter departed with the total on 28. As Wessels emerged from the pavilion, he looked up and saw Lloyd gesturing towards Garner at fine leg. Next over, Joel. It's your man again. In Brisbane, the bunny had shown his teeth. In Adelaide, the bunny bit back.

Get into line, each time. Get on top of the rising ball. Know which balls to let go. Latch on to anything off line, and punish it ruthlessly. Don't let them see you're scared. Fight with mind, fight with body, fight.

Wessels held firm until five minutes before six o'clock when he misjudged a bouncer from Walsh. Crack! His elbow exploded with pain. Wessels dropped his bat, reeling away in agony. He felt sure the joint was broken and was driven to hospital where X-rays revealed only bruising. At 9.30 the next morning, Wessels walked into the nets with a heavily strapped elbow and an undaunted spirit. Batting was painful but he would resume his innings down the order.

After lunch, with the Australian innings in trouble at 145 for six, Lloyd and his team were amazed as Wessels approached the crease, wearing a makeshift elbow guard. 'He was an exceptionally gutsy player,' the West Indian captain recalls. 'I think we all respected him very much for that.'

In partnership with Lawson, Wessels started to haul the innings towards respectability. They added 87 runs before Lawson nicked a catch to wicketkeeper Dujon just before tea. Lawson waited for the umpire's decision. Dujon thought that was ridiculous and said so. Wessels, who had been verbally abused by Dujon in Brisbane, saw red and waded in with his most descriptive nouns. Never mind the pain of his elbow, Dujon was a *****. As the players walked off the field for tea, Viv Richards became involved. Fine, he was a ***** as well. The group reached the pavilion amid wagging fingers and raised voices.

Fight. Fight. Fight. Wessels thrived into the evening, edging towards three figures. On 90, he drove Marshall for successive boundaries. Rod Hogg was surviving at the other end but Wessels sought a single to keep the strike, so he shaped to run the ball to third man. An inside edge. He was bowled for 98, a hero none the less. Australia 284 all out, 72 behind.

A century by Gomes enabled the West Indies to declare at 292 for seven, challenging Australia to score 365 on the fifth day, or simply to survive for the draw. They managed neither, as only one player passed 20: Wessels. Again, he had manned the bridge alone. Again, he had defended by attacking, striking 70 in just over two hours (56 of his runs were scored in boundaries) but to no avail. Australia were all out for 171, beaten by 191 runs.

Hughes, who had retained his place in the side after resigning as captain, went out of his way to congratulate Wessels but there was little to be said in reply. The former skipper, striving desperately to rediscover form, had been caught behind first ball in the first innings and then scored only two in the second. What was there to say? There were now widespread calls for him to be dropped from the side altogether. The hounds were still chasing. He remained for the fourth Test in Melbourne but there was no respite. Australia forced a draw and Hughes scored not a single run: caught behind for 0 in the first innings, LBW Garner for 0 in the second. He could take no more, and was left out of the side. In a wretched twist of fate, his demise coincided with the team's long-awaited revival.

Richards had scored a monumental 208 in the West Indian first innings at the MCG but Australia avoided the follow on, thanks to Wessels, who scored 90, and a defiant last wicket stand between Hogg and Murray Bennett. The eventual West Indian declaration again challenged Australia to survive the fifth day for a draw and, in spite of a sudden collapse during which Wessels' new confidence was punctured, bowled by Garner for 0, Andrew Hilditch, returning to the team after five years, scored 113 to stave off another defeat.

The draw, celebrated as a moral victory, was followed by a genuine triumph in the fifth Test in Sydney. Australia prepared a turning pitch to suit Bennett and Bob Holland, and then managed to do what the West Indies had been achieving all summer: put a large total on the board, apply pressure on the opposition and bowl them out twice to win by an innings. 'Dutchie' Holland finished with match analysis of ten for 144, and most of the glory.

However, Wessels had played a decisive role in establishing the dominant first innings total. He scored 173 and would cherish his innings at the SCG as one of the greatest of his career — because he had been written off and fought back, because Australia, once ridiculed, had beaten a seemingly invincible foe, because he had proved himself at the very highest level.

He had arrived at the crease with the total 12 for one and barely managed to survive on an uneven pitch. Dropped in the gully on 13, he had scored 30 by lunch and accelerated into the afternoon, reaching tea on 73. Walking out for the last session of the first day, Wessels was approached by Haynes.

'So, are you finally going to get that hundred now?' the West Indian opener had asked. Wessels, who had scored 61, 98, 70, 90 and 0 in his previous five Test innings, smiled.

'I hope you do,' Haynes added.

Through the 80s, into the 90s, Wessels progressed. A studious drive for four past cover off Marshall took him to 98. Keep it tight. Get in line, get in line. Marshall bowled, well pitched up. Wessels moved across and pushed through extra cover, ran one, and then came back for the second. He'd done it. The bat was pumped furiously towards the home dressing room on the ground floor to the left of the Members' Pavilion at the SCG. Haynes grinned.

Back at home, Sally Wessels, emotion welling in her eyes, dialled a number in George, South Africa. 'Hello, Ma?'

'Yes,' Marguerite Wessels answered.

'Your son has just scored a century.'

Australia reached the close at 252 for two, with Wessels 120 not out. Bob Hawke, who had replaced Fraser as the prime minister, visited the dressing room and offered his congratulations. This was the Australian way, never to give up. Many miles away, South Africa celebrated a surrogate triumph.

The next morning, Wessels advanced in partnership with Border, scoring well despite a slow outfield. He departed on 173, dragging a ball from Holding on to his stumps, but Australia reached 471 and the spinners completed the job, dismissing the West Indies for 163 and then 253 to win by an innings and 55 runs. Only Richards and Lloyd, battling hard to save his last Test match before retirement, offered significant resistance.

Wessels had completed the series with a total of 505 runs at an average of 56.11 (no other Australian had passed 250). His average after three innings had been 4.33. By any standards, it had been a rare recovery.

As usual, the Australian summer was concluded by a deluge of one-day internationals; and, as usual, Wessels' shares plummeted amid the now familiar refrain that he batted too slowly. This year, the flood was of unprecedented proportions. The Sri Lankans joined the West Indians and Australians in another triangular tournament, and that was followed by a six-nation event to celebrate the state of Victoria's 150th anniversary... and, in a schedule that beggared belief, that was followed by a four-nation jaunt in Sharjah.

Performing at this circus, the Australians won more than they lost and were content with that. Border and most of his yellow-clad team-mates enjoyed the upbeat vibe of one-day cricket but did not lose sleep over the results. You win some, you lose some. When does the next Test series begin?

The selectors took a less sanguine view and, pathetically influenced by the hue and cry, constantly shuffled their team on the basis of one smash-bang result after another. Wessels, of course, was easy meat.

When Australia lost to Sri Lanka, he was dropped to No.8 in the order, but after they had collapsed against the West Indies, he was returned to No.3, from where he scored 82 in only 92 balls. So he remained No.3, until he slipped to No.6, and then No.7. Was this a record in the pop charts, or was this the most consistent batsman in Australia being mishandled?

A strategy evolved, for which Border was partially responsible, whereby Wessels batted high in the order when times were tough against the West Indies but then sank into the tail against the Sri Lankans. Lloyd, whose West Indian team ultimately defeated Australia in the series final, was surprised: 'Kepler should have opened. There was nothing he could do late in the order and, in one-day cricket, you need someone to provide a platform. His style was to settle in and push it around. Desmond Haynes may have had a wider repertoire of strokes, but he filled that anchor sort of role for us.'

Such basic tactical sense finally dawned on the Australian selectors when Wessels was chosen to open the innings for the tournament in Victoria. Hughes, who had played himself back into form, was recalled to the team for Australia's fixture against England but his luck did not change: out for 0. Australia won that match, the first played under floodlights at the MCG, but defeats against Pakistan and India eliminated them from their own tournament.

Still, there was the trip to Sharjah, a cricket ground in the desert where major cricket nations competed in a knock-out one-day competition. The annual exercise confirmed the principle that most sportsmen and administrators will agree to play anywhere if the cheque is good. Both Wessels and Hughes were included in the squad which played two matches in a fortnight, beating England and then losing to India in the Sharjah final.

Wessels was once again being troubled by his knee. He played in both games but was booked to fly home for another operation two days before the rest of the squad. Disappointed, he became tense and irritable. There was nothing to do, nothing to say. Hours before his flight was due to leave, Wessels attended a routine net practice, standing by, watching, grumpy.

'Come on, Kepler, what's the matter? Can't you see the tour through to the end? What's the matter this time?' Hughes was joking, only teasing, but he misjudged the turbulent state of his team-mate's mind.

In a blur, Wessels hurled himself at Hughes, wrestling the former captain to the ground and rubbing his face in the turf. Team-mates stepped in to break up the brawl. Hughes clambered to his feet. He was obviously shaken and there was blood above his ear. Wessels walked away.

The nets finished not long afterwards. Hughes gathered his kit and strode deliberately towards where Wessels was waiting.

'Mate, I'm sorry.'

'Yeah, I'm sorry too.'

'No hard feelings?'

'No hard feelings.'

Bygones immediately became bygones. It had been a mad minute, the final episode in their odyssey around the cricket world. In two years from March 1983, Australia had played 16 Test matches, won four, drawn six and lost six. Wessels had played in all 16, Hughes in 13.

Wessels, who began as an uncertain import striving to establish himself, finished as an automatic selection for the 1985 Ashes tour to England. Hughes, once the most favoured player of the Australian Cricket Board, ended up disillusioned and angry, omitted from the squad selected to play England.

Their paths, however, would cross again. Both the dark, quiet one and the fair, emotional one would soon be caught in a turbulent storm which, amid much bitterness, would end their careers as Australian Test cricketers.

Around Australia, the good names of both Hughes and Wessels would be tainted by their involvement in the rebel tours of South Africa. Yet nothing subsequently said or done can detract from the fact that, for two years, no one tried harder, cared more or suffered more for the cause.

They had given everything for Australian cricket. How many people, in any walk of life, can say that? They had given everything.

# 7

# Wrecked in a Storm

In some quarters, Kepler Wessels' reputation has been ruined by the perception that he played a role in organising the rebel Australian tours to South Africa during the mid-1980s, effectively biting the hand which had fed him an international career.

The falsehood lives on, festering in official circles as the 'real inside story', but it emphatically IS false.

In sport, as much as anywhere else, yesterday's newspaper scandal is the next day's fish and chips, but the record does need to be set straight because what one man struggled so long to build up was cruelly torn down by mistaken officials...

By May 1985, Wessels was established in the Australian side, a senior member of the squad to tour England, a close associate and friend of Allan Border, in excellent form and apparently all set to pursue his Test career for some time to come. One year later, his entire world had come crashing down around his head. He had retired from international cricket at the age of 28, left Australia and taken his family to start anew in South Africa.

The 'perception' holds that this was the intention all along, to reap the benefits of a Test career and then to scurry home with a rebel's booty. It was not. Wessels did not quit Australian cricket. He was driven out by the Australian Cricket Board.

The ACB rid themselves of the player who had worked hardest to represent them because of three misconceptions: (i) that he had played a role in facilitating the rebel Australian tours to South Africa in 1985/86 and 1986/87; (ii) that he had signed a contract to take part in the tour as a player; and (iii) that his overwhelming intention was to return home to South Africa.

Wrong. Wrong. Wrong. In the minds of panicked officials, two plus two equalled five, and Wessels paid the price.

Panic set in when, only six years after the Packer schism, the ACB was suddenly confronted by another mass exodus of leading players. The rebels to South Africa issue prompted yet another year of perpetual crisis, of crippled team morale, of the Ashes lost, of rumour, suspicion and threats. Wessels, defensive, maybe naive and certainly impulsive, was cut down in the crossfire.

Hindsight allows a clear perspective on a frantic time when the truth was obscured and justice was lost. The ACB was mistaken in driving Wessels away, wrong on all three counts:

### (i) *Wessels played no role in facilitating the tour*

Since early 1983, the South African tour issue had followed Wessels around. The South African organisers wanted his views on the merits of various Australian players, and team-mates in Australia, unsure whether to accept an invitation to tour or not, sought his personal opinion about conditions in South Africa.

Wessels was everyone's sounding board. Sometimes, he obliged by answering the enquiries. Other times, he changed the subject. Short of slamming down the telephone or walking out of the room, he could have done very little else.

This series of informal chats was not, however, facilitating the tour. Yes, he did discuss the issue with John Dyson over supper on January 25th, 1983. Yes, he did join Graham Yallop to have dinner with Ali Bacher, then a special consultant to the SA Cricket Union, at Leeds during the 1983 World Cup. Yes, he was one of many players contacted by Bruce Francis, the former Australian cricketer and the rebel tour organiser, during 1983 and 1984. But he never signed up, or tried to sign up, any player. Bacher confirms: 'Kepler was never part of our organising strategy.'

Wessels' unique status as a native South African playing for Australia placed him in a position where he was often aware of the plans but he played no role in making them.

### (ii) *Wessels never signed a full tour contract*

Through the planning process, there were times when Wessels, in a passing mood of despair, was sorely tempted to join the rebel tour. When he had dinner with Bacher in Leeds, he had just been dropped from the Australian side at the World Cup. Through the bad days, when he felt he had no future in Australian cricket, the A$200 000, after tax, which the rebels had been offered, made the tour seem a lucrative route back to South Africa, back home.

During one of these mental dips, on November 9th, 1984, as the West Indies' tour of Australia was gathering pace, Wessels sank to new depths of despair. Regularly dismissed by Joel Garner, he could not score a run. Criticism was mounting in the media. There seemed no escape. The West Indian fast bowlers were issuing him a one-way ticket to oblivion... that day, Bacher phoned.

The SACU organiser wanted a final answer. Wessels hummed and hawed but was then persuaded to sign a Power of Attorney document giving Bernie Knapp, a Brisbane lawyer, the legal authority to sign a rebel tour contract on Wessels' behalf in Johannesburg — but only if, at some time in the future, Wessels so instructed.

Bacher stressed the document did not oblige Wessels in any way but was practically necessary in so far as legal technicalities meant all tour contracts would have to be signed outside Australia. A further letter stressing that Wessels was in no way committed to the rebel tour was then attached to the document. The effect of signing, he was told, was simply to keep his options open.

Nine of the Australian team selected to play the first Test versus the West Indies had, by November 9th, signed to join the South African tour, a fact that reflected not only the lure of A$200 000 but also the profound discontent about the manner in which the ACB, in tandem with Kerry Packer, was running the game. With Kim Hughes joining the rebel squad later, only Border and Lawson in the Perth XI were not involved, and neither was ever invited.

However, alone among these nine rebels, Wessels did not sign a full tour contract and consequently did not receive a signing fee of A$25 000. Fact: he was paid no money at any stage.

As the series versus the West Indies ran its course, Wessels recovered his form, batting with singular courage. His prospects in the Australian team soared and, early in 1985, he finally confirmed to Bacher his earlier indications that he would not join the rebel tour, that he did not want to return to South Africa. Bacher told him the Power of Attorney document would be destroyed, and Wessels duly travelled to England with the Australian squad, relieved that an awkward issue had finally been dealt with.

Open-minded and innocent, he had been tempted but he had pulled out once he realised what the full implications of joining the rebel tour would be. There were two other factors in Wessels' decision, both linked to a growing lassitude on Bacher's behalf as to whether Wessels took part or not.

First, Bacher had conceived a plan where Wessels would play in the first tour and then be welcomed back into the South African fold (playing for Eastern Province etc.), thereby creating a place on the second tour to be filled by David Hookes. This option did, however, effectively cut the carrot dangling before Wessels from a full A$200 000 to A$100 000 for one tour.

Secondly, Bacher held a wider perspective. Believing the spectacle of South African-bred sportsmen playing for other nations was beneficial to the cause of sustaining South African sport in isolation, he was reluctant to actively lure Wessels away from a high-profile position where he was reflecting positively on South African cricket. It didn't feel right.

At any rate, Wessels never signed a tour contract.

## (iii) *Wessels had no intention of leaving Australia in 1985*

The ACB were convinced Wessels was on his way home. David Richards, the ACB's chief executive, telephoned Wessels during the tour of England and repeatedly suggested this was the case. Wessels always denied it. Richards would never believe him.

The ACB's sole grounds for believing Wessels was connected with the tour and planning to return home was the Power of Attorney document which Bacher had said would be destroyed. Instead it was presented to the ACB as part of the 'discovery' in the legal action which SACU brought when the ACB threatened to ban the rebels from all state and club cricket in Australia. It was presented, what's more, without the attached letter setting out the undisputed fact that Wessels was not in any way obliged to the tour.

SACU had been scrupulously honest in their approach to the discovery, releasing all documents in their possession to the ACB, and the matter was subsequently settled out of court. For Wessels, that made no difference. The damage was done.

Bottom line: when SACU handed the Power of Attorney document to the ACB, they effectively ensured the premature end of Wessels' hard-earned cricket career in Australia.

Why? Because in April 1985, Wessels had told the Australian media that he would not join the tour and had had no dealings with the SACU.

The release of this document appeared to reveal that he had misled the public and ACB over his role in the tour.

It could be persuasively argued that, during these days of rumour and confusion, Wessels lacked the maturity and confidence to confront the issue and to state his case clearly. He had, in truth, done nothing wrong. He had nothing to hide.

Yet it was his deep suspicion of the media that prevented him from doing this and it cost him dear. He simply did not trust anyone with the truth and, in hindsight, that was his error. The rumours spread, unchallenged. He left his position unclear enough for some people to believe that 2 + 2 = 5.

The ACB was able to seize upon the fateful Power of Attorney document and proclaim that Wessels had lied about his involvement in the tour. Like salivating hounds with the scent of treachery in their nostrils, the discovery of one signed piece of paper, however meaningless, convinced them that he had lied all along, that he had other skeletons in his cupboard and that he was planning to join the rebel tour some time in the future. There were no grounds for such conclusions, but the hunt was already underway.

Wessels repeatedly protested his loyalty to Australia but his words fell on deaf ears. His only crime had been seriously to consider joining the tour to South Africa, and that was a 'crime' of which the vast majority of leading Australian cricketers were guilty at some stage between 1983 and 1985.

He did not want to return to South Africa. He wanted to stay in Brisbane, he wanted to play for Australia...

The ACB would not believe him. They accused this man who had stood firm at the crease amid the West Indian barrage of disloyalty to Australian cricket. That was some disloyalty. Regarded as guilty till proven innocent, Wessels was swiftly doomed. The ACB moved to force him out of Australian cricket.

Their strategy was simple. Australian players were paid on a three-tiered structure ranked according to experience and form. On the Ashes tour, Wessels had shared the highest tier with Border and Geoff Lawson, earning around A$35 000 per year but, when he arrived back from England, the ACB offered him a three-year contract on the second lowest level, paying only A$12 000 per year (the bottom tier was reserved for uncapped players). His previous three-year contract still had a full year to run but the ACB were offering new deals to roll over and supersede the earlier agreements.

The ACB attempted to justify Wessels' demotion by claiming they were only following the selectors' suggestions, as usual, but this was not the case. How could it be when Wessels had scored more Test runs than Border during the previous year? Their offer could not be justified in cricketing terms.

Some years later, a prominent ACB official finally conceded: 'We were basically telling Wessels to buzz off.'

The message was received. Initially, Wessels stalled on the new contract offer and played in the first Test of the home series against New Zealand. Facing Richard Hadlee on a green pitch at the Gabba, Wessels, alone among the Australian batsmen, showed courage and skill. Such heroics were unbecoming of a player who, according to the ACB officials, was on the verge of quitting.

His efforts cut no ice. The ACB coldly informed him that he would not be considered for the second Test match unless he signed the contract on the table. Wessels reacted impulsively, announcing his immediate retirement from international cricket.

November 1985 — The ACB had won. Wessels was out.

* * * * *

April, 1985 — Allan Border knew nothing and it irritated the hell out of him. He was supposed to be the Australian captain, preparing his team to defend the Ashes in England, yet all his efforts were being undermined by the rebel tour rumpus. 'Everyone else seemed to know what was going on except me,' Border recalls.

Life would certainly have been easier for the captain if the players who had signed to tour South Africa had then gone to South Africa, and those 'best-of-the-rest' selected for the England tour had followed him, but life was not so simple.

His problems started when three players who had agreed to join the rebels (having signed SACU contracts and received their A$25 000 signing-on fee) suddenly changed their minds, returned to the ACB cuddle and were selected to tour England.

The rumour spread like fire through the tinderbox world of Australian cricket that this trio — Graeme Wood, Wayne Phillips and Dirk Wellham — had been bought back into the official fold by PBL, one of the companies owned by Kerry Packer. Tony Greig, a faithful Packer employee at the time, confirms the whispers, recalling: 'I had to go and get a couple of the players back.'

What's the buzz? Tell me what's-a-happening? If there is one guaranteed way to upset a professional sportsman, it is to tell him that some of his team-mates are being paid more than he is. Hit them where they can feel it: not the brain, but the wallet. The word was loose and burning in the Ashes squad. The players had been promised A$21 000 each for the tour. Everyone knew that. What everyone now wanted to know was how much the three 'ex-rebels' had been promised to persuade them back into the official side?

There was a vital supplementary question too: Were the ACB involved in a counter-offer to Wood, Wellham and Phillips? And what exactly was the nature of the ACB's relationship with Packer? Who was running whom? Plenty questions. Few answers.

Amid anger and dismay, Border acted with purpose and speed. He wanted this divisive issue resolved before the Ashes tour began, so the captain called a full players meeting on May 29th, the eve of their departure for England. Cards on the table, please guys. Wood, Wellham and Phillips would be confronted at the meeting and asked how much money they had been promised by PBL.

In the event, all three denied receiving any extra payment and claimed PBL had promised no more than future employment. The squad was not convinced, and duly voted by a large majority that all three players should withdraw from the tour.

The players' view was conveyed to the ACB, and ignored by the ACB. Once again rumours ran loose. Wasn't it true that the ACB had been placed under pressure by the Packer organisation to stand by the trio? The rumour-mongers said it was.

Kim Hughes, who, until this time, had pledged his efforts to regaining his place in the Australian side, was outraged. 'Who was running Australian cricket?' he demanded. Through six years playing for his country, Hughes' loyalty had never once been questioned. On the contrary, he was a loyal subject of the ACB. But now, disillusioned by the way in which Australian cricket was being run, he agreed to lead the rebel tour to South Africa.

Wealthy Victorians in 19th-century England had a saying that they felt was appropriate to them and their servants. It could also be applied to 20th-century sports administrators and their players: 'If one of them is rude to you, you give them a spoonful of castor oil as punishment, but if two or more are rude, you swallow a dose of castor oil yourself.'

The ACB might have kept this in mind.

Wood, Wellham and Phillips remained in the squad. It may be difficult to believe that the same ACB officials who were content to forgive these three men, all of whom had signed a contract to tour South Africa, should later so relentlessly hunt down Wessels, who never signed, but that was their decision.

The shadow of Kerry Packer was everywhere.

Against this background of confused administration, Border and his team flew to England. Who ever said sport was supposed to be fun? This was the Ashes tour, the pinnacle of an Australian Test cricketer's career. But the magic had been lost amid the shambles of rumour and counter-rumour. Fun? No fun.

Spirits within the squad sagged. Border could not live with that and, as captain, he worked manfully to revive the tour: first, by the brilliance of his own form, he scored centuries in each of his first four first class innings; and, secondly, by striving to build morale within a squad that plainly didn't trust one another. It was not his nature to blithely accept the furtive glances, the visible divisions and the occasional sniping as part of the daily schedule. He urgently sought the camaraderie and shared goal that is distinctive of almost every winning team.

Sitting in the dressing room after Somerset had been soundly beaten in the opening first class match of the tour, the captain went to work. He looked around at his players, and sensed the vibe. The vibe, the vibe... it was not good.

Someone needed to laugh. He glanced at Wessels, his old mate from Brisbane, and worked an old routine.

'Aren't you getting a bit fat, Chopper?' Border asked.

'What do you mean?'

Border started pinching fat around his ribs and pointing at Wessels' waist. 'No, maybe not. I just thought you'd put on a bit of weight around the waist... although, I reckon...'

Wessels was unsettled. 'No, there's nothing.'

Border kept looking, squinting, pinching. 'Well, you'll know best, mate, but I should just be a bit careful.'

Wessels swallowed the bait every time. Before too long, he would change into a pair of shorts and set off on yet another run around the ground at the end of the day's play. Border and the rest would endlessly play on the opener's severe approach to his fitness and, as Wessels ran, at last, the squad laughed.

Border and Wessels: good mates from way back in the days of Ron McConnell Holdings in Brisbane, good mates whose wives often kept each other company whenever their husbands were away playing cricket, team-mates for club, for state, for country.

Not for much longer.

At the ACB offices back in Melbourne, officials had started to inspect the documents handed over by the South African Cricket Union. What's this? Look at this over here.

The Power of Attorney document signed by Wessels was swiftly found and, within days, Border was contacted in England and warned that Wessels had not been completely honest about his contacts with the rebel tour to South Africa. For Border, this suggestion came as a bitter disappointment. Where was the loyalty now?

He said nothing, and Wessels said nothing. There was no real communication, so Border never heard the full story and Wessels was not made specifically aware of his captain's misunderstanding. If they had only talked, matters might have been different. But they didn't. Many years later, Border would still be labouring under the ACB-induced and ACB-approved impression that Wessels was, somehow, organising the rebel tour. But it was in England, during the 1985 tour, that their friendship started to dissolve.

Where once there was trust, now there was doubt. The Ashes, however, were still there to be won. Victory in both the first and second one-day internationals boosted the Australian dressing room, and, although Graham Gooch, returning from a three-year ban after touring South Africa in 1982, took England to victory in the third game of the series, Border's side were able to approach the first Test with an injection of renewed confidence.

It was soon shattered because their bowling attack relied far too heavily on an unfit and unwell Lawson. This would turn out to be the recurring weakness of the 1985 Australians, and it was swiftly exposed. England amassed 533 in their first innings and won the Test match by five wickets. For all his restless fidgeting at first slip, Border could but stand and sigh.

Wessels, whose troublesome left knee, operated on barely two months before, was already requiring more cortisone injections, produced innings of 36 and 64. It was not enough. Through the tour, he would frequently threaten a major contribution but, to his great frustration, never quite produce it. Australia required cast-iron centuries from his bat, not mere 30s and 40s.

If he struggled to remain focused on the task at hand, that was not surprising. The acrimonious telephone calls had started: to Melbourne, protesting his loyalty and innocence to Richards at the ACB; and to Johannesburg, asking Bacher to explain how the Power of Attorney document that he had said would be destroyed had turned up in Melbourne, in the hands of the ACB. 'Kepler was always on the phone,' Border recalls, not understanding why.

Blow winds, and crack your cheeks! Rage! Even Shakespeare's Lear would have been distracted. The storm was breaking.

At Lord's for the second Test, the touring bowlers produced their best effort of the series to dismiss England for 290, and the advantage was pressed home by Border's brilliant 196. When England mustered only 261 in their second innings, Australia were left to score 123 for victory. Botham bounded in again and reduced his old rivals to 9 for two wickets, but the innings was steadied by Border and Wessels, still together at the crease at least.

When Wessels was dismissed for a careful 28 in more than two hours, unfortunate to be run out by Gower's instinctive flick from silly mid-off, the crisis had passed. Even as further wickets fell, Border guided his side to a four wicket victory.

Wessels had been disappointed by the freakish manner of his dismissal but, on this occasion, he could not simply slink away to a corner of the dressing room and sit quietly alone. According to tradition, the touring team was to be presented to the Queen during the tea interval on the fourth day of the Lord's Test. So, in their blazers, the Australians lined up to meet their monarch.

He had been forewarned of the protocol that you may not ask questions of the Queen but Wessels mistakenly understood this to mean that you may not actually speak to her. So, when she asked him whether he was enjoying the tour, he silently nodded.

'She must have thought I was an idiot,' he recalls, 'but, to be honest, I was still a bit grumpy about getting out.'

The storm raged on. ACB indignation had begun to spill over into evidently leaked newspaper articles connecting Wessels to the rebel tour. The rumours, like wild horses, were running free and no amount of slamming of stable doors would restrain them.

A four-way conference call was arranged between Richards, Fred Bennett (the ACB chairman), the ACB's solicitor and the player in his hotel room in England. It proved a useless exercise. Wessels believed he had already been found guilty in ACB minds and was soon convinced that the other three men were only interested in coaxing out of him some kind of confession. He couldn't make himself clear. He was being defeated. There seemed no way out.

Head down, chin in, concentrate, concentrate. Back to work. The tour went on and the third Test finished as a high-scoring draw at Trent Bridge. Wessels scored 34. All right, but all right was not enough. The runs were not coming easily. Life was becoming hard for him. Nothing was going right. Stay calm.

He struck the first ball of the fourth Test at Old Trafford to the boundary but again progressed no further than 34. Australia were bowled out for 257, to which England replied with 482. Border again emerged as the admired hero, compiling an unbeaten 146, and the match, curtailed by rain, ended as another draw.

As Border blazed across the headlines, Wessels should have been the first person to congratulate him but this was no 'should-have' tour. Everything felt odd, somehow wrong. Instead Wessels was cursing his captain. Yes. Another incident.

Was he too uptight? Was this an incident that a more relaxed type of player would have casually brushed aside? Or was his anger justified? At the time, at the place, who can say?

Greg Matthews, the all-rounder, had approached Border during the fourth Test and asked if he could open the second innings. The captain had no objection and asked Wessels if he would mind moving down the order to No.3. 'If that is what you want, A.B.,' Wessels replied, 'then it's not a problem for me.'

WESSELS ASKS TO DROP DOWN ORDER declared the following day's headline in Sydney. Wessels was told of the story and the matter was raised at a routine tour Press conference that afternoon. 'Did Kepler ask to move down the order?' Border was asked. In reply, he waffled. He was ambivalent. He didn't deny it.

Wessels was livid. They could say what they liked about him but they could never question his courage. He had never ducked out of a challenge in his entire career. Not once. Why hadn't Border told the Press that Matthews had asked to open? Increasingly alone and sad, Wessels began to sense a carefully orchestrated campaign being waged against him in the media.

A familiar explosion of his pent-up frustration and anger was imminent. It occurred during the Australians' match against Middlesex. As the tour progressed, he had grown increasingly vocal at team meetings on the subject of what he believed was indifferent bowling. On several occasions, he had warned Border that the Ashes would be lost unless a solution was found. The fast bowlers reacted to this typically blunt view with understandable irritation. 'That Wessels is mad. He's a fanatic,' one grumbled. As a senior player, however, the opener felt entitled to his opinion.

When the Australian bowlers were tamed by Middlesex, who had eased to 397 for four by stumps on the first day, Wessels lost all patience. Someone would suffer. Unsurprisingly, it was Border. The captain, rested for the match, had been playing golf and arrived at the ground before the close in cheerful mood.

'Where have you been?' Wessels asked, aflame.

'What's the matter with you?'

'What's the matter with our bowlers is a better question. I think it would have been helpful if you'd been watching...'

The dispute escalated, tempers were lost. Mate against mate. Wessels against Border. Around the dressing room, jaws dropped. It had been another crazy minute, another emotional release. Wessels looks back and concedes that he was wrong to have criticised his captain. Border was within his rights to take a day off during the tour. 'It was just the pressure,' he says.

Onwards, ever onwards to the fifth Test at Edgbaston. With his parents visiting from South Africa in the stands, Wessels put together his most impressive innings of the series, scoring 83. It was, none the less, in vain.

Australia reached 335 all out but their bowlers were again mauled with Gower, thriving as captain, and Robinson adding 331 for the second wicket in six hours. England, happy England, declared at 595 for five. On the rack, the tourists looked to the heavy clouds overhead and they weren't disappointed. Persistent rain delayed the start of the Australian second innings until 95 minutes before the close on the fourth afternoon.

Amid the grizzle of a grey Monday evening in Birmingham, and with still more rain forecast, another draw seemed inevitable. That prediction, however, did not take into account the feeble nature of the Australian challenge. For once, they rolled over. Reduced to 37 for five by stumps on the fourth day, more rain meant they did not have to bat again until after 2.30 p.m. on Tuesday but that left plenty of time for them to lose the last five wickets. The tourists were beaten by an innings and 188 runs. It had been one of the most degrading defeats of Wessels' career.

There is little better in cricket than a tour going well but there is little worse than a tour gone wrong. The sixth and final Test at the Oval offered Australia a chance to level the series at 2-2 and thus retain the Ashes. Border's side did not, however, have the stomach for the challenge, and England roared. Rarely since the Honourable Ivo Bligh was presented with the tiny urn containing the 'Ashes' of English cricket by his future wife at Melbourne in 1882 had the side wearing the green caps seemed so pedestrian. By stumps on the first day, England had eased along to 376 for three. Gower, genius, had stroked 147 and Gooch was 179 not out.

They 'collapsed' to 464 all out the next morning but such a total proved more than adequate to secure the Ashes. Australia were dismissed first for 241 and then 129, and humiliated, defeated by an innings and 94 runs before lunch on the fourth day. Wessels had scored 12 in the first innings, undone for no less than the sixth time in the series by Emburey's off-spin, and for seven in the second innings. He was profoundly disappointed with his final tour average of 33.45. His miserable tour ended in the gutter.

So did Wayne Phillips.

The wicketkeeper-batsman was precisely the sort of character who regularly irritated Wessels. Smart, swish, quick-witted, he represented the antithesis of the sober, hard-working attitude that Wessels so admired, and indeed epitomised.

At the end of a long, difficult tour, this irritation was liable to become anger, and it did when Phillips and Border turned up late for a prearranged meeting with Wessels. They had organised to meet at the Wellington pub, on the corner of the Aldwych and the Strand, not far from the Waldorf Astoria, the team hotel. The time had been set for 6 p.m. Wessels had arrived, and waited, and waited. At 7.25 p.m. he got up to leave and, on his way out, he came across Phillips and Border on their way in.

'About time,' Wessels said.

Phillips made some flippant remark. Wessels didn't much appreciate his attitude. Border intervened but the tempers began to fray. Another storm in another teacup. Wessels, flustered, returned to the hotel. He was tense and he was defensive but these were very difficult times. At least the tour was over. His thoughts turned to the reception for him back in Australia. What could the ACB have on their minds now? What would happen?

Deep in his heart, Wessels began to fear that his Australian career was drawing to a conclusion. If the ACB really didn't want him around, there was little he could do. Privately, he started to consider the options: remain in Brisbane and continue playing for Queensland, or return to South Africa. Hard days.

Greg Chappell, for one, was not about to desert this ship in distress. Now installed as a national selector, it was he who told Wessels that the ACB were preparing to drop his contract to a lower tier; and it was he who urged Wessels not to let the problem get him down. It would pass, Chappell said. Keep going.

So Wessels went back to the Valleys club in Brisbane, his sanctuary, to the Institute Gym, another safe haven, and then to the Queensland nets, and worked harder. At club and state level, he sank back into the same old routine, relaxed, started to enjoy the game again and swiftly discovered his best form.

His early season performance was such that the Australian selectors could not leave him out of their team to play the first Test against the touring New Zealanders. His contract was still in force and he was still, by general consent, the best opener in the country. So, grimly clinging to his green cap and blazer by his fingernails, Wessels prepared for his 24th Test.

It was, by strange coincidence, to be played at the Gabba, the ground where he had launched his Australian career with 162 on his début almost exactly three years before. Was the wheel about to come full circle? Only Border, Lawson and himself had survived from the side which defeated England in 1982. Going through the same old pre-Test routine, Wessels felt the emotion welling.

Relations with Border had scarcely improved since the Ashes tour. They spoke, of course, and their wives remained close but the trust had been broken. The captain, however, had no inkling that Wessels was on the brink of retiring from Australian cricket. When the news broke, he would be genuinely astounded. In every walk of life, the saying goes, communication is the key.

Australia lost the toss against their country cousins from across the Tasman Sea and were invited to bat on a green pitch in overcast, muggy Brisbane weather. Richard Hadlee, very probably the world's most lethal bowler in these conditions, stood at the end of his run-up and prepared to put on an exhibition. He moved the ball this way and that, through the air and off the pitch. With unique skill, he took nine wickets for 52 runs and Australia were bowled out for a wretched 179. It was Hadlee *in excelsis*.

Only one man had resisted, only one batsman had put his head down, tucked his chin in and concentrated with all his might. If it was going to be his Test swansong, Wessels would not throw it away. His memorable innings of 72 represented the enduring image of his mental strength. It was a masterpiece of resolve.

Rising to the challenge, he judged each swinging and cutting delivery with meticulous care, not offering a stroke at balls which passed his off-stump by the merest inch. That was fine. The merest inch was enough. Into line, careful, careful . . .

Such was the spectacle of this classic confrontation between a dazzling bowler and a batsman of unshakeable resolve that a video tape was subsequently produced, compressing all the deliveries that Hadlee bowled at Wessels into an hour or so. In any context, it was a remarkable performance. In the context of ACB wrath, his innings matched his heroics against the West Indies.

When New Zealand batted, it seemed as though all the snakes in the pitch had suddenly dispersed. The tourists tore into a weak bowling attack and, strutting, finally declared at a mammoth 533 for seven. Australia subsided, and lost by an innings. Wessels sat quiet in the Gabba dressing room he knew so well, alone with his memories and his fears. He said nothing. No one said anything. The team had been humbled. What was there to say? He gathered his kit, packed it away and left. That was it. The End.

Soon after the Test, Wessels yielded. Told that he would not be considered for the second Test unless he signed a new contract, he acknowledged the point of no return and issued a media statement declaring his retirement from international cricket.

He was emotional and upset, but was he rash?

'I don't know what else I could have done,' he reflects. 'I was getting a clear signal from the ACB and there didn't seem to be much I could do about it. Some people thought I wanted to withdraw for a short time and let things cool off but, in my mind, it was a final decision. I couldn't go on in the same way.'

If Wessels, ever expecting the worst rather than the best and somehow more comfortable with the idea that people were against him than behind him, suspected his announcement would be met with a chorus of 'good riddance', he was mistaken. Heavyweight newspaper opinion fell clearly on his side and there was no doubt where the cricketing public stood on the issue. They might not have seen any documents but they had witnessed the brave manner in which Wessels had played for Australia and they respected him for that. The fact that Wessels was evidently disliked by certain officials should not distort his wider status as an admired cricketer.

In and around the Queensland Cricket Association, even the administrators supported him. Players and followers alike urged him to reconsider his position. Don't give up, mate.

Wessels was happy in Brisbane. In his book *Guilty,* relating the background to the South African tour, Bruce Francis wrote: 'My belief is that he (Kepler) never felt comfortable in his new world. From the day he arrived, he felt people were against him.' This may well have been the case everywhere beyond his closest enclaves: his family, his gym, his club and his state side.

Wessels reflects: 'Queensland was a fantastic place to play. In 1979, when there was pressure to sign for New South Wales, I had insisted on going to Brisbane and it was one of the best decisions I made. I really felt as though I belonged.'

Administered by officials such as Allan Pettigrew and Norm McMahon, the state side structure was friendly and relaxed, and the player responded. It was sometimes claimed that Wessels had no loyalty, that he would take what he could get and steal into the night, that he was a jackal among cricketers. His experience with Queensland explodes the perception. If he feels badly treated, Wessels will walk away. But when a person or organisation shows true loyalty to him, he is nothing less than ferociously loyal in return.

Through tough times, Queensland were loyal to him and he was keenly aware that the best way of expressing his gratitude would be to bring the Shield to Brisbane for the first time. 'Nice guys come second' — throughout their history, Queensland had.

The previous season, 1984/85, they had fought through the log matches to play New South Wales in the Shield final at the Sydney Cricket Ground. When, set 220 to win, New South Wales floundered at 175 for eight, the elusive prize seemed within reach. But the home side had scrambled to their target and snatched the Shield. Big men had wept that evening in the Queensland dressing room.

Sweating their disappointment into yet greater resolve, the team again challenged boldly during the 1985/86 season. Wessels, now released from international duty, was ever present in the side and proved wonderfully prolific. He was batting with a point to prove, even a chip on his shoulder, and batting brilliantly.

Furthermore, Wessels was appointed to lead the side when, as often happened, Border was away playing Test matches. This was his first sustained experience of captaincy since leaving school and he relished the responsibility. As the season became a crusade, his team ended in second place on the completed log and qualified for the final: against New South Wales in Sydney, again.

The script was perfect, the stage was ideal. Days before the Shield final, Kepler and Sally Wessels had reached a firm decision to leave Australia and return to South Africa but they would keep their verdict secret until after the match. Only Wessels, then, was aware that this would be his last game in Australia.

With Border away, Wessels was confirmed as captain for the final, leading his team with a flock of ACB officials watching from the stand. Prove them wrong there on the field, Kepler. Show them up one more time. As 'psyched out of his mind' as he had been in his very first match for the WSC Australians seven seasons before, Wessels won the toss and decided to bat.

Just before stumps on the first day, he steadied himself and carefully chopped another single to third man. The Sydney Cricket Ground, scene of so many of his triumphs in the past, rose to cheer a century scored by the sheer power of one man's will.

K. Wessels... 100 not out. Again. The Queensland captain had not reached three figures because he happened to feel in good form or because he had had a little luck and was dropped at some stage. He dominated the first day because he was intensely resolved. The next morning, he advanced his score to 166; and, with Glen Trimble making his maiden first class century, he was able to declare the innings closed at 436 for nine. The large first innings total was ideal, just what Ian Chappell would have wanted.

New South Wales were bowled out for 292 but Queensland began anxiously to eye the clock. Only an outright victory would take the Shield to Brisbane and Wessels ordered a second innings blitz to leave his bowlers enough time to dismiss New South Wales again. The team responded and the home side was set 270 to win in just over a day. It appeared an eminently astute declaration.

Carl Rackemann, tall, fair and angular, ran in and ran amok among the home team, reducing them from a secure 109 for two to 113 for five soon after lunch. Queensland appeared in charge. Wessels, urging, clapping and calmly directing, was keeping his team on the boil. It was perfect pressure cricket.

Mark Waugh and Wellham then staged a recovery and, with the score 175 for five, Queensland were in urgent need of a wicket. In crisis, Wessels backed himself. He brought himself on to bowl. Off 12 paces, he trundled in and hit the seam. Waugh played forward... an edge... a sharp catch at short leg. Out.

Twenty minutes later, Wellham, the home captain, was run out for 80. With ten overs remaining, New South Wales stood at 218 for eight. Two wickets were required in 60 balls. Murray Bennett and Bob Holland stood at the crease, denying the dream. Jeff Thomson, also playing his last match for Queensland, took the ball and ran in, just as he had run in to demolish England 16 summers before, but the wicket would not come. Scratching and scraping, Holland and Bennett would not be moved, would not be moved...

New South Wales survived, and retained the Shield. There had been no happy ending for Wessels. He had tried everything he knew, done everything he could, but that was that.

At the prize-giving ceremony in front of the pavilion at the SCG, he stood between two thickset friends of Thomson, laughingly referred to as his 'bodyguards'. With members of the ACB hierarchy, notably Fred Bennett, standing by, Wessels picked his moment. 'And now for a word from the losing captain...'

All of a sudden, he had the microphone in his hand and the ACB at his mercy. Set the sights, trigger, fire.

'I want to thank the ACB for forcing me out of the Test side and giving me the opportunity to play with the best guys I've ever met,' Wessels told the crowd. Bennett was livid but the player was only being honest, telling it as he saw it.

It may have been the wrong thing to say at the wrong time. Wessels looks back and regrets the outburst. Even Border, who soon heard about the incident, thought it was unnecessary. But was it so wrong for a player who had been so seriously mistreated to let off steam? Sportsmen, in general, won't take on administrators for fear of the reprisals. Wessels had no such fear. That may have cost him dear, but it wasn't necessarily wrong. The administrators, at the end of the day, are not gods. They make mistakes, too.

Reflecting on his seven-year adoption, time has healed most of the disputes with the ACB. Returning to Australia for the 1992 World Cup,

Wessels was happy to bury the hatchet with Richards and Border. What was past, was emphatically past.

'Look it would be stupid for me to pretend that I didn't make mistakes,' Wessels concludes. 'There are things I could have done differently and I would certainly have preferred to leave on a much better note with the ACB but that wasn't possible. Overall, I know I gave my best for Australia and I look back on my time there as a fantastic period of my career. The positives far outweigh the negatives. I had the chance to play with some great players and I think, at least I hope, I was worthy of them.'

Beyond the committee rooms and corridors of power, Wessels had only ever been a gutsy cricketer giving it all for his country. His popularity among Australian cricket followers was also a matter of conjecture until the 1992 World Cup, but there it was decisively proved. Whatever else had happened, he had performed nobly on the field and that, ultimately, is what counted.

There remained doubts about his aptitude for one-day cricket and he had been treated like a yoyo, whirled up and down the order, but there was no mistaking his distinction in the Test match arena. For three years from November 1982, Wessels played in every Test for which he was fit. Injury ruled him out in the West Indies but he was never actually dropped from the Test side.

Finally, as ever, there are the statistics, the final proof that his adventure in Australia can only be judged as an astounding success. Beyond the tiffs, there were the runs.

He had played in 24 Tests for Australia (10 against England, seven against the West Indies, five against Pakistan, one against Sri Lanka and one against New Zealand) and scored 1 750 runs at an average of 43.00. He also played 54 one-day matches. Not bad for the 21-year-old from Bloemfontein who had nervously arrived at Sydney airport knowing nobody at all.

Seven years on, it was ending at Brisbane airport.

A succession of farewell functions had been held in his honour, at his club, at the Queensland offices, and many people had asked him to reconsider his decision. Guts it out, mate, the ACB will change their position. Just be patient. For better or worse, however, Wessels had made up his mind. He was on his way.

Together with Sally and his four-month-old son, christened Mattheus Hendrik but known as Riki, Wessels drove to the airport for the last time. His parents-in-law and several close friends gathered to bid farewell to the young family.

The group, huddled around a pile of suitcases and cricket equipment, looked forlorn and poignant. The adventure was over. Sally glanced across at her desolate husband: 'He just looked so sad that it was all over. I felt so terribly sorry for him.'

# 8

# The Reluctant Rebel

W essels left South African sport isolated, cowering in the corner, bemoaning its fate and whimpering like a kitten.

He returned in April 1986 to discover the kitten had become a tiger, still locked behind bars, but now snarling at the rest of the world, seizing any scrap of international opposition that could be lured within reach. With no political reform in sight, no joyous readmission imaginable, the rebel era was in full swing. Sign up, sign up for the cheque of a lifetime...

Within days Kepler, Sally and Riki Wessels were followed into the arrivals hall at Jan Smuts airport by the best 30 rugby players in New Zealand. The All Blacks, in all but name, had been lured to break the boycott. 'Stuff the world,' starved sports fans cried. 'If they won't tour officially, we'll buy them as rebels.'

Drawing on vast reservoirs of public money, thinly veiled as tax breaks, South African sports administrators covertly crept into the outside world and offered colossal sums to tempt the discarded and disaffected (just occasionally they coaxed current players) to come and play the raring Springboks.

The tours were ostensibly financed by sponsors but, in truth, the government footed the bill through a system whereby sponsors could recoup as much as 90 per cent of their outlay as a tax rebate. The National Party moguls, like the Emperors of post-Augustan Rome, knew how the provision of sports and games could maintain both the morale of the people and the prestige of the nation. No matter the cost, South Africa had to have tours.

South African cricket, grown frail and dull on a simple diet of domestic competition since 1970, pioneered the rebel route when two high-spirited entrepreneurs, Peter Cooke and Martin Locke, arranged an unofficial England XI tour in 1982. Geoff Boycott, Alan Knott, Graham Gooch and Derek Underwood headlined the rebel squad who accepted three-year Test bans for financial security. For South Africans, the tour was an unmitigated triumph: once again, they could watch the likes of Richards, Pollock and Procter pull on the Springbok cap and tear into Test-class opposition.

An unofficial Sri Lankan squad followed, signed up not just to keep the Boks rolling but also to demonstrate that the country where non-white sportsmen were once not welcome would now embrace them. In their footsteps, to worldwide amazement, marched a rebel squad from the West Indies, captained by Lawrence Rowe, featuring Sylvester Clarke, Colin Croft, Alvin Kallicharran, Collis King and Franklyn Stephenson. This tour, played over two legs in 1982/83 and 1983/84, galvanised the sport at all levels. Suddenly, the stadiums were full. The coup was masterminded by a special consultant to the South African Cricket Union (SACU), Dr Ali Bacher.

One of the most brilliant organisers in any sporting code, of any era, Bacher had relinquished his medical practice to join the administration of the game he had once played with distinction. As captain of the glittering Springbok team that whitewashed Australia by four Tests to nil in 1969/70, he had displayed a rare gift for leadership and direction. Showing these same qualities, he swiftly advanced to a position where, invaluably supported by the financial acumen of Joe Pamensky, a sometime SACU president, he was entirely responsible for the organisation of international tours.

Other sports, such as rugby and athletics, followed the same rebel route at one stage or another but very few of their officials could hold a candle to Bacher. In terms of being clever, clinical, professional and simply producing the goods, Bacher quickly became an acknowledged master of the rebel art.

Why? Because you could look into the face of this decent man, listen to his sensible, coherent explanations and you could trust him. That was his primary gift: his skills with people. He was also alert, tactful and almost always available, ever ready at the end of a telephone to react to new developments. After his success with the West Indians, Bacher set about concluding arrangements for an unofficial Australian tour.

He reflects: 'There was no question that the tours maintained interest in the game. Through the huge tax perks, we were able to attract very substantial sponsors and I would be lying if I said there was not a certain sense of exhilaration at the time. Meeting the Australian players in Singapore to sign them up on their way home from the tour of India was exciting.'

Subsequent developments have completely doused any glowing embers among Bacher's memories of his cloak and dagger days around the cricketing globe. 'It never entered my mind, or anyone else's mind, what the reaction to the tours would be beyond our world,' he says. 'We were living in a cocoon.'

In fact, in townships around the country there was some anger but the overwhelming majority of black people showed no interest in cricket. It was a sport which did not feature in their newspapers, in their schools or in their lives. For these non-white inhabitants of a frighteningly divided land, cricket was largely a game played on the other side of the fence.

It might now be politically correct to look back on the rebel tours and denounce them as folly, yet constructive history can't be viewed through binoculars and without taking into account views and circumstances at the time. It would be quite wrong to expediently forget what sort of atmosphere there was at the floodlit Wanderers when Graeme Pollock imperiously swept a straight ball from Rod Hogg high into the main scoreboard, or how Newlands roared when Carel du Plessis dived through the mud to score the winning try in the dying seconds of the first Test against the New Zealanders.

The fact is that these tours did exhilarate the public. They kept sport alive in the dreams and minds of eager youngsters during two decades of international isolation. It was a unique period. No other country on the planet, before or since, has been judged evil enough to receive a similar punishment, the far-reaching effects of which most nations cannot begin to imagine.

Yes, the sports boycott was justified in so far as it proved a neatly effective reminder to the white population that the world would not tolerate the system of apartheid but, even so, what were South African sports officials to do? Watch their sport gradually decay and wither away? Were they supposed to do nothing until the government, over which it had minimal influence, happened to see the light and reform its crazed ideology?

South African sport was in the position of a prisoner serving an indefinite sentence. Even if the sentence was justified, the top administrators simply had to make the best of it, try whatever they could to sustain interest in their code. In similar circumstances, any country would have conceived rebel tours.

There was, however, another view. Eddie Barlow, the former Springbok cricketer, was appointed to launch a South African sports office in London which would strive to argue against the boycott by lobbying journalists and politicians, and making speeches wherever possible. Barlow, independent of mind and style, expressed personal reservations about the rebel tour strategy.

'They were a contradiction,' Barlow reflects. 'It seemed at the time that, like Packer, we were saying, "Stuff the world, we're right. We don't deserve this treatment, so stuff you." We were just saying we weren't wrong and saying how much the world needed South Africa. How arrogant could you be?

'I remember arguing that it's apartheid they don't want, not South Africa. Others would say they wanted one man/one vote and a black government. I would say they don't want that. They demand the end of apartheid because it is a blatant violation of basic human rights. The only way forward was to come out against apartheid. The rebel tours didn't seem to take us forward.

'Our approach was all wrong. When Sam Ramsamy said there can be no normal sport in an abnormal society, we replied, "Russia is an abnormal society, so why do you play against them?" It was a futile response. It didn't take us anywhere. So, in London, we attempted to follow a new tack, stressing the benefits of equal opportunities through sport as a powerful social influence, as it had been in the US and in Britain, and arguing positively how sport could be used to break down apartheid. The rebel tours were a negative, defiant and frankly un-helpful approach to the problem.'

The consensus of South African opinion, however, had little time for rational and advanced initiatives of this sort. There was anger and there was impatience. They wanted tours and they wanted them now. So, the 1980s became the decade of rebels. 'Stuff the world, we're already off.' As each tour was triumphantly announced, a clear pattern of policy and behaviour emerged.

Welcome to the Theatre of Necessary Delusion...

Act One — The Arrival.

Exhausted and bleary after their overnight flight, the rebel squad would parade into Jan Smuts airport, squinting beneath the glare of television lights. Some would look nervous, others would appear defiantly relaxed and confident. All would be ushered to one of the VIP lounges for a media conference.

'Are you aware of the reaction to your tour at home?' one of the foreign correspondents taking time off from the townships would ask. The tour captain would apprehensively reply that his team was there to play sport and not to talk about politics. South African sportswriters, more interested in form and injuries, would scowl at the foreign correspondent. Don't rattle our cocoon.

An obligatory photo opportunity would follow, with the squad posing beneath a giant sponsors' banner. They would then be driven by luxury bus to their Sandton hotel. A few would peer uneasily out the window as they cruised up the N3 past the dense, grim, smoky township of Alexandra on the left: others, tuned to their personal stereo, would be happier hiding behind sunglasses.

For a few weeks, these grotesquely overpaid sportsmen would be hailed as courageous heroes. They would become some of the most celebrated visitors in the country, endlessly invited to official functions, showered with gifts and souvenirs. Their photographs would appear in the newspapers each day, and not only on the sports pages (after the first week, some of the captions would actually be correct: erroneous captions were a tradition). Wives and children, frequently invited along with all expenses paid, would share in the publicity binge, all pampered and praised by the beggars who can't be choosers... 'Mrs X loves South Africa!' By accepted standards, they would be treated like minor heads of state.

Act Two — The Hype.

Hold on, this is a sports event. 'Indeed it is, Martin, and we are absolutely delighted, overwhelmingly privileged, in fact, to have in our country one of the strongest ...... (fill in the sport) sides ever to leave ...... (fill in the country). Yes, fine, we know about the official team playing ...... (fill in the next real opponents for the real team), but most neutral observers would say this is THE team, and I would have to agree with them. We truly are extremely privileged, quite thrilled in fact...'

The process of convincing the South African sporting public at large that the touring squad was of genuine international class was crucial to the success of the tour. They were beggars, yes. But not suckers. No one would pay to watch clowns. They were desperate to believe the rebels were worthy opposition for the Springboks. It could perhaps be put like this: the punters didn't want to see Dad climbing into the Father Christmas outfit.

Tour organisers were invariably assisted in this task by an enthusiastic and excited media. If the Emperor had no clothes, very few were prepared to say so. Not in public, anyway.

The hyping of the rebel Australian cricket tour was largely achieved by the England team which defeated Allan Border's official side in the 1985 series. That result enabled Kim Hughes' squad to be jubilantly hailed in South Africa as the 'real' Australian team. Was that right? What was the actual truth? It didn't really matter. The 'truth' was what most South Africans believed.

Act Three — The Celebration.

When the Springboks had triumphed, as they invariably did in a contest where they were straining at the leash for national glory and their opponents were trying (most of the time) to give value for money, they would be mechanically applauded as 'still amongst the finest teams in the world'. They had, after all, beaten a Test side in all but name (as proved in Act Two).

'There are obviously a few problems that we have to work on,' the Springbok coach/captain/manager would say, 'but I think we can be satisfied with our performance. Personally, I doubt if there is a better all-rounder in the world than Clive Rice/left-hander in the world than Graeme Pollock/ wicketkeeper in the world than Ray Jennings/flyhalf in the world than Naas Botha/hooker in the world than Uli Schmidt/ fullback in the world than Johan Heunis/wing in the world than Carel du Plessis/centre in the world than Danie Gerber/eighthman in the world than Jannie Breedt . . .'

The coach/captain/manager may very well have been right but, sadly, outside real and regular international competition, no one could measure Springbok heroes on a global scale. To be the 'best in the world' ultimately meant nothing at all.

At the conclusion of the tour, everyone would go home, the sponsors would go to collect the tax breaks from Pretoria and the white population would have been cheered, enthused and exhilarated, their self-confidence effectively restored.

This was the Theatre of Necessary Delusion: necessary because there was no other way to sustain interest in isolation; delusion because the opponents very rarely were 'Test-class'.

The South African Cricket Union's 1985/86 production, 'Hughes' Australians Part I', had been a qualified success. With Carl Rackemann leading the attack, the touring team had more than held their own in the field but their batting was fragile. Yallop, one of those who found real motivation beyond him, struggled and too much was left on the shoulders of Kimberley John Hughes. Since his natural inclination was to open those shoulders at every opportunity, he was never likely to be the most secure of anchors. South Africa had rolled to victory in both the one-day series and the Test series. Yes, it had been a contest, but only just.

SACU were growing anxious. When the plummeting value of the Rand dramatically raised their costs, the need to sell more seats became imperative. They needed to promote a better contest, make more money... essentially boost the Australian batting.

Hello, Kepler.

A dispirited refugee from Australia, one of that country's most consistent Test batsmen in recent years, had recently arrived in South Africa, in their lap. SACU thanked their lucky stars and, according to their settlement with the Australian Cricket Board, applied to the ACB for permission to recruit a new player for the second leg of the tour. This was gracefully granted and Bacher was empowered to open negotiations with Wessels.

'Well, not really, Dr Bacher.'

Wessels was hesitant.

First, he was centrally involved in the rebuilding of Eastern Province cricket and he did not seek distraction. Secondly, he was heartily fed-up with the rebel tour issue which had led to his being forced out of Australia. Thirdly, he was not certain that he would be welcomed by Hughes' squad, some of whom resented him for pulling out of the first tour at a relatively late stage.

His inclination was politely to decline the offer.

But... then... there was the money.

As an Australian living in South Africa, Bacher felt Wessels fell between the two sides. He could not be paid the R230 000 which the Australians would receive for the tour but he ought to get more than the R50 000 per man paid to the South African players. Bacher offered R70 000 for the tour plus prize money.

Wessels stopped to think. It was a substantial sum. To a man who had started to feel increasingly isolated and who realised his future beyond South African domestic cricket was bleak, it suddenly seemed the last big payday of his career. He began to doubt whether he could afford to turn down the SACU offer.

'OK, it's a deal but on two conditions,' he informed Bacher. 'First, I want to miss as few Eastern Province matches as possible, so I would like to skip three of the tour games.'

Bacher agreed.

'And secondly I want to reserve the right to withdraw at the very last moment if I feel that I'm not welcome. It's impossible for me to tell how the guys will react but I want to avoid another confrontation. I just don't need the hassle.'

That was fine too.

With Wessels on the horizon, the Australian squad gathered to discuss the issue soon after their return to South Africa before the second tour. There is a difference of opinion about the extent of opposition to Wessels' arrival but there were certainly some mixed feelings. Mike Haysman recalls: 'The guys felt pretty dark about anyone who had pulled out of the first tour.' Haysman himself had no objection.

'There was some grumbling,' says Bruce Francis the manager, 'but most of that was cleared up when we told them that Kepler had not received a signing-on fee. Some of the players were simply not aware of his position. By the end of the discussion, the squad was virtually unanimous in accepting him.'

Francis felt the meeting had been unnecessary, believing SACU, as the players' employers, should have imposed their decision without argument but the 'cards-on-the-table' approach smoothed the path for Wessels' eventual arrival on December 1st.

He joined the side on board an SAA flight from Johannesburg to East London. The aircraft had stopped in Port Elizabeth and Wessels strode alone into the cabin where the rest of the squad and members of the media were already strapped in. Would they look the other way? Would some of the players ignore him?

The nervous moment was eased by Hughes. Leaping out of his seat, the captain shook Wessels warmly by the hand and invited him to sit down next to him. With Kim, again. That was fine. How are you? All right, mate. Yeah, fine. It was OK.

Hughes was genuinely pleased to have Wessels at his side, and at No.3 in the batting order. Typically, the captain had approached the rebel tour as diligently and whole-heartedly as if it were an official Test series. To a proud man, it mattered.

To his frustration and sadness, however, this attitude was not shared by some members of his squad who, content to saunter and moan their way through the tour, were excited only by the prospect of banking the cheque. Discipline was a problem. Hughes hoped that some of Wessels' famed professional approach would rub off on those around him and give the team a sharper edge.

His 12-cylinder optimism was, not for the first time, dashed. Hard though many tried, the Australian rebels did not fulfil their potential. A team which boasted Steve Smith and John Dyson as the opening batsmen, followed by Wessels, Hughes and Yallop, and a fast bowling quartet of Rackemann, Terry Alderman, Rodney Hogg and John Maguire, ought seriously to have challenged the Boks.

They did lack a top-class all-rounder, and this cost them dear in the one-day series, but perhaps the harsh truth was that, like many rebel squads touring South Africa, they ultimately lacked the motivation to turn potential into performance.

Too many players were not prepared to pull their weight and Wessels, fresh from a year of controversy, was not about to stand and shout at them in the dressing room. Keen to dodge conflict, he would work hard and try his best at the crease... but, finally, he would also collect his cheque and return home.

This makeshift quasi-international squad was confronted by a venerable South African XI, proudly wheeled out from the garage of isolation like a vintage Rolls Royce, a classic construction with parts of timeless quality, yet covered in dust.

Fiercely led by Clive Rice, the 1986 Springboks were a plush combination of princely batting and sprightly bowling. They may have been ring-rusty and sometimes unable to move in for the kill, yet they rarely failed to entertain their supporters who longed to cheer. Never mind the rust, feel the quality.

Opening batsmen: Jimmy Cook, dark, moustached, upright and a teacher from the primary school around the corner from Wanderers, and Henry Fotheringham, fair, freckled, broad, hugely gifted. More often than anyone could remember, this accomplished pair had opened the Transvaal innings in a blaze of stroke-making. From the first, if the ball was there to be hit, they would hit it.

There would follow Peter Kirsten, the fighting bantam, nervy, twitchy, brilliant, prolific, once of Derbyshire — or perhaps Kenny McEwan, the gentleman stroke-player, once of Essex: both batsmen of globally acknowledged quality and stature.

At No.4, Graeme Pollock. He was, as the Wanderers scoreboard would post it during the final match of the Australian tour, his last game for South Africa, simply the MAESTRO.

Supported by Kevin McKenzie and Rice, the batting was packed with big guns. Garth le Roux, maybe a yard slower than during the Packer series but several yards wiser, led a bowling attack which called on the young talents of Hugh Page, Corrie van Zyl and, later in the series, the gangling Allan Donald. With Dave Richardson as wicketkeeper and Brian McMillan, the fiery Transvaal all-rounder, also in the frame, the South African squad included all the basic ingredients of a top-class international side.

What they lacked was experience, the street-wise proficiency that comes from regular competition and nothing else. It was a fact that, no matter the sumptuous mahogany panelling and real leather upholstery, this Rolls Royce would probably have been troubled, but not outclassed, by most of the modern conveyor-built sedans around the highways and byways of international cricket.

Wessels, a more than averagely interested opponent, recalls the 'superstars' with awe and respect but, having worked several shifts at the hard, grimy coalface of Test cricket, adds: 'I would like to have seen them against the West Indian pace attack. They might have found it pretty tough.'

The opening day/night series against Hughes' Australians in 1986/87 was, however, a breeze. The Springboks led the series 2-0 (it would have been 3-0 but for rain at the Wanderers) until some Australian pride was salvaged in the final game. The tourists had been humiliated at Newlands, reduced to 15 for seven at one stage, and the tour's credibility teetered on the brink.

Once again, the tortured issue of 'the real thing' nagged at the public conscience. When the Springboks won the first Test match at Wanderers after a helter-skelter scramble on an under-prepared, green wicket, the question begged: was this real Test cricket, or was it an artificial imitation? The people fretted.

The Wanderers pitch had not been conducive to a fair contest between bat and ball, and it prompted the uncomfortable suspicion that South African strategy was to win a shoot-out first Test, and protect that 1-0 advantage by playing the next three Test matches on featherbed batting pitches.

Such suspicions did not ring true but rebel tours were always vulnerable to scepticism because, like Kerry Packer's World Series Cricket, these games were essentially an exhibition series arranged by a single paymaster, not an even contest between two countries played according to agreed guidelines.

An undercurrent of unease was felt by some players. Ray Jennings, the world class South African wicketkeeper against the West Indies, recalls: 'The rebel tours were built on money. Test cricket is not like that. Against the West Indies, it sometimes felt as though we'd win the first match, they would win the second, we'd win the third and then everyone would hope they win the fourth to make it 2-2 and set up a decider. That was the vibe. In real Test cricket, the mood is "let's go out and kill the guys". We wanted to believe it but the rebel tours weren't the real thing.'

The first Test also identified the poor standard of umpiring as another faultline running through the rebel tours, another area where South African cricket had decayed in isolation. The match was peppered with bizarre decisions, one of which was overturned by the South African fielders after Hughes had been given out. The most glaring error involved Mick Taylor, the Australian batsman, who was given out caught behind with his bat apparently far from the ball. The senior local umpire compounded his error by later explaining to Taylor: 'Sorry, Mick. I was not absolutely sure that you had got a nick but I thought it might have been LBW anyway.'

Taylor's dismissal proved crucial as the Australians fell 49 runs short in the pursuit of 249 to win on the fourth day. Hughes, ever brave, had scored an unbeaten 56. Dyson and Haysman showed a similar resolve, batting to salvage honourable draws from awkward positions in both the second and third Tests. At Newlands and at Kingsmead, the batsmen held sway. But not Wessels.

His slump was broken in the drawn fourth Test at St George's Park in Port Elizabeth: a century in the first innings, a century in the second innings. He enjoyed some luck, being adjudged not out when television replays showed him to be run out and he was dropped twice, but the centuries were made and they served to re-establish Wessels as a main man in South African cricket.

His achievement was eclipsed, however, by an event which many of those present will recall as long as they live: the day Pollock scored a century in his last Test for South Africa. The great man's feat provided the series, perhaps the entire tour, with its single defining moment.

What set Pollock apart? Perhaps it was the sheer simplicity of his stroke, the technique which made batting seem so simple and natural. As Muhummad Ali boxed, as Carl Lewis ran, as Jack Nicklaus swung a golf club, so Pollock batted, with ease.

Or was it the power of his stroke, so great that fielders on the cover boundary would ring their throbbing hands after turning four runs into two? 'It felt as though we were catching bullets,' said one of the awe-struck Australians.

Or maybe it was the sheer volume of runs he scored in each of 26 seasons since he was named Cricketer of the Year in 1961. Or was it the expectant buzz that rippled around the ground whenever the upright figure stepped out towards the crease?

Whatever the reason, Pollock towered above the game. With his 43rd birthday in sight, he had announced that the fourth Test against the Australians would be his last, finishing a career that began at Grey High in Port Elizabeth, reached the highest level of the game with an innings of 122 against Australia in Sydney at the age of 19, and had sustained a majestic aura ever since.

Pollock played 23 Tests before isolation, scoring 2 256 runs at an average of 60.97. A further 15 unofficial Tests completed his sadly truncated international career. This was enough, however, for the world to know his immense talent.

It was, of course, fitting that he should bring the curtain down in Port Elizabeth, the city where he had grown up as the son of a newspaper editor, and where he had made his Currie Cup début for Eastern Province. It was also appropriate that he would close against Australians, if not quite Australia.

When the second South African wicket fell at 42, chasing the tourists' 455 for nine declared, there was still half an hour to be played before lunch on the second day. A hush. A roar. Pollock, so tall, thin, and angular, paced into the sunlight. There were three balls left in Hogg's over. The idol took guard. These three balls would provide the most dramatic action of the series.

Hogg stood at the end of his run-up. Hard, fast, aggressive, sometimes grumpy, usually caustic, he had not enjoyed a prosperous tour but this was his chance. The scourge of England in 1978/79 was awakened from lethargy, inspired by the sight of the prize scalp. Pollock's eyes darted this way and that. Nerves?

Torso bent familiarly forward like Groucho Marx, Hogg ran in, and bowled . . . fast. Pollock was surprised. He fended. An edge. The crowd gasped . . . and the ball scuttled between the wicketkeeper and slip to the boundary for four. The master gulped.

No time to settle. Hogg, now aflame, was running in again. He dug in a bouncer . . . very fast. Pollock ducked in the nick of time, and

135

wicketkeeper Steve Rixon gathered the ball above his head. Bold Hogg puffed out his chest and stood in the middle of the pitch, his chin resting on his left hand, and stared at his prey.

One ball left. Hogg ran in again and bowled... the fastest of the three, slanted across the left-hander, lifting. The batsman was startled. He fended desperately. The ball hissed at the bat but did not lure a fatal edge and safely passed by.

'Over!' National relief. Pollock puffed out his cheeks, Hogg grinned and slunk away towards third man.

What followed was Pomp and Circumstance. Pollock hardly moved his feet before crashing a short delivery in Hogg's next over for a redeeming boundary past cover point. Wielding his abnormally heavy bat, a veritable Excalibur, he then swept a ball from Trevor Hohns, the spinner, into the main stand and he was on his way.

Easing past 50, his innings began to assume an unstoppable momentum. With destiny at his side, he prospered. The circumstances of the Test were insignificant. Past 90, past 95.

Alderman moved in again, and bowled on the off-stump. Pollock rocked back, chopped the ball to third man and cantered gently into history. Three figures, again. St George's Park, scene of the first Test ever played by South Africa, bellowed delight, and a modest, quiet, even shy man raised his bat in thanks.

There followed a raw and ruthless demolition of the bowling. Pollock erupted and Alderman, who would torment England two years later, was humiliated, driven and pulled with disdain by a genius in relentless flow. Finally bowled by Hogg, the persistent terrier, Pollock had scored a regal 144 in 221 balls.

Wessels stood in awe, and then went back to work and scored a second century as the Test meandered to a draw.

Pollock and Wessels: the comparison was unavoidable. Both were left-handed batsmen, both had consistently proved themselves at the highest level, both were South African.

There the comparison stopped.

Pollock was so natural at the crease, putting his foot down and playing straight. Wessels seemed calculated and manufactured, prefacing every shot with an instinctive inward twitch of his toes. Pollock sailed, Wessels swam. Pollock inspired unconfined delight, Wessels earned everyone's respect. Pollock's innings is jubilantly remembered, Wessels' contributions to this fourth Test are not.

It is, of course, unfair to rate anyone alongside the genius but does it hurt, does it ache that, no matter how hard he trains, how far he runs, how much he sweats, Wessels will never bat like Pollock batted that day at St George's Park?

'No, not at all,' he responds. 'Every side needs players of all types. You can't have a team of Wessels and you can't have a team of Pollocks. You need a blend of grafters and stroke-players. You need different types of batsmen who are suited to different types of situation. It takes all sorts.

'I was aware early in my career that I would never play like Graeme Pollock or Barry Richards. That wasn't a problem. I suppose I would love to have batted like them, to have made it all look so simple and easy, but I didn't and I accepted that. I set my sights on being the best player I could be. So long as I achieved that, I was happy. Pollock was brilliant, but he was a freak. You could say he was one in a million. Only he could bat in that way.'

A quartet of one-day matches would complete the tour and the first of these was played in Port Elizabeth only three days after the Test. St George's Park was packed with 16 000 people who were wowed on a momentous day when, as Hughes graphically recalls, 'the crowd were hanging from the chandeliers'. Limited overs cricket is often predictable. But, sometimes, it is magical...

The breeze gusts in off Algoa Bay, the sun is up, the crowd is in its place and Rice wins the toss. All is set. Cook strides out to open the innings with Roy Pienaar, another massively gifted player drafted into the side. Hughes has instructed his pacemen to keep it tight, but they have not listened. Their asinine tactic of bowling short is mercilessly punished.

Pienaar disdainfully hooks Hogg for six. We are watching a rout. After 23 crazy overs, South Africa have raced to 151 without loss. The big guns are blazing. Cook departs with a princely 70 and Pienaar is soon quenched with 74 but Kirsten and Pollock move into the front line and the amazing pace never slackens. When 60 overs have been bowled, the Australians troop sadly off the field. If the match had been a boxing bout, the tourists would be retired. South Africa had amassed a towering 313 for six.

Festival! Between innings, the sun-kissed crowd are treated to skydivers and whirling, twirling drum majorettes. This is white South Africa at play, wallowing in pride.

Bring on the lambs. Dyson and Smith, both of New South Wales, launch the Australian innings. Chase 314 to win? They might as well be chasing the wind. Dyson is run out with the total on 33 and as Wessels walks out to the crease, some of the crowd applaud. He is, after all, the Eastern Province captain, the new local hero. The tourists need almost six runs an over. Give it up.

It is hard to explain what suddenly possesses this man whom so many dismiss as unsuited to one-day cricket. Perhaps the apparent hopelessness of his task releases from his mind the pressure that has seemed to restrict him in the past. Maybe he simply relaxes at the end of a tour which had seemed so unreal.

Whatever the reason, he plays magnificently. He exhilarates thousands in the ground, and millions more watching on television. This is the sportsman's high life. He breathes deeply.

Anything loose outside his off-stump is driven or cut, sent thundering into the boundary boards. Anything on line is cleverly run down to third man. He is scoring off almost every ball, the Springboks cannot contain him. Kepler? What's he on?

When the talented Smith is dismissed, Hughes joins his old team-mate with the total at 139 for two. The impossible has become improbable. All right, let's go for it.

There is nowhere to bowl. Hughes repeatedly steps back from his stumps to crash the ball through cover, and Wessels sustains his assault. The Springboks are struggling. Rice knows the deal. He calls for calm and bravely holds himself back to bowl at the death. Where the battle is fiercest, you will find him.

Hughes and Wessels add 157 runs in 18 overs. They are Butch Cassidy and the Sundance Kid, the straight man and the wild man. Hughes has effectively gone berserk. When he hurls himself towards another wayward delivery, his body convulses with excitement. When Wessels drives Rice for four past extra cover, Hughes takes it upon himself to signal the boundary at the non-striker's end.

Wessels has seen his captain in this sort of mood before. It is a wondrous sight, and he knows what he must do: keep talking to him, encourage him, just keep him on this high. 'Keep going, Kim. Yeah, it's fantastic. Keep going.' Something quite remarkable is happening. His job is to make sure it doesn't stop.

This heroic partnership takes the innings to the brink of an astonishing victory. Only 19 runs are needed from 21 balls. It's a stroll for the Australians. Hold on. Wessels pulls Le Roux towards the square leg boundary where McEwan arches back over the rope and holds the catch. Wessels is hailed. He has scored 122 from only 112 balls. Even the Springboks stand and applaud.

Exhausted, he heads for the dressing room which, originally built for a rugby team, is buried deep within the bowels of the old grandstand and has no view of the middle. He lies on the bench and places a towel across his forehead. Tired but happy. It had been a good day. No, it had been a bloody fantastic day.

Soon, he is startled by an immense roar reverberating around the stand above him. He knows immediately what has happened. Hughes is out. All right, there's no need for panic. Hughes arrives in the dressing room. 83 from 57 balls. Well batted, mate. Thanks. And you. The captain rips off his pads and rushes outside to watch. Wessels stays put. On his back, listening to the game.

Another roar. Peter Faulkner has been bowled by Rice. Another roar. Rixon is out. The stand seems to be shaking and the dressing room has become chaotic. Lower order batsmen, who hadn't expected to be required, rush down from the stands to pad up. The innings is collapsing. Two more roars. Hohns and Maguire gone.

Wessels lies still. There's more bedlam. Haysman is run out. From somewhere high above him, he makes out someone shouting that the Australians need seven from the last two balls. Hogg is facing. One last, lingering roar. He can't believe it.

Outside, Rice stands with legs planted in the middle of the pitch and pumps his fists. He has ripped through the Australian batting. Spectators dash on to the field. South Africa have won. Remember all this. You're going to tell your grandchildren.

The Australians are stunned but the mood soon changes from shock to anger. Some of the fast bowlers openly criticise Hughes for playing a wild shot and getting bowled. They say he threw the game away. Tempers explode. Wessels supports the captain. You can't criticise the way he batted when it was that kind of batting that put us in position to win the game at all. The bowlers don't agree. It had been a long day, still a great day...

Inevitably, the rest of the series seemed an anti-climax. South Africa won comfortably at Newlands, the Australians kept the series alive and kicking by winning in Verwoerdburg and the South Africans duly wrapped up a 3-1 triumph at Wanderers.

'And the Man of the Series is... Kepler Wessels.' Can't play one-day cricket, they said. For the third time in his international career, Wessels had won the main award from a limited overs series. He simply batted the critics into the ground.

As the 30 000 crowd drifted homeward from the Wanderers, the tour came to its conclusion. SACU were satisfied. The presence of the Australians had sustained public interest in the game and given the Springboks another chance to flex their muscles.

Hughes had been the tour's salvation. There had been breaches of discipline within the team, some of which forced the captain to take on the duties of a sole selector midway through the tour, and some players, notably Yallop and spinner Tom Hogan, had contributed very little but Hughes kept his standards high.

With his easy grin and his up-front manner, he had earned respect around the country. Young South African cricketers, hanging on his every word, would ask his advice and he would oblige. After the relentless mauling he had grown accustomed to from the media in Australia, he seemed to relax in South Africa and, in many ways, he came powerfully into his own. What sort of tour would it have been without Hughes? SACU shuddered to imagine.

Utterly convinced he had done nothing wrong, Hughes returned to Perth and became embroiled in a series of legal suits with the Western Australia Cricket Association, but his career in Australia was effectively over. He eventually returned to South Africa to captain the Natal side, a role he fulfilled with dynamic enthusiasm and some success for two seasons before retiring.

Thus, the distinguished career of an exhilarating batsman ended quietly and a little painfully. Few would dispute that Hughes deserved better. He may have been emotional and impulsive, may have said the wrong thing at the wrong time but his motives were right. There seemed to be no malicious thought in his head. He simply wanted to play for Australia — that was all, he never robbed a bank. History should judge him more kindly than his contemporaries.

It was his misfortune that his captaincy of the national team had been derailed by a great West Indian side, his bad luck that he should catch most of the fall-out from the rebel tour.

When the South African side arrived in Australia for the 1992 World Cup, they were welcomed at a function in Perth. The Western Australian cricket authorities seemed to extend a forgiving gesture to Hughes by sending him an invitation. He accepted, and turned up for the cocktail party wearing his rebel tour blazer. That was Kim Hughes, forever wearing his heart on his sleeve.

Others discovered a much better life after the South African adventure. Alderman, Rackemann and Hohns served out their bans and slid quietly back into the official team, all playing a major role during the Ashes tour of England in 1989. Still others such as Rod McCurdy, Haysman, Smith and Maguire, sooner or later, returned to play for provincial sides in South Africa.

Wessels simply caught the next flight to Port Elizabeth. His rebel experience had felt strange. It had not remotely compared to either official Test cricket or even the Packer series, but it had been hard and competitive. As such, he had enjoyed it more than he might have thought possible at the outset.

His main business, however, was in Eastern Province. There, nothing less than a miraculous revolution was underway.

# 9

# The Eastern Province Revolution

F asten your seatbelts. We have started our descent.

The aircraft flies out above the Indian Ocean before making its final approach to H.F. Verwoerd airport and there, in a brief twinkling of an eye, is Port Elizabeth, gently stretched out along a broad bay on the southern coast of Africa.

From the beaches, to the old town, to the port, to the green suburbs, to the motor factories and the sprawling townships beyond, Port Elizabeth has the appearance of a strong and established city, but it has preserved the atmosphere of a village.

The Friendly City, they call it. So it can be, and yet the close-knit community can also be quick to condemn, eager to gossip and prone to suffer a deep inferiority complex. Anything or anyone from the Transvaal is viewed with suspicion.

In April 1986, PE had little to feel superior about. Unrest simmered in the townships and the Eastern Cape economy was drowning in a pool of despondency. Unemployment was rising.

Sport offered little reason to cheer. The muscular Despatch rugby club had won the national club championship, but the pattern of 'flattering to deceive' had been predictably upheld by both the Eastern Province cricket and rugby teams. In almost a hundred years of trying, neither had ever won the Currie Cup.

The region boasted some of South Africa's finest schools and produced many players of great talent but the provincial teams had lost, and lost again. Year after year, initial optimism would drain away and be followed by another orgy of recrimination and blame. PE sport became infamous for its infighting.

In April 1986, one man arrived in Port Elizabeth who would make his own rules, establish his own order and teach the province how to win. Kepler Wessels. In a career full of achievement, the sporting wonder he worked in the world of Eastern Province cricket would rank alongside any other feat.

He inspired the bridesmaid team beyond its first Currie Cup triumph to a position of sustained dominance within South African cricket. In doing so, he revived the sinking spirits of the region. He gave people a reason to feel good about PE.

Every team, in any sport, in any league, wants to win. That is why they play. Between 1986 and 1990, Wessels provided a model of how to earn sporting success by transforming 97-year losers into consistent winners. Of course, many people helped him along the way but it was he who provided the central impetus.

He was the leader, the hero of the revolution . . .

* * * * *

April 1986 — The choice facing Wessels when he returned to South Africa from Australia was clear: snuggle cosily into a soft landing and settle down or leap straight into another frying pan and fight some more. Join Transvaal or join Eastern Province?

Transvaal, the premier province of the previous decade, were starting a rebuilding phase during which their captain, Clive Rice, would work to replace the pillars of the legendary 'Mean Machine' with new talent. Wessels was lured to Johannesburg to stabilise the top order batting during this transition, receive a healthy salary and, everyone expected, help win trophy after trophy.

Eastern Province, by contrast, was the inferior province of the previous century. There was plenty of talent but no discipline, direction, purpose, or prospect of success. Wessels was invited to score the runs, captain the side, organise the training, develop a squad, recruit players . . . everything but mow the grass.

Transvaal or Eastern Province? Settle or struggle? Stupid question. Wheeling the guns back on deck, manning the battlements of his mind, Wessels set full sail for Port Elizabeth. In this most relentless career, there would be no respite.

Ahead on the wind-whipped shores of Algoa Bay, the people slept in their beds, unaware of the coming invasion that would turn their lives upside down, their cricketers inside out. In their very midst, however, the groundwork was being laid by the professor of Greek at the University of Port Elizabeth (UPE).

Kotie Grové appeared every inch the outlandish academic. His dark, curly hair and thick spectacles framed eager eyes that seemed never at rest, ever plotting. An eager admirer of Aristophanes, the ancient Greek author, Grové had sparked official outrage in 1983 by directing a UPE production of *Lysistrata,* the raunchy play about love and war first staged in 411 BC.

His second passion was cricket. Born in the Free State and educated at Stellenbosch, Grové found the UPE cricket club struggling but he set about recruiting talented schoolboys and establishing a new structure. Year after year, the club grew and Grové's cricketing interests began to broaden. He became frustrated by the form of the Eastern Province side. 'They were nicknamed the *aandblomme* (night flowers),' he recalls, 'because they looked so good on paper, i.e. at night, but they never bloomed during the day.'

Gavin Cowley, Graeme Pollock and Kenny McEwan were three of many top-class cricketers who had emerged from the Eastern Cape yet Eastern Province continued to struggle. Grové, once elected to the EP cricket union executive, conceived a plan.

Central to his ambition for the province was the recruitment of one all-powerful man who would encourage a new approach, inspire confidence, lead from the front, tolerate no opposition, accept no compromise, follow his own conviction, nobody else's.

Grové believed Wessels was the man for the job.

One day in 1973, when he was working in Bloemfontein, Grové had been driving past the Grey College cricket nets when he noticed a boy batting. Almost two hours later, Grové passed again. The boy was still in the nets. On impulse, he stopped his car and asked one of the young bowlers who it was who wanted nothing else but to bat. Since that day, he had not forgotten the name.

Through the years that followed, he had traced the boy's progress into Currie Cup cricket and on to Australia, becoming ever more impressed by what he recognised as a rare resolve.

In September 1982, Grové heard that Wessels was planning to visit his parents in George, just along the coast, and seized the chance of inviting the batsman to visit UPE and then be the guest speaker at a UPE cricket dinner. It seemed a long shot.

Wessels accepted. At an uncertain stage of his career, when he was afraid the Australian selectors would not choose him because of his background, he was prepared to hear what sort of offer Grové could make. It might, he calculated, be useful to have an option in South Africa in case his Australian hopes collapsed.

Grové all but rolled out the red carpet. A car was waiting for Wessels at the airport and the reception committee at UPE was exhaustively briefed. The cricketer was ushered to the main tower block on campus and taken to the 11th floor.

'This way, Kepler.' Grové walked on towards an office in the university's public relations department. 'This will be yours,' he told Wessels. 'It's ready when you are.' That was the offer: take over the Eastern Province team as captain and work for UPE as a public relations officer. Wessels was impressed. He assured Grové that if he ever returned to South Africa, he would very much like to take up the challenge in Port Elizabeth.

That evening, Wessels told the UPE dinner that the secret of cricketing success was a professional attitude and hard work. There were, he said, no short cuts. Unbeknown to anyone sipping his coffee, four years on, he would prove it.

Grové was encouraged by Wessels' response. He became more excited when his target was not included in Australia's team for the first Test against England in November 1982. If they weren't going to pick him, he could be in PE by the end of the season. But his hopes dissolved when Wessels was selected for the second Test and set out on his Australian Test career.

'It sounds odd,' Grové recalls, 'but I always had this idea that Kepler would come to Port Elizabeth. People in town used to tease me about it, saying I was completely mad but I knew Kepler would captain Eastern Province. I was sure.'

Not mad, just patient. When Wessels' difficulties with the Australian Cricket Board began in 1985, Grové moved into action by writing letters to reach Wessels on tour in England, confirming the UPE offer was still on the table. Still 'ready when you are'. By the time Transvaal reacted to growing rumours of Wessels' return, Eastern Province were way ahead in the race to sign him.

On April 15th, 1986 — Grové recalls the date — Wessels arrived in Port Elizabeth. Sally, his wife, was naturally apprehensive. She had started to speak Afrikaans and she knew South Africa well after a number of extended visits but this was different. The country had been placed in an official state of emergency for nine months and the political temperature was rising... yet the move was best for her husband's career. She understood that, and she supported him. With their four-month-old son Riki (he had been born shortly before Christmas 1985), the Wessels family moved into a flat.

Fully five months before the start of his first season in charge, Wessels might have been expected to ease gently into his new environment. He didn't. He headed straight to St George's Park and, in a manner of speaking, ripped up the floorboards. He met the staff, the administrators and some of the players, and was pleased. From the very start, he saw potential: 'The set-up was everything I wanted,' he recalls. 'It seemed as though the people were tired of the old ways, and of losing. They wanted change.'

Some of the administrators were perhaps more braced than ready. For 97 seasons the Eastern Province cricket union had been essentially run by the old, established families of Port Elizabeth, some of whom were directly descended from the original settlers of 1820 and many of whom were connected to the Grey High School. There was a kind of time-honoured elite, a ruling class.

Now, prompted by the zealous Grové, these men had agreed to hand the keys of their castle to this Australian. After the years of failure, they hungered for success as well.

Colin Rushmere, a former opening batsman for the province and a successful local businessman, was the EPCU president with the vision to put all his eggs in Wessels' basket. 'All you need from a president is an open line of communication,' Wessels remembers, 'and Colin Rushmere was brilliant in that respect. He knew exactly where we were going and everyone respected him.'

There were other lions in the Port Elizabeth jungle. Geoff Dakin, another former Eastern Province player, was serving as the South African cricket union president, and Peter van der Merwe, a former Springbok captain, was in position as convener of the South African selectors. While neither played a direct role at the EPCU, both retained influence and both backed Wessels.

To each of these substantial men, Eastern Province cricket was not a paid profession. It was a passion, and they gave their time freely. Wessels, by contrast, was an employee, in effect their employee. Thus, while the captain was handed absolute control of day-to-day team affairs, the EPCU board remained emphatically in overall authority. This was right and proper, but, from the outset, the alliance between a hard-headed, disciplinarian Afrikaner and a generally genteel English-origin board was brittle. It would buckle and fracture, but that was in the future...

In 1986, at least, there was cosy cohabitation. David Trist, a livewire New Zealander, was appointed as Director of Cricket and assumed responsibility for marketing and coaching. His extrovert manner complemented Wessels' approach, and they began to work well together. Finally, there was Grové, who was elected as chairman of the union's Playing Affairs Committee, a committed Wessels man in an influential position. That was important.

Wessels was thrilled by this administrative structure. There was a unity of purpose, there was a clear goal, and he very clearly was the apex of the pyramid. Whatever he wanted, he would receive. Whoever he wanted to play, would play. He began to feel the burden of expectation, the weight of responsibility.

Stand and deliver. And so to work.

The players were summoned to attend pre-season training. It was May. Barely six weeks after one season had ended, they gathered to meet the new leader. Welcome to a new world. The presence of one man had energised the whole atmosphere.

Dave Richardson, the wicketkeeper, had led the side during 1985/86 and was initially wary of the new regime. Was it right that someone should be brought in from outside? Before long, even he had started to wonder whether that wasn't exactly what the province had needed all along to release its potential. 'Most of us were brought up in a different era,' he recalls. 'We went along to the nets, and played squash or some touch rugby to keep fit. We thought we were fit because we could run around the park.

'Kepler showed us that was not enough. You had to do what he asked, or you fell away. There was no dodging the work. He wouldn't accept a situation where you were still doing your stretches when the other guys had already started the running.'

The running, the running. Wessels wanted his players to be fit and, more importantly, he wanted to discover who was prepared to sweat and who wasn't. Just like Ian Chappell eight years before, Wessels was looking for his 'infantrymen'.

Shuttle sprints. Longer sprints of 200m and 400m at the UPE athletics track. A four-kilometre run inside a 15-minute time limit or you do it again. Even longer hauls through the sinking sands of King's Beach. Run, run, run. This was the rugby season, mid-winter. Wessels just kept running, leading the pack and always keeping one eye over his shoulder to see who was lagging.

Neatly delegating the role of taskmaster so he could more easily concentrate on the players' reactions, Wessels had invited a broad-beamed policeman named Neil Schultz to run the sessions. Schultz proved the perfect sergeant-major, caring little whether a preening cricketer secretly cursed him. 'Schultz gave the orders,' Dave Callaghan, a young all-rounder on the fringes of the squad, recalls, 'but we all knew who was behind it.'

Callaghan was one of several young players who were prepared to serve in the trenches with Wessels. Whatever he asked, they did. Mark Rushmere, the talented son of the union president, was another to follow without question. 'Kepler was a big name and there were not many big names coming to Port Elizabeth,' Rushmere recalls. 'We saw him as a God. We'd have done anything he said.'

So they ran, day after day. Vangelis' score from *Chariots of Fire* might have been playing in the background. A group of emerging players had begun to live a dream, so they ran.

Some struggled to keep the pace. Tales began to circulate of exhausted EP cricketers driving home after training and pulling over to the kerb before vomiting in the gutter.

Others opted out of the new deal. Terry Reid, until then the regular No.3 batsman, attended a practice at UPE and began running on the grass just inside the athletics track. Wessels asked what he was doing. Reid explained that his knees were sore.

'Mate, I've had four operations on my knee and I've got no problem running on the track,' the captain barked. 'Don't you think you should rather go home and rest it?' Reid soon went.

Kenny Watson was another to struggle. Strong and willing, he had played two Tests for South Africa versus the rebel West Indians but the exertion was too great. He explained to Wessels that he was sorry but he couldn't keep up, and he departed to East London where he pursued his career for four more years with Border.

What Wessels didn't know, but later learned, was that Watson was scared of suffering a similar fate to his father, who had died from a brain haemorrhage on the cricket field. That same condition later forced his retirement. 'If I had known that, I wouldn't have made him run,' Wessels reflects, a little late. Yet he could hardly be blamed. There was no time to discover such personal details when the player preferred to keep them to himself.

Each time a player dropped by the wayside, the others would look for a sign of weakness in Wessels, the merest hint of remorse or pity, the slightest suggestion of mercy. There was nothing. His resolve was forged in gleaming steel, without a blemish or scratch. Follow or fall. There would be no middle way.

Beneath the ruthless, authoritarian exterior, there beat a human heart as vulnerable as any. No one but his family ever glimpsed his moments of weakness but Wessels was as concerned and fretful as ever. What if the players didn't want to run? What if the team didn't win? He was putting himself on the line ... No one glimpsed inside his head because no one ever got close enough. If he was to instil genuine discipline, he couldn't be everybody's mate. If the players didn't like him, and he suspected many of them didn't, that was hard luck. He wanted to win trophies, not popularity.

Wessels recalls: 'I came in hard and I made enemies but I had to challenge the players' approach. I had to be extreme. I had to find guys who were prepared to work. That mattered much more to me than their level of talent. I would rather have had an average player prepared to work than a brilliant cricketer who wasn't. If they weren't willing to join in, I really didn't want them around, no matter how dazzling everyone said they were.

'I wanted to know how they thought, how they reacted under stress and pressure. One routine that worked well was to run them until they were extremely tired and then see how well they batted in the nets. Some of them made it, others didn't. I was lucky that there were enough young guys in the squad to make it work, and we formed a nucleus from there. They did really well.'

As the training succeeded, so Wessels began to settle into his new role. After a year of things going wrong in Australia, this was working. He grew in confidence and started to introduce more of the training drills he had learnt in Australia, most of which were new and exciting in stagnant, isolated South Africa.

When in September 1986 the Eastern Province cricket players attended a joint training session with the provincial rugby squad and proved themselves to be fitter, Wessels was exhilarated. His side was ready and set for the forthcoming season.

Around the country, rival provincial sides were just getting together for the first time. Have a bit of a net, chappie? How was your winter? Played a bit of golf? Durbs? Caught in a virtual time warp since isolation, gentleman players were turning up for the new season. Professional? What does it mean? Well, it means being paid, doesn't it? Not in Port Elizabeth. There, it meant running from May until

September. It meant total sacrifice. Before a single ball was bowled, EP had already moved ahead of the pack.

Wessels, however, was realistic. He knew he did not have the players required to win. Better acquainted with the challenge, he sat down with Rushmere, Trist and Grové and hatched a three-season plan for the province: in 1986/87, simply compete; in 1987/88, win a limited overs trophy; in 1988/89, win the Currie Cup.

Many such plans are made, but never realised. 'We had two things going for us,' Wessels recalls. 'First, we had the talent, and second, everyone was pulling in the same direction. I was very positive. It was an exciting time for all of us.'

Season One's objective was achieved. The team did not thrive in either of the limited overs competitions but they competed well in the Currie Cup, finishing second on the completed log table and earning a home semi-final against Western Province, the winner of which would advance to play Transvaal in the final.

Wessels, who had scored more than 1 000 runs in the season, was satisfied with the immense improvement. The semi-final was seen as a bonus. In the event, Eastern Province secured a first innings lead and seemed in command before, set a target of 213 to win, they collapsed from 124 for two to 166 all out. Rod McCurdy, the burly Australian fast bowler recruited directly from the rebel tour, had taken nine wickets in the match and Wessels had scored a gutsy 83 in the second innings but it was insufficient. The general lack of experience took its toll. The players would learn.

Some of the less perceptive sportswriters lambasted Eastern Province for throwing the game away, but the astounding progress of the team had been noticed in the other provinces. So long a nobody, Eastern Province had swiftly become a somebody under Wessels.

Rice, for one, was impressed by what he saw. 'EP had always lacked basic discipline but Kepler sorted that out. There are many different formulae for success but Kepler's approach worked for EP and he should get the credit. I think he led very much by example. That was the key. The guys saw how the extra training had worked for him, so they followed. It was quite dramatic.'

Ray Jennings was another to recognise the signs. 'I recall our match against EP that year,' the Transvaal wicketkeeper says. 'We could see the difference in their set-up immediately. Kepler was the king. Every successful side must have a king who runs the show, takes the decisions and accepts responsibility. He must be the guy who lays down a clear direction which everyone can follow. It's the same in all successful businesses. Ali Bacher plays that role in the administration of South African cricket, Ricey did it at Transvaal, and Kepler was the king in Eastern Province. That's why things were going so much better for them after he took over.'

The younger players were responding to Wessels' professional and disciplined leadership. He was not the sort of captain to throw his arms around a player in bad form. He led the way and challenged his team to follow. Such an uncompromising approach might not have been so successful with older, more experienced players prepared to question the captain's conviction, but it was ideally suited to the appetite of the Eastern Province youngsters.

They cried out for guidance, and Wessels gave it. In return, they respected him, profoundly; and, particularly during the early years, they were scared of him. 'It wasn't fear,' suggests Grové. 'It was just that they didn't want to disappoint him.'

Whatever the terminology, there were occasions when one of the younger players, sipping on a can of beer in the dressing room after the day's play, would suddenly hide the can when Wessels came in. Others would hastily extinguish cigarettes.

Was this healthy? Of course it was. Wessels' message was that you could not expect to be a star in the bar and bowl 25 overs the next day. He would not waver. Wessels' message was that there was a heavy price to be paid, and it had to be paid on the training field and in the nets. There was no other way. Wessels' message was do all this and you will be the best you can be.

No other way. The Eastern Province team accepted his rules and reaped the rewards. Ask Dave Callaghan about the rewards. When Wessels arrived in Port Elizabeth, the young, sturdy all-rounder was on the brink of giving up cricket. Six years of life-under-Wessels later, Callaghan was playing for South Africa.

April 1986: Callaghan, 22, a fine sportsman, has established himself as centre in the Eastern Province rugby team. He's playing so well he's invited to play club rugby in Italy from October until March. At last, the big decision nears. Rugby or cricket? He tends towards rugby because he has only been hovering around the fringes of the Eastern Province cricket side.

Soon he hears about the cricket squad training in May. He is intrigued. He goes along to see this Wessels character, and settles into a new routine. Cricket training in the afternoon, rugby in the evening, day after day. Wessels watches Callaghan, sees a man ready for the trenches and tells him to hang around.

'No thank you, Italy.' Callaghan remains in South Africa and his cricket prospers. Bowling accurately, batting powerfully, he wins a place in the team and blazes a few headlines by carrying the side to a last ball night series victory over Natal.

The Currie Cup semi-final approaches, and the selectors say Callaghan isn't suited to that type of cricket. They don't think he should play. Wessels disagrees. Callaghan plays. In the years that followed, his place would rarely be in doubt again. He would become a cornerstone of the side, and an international...

With Season Two on the horizon, the plans once again began in June when the players received off-season fitness programmes in the post. 'Kepler never stopped training,' Rushmere recalls with awe. 'He set the pace and we all tried to keep up.' The clear goal, as everyone at St George's Park knew, was a trophy.

In February 1988, Eastern Province beat Northern Transvaal to win the Nissan Shield final at Centurion Park. Wessels received the Shield and raised it above his head. He took the microphone and addressed the milling crowd: '*Hierdie is 'n groot oomblik vir my, en vir die Oostelike Provinsie,*' he declared. In English, 'This is a great moment for me, and for Eastern Province.' So far as anyone could recall, it was the first Afrikaans victory speech in the history of South African cricket.

Oh, happy day.

Wessels sat back in the changing room, smiling broadly. This was the sort of moment that made his intense life worth while. Sweet victory. For what seemed the first time since he had taken control of the side, the captain removed his steel armour and relaxed with his team. Callaghan teased him playfully. Wessels laughed, snapped open a beer, drank deeply and let his eyes wander around the room of thrilled cricketers, still grinning, looking...

... at Kenny McEwan, the richly talented, richly experienced batsman whom he had recruited at the start of the season and who had stabilised the middle order. Upon leaving Western Province, McEwan seemed to be edging towards retirement. He settled on a dairy farm two hours' drive west of Port Elizabeth, but was asked to play for Eastern Province again, back on his old stamping ground. Well, he would like to but it's difficult with the farm.

Grové and Wessels made it easy. Bennie Melville, the UPE groundsman, drove out to McEwan's farm and built him a net where he could practise on his own, and Wessels accepted there would be days when McEwan would not be able to attend the team net sessions. He was later provided with a flat in Port Elizabeth. Compromises flew in every direction. Whatever needed to be done to get McEwan into the side, would be done. The operation was an example of effective and efficient sports administration.

... at Greg Thomas, the Glamorgan and former England fast bowler, whom Wessels had approached to join McCurdy in a successful new ball partnership. The Welshman and the Australian had roared in all season, a blur of bounce and aggression. There was some sorrow that both frontline fast bowlers were imported, but Wessels needed his big guns. They were a crucial part of his plan.

... and at Callaghan, now 23. The all-rounder had played the match-winning innings in the Shield final, crashing a blistering 92 from 88 balls. Earlier in the season he had batted with a wired-up jaw, showing the type of guts his captain admired. 'If a Springbok touring squad was chosen now, he'd be in it,' remarked no less an authority than Ali Bacher. 'He's the find of the season.' In March 1988 Callaghan retired from top-class rugby.

Others sat smiling: Philip Amm and Rushmere, the young and consistent opening batsmen; Tim Shaw, the tall, economical spinner; Richardson, the safe pair of hands behind the wicket. This was the nucleus of Wessels' side. They had become the hard-working epitome of everything that he admired. It was, you might say, a team with their heads down, chins in, concentrating.

Eastern Province net sessions were a wonder. Bowlers running in off their full run-ups, batsmen playing each 'net' as if it were the first 15 minutes of a major innings. There were no bouncers, no wild swipes, no chatter, no jokes. In every face there was a firm purpose and a resolute concentration. Keeping a quiet, alert eye on everything, and unafraid to bark at anyone who allowed the standard to drop, was the king-captain. 'If there's one thing I simply can't tolerate,' Wessels said, 'it's a sloppy practice.'

Some outsiders peered into Eastern Province's new order and asked: 'Fine, but is this cricketing army camp much fun?' Fun? Is winning the Shield at Centurion Park fun? Yes it is.

'What pleased me above all,' Wessels recalls, 'was that our hard work and preparation had moulded the squad into a strong and confident unit. You could judge that from the way we played when a one-day or night match went down to the wire. When the bowlers had to bowl straight or when the batsmen needed to score the runs, our guys kept producing the goods under pressure. I probably never let them know it but that really delighted me.'

In the second leg of the Shield semi-final, Eastern Province had defeated Western Province off the last ball, thrilling another cheering, chanting capacity crowd at St George's Park. 'There was a new atmosphere around the whole town,' Richardson recalls. 'People were coming to St George's expecting the side to win. It was never like that in the old days, and this sort of confidence got through to the team. We had this fantastic hunger for success. Youngsters came in to the side expecting to win. Before, you would come in and hope to score 30-odd just to keep your place.'

Shield success established Wessels as a celebrity in Port Elizabeth, perhaps *the* celebrity, admired as much for the fact that his team was winning as for the suggestion that others 'up-country' were irked by his achievement. The Transvaal Press, widely resented as the mouthpiece of all enmity, had begun to carp at his style of captaincy, at conservative tactics. In doing so, they effectively whipped up more fervour in the Eastern Cape.

Leading UPE to victory at the national club championships in Johannesburg, Wessels was fiercely sledged. In one innings, he had survived two confident appeals before finally being caught behind. As he left the crease, the bowler graphically summed up Wessels' career by shouting, '**** off, you Aussie Dutchman.'

'I'll see you after the game,' Wessels muttered in reply. He would stand back for no one. Neither would his team.

Season Three drew near. '1988/89: win the Currie Cup.' That was the goal, crystal clear in everyone's mind. It does not happen very often in the fickle, mercurial world of sport but the players, office staff and administrators all stood together. As the season progressed, the bandwagon rolled on, through each serious practice, each teamtalk, each high-five. Like the New York Mets baseball side in the 1986 World Series, they had the teamwork to make their dream work. And all the time, the paramount, overriding objective — the Currie Cup — remained in perfect focus.

It is March 10th, 1989.

Who wrote this script? It's perfect.

Eastern Province, led by Wessels, are to play Transvaal, led by Rice, in the five-day Currie Cup final at St George's Park, Port Elizabeth. Amid festival. The match is the centrepiece of the South African cricket union's centenary celebrations, and various cricket VIPs have been flown in from around the world. There are banquets, and vintage car parades, and banners; and, in the middle of it all, there is a team within reach of its finest hour.

'I was very excited,' Wessels recalls. 'The build-up and the whole situation reminded me very much of the two Sheffield Shield finals I had lost with Queensland. The big difference was that we were playing at home. That was a major advantage and I was really quite confident going into the game. I knew we had the team. It was a question of producing the performance on the day; and, of course, of winning. I was getting tired of going into these big occasions and finishing on the losing side. I was really desperate to beat Transvaal. It was a personal thing.'

Few neutral observers were ready, however, to bet against the Vaal. Giants such as Graeme Pollock, Kevin McKenzie and Alan Kourie might have shuffled off the stage but the team still reeked of big-match experience, class and quality. Cook and Fotheringham, Roy Pienaar, Brian McMillan, Jennings and, above all, the great Rice. These were the big names representing the big province from the big city. What would Port Elizabeth be in Johannesburg but just another suburb? Surely class would prevail.

Across the corridor in the players' area, a quite different kind of team was completing their preparations. Younger, fitter and probably more hungry than their opponents, eleven Eastern Province players were approaching what was for most of them the biggest game of their careers. Nothing had ever mattered so much.

Rushmere, Amm, Wessels, McEwan: big batting guns. Thomas and McCurdy: shock bowlers. Shaw and Hobson: solid spinners. Callaghan: all-rounder. Michau: broad big-hitter. Richardson: wicketkeeper. The balance was right, the mood was right.

Wessels won the toss, and decided to bat. His strategy for the final was taken directly from the Ian Chappell guide to winning cricket matches: bat first, steadily build a first innings total so large that you don't have to bat again, utterly rule out any chance that the other side might have of winning, then apply the pressure, tighten the pressure, increase the pressure and bowl them out twice to win by an innings and some.

In Wessels' opinion, this kind of victory represented the ultimate triumph in his sport. It was the hole-in-one, the perfect ace, the slam-dunk basket and the one punch knock-out all rolled into one wonderful, satisfying, vindicating experience. Viewed in a different way, it could be seen as subdue and penetrate, cricket's equivalent of ten-man rugby. Power. Grind. Win.

That was the plan but, after only an hour's play, the plan was in trouble. Rushmere and Wessels were out. The score was 42 for two. Amm and McEwan came together, and settled.

They stayed together until lunch, until tea, until stumps on the first day, past a second lunch break and well into the second afternoon. By then, the score had moved along to 379 for two. They had added 337 in seven hours and 17 minutes.

Wessels sat quietly and watched this monumental partnership, marvelling at McEwan's application and strokeplay. He had ridden his luck, dropped by Clive Eksteen on 32 and by Rice on 44, but found a splendid momentum. He finished with a magnificent 191 that included no fewer than 25 boundaries and one six.

Amm's powers of concentration were yet more astonishing. He ended with 214, having batted for almost eleven and a half hours and offered not a single chance.

There had been times when Wessels questioned the application of the talented opening batsman, whose relaxed nature occasionally concealed his determination. One day, when Amm misfielded at third man, Wessels had turned to glower at him in a disapproving fashion. Amm responded by flinging out his arms, as if to declare: 'OK, I'm sorry. It's not the end of the world.' Team-mates laughed and made light of the event, but Wessels and Amm, different personalities, seemed occasionally to be operating on different wavelengths.

Such reservations were set aside, at least temporarily, when the opener played the crucial innings and Wessels congratulated him warmly. The ideal platform had been laid. Michau's hard-hit 79 on the third morning consolidated the advantage, and Eastern Province were eventually all out for a dominating 561. Curiously, only three batsmen had scored more than 12, but all three had scored a great deal more than 12 and the strategy was on course.

Meanwhile in the President's suite, a luxurious room removed from events in the middle by 60 metres and by a generation or two, criticism of the home captain had been mounting since the close of play on the second day. When Eastern Province batted deep into the third day, it began to reach a crescendo: 'Wessels is killing the game... he should declare, make a match of it... this is supposed to be a showpiece... they're batting too slowly... someone should go and tell him this simply isn't good enough... does he realise we've got overseas guests here...

it's a national disgrace... he really should declare... is he playing for a draw?'

In traditional fashion at St George's Park, opinions in the President's suite tended to overflow into the neighbouring Press box and miraculously appear in print the next morning. Anonymous Transvaal officials, outraged by Eastern Province's decision to bat on, were quoted as saying the game was dead and their team would now bat out the rest of the match to 'teach Wessels a lesson'.

There were certainly some lessons to be learned, but who was teaching who? Wessels had extensive experience of winning five-day cricket matches. His critics, with respect, had virtually none. He knew exactly what he was doing. His critics, with respect, had very little idea of what they were talking about. Glorious vindication, Wessels suspected, lay just around the corner.

Transvaal launched their innings in the depressing position of being unable to win the match. Their task was to bat through two and a half days with an effective 20 wickets standing. Wessels let McCurdy and Thomas off the leash and applied the pressure. His team were hyped up from their heads down to their heels.

'The atmosphere got really heated in the middle,' Wessels recalls. 'Our guys were very determined and the sledging was pretty severe at times. After all the years of losing to Transvaal, this was the payback day. I think we all wanted it so badly and I wasn't going to tell our bowlers to go easy on the batsmen. I encouraged them to go for it. I wanted them to be angry.'

Seeking 362 to avoid the follow-on, Transvaal slumped to 52 for three. Pienaar and Rice managed to withstand the onslaught but both were removed by the persistent Shaw and the visitors limped to the close at 147 for six, in dire straits. Next morning, Jennings resisted bravely but the innings ended on 203. Still, with only seven hours left to play, Transvaal seemed to have a fair chance of salvaging a draw as they began their second innings.

Callaghan recalls: 'It all came down to the fifth day. When we went out to field, there were only a couple of thousand people in the ground and I remember feeling a bit deflated. It was almost as though people expected Transvaal to hold out. But we just kept plugging away and the wickets started to come. Into the afternoon, we could see a steady flow of people arriving in the stands. They must have been waiting to see what would happen. By tea, there were nearly 10 000 people there. It was an amazing thrill to be in the middle of it all. We just kept going.'

Transvaal would not lie down. Cook scored 28, Fotheringham 33 and Pienaar 30, but their less experienced batsmen, Mark Venter and Kevin Rule, managed a total of nine runs between them in the match. Not for the first time, it was left to Rice. In as truly gallant a display as graced any of his triumphs, the courageous veteran dug himself in... 'If you want the Currie Cup, get me out.'

He was joined by another legendary figure brought up in the invincible years. Jennings also refused to yield, holding firm in a torrent of accurate bowling and ferocious abuse. Rice and Jennings, the old troopers, held the bridge and batted on.

Amid this admirable resistance, Wessels was not swayed. He would not be panicked by any stolen glances at the clock where time kept tick-ticking away, and his bowlers served him well. McCurdy and Thomas claimed three wickets each, and Shaw kept such an accurate line that, in 46 overs, he bowled 31 maidens and took three for 32. The second of those wickets was the decisive breakthrough, the last remaining obstacle between Eastern Province and the cherished trophy they had waited 100 years to win.

With barely an hour and a half left to play, the shadows now lengthening and the Port Elizabeth crowd growing anxious, Rice took guard for the umpteenth time against Hobson. He had batted for more than five and a half hours in scoring 75, at one stage receiving nine minutes of treatment after being struck in the groin by Thomas. Now he took guard again, and pushed forward, an edge on to the pad, the ball lobbed up, Michau clutched it. Appeal. Out!

The Eastern Province players converged in delight, and Rice appeared to stop in his tracks and sigh before slowly trudging back to the pavilion. The dam had broken. Next over, Shaw wheeled in to Jennings and had him caught behind for 27. Eksteen quickly followed him in, and out, LBW to Shaw. Three wickets had gone with the total on 249. Suddenly, St George's Park came to life.

Wessels recalled Thomas for the kill, and the fast bowler obliged by shattering Radford's stumps. Transvaal were all out for 255. Eastern Province had won by an innings and 103 runs.

Tears welling in their eyes, the Eastern Province players gathered in front of the newly constructed Centenary Stand for the presentation of the Currie Cup. For all the running, for all the hard work, this was their reward. Several of the players would reflect on this moment as the greatest of their career, greater than being selected for South Africa, greater than anything.

Transvaal, who had not lost a Currie Cup match since 1981, stood by, sad but gracious, as Wessels stepped forward to receive the Cup. He was wearing a short-sleeved sweater without any sort of shirt underneath. Some thought it inappropriate attire.

'Dr Danie Craven sent me a message saying I should have been properly dressed for such a historic moment,' Wessels recalls, 'but he didn't know that someone had poured Coke all over me as we ran off the field. I was drenched and when we had to rush back out for the presentation, I grabbed the first thing I could find. I suppose I should have looked a bit harder.'

So there it was. The Currie Cup at St George's Park.

What now? Anti-climax? No, the task was simply to make sure that Eastern Province would not have to wait another century before winning the Currie Cup again. In fact, they had to wait no longer than 12 months. In the 1989/90 season, when the lessons of history seemed to point towards a slump, Eastern Province scaled new peaks and confirmed their dominant status in domestic cricket. They won the Shield, they retained the Currie Cup after a drawn final at St George's Park against Western Province, and they won the Benson and Hedges night series. They had captured the fabled treble.

How? If the application of Wessels' discipline and guidance to a talented group of young players led to the realisation of the original three-year plan, success was sustained first and foremost because the strong discipline was sustained. Without that, without the shared purpose, without the unity, there would be no trophy, no glory. Everyone involved understood that. For now.

Beyond that, Wessels and Grové continued to work tirelessly from their tower block base at UPE, recruiting both emerging young players and overseas professionals. 'There was no point having all the discipline in the world if we didn't have the talent,' Wessels recalls. 'Kotie Grové did a brilliant job in that respect. It was a competitive market but, more often than not, if we really went for someone, we ended up signing them. We had earned a good reputation.'

The youngsters were the prime target because, all going well, they would safeguard the future of the province. Wessels' job of selling UPE to high schools in the Transvaal and Natal put him in a perfect position to get wind of exceptional schoolboy talent looking for a university home, and Grové's involvement in student sport meant he also had his ear to the ground.

In most cases, the process was simple. Wessels would make the first approach and sound out the young man. If the response was favourable, Grové would then move in to apply the nuts and bolts of the offer and tie up the financial arrangements. They were usually talking about an overall package in the region of R20 000 to secure the enrolment at UPE of a talented cricketer.

As a result, UPE cricket boomed. They regularly shone at the national club championships and gradually dominated the leagues in Port Elizabeth. The university became an invaluable breeding ground for the province, something it had not been before.

To the irritation of rival provinces, much of South Africa's bright, young talent found its way to Port Elizabeth...

Brett Schultz, a tall, left-arm over the wicket fast bowler, was vigorously pursued by Transvaal who regarded him as a potential Test player. Grové nipped in... sold to UPE and EP.

Louis Koen, a compact, talented middle-order batsman, scored 90 for Boland against Eastern Province. Wessels was impressed and sounded him out. It was awkward because Koen was a policeman. Grové located an SAP contact... sold to EP.

Ross Veenstra, a tall fast bowler, was taking wickets for Maritzburg College and seemingly headed for the Natal team. Grové was alerted. He telephoned... sold to UPE and EP.

The second dimension of the recruitment drive was to appoint overseas professionals who would make a major contribution to the side rather than enjoy a six-month South African holiday. Wessels usually made the final decision, and the quality of his judgement became a feature of Eastern Province's success. The balance of his squad always demanded the signing of foreign fast bowlers.

McCurdy was the first and, for four years, the Australian proved himself one of the most aggressive bowlers in the country. Then there was Thomas, an outstanding choice.

The third would be John Maguire, another ex-Australian rebel whom Wessels had known well in Queensland and who would regularly produce long and accurate spells. Despite initial murmurings, he too had proved a sound investment for the province.

Later, there would be Eldine Baptiste, an all-rounder from Antigua who fitted in so well that he would captain the side when Wessels was away on Test duty. Wessels appreciated the West Indian in blunt terms. 'The best signing we made,' he said.

Grové, content to leave Wessels most of the credit for the regular attraction of talent to a city which, scarcely five years before, was regarded as a backwater, looks back with enthusiasm on the days when he was armed with a chequebook and pen: 'I reckon we did a good job. People in Port Elizabeth were always quick to say they thought we had made a mistake but most of the signings worked out well. We worked well together. I would do the groundwork but Kepler was the big chief. He was the key, and he was the reason why so many top players wanted to come and play.

'Of course success bred success to a certain extent and when people saw we were winning, they started contacting us. But my line of approach in selling UPE and EP cricket was generally the same. I would say we have this plan, Kepler is in control, and he wants you to be part of it. That usually did the trick.'

The success of this diligent and skilled mining for talent was reflected in the succession of glittering trophies that flowed into Port Elizabeth during the 1989/90 season. First, the Shield after Northern Transvaal were defeated in the final. The Currie Cup stayed where it was (in the St George's Park trophy cabinet) after the stalemate final with Western Province, and, once Wessels had endured the trauma of representing South Africa during the English rebel tour (see Chapter 10), this season of 24-carat triumph ended at the Benson and Hedges night series final in Durban.

Friday, March 30th, 1990. Life goes around in circles. Wessels strides out for the toss before a capacity crowd at Kingsmead. The Natal captain is Kim Hughes. Old rivals, old team-mates, a wealth of shared memories, another game, another job.

Natal, in outstanding form under lights all summer, managed only 202 in 45 overs, but Eastern Province were then reduced to 30 for three before Wessels and Callaghan staged a recovery. Wickets fell, runs were scored, the game hurtled towards one of the tense conclusions which occasionally make the smash-bang worth while: 23 runs were required from the last three overs, 12 from the last two and then six from the last. Karl Bauermeister, a strong all-rounder, had connected with several hefty blows for Eastern Province.

Amid creeping frenzy, Hughes fought to keep his team under control in the field. Wessels, who had scored 41, sat still, eyes fixed on the middle as he watched from the players' area. A hectic last over produced all the fun of the fair: two dramatic run-outs and several scampered runs. Finally, one run was required off the last ball. Dave Norman bowled to McCurdy, and McCurdy swiped the ball to the square leg boundary. Victory, again.

The treble was widely viewed as the absolute justification of all Wessels' methods. He was a hero to almost every man in the Port Elizabeth street, the totem of his region. A winner. He could do no wrong. Among the people, he was idolised.

Around a small town, that was not necessarily a good thing to be. Idols breed jealousy. Winners prompt envy. The adulation was becoming too much for some people to bear. The more Wessels became a hero to some, the more antipathy he aroused in others.

In general terms, that is why the Eastern Province fairytale turned into a living nightmare during the 1990/91 season.

Wessels suddenly found himself opposed by a small number of leading administrators and players. They wanted him to be replaced as captain. Four magnificent seasons of unity were torn up amid the rumour and recrimination that followed. It was as if the province had climbed a ladder to the top of the tree but, maybe overwhelmed by the view and the speed of their ascent, were now prepared to cast aside the ladder, the means of their rise.

The opposition to Wessels existed on two levels: (i) at board level where Peter van der Merwe, who had succeeded Colin Rushmere as the EPCU president, favoured the appointment of Mark Rushmere as a new captain of the provincial side; (ii) in the dressing room, where McCurdy became a catalyst for grumbles in the team that Wessels was too dictatorial, too strict, too much of a despot.

Van der Merwe's suggestion that Wessels should step down as captain, made during a private Eastern Province meeting towards the end of the 1990/91 season, was all the more extraordinary for the fact that, hardly ten months later, he was instrumental in choosing Wessels as captain of the South African team. His line of thought appears to defy rational explanation or logic.

'I sensed a change in the officials' attitude at the start of the 1990/91 season,' Wessels recalls. 'Up until then, I could be fairly sure that whatever I asked for, I would get. But I began to get the idea that if I asked for something, I definitely would not get it. It was a gradual thing, but I felt it very clearly.'

Soon after the season began, Van der Merwe outlined to the captain his concern about a period of stagnation after the winning of the treble. It seemed to Wessels that Van der Merwe wanted some changes in the side to sustain the hungry atmosphere. Wessels did not agree, saying it would be wrong to change a winning side. There was clearly a difference in basic philosophy.

Rightly or wrongly, and it is impossible to prove intent, Van der Merwe seemed to regard Wessels' prime task of instilling discipline to the side as essentially complete and saw the time as right for the younger Rushmere to take over the side. Such thinking was interpreted, again rightly or wrongly, as representing the old Eastern Province elite's attempts to re-establish control over the side. Rushmere, perhaps unwittingly, was their man. Ever since his début, the local boy had seemed destined for the captaincy. It now appeared as though Wessels was in the way.

Whether this analysis is true or not does not alter the fact that it was believed by enough people for the ship to be unsettled. Trust dissolved, suspicion spread like the plague.

The second level of antagonism towards Wessels was sparked when McCurdy and Michau subjected their team-mates to a 3 a.m. wake-up call after a pre-season friendly against Boland. Wessels protested that McCurdy was leading younger players astray. McCurdy resented what he saw as the captain's schoolmasterly approach. Again, the battle lines were clearly drawn and trust drained away.

As the season progressed, McCurdy became bolder and more defiant. Idolised by the less experienced players, the Australian took Rudi Bryson out drinking one evening. The next morning, Bryson was scarcely in a fit state to bowl. Wessels repeated: You cannot be a star in the bar and then bowl 25 overs the next day. Was this a dictatorial attitude? What else was a responsible, professional captain supposed to do? He felt he had to act. Once again, he told McCurdy that his behaviour was unacceptable.

McCurdy, for his part, reflects that the chief problem was communication. 'Kepler couldn't communicate. It's OK to be a disciplinarian, but when you start looking at the guys and saying they shouldn't be going to the pub because the younger guys might see you there, I reckon it's going too far. I think I was old enough to know when to go to bed.'

As a truce between McCurdy and Wessels became increasingly unlikely, the fast bowler decided to go out with a bang, writing an article with a friend in newspapers which catalogued his complaints about Wessels. The 'bombshell' was offered to the mass-circulation *Sunday Times,* rejected, and eventually printed in the Port Elizabeth-based *Weekend Post*. The row had become public.

The simmering confrontation turned the spotlight on Wessels' relationships with his own players. His authority, once absolute, became a topic of discussion. Some members of the team complained they could not get close to him, that he sometimes appeared cold and distant, that he was sometimes unfriendly.

Wessels says he is aware of the comments: 'But that was how it had to be,' he adds emphatically. 'If I was going to impose a degree of discipline, I couldn't be buying drinks in the bar at the same time. In a way, I had to be distant.'

For a period, it seemed as if the hostility towards Wessels was snowballing. McCurdy's cry that other players agreed with him, but were too scared to say so, may have been proven by the growing list of grumbles about Wessels which surfaced in the media, many of them asides obviously planted by the disaffected.

Other top order batsmen had the audacity to accuse Wessels of rearranging the batting order to suit himself when, in truth, it was they who had demanded changes, even going so far as to petition the Board to bat where they wanted. Then they said he arranged pre-season first class friendlies to boost his batting average when, in fact, he simply believed they were the most effective kind of warm-up match. Of course, the captain was not entirely blameless. In any quarrel, no one ever is, but the complaints were largely unfounded, malicious and designed to undermine him.

Discipline. It came down to discipline. Were these grumbling players so foolish that they believed discipline was only necessary when you're a young team learning to be the best? Were they under the impression that, once at the top, you can go back into the bar and have a good time? Sadly, it seems they were.

So these were the two levels of opposition to Wessels which developed during the 1990/91 season. Was there a connection between the two? McCurdy has since bemoaned that fact that people who said they would back him failed to do so when push came to shove.

There are no answers but the campaign against the captain, and that is what it became towards the end of the season, escalated to levels of intimidation that were entirely inappropriate to what was still a sporting matter. Decent men behaved very badly, and the atmosphere became unimaginably unpleasant.

Wessels' personal life became the subject of gossip around Port Elizabeth and his car was repeatedly vandalised whilst parked at St George's Park. Three times his car tyres were let down, and twice the side panel was scratched with a coin. He was eventually forced to remove the sponsor's logo on the door that identified the vehicle as belonging to him. He was telephoned, at work and at home, at all hours and warned to leave Port Elizabeth. These calls only stopped when he told the anonymous voice at the end of the line that the Post Office had traced the call.

His life, and that of his family, was becoming intolerable.

On cue, the Free State cricket union asked Wessels to return 'home' to Bloemfontein, captain their fast-developing side and work for the local municipality. Wessels was sorely tempted. He may have been better off in financial terms and he would have escaped from the incessant harassment in Port Elizabeth. Tempted...

'But I turned them down,' Wessels recalls. 'I just decided that I wasn't going to run away again. We liked Port Elizabeth as a place and we liked being at the coast. It was a difficult time, but Sally and I decided we would stick it out.'

His firm decision to stay in Port Elizabeth encouraged him to confront his opponents and resolve the situation. He arranged a meeting with Geoff Dakin and told the South African cricket union president the whole story, from start to finish.

Dakin was appalled and, to his great credit, he acted with speed by confronting various individuals and inviting them to be plain about their criticism of the captain. Boldly challenged by a strong man, the opposition seemed to melt away.

It was soon decided that Wessels would be retained as the captain for the next season. McCurdy left to join Natal, sustaining the vagrant pattern of his entire career, and some calm returned.

Three months later South Africa was joyfully readmitted to the International Cricket Council and Wessels' prime focus would move from Eastern Province towards the national side. He was able to leave all the uncertainty behind. The issue eventually died a natural death, the storm blew out and passed.

Grové, sitting on the board, had been shocked by the effort to oust Wessels: 'This clique was always there in PE. I don't think Kepler was ever totally accepted by the clique. After the success of winning the treble, they were actually trying to pretend they could have done it all without him. It was ridiculous. There's one major problem in the Eastern Cape. If you're up, they only want to cut you down. You'll never get it out of the place.

'Kepler was criticised, but I honestly don't know what more he could have done for Eastern Province. Some of the administrators didn't like him, and that was because he was so straight with them. He thought some of them weren't doing their job properly, and he was prepared to say so. He never crawled to anyone.'

In conclusion, the invidious backlash to Wessels' absolute authority may have been predictable. He had revolutionised Eastern Province cricket and, as Robespierre and Marat discovered in France during the late 19th century, profound revolutions have a curious habit of claiming their leaders as a victim.

Wessels, at least, survived.

In 1990/91, through all the infighting, Eastern Province won nothing. No discipline, no unity, no trophies, no glory.

* * * * *

March, 1991 — The Port Elizabeth taxi driver has just collected a passenger from the airport. He's driving into town. The man in the back seat asks him how's life in the Eastern Cape. He replies that it's fine, considering, you know, not bad.

'So, who are your heroes down here?'

'What do you mean?'

'Who are your heroes? You know, in sport or something.'

'Oh, there's only Kepler Wessels and the cricket team. The rugby aren't up to much. It's only Kepler really.'

The man was surprised. A cricketing friend had told him of dissent and feuding in the Eastern Province side. 'But hasn't he been having a few problems over the past few months?'

'Oh, there was something in the newspaper,' the taxi driver replied, 'but I don't know about that. I don't care. I'm just an ordinary cricket fan and, as far as I'm concerned, he's the one who made us winners. Yup, Kepler's a hero in Port Elizabeth.'

The man was intrigued. He asked about McCurdy.

'No, he's not so good now. I don't know.'

'And Peter van der Merwe?'

'Who? Is he a Springbok selector or something?'

# 10

# The Darkest Hour, the Brightest Dawn

In February 1990, South African cricket lay in ruins, racked by demonstrations and dissent, condemned around the world, spat upon by black compatriots, apparently without hope.

Only 20 blurred months later, the South African cricket team was saluted as heroes by 100 000 people on the streets of Calcutta at the start of an official tour of India. Readmitted to international cricket, the dawn had broken.

This transformation from despair to delight was mirrored in the dramatically changing fortunes of Kepler Wessels.

In February 1990, he walked out on the South African side, feeling unwanted, alienated and desolate. Within 20 months, he was named Man of the Series in India. His unique international career, seemingly over, had been resurrected.

\* \* \* \* \*

Geoff Dakin, president of the South African cricket union, stands full square in the middle of the international arrivals concourse at Jan Smuts airport, Johannesburg. Jaw set, he is bravely holding court in a jungle of notebooks and microphones.

'You people, you call us wicked and evil but I want to tell you something: I pray 15 minutes every morning...' Battle-hardened English journalists devour the choice quotes. A forthright man is wearing his heart on his sleeve, and being mauled.

The air is thick with uncertainty, thrill, rumour and fear. The flight carrying Mike Gatting and the rebel English cricketers from Heathrow to South Africa has been delayed three hours. Anti-tour demonstrators are expected. How many? No one knows.

Some protesters have already been cornered by police dogs. Journalists arrive at the airport two hours after the incident and scurry round, catching up on the story. 'The blood was still wet on the tarmac when Mike Gatting...' began one report the next day in a London newspaper. The journalist had written fiction. Before it has begun, the tour seems fated to be a shambles.

Armed police constables are hovering throughout the airport, nervous, watching for any problems. Officials and journalists, all discussing earlier events, stand around too, waiting for the flight to arrive. Dakin tries to put matters in perspective: 'We're doing what we think is right.' It is January 19th, 1990, and South African cricket is hurtling towards the precipice...

Some metres away, across the concourse, stood Dr Ali Bacher, managing director of SACU and organiser of the tour. 'It somehow didn't feel right,' he reflected later. 'I had been involved in the West Indian and the Australian tours but there was something about this one which worried me. It wasn't right.'

Bacher had travelled to England to sign the players, at one stage taking the train to Manchester to meet Phil de Freitas in a coffee shop at the station. As he left, another contract securely in his briefcase, he suddenly sensed a chill. It felt wrong. There was no excitement. Back in his hotel room, he switched on the TV and watched a report of a major ANC march in Cape Town.

He was concerned and, soon after returning to South Africa, he consulted key politicians to assess the fast-changing climate. Wynand Malan, the Democratic Party MP, among others, assured him it would take 'ten years' before the National Party government abandoned apartheid. On that basis, Bacher concluded, the tour had to go on. That was SACU's double-edged policy to survive isolation: develop the grass roots of the game in the townships and maintain the upper levels with rebel tours. The English squad would come. 'It was,' he recollects, 'too late to start turning back.'

The flight from London touched down soon after noon and Mike Gatting led a weary, wary squad into the VIP lounge for the opening Press conference. Not for the first time, SACU had taken advantage of an unsettled era in the victim nation's cricket fortunes to lure a group of top players. Gatting had been sacked as England captain after describing Shakoor Rana, a Pakistani umpire, as a cheat, and featuring in some tabloid tales about a barmaid. First, Kim Hughes, now Gatting: in both cases a ferociously loyal and patriotic man, not a rebel by nature, had been estranged by his own authorities and effectively dropped into South Africa's lap.

Gatting had agreed to lead a talented squad with bowling might in Neil Foster, Graham Dilley, Greg Thomas, Paul Jarvis and John Emburey (De Freitas had withdrawn) and Test-class batsmen in Chris Broad, Tim Robinson, Matthew Maynard and Bill Athey. Managed by the Gloucestershire spin bowler, David Graveney, the 16-strong group had planned to join a mortgage-clearing tour, but they soon found themselves caught in a political whirlwind.

Krish Naidoo, a clever, well-spoken lawyer, was leading the newly formed National Sports Congress (NSC) in persistent protest against the tour. First, black waiters and waitresses at the Sandton Sun hotel refused to serve the touring cricketers, a gesture that was repeated at almost every hotel the squad visited. Embarrassed white managers standing in as waiters, hurrying between the tables, would become a feature of the tour. After a steady week of hard practice, Gatting's side travelled to Kimberley for the opening match versus a Combined Bowl XI. Their chief opponents, however, would be 1 500 chanting demonstrators outside the ground.

Gatting stood firm. On arrival at Kimberley airport, he had been passed an urgent message from the hotel warning the squad to stay away until 2 000 protesters gathered outside the main entrance had dispersed. Gatting refused, and bluntly instructed the bus driver to go directly to the hotel. As policemen looked on in amazement, the English captain strode into the middle of the large and swaying crowd, met the leaders of the demonstration, accepted their petition which demanded that the tour be called off, and then thanked them for ensuring that their protest had been orderly and peaceful. He had shown immense courage and sense in an explosive situation.

January 26th, 1990 was the opening day of play in Kimberley, a difficult and momentous day which changed the face of South African cricket, perhaps of all South African sport.

It began quietly, with some 800 people turning up at the De Beers country club, arranging themselves around the white boundary fence with their beers, braais and colourful umbrellas. The sun was already up. It was going to be a long, hot day.

Meanwhile, in nearby townships, the NSC organisers, who had promised an anti-tour demonstration at the ground, were rounding up supporters, most of whom understood little about either the tour or Gatting. They were simply attracted by an opportunity to march into a white area, to protest and express their anger against the daily injustices of their lives. In this sense the cricket tour became a vehicle for, rather than a cause of, protest.

When play started, there was no sign of any protesters near the barbed wire barricades set up to the west of the small ground. By mid-morning, there was still no sign. White supporters sank into their deckchairs and laughed off the threats. 'You see, I told you nothing would happen. They couldn't organise a . . .'

At 12.10 p.m., there was a sudden burst of activity around the main gate. Startled unease rippled through the crowd. Naidoo soon appeared wearing a yellow T-shirt. Bacher, breathing hard, left his seat in the stand and briskly marched over to meet him, a gaggle of journalists and photographers in his wake.

'Do you believe in the right to protest?' Naidoo demanded.

When Bacher replied that he did, Naidoo asked him to come to a point several kilometres from the ground where demonstrators had been halted by the police. Bacher agreed, winning acceptance from Naidoo that people also had a right to watch cricket.

The situation was unbearably tense. There was, it was clear, the potential for an appalling confrontation. As Bacher and Naidoo left the ground, play continued. Gatting was batting, driving past cover, moving the total serenely to 34 for one.

Down the road, a restless crowd of 1 200 was being prevented from advancing to the ground because local police commanders, whose first instinct was to call in the teargas, were unwilling to allow the march. They hadn't seen this sort of thing before in Kimberley. Hordes of angry blacks in the suburbs? No, man, they would have to consult their superior officers in Pretoria.

The crowd was growing impatient, and Bacher realised his main task was to gain permission for the march before the situation became violent. The sun beat down. He loosened his tie and knocked on the door of the nearest private house, and asked if he could use the telephone. 'Yes, of course, something should be done about all this,' replied the man inside. 'Please come in.'

Bacher phoned Gerrit Viljoen, a senior Government minister in Pretoria, who told him to get hold of Adriaan Vlok, Minister of Law and Order, and gave him a number. Vlok was out, but called back 20 minutes later to say he needed to consult.

While the highest powers in the land dithered, Bacher faced increasing difficulties back outside in the street. The protesters were becoming angry. Tempers flared. Suddenly the police pulled on their riot helmets and formed a line. There was more shouting and pushing. Bacher, sweat dripping from his brow, begged the policemen to move back and not to confront the crowd.

'Keep calm, please keep calm,' he pleaded. As he spoke, the barrel of a police rifle rested on his chest.

The protesters, who had been standing in the sun for several hours, began shouting for water. Bacher hurried off to find some empty plastic bottles, filled them with iced water from the houses further along the street and handed them out himself. Somehow, the people had to be kept cool, and calm.

Vlok finally called back. He said the protesters needed to get a permit from the Kimberley magistrate. Bacher, commandeering a car, drove into town. The chief magistrate was away and his deputy was not prepared to make a decision. Bacher called Vlok. Vlok said try the Town Clerk. Finally, at the Town Clerk's office, the permit was typed out. The march was legal, and Bacher, exhausted, was able to return to the cricket. English XI: 182 for four.

The next morning Bacher sat thoughtfully eating his favourite breakfast of sweet melon and water melon slices. Another march was planned and the permit had been arranged. The previous day many of the demonstrators had eventually lost patience and drifted home but this time they would get to the ground. He was suffering. Was he to blame for this confrontation? Was it his fault?

Soon after the tourists resumed their innings, more than 1 000 black protesters arrived outside the barbed wire and began chanting and dancing. As they did so, a group of white cricket fans gathered on the opposite side of the fence, inside the ground. Soon insults were being catapulted this way and that. 'Kill a Boer'... 'stupid kaffir'... 'kill a Boer'. Angry men on both sides began to spit and swear. The scene became a grotesque image of the recurring South African nightmare. Everywhere, etched in the black faces and the white faces, there was hatred.

In this anger, a strange kind of healing began. The English rebel tour would ultimately prove a medicinal experience for most white sports followers. Their cocoon was broken.

For the first time, the right to demonstrate peacefully at a South African sports event was established and significant marches took place as the tour passed through Kimberley, Bloemfontein and Pietermaritzburg. Day after day, whites were physically confronted by black opposition. It hadn't happened before.

Establishment sports administrators began to recognise the need for unity with their previously resented rival bodies and to meet demands for development in the townships.

In basic terms, before the harsh confrontation at Kimberley, 'white sport' was able to go ahead without stopping to consider the needs and dreams of 'black sport'. After Kimberley, that was not possible. Out of conflict, reconciliation was born.

As the dark clouds were massing above South African cricket in general, so they had gathered around the habitually storm-clad brow of Wessels. The controversy was simple: should he be eligible to play for South Africa against the English XI?

On August 2nd, 1989, the SACU announcement that Wessels would qualify to represent the country of his birth provoked unrestrained anger among a significant number of provincial players. In feisty dressing rooms around the country, none more angry than the one at the Wanderers, Wessels was accused of wanting to have his cake and eat it. It was said that he had deserted South Africa when others remained loyal to keep the home fires burning through the dark and cold nights of isolation, that he had reaped all manner of rewards from Australian cricket, and that he had then been paid even more money to join the Australian rebels in 1986.

This, they concluded, was quite enough. And now he wants to play for South Africa too! He didn't seek the best of both worlds, they grumbled, he wanted the best of all three.

Amid increasingly vocal opposition, the Players' Association was invited to gauge the mood of its members and report to SACU on its findings. André Bruyns, the association's president, personally felt Wessels' eligibility was justified by the 'abnormal times' but he was in Lisbon on business. In his absence, Clive Rice and Jimmy Cook, two senior members of the association, set about the task. A series of meetings was held, and petitions drawn up.

Asking Rice and Cook to conduct a survey on whether Wessels was qualified to play for South Africa was something akin to Bill Clinton running a poll on George Bush in 1992. They were simply too involved in the issue to be credible.

Both Rice and Cook were at pains to stress the issue was not personal, claiming the debate was about other borderline cases such as South African-born England players like Robin Smith and Allan Lamb, and Australians like Rod McCurdy and Mike Haysman playing in

South Africa. But these were red herrings because the first two did not want to play, and the second two did not expect to.

Wessels was the issue. 'Do you want Kepler to play for South Africa or not?' That was their essential question.

To his credit, Rice approached the issue in an appropriately detached manner, claiming no strong feelings. In 1986 he had argued publicly that Wessels should play for South Africa. 'Kepler did get the best of both worlds,' Rice reflects, 'but the world is about opportunity and he took it.'

In contrast, Cook set about the matter with zeal. Setting aside his public image of a perfect gentleman, Cook used the occasion of Transvaal's night series match against Eastern Province in Port Elizabeth to press his case. Waiting until Wessels had left the ground after the match, Cook walked across to the home dressing room to confront Mark Rushmere and Philip Amm.

The Eastern Province player sitting beside Rushmere recalls: 'Cook only spoke to those two. I suppose he thought he had a chance of getting them round to his way of thinking because they were the only ones who might have been competing with Kepler for a place in the South African side. He probably knew the rest of us would stick by our captain, whatever he said.'

In the event, Cook's approach failed. Amm and Rushmere not only declined to join his crusade, they also went to the trouble of visiting Wessels at his house the next morning to inform him what Cook had said and done. 'Jimmy wanted us to sign a petition but we weren't going to go against Kepler,' Rushmere recalls. 'I could see why they were upset but it seemed to me that other players had had the chance to do what Kepler did but only he had the guts to go and do it. You couldn't really hold that against him.'

Wessels was livid and, ironically, phoned Rice to complain about the campaign being conducted behind his back. 'They had no right trying to turn members of my team against me,' he says. 'They were entitled to their opinions. They may even have been right but I felt their methods were all wrong.'

His wrath was vented during a subsequent Nissan Shield final when he gave Cook an amazingly public 'send-off' from the pitch. As the Transvaal batsman headed back towards the pavilion after being dismissed, Wessels appeared to walk after him, releasing his anger in a flood of wide-eyed, pent-up abuse.

At any rate, their discussions complete, Cook and Rice told SACU of their unsurprising conclusion that a majority of provincial players believed Wessels should not be eligible until another two years had elapsed. 'Dakin (the SACU president) basically told us to buzz off,' Rice recalls.

Unbeknown to Cook and Rice, although they may have suspected as much, SACU's hands were effectively tied by an earlier agreement with Wessels. During negotiations before Wessels agreed to join the Australian rebel tour in 1986/87, SACU, desperate to make a deal, accepted as a condition that he would become eligible to play for South Africa two years from the end of that tour.

This arrangement flew in the face of accepted International Cricket Council rules that a player can represent a second country only after serving a minimum four-year residential qualification, but this was South Africa in isolation, expelled from the ICC and free to make up its own regulations.

For his part, Wessels was ambivalent. As the row raged, he contacted Bacher and told him that if SACU wanted to rule him out, then he would not protest. 'It was up to them,' he recalls. 'If they wanted to lengthen my qualification period, that was fine with me. I never insisted on being eligible.'

The issue, which could hardly have been handled in a more unsatisfactory manner, had become a mess, a shambles, a bore. But its consequences were far-reaching.

In the first place, Wessels felt unwelcome and unwanted in the South African team. He was once again overcome by his tendency to become pessimistic and defensive. It was not true that everyone was against him, but he started to believe it.

Secondly Rice, and not Cook, appears to have been blamed in upper SACU circles for persecuting Wessels. Dakin, as quoted in *Die Transvaler* of January 14th, 1990, criticised Rice for leading a smear campaign against Wessels. Cook seemed forgiven.

On January 31st, the South African side to play the first Test against the English XI at the Wanderers was announced on the SABC evening news. Peter van der Merwe's selection panel delivered their verdicts. Wessels: in. Rice: out. Cook: captain.

Van der Merwe had taken Cook to lunch to give him the good news but had not even telephoned Rice. The national captain for six seasons heard of his sacking on the news. Whether the decision was right or wrong, it was grubbily executed.

Rice appeared to be the victim of a long-running personality clash with Van der Merwe, stretching back to 1986 when Rice had handed a

Springbok team list back to the convener, suggesting that his panel should select again. His prominent role in the storm over Wessels' eligibility cannot have helped, yet the same issue did not seem to have damaged Cook at all. The new captain, who nobly told Van der Merwe that Rice should have been retained, was widely regarded as a compromise choice to lead the side. He had not captained any sort of team regularly since leaving school.

Wessels, meanwhile, heard the news of his selection to play for South Africa and felt pitifully deflated. This was the moment which had inspired him through school, the ultimate honour. His own name would now be inscribed on the walls of the Reunie Hall at Grey College, but he felt flat because he was led to believe a majority of his team-mates did not want him in the side.

He spoke to Johan Volsteedt, his friend from the old days. 'I could tell Kepler was very upset,' he recalls, 'but I just said that he should get on with it. Whatever anyone else did, he had been selected and he should do his best.'

The team assembled at the Sandton Holiday Inn. The veteran of 24 official Tests had been reduced to a quiet 32-year-old lining up with two other débutants to be kitted out in Springbok colours. He had played in two Ashes series, two full series against the West Indies and a World Cup, scored runs off every leading bowler in the world but here he stood, anxious, nervous and wary. His Springbok début was starting to seem more of a trial than a dream.

The Test unfolded as a frantic shambles on a green, under-prepared wicket. South Africa had secured a seven-wicket victory by five o'clock on the third day. Frequently interrupted by rain, the match had lasted a few minutes over 15 hours. It was hardly worth crossing the road to watch, let alone crossing the globe to play. The English XI had been dismissed for 156 and 122, wickets fell at an average ratio of one every 16 runs and no one emerged with any credit, least of all the Wanderers groundsman.

Wessels had endured a predictably dismal match. He had been stumped off Emburey for one in the first innings, then trapped LBW to Gatting for only two in the second. At one stage of his nervous and brief stay at the crease, he over-balanced and nearly tripped over his stumps as he tumbled to the ground. Some of the Wanderers crowd had laughed. He had felt humiliated.

In the depths of despair, Wessels was sitting quietly in the South African dressing room towards the end of the Test match when he overheard a conversation between his captain, Cook, and another senior player. They were discussing plans for the second Test, due to be played at Newlands the following week.

'You see,' said Cook, 'if we drop Kepler, then I think we'll be able to get Ricey back in the side.'

This was the straw that broke the camel's back. How could he play in a side where the captain was a man who had first campaigned to have him ruled ineligible and now was continuing to work against him? He began to sense his position was untenable.

Emotion flooded his mind. Wessels decided to withdraw from the Springbok team. He knew he was in bad form but he did not want to give Cook the satisfaction of having him dropped. At the end of the match, he informed Cook and Van der Merwe of his decision. He told them he felt emotionally exhausted and drained.

That sad Saturday evening, Wessels rearranged his flight to Port Elizabeth and called his brother, Wessel, asking him to drive through from Pretoria and give him a lift to the airport early the next morning. Wessel, naturally, said he would.

'When I arrived to fetch Kepler early that Sunday morning, he was in a real state,' Wessel recalls. 'I didn't ask him what was wrong because I could see it was hurting. His entire body language was clear but I knew he'd come out of it. There was a determination in his eyes. You can always look into Kepler's eyes and see what is happening. I knew he would get over it.'

He was met at the airport in Port Elizabeth by his wife. 'He looked terrible,' Sally recalls. 'He was shattered. He looked as if his entire world had just fallen apart.'

That afternoon, Ray Jennings called. With Peter Kirsten, the wicketkeeper had made a special effort to cheer up Wessels during the Test. That had been appreciated. Now he telephoned to say that he was sorry. That was all. He was just sorry. 'I think Kepler knew he was going to be dropped,' Jennings recalls. 'He was obviously in a bad way but I didn't notice much during the game. He fielded in the slips beside me quite a lot, and he seemed OK.'

Others took a much harsher line, accusing Wessels of being a quitter. Gin-sodden veterans gurgled their vitriol. Bacher was not among them, but the SACU managing director was disappointed: 'I did speak to Kepler after what had been a bad game for him but it was unlike him to run away from a problem. I must say I felt he had let us down because we had backed him right from the start against the players. I don't think he should have walked out.'

Wessels was profoundly depressed. 'For about a month, I just didn't know which way to turn. Some days, I thought about staying where I was. Other days, I would think about going back to play a season with Queensland, and sometimes I even considered giving up the whole game. I was tired of the hassle.'

His enthusiasm was ultimately recharged by the success of his Eastern Province team. 'Kepler just came back to the nets after the Gatting tour,' Dave Callaghan recalls. 'We knew there had been problems but he just went back to work.' Within three months, his team had clinched all three domestic trophies.

Reflecting on the entire saga, Wessels predictably concludes that he should not have played against the English XI. 'It was all too early,' he says. 'I should have insisted to SACU that I sit out a four-year qualification, but that's easy to say now.'

There was a final irony to Wessels' walk-out. If he had waited just another 48 hours, he would not have had to make any decision at all because, on February 13th, SACU decided to curtail the English tour 'as a gesture of conciliation in times of change'.

All around the cricket tour, the country had moved into a state of turmoil. On February 2nd, 1990, State President F.W. de Klerk announced the dismantling of apartheid. On Sunday, February 11th, the selfsame day that Wessels walked out of the Springbok side, Nelson Mandela, walked free from prison after 27 years.

These historic events created such a wave of public emotion and hope that the ongoing conflict aroused by the tour was made to seem an untimely embarrassment. After discussions with the NSC and a senior government minister, the second Test and six one-day games were replaced by a quartet of one-day matches. These were played, without Wessels and without protest, South Africa winning by three matches to one. The English players returned home, 16 unfortunate men who had been in the wrong place at the wrong time.

Bacher had nowhere to go. His struggle would continue, but not against the NSC. His fiercest opponents were now the stubbornly conservative members of his own board who deplored his decision to curtail the tour as capitulation to mob rule. A full SACU board of control meeting was to be held in East London, and the handling of the English tour dominated the agenda. The managing director's job, it was reported, would go on the line.

Armed with video tapes of BBC news bulletins showing scenes of anti-tour demonstrations not seen in South Africa, Bacher strode into the meeting, passionately outlined his own blueprint for the future and then excused himself. He was due to receive an award in Johannesburg that same evening. Arriving at the function in black tie, surrounded by his family, he appeared emotional and exhausted. He had challenged the board to back him or sack him, and he hadn't heard their response. It was out of his hands.

'The problem was that some of them had been sitting in the Long Room watching the Test at the Wanderers while all the trouble was taking place in Alexandra,' Bacher recalls. 'I felt I had to show them what had really happened and to demonstrate why it had been so necessary to cut short the tour.'

They backed him. Bacher was given a clear mandate to put his blueprint into action, and South African cricket was set on course to keep pace with the fast-changing times.

Longed-for political reform started to change Wessels' life as it changed the life of every South African. Suddenly, the clouds lifted. As the pillars of apartheid crumbled one by one, it became clear that the gates to international sport would soon swing open. The challenge for South African sports officials was to acknowledge the sea-change, replace hard-headed defiance with soft-spoken tact and, above all, pursue unity with the previously untouchable rival bodies under the SA Council of Sport (SACOS) umbrella.

Unity became the new watchword. It was not an easy process because many of the SACOS bodies were disorganised, ramshackle and blatantly unworthy of a 50/50 unification in every sense except the one that really mattered: the political sense. A new consensus had to be reached on playing kit, on logo, on selection, on committees and on the generic name of national sides (the Springbok was seen as a symbol of the divided past and widely dropped).

Some administrators resisted these inevitable changes and served only to delay the readmission of their codes. Athletics and rugby, for example, were slow to recognise the key role of the ANC-backed National Sports Congress (NSC) and wasted time.

Cricket, by contrast, set a dazzling pace. Under Bacher's politically sensitive stewardship, the SA cricket union established notably close ties with 'the other side'... the NSC were treated with the respect they craved... Sam Ramsamy, who had returned home from London to lead a new Olympic body, was given use of the SACU offices... and the initial steps were taken on the road to unity between SACU and the SACOS-aligned SA cricket board.

This complex, flannelled code was soon being hailed as 'the model sport of the new South Africa'. SACU secured such status because it had committed itself to running the most advanced and ambitious development programme introduced in any code, at any time. Since 1986, a series of coaching schemes had been launched in townships countrywide with the aim of introducing cricket to thousands of young Africans.

Many of these initiatives had been suspended amid the angry recriminations of the English rebel tour — in Mamelodi, the township outside Pretoria, for example, ANC leaders had stamped out cricket, coaches were unwelcome, the boys had stopped playing — but, with a mood of reconciliation, progress was revived.

Astounding progress. Bakers Biscuits, following through one of the most distinguished sports sponsorships, backed the growth of mini-cricket. Thousands of T-shirts, bats and stumps were provided as boys as young as five were taught the game. Coaching academies were established and, everywhere, smiling boys began to demonstrate remarkable natural talent. The old refrain that 'blacks only play soccer' was exploded in a cascade of enthusiasm.

Teams were soon formed and these were entered into leagues once reserved for white schools; cricket fields were built and the most promising players were awarded scholarships that enabled them to attend traditional cricketing schools. As the programme grew, so did the challenge. There was so much to be done.

Before long, SACU could claim cricket was being played in 25 townships by more than 50 000 boys. Energetically and dynamically, Bacher started to spread the news. Only cricket, he would regularly argue, allocates millions of rand to actually put right the wrongs of apartheid. Only cricket, the sponsors and media were ceaselessly told, is helping to build the new nation.

A succession of high-profile foreign dignitaries and cricket celebrities were taken to witness bold developments in Alexandra or Soweto. Sir Gary Sobers, Sir Colin Cowdrey, Sir Richard Hadlee, Douglas Hurd, Sunil Gavaskar, Sir Clyde Walcott, Wes Hall, Clive Lloyd and others were escorted to watch the saplings, almost always with invited journalists and photographers in tow.

The stories would be written and the pictures taken. Before long, the success of the scheme had been reported, at one stage or another, in almost every magazine and newspaper around the cricket world. There was nothing sinister in this. SACU simply had a story to tell and they wanted to make sure it was told.

There were, however, some raised eyebrows at the remarkable transformation in Bacher from the master of rebel tours to the new world administrator with a missionary zeal. Was he riding on some bandwagon, using development as a means to an end, currying favour to propel South Africa back into international cricket?

No. He was genuine. Bacher drove the development programme because he believed in it. It was, in many respects, his child. He lived it, meeting after meeting, day after day.

One warm evening in Soweto, as wafting columns of smoke puffed into a clear sky, amid the gentle buzz of township life and the distant roar of the commuters' traffic, Bacher was to be found pacing the nets at the Elkah cricket stadium. He had driven out to the township at the end of his working day because he was worried not enough room had been left for the bowler's run-up. No, it was fine. Satisfied, he finally returned home, no media in tow.

Another time, Bacher strode into his office at 7.30 a.m., as usual, and started scribbling a list of things to be done that day. At the very top of the SACU managing director's list was a reminder to pay R10 petrol money to a woman coach in Alex who had had to use her own car to ferry boys to nets the previous day.

Whenever Bacher stood and watched another youngster run in, laugh and play, and was moved to remark that he found more pleasure watching Diepkloof under-14A than a Currie Cup match, no one close to him could possibly doubt his sincerity.

Perhaps he had seen a light, not on the road to Damascus but on the road to Kimberley. His own physical confrontation with the might of the previously ignored majority had left him utterly aware that no sport would advance towards readmission without the backing of the majority's premier representatives, the ANC. That might seem obvious with hindsight, but it wasn't at the time.

Eddie Barlow, a keen and independent observer, recalls: 'You could say that Ali was converted before the others, and cricket was able to reap the benefit of his vision.'

SACU certainly profited from a close relationship with the ANC, the product of the extraordinary mutual trust which developed between Bacher and Steve Tshwete, the ANC spokesman on sport. 'I love Ali Bacher because he admits mistakes he made in the past and then he

The darkest hour (*above*) before the brightest dawn (*right*). After playing against the English rebel team in February 1990, Wessels walked out on Jimmy Cook's Springbok side because he felt unwanted. Fifteen months later, South Africa was voted back into international cricket. The UCB delegation of (*from left*) Steve Tshwete, Geoff Dakin, Krish Makerdhuj and Ali Bacher joyfully faced the media at Lord's.

(*above*) November 10th, 1991: Thank you, India. Clive Rice leads the South African side out to greet the 92 000 crowd Eden Gardens in Calcutta before the momentous first match after readmission. Wessels carried the batting, scoring 50 then 71 in Gwalior (*below*) and 90 in victory at New Delhi.

(*above*) Hurled in at the deep end. Leaving the selection row behind him, Wessels gathered with the other eight captains on the eve of the 1992 World Cup. Aboard the *Canberra* in Sydney harbour are (*from left*) Gooch of England, Imran of Pakistan, Azharuddin of India, Houghton of Zimbabwe, De Silva of Sri Lanka, Border of Australia, Crowe of New Zealand, Richardson of the West Indies… and Wessels of South Africa.

(*below*) Swimming in the deep end. Wessels directs his young team during their opening match against Australia.

Oh, starry, starry night… Billed as lambs to the slaughter against Australia at the Sydney Cricket Ground, South Africa stunned the world with a nine-wicket win. Wessels (*above left*) finished unbeaten on 81 as his unique career came full circle. *Above right*, Allan Border, his friend and team-mate from Queensland and Australia days, congratulates him.

(*above*) The image to endure: Steve Tshwete arrived in the South African dressing room after victory over Australia and, in tears, embraced the captain. One country, at last.

(*below*) Pressure, tension, despair … Wessels, heavily criticised after the World Cup defeats against New Zealand and Sri Lanka, sits alone. 'Sometimes I get so tense. I know it's wrong. I can't help it.'

Beaten by England and the rain. After all the effort and strain, Wessels and his side gazed at the scoreboard on a sad, wet night in Sydney and realised that their World Cup would end with an honourable semi-final defeat. 'We had no real complaint. The rain rules had helped us defeat Pakistan earlier in the tournament,' Wessels reflected.

SIR GARFIELD SOBERS PAVILION

History for the taking:
April 1992, South Afric
played their first Test
since 1970 and their
first ever against the
West Indies. After the
historic photograph
(*above*), a winning
position was forged,
only to be thrown awa
during the final day
collapse. Defeat did n
however, diminish the
reputation of Allan
Donald (*left*) as one o
the world's finest
bowlers.

(*previous page*) In
Barbados, Wessels to
the attack to the Wes
Indians, hooking at
anything short, scorin
quickly and giving hug
encouragement to his
players.

(right) Captain courageous or Captain conservative? Wessels' tactics were widely criticised during the home series against India, but both the Test and one-day series were won. He is seen here with Trevor Quirk, a former team-mate, and Mohammed Azharuddin before the first Test at Kingsmead.

(below) The triangular series which followed against the West Indies and Pakistan ended in failure, but Wessels and Procter (centre) found some consolation in two victories over the West Indies. Richie Richardson stands to the right.

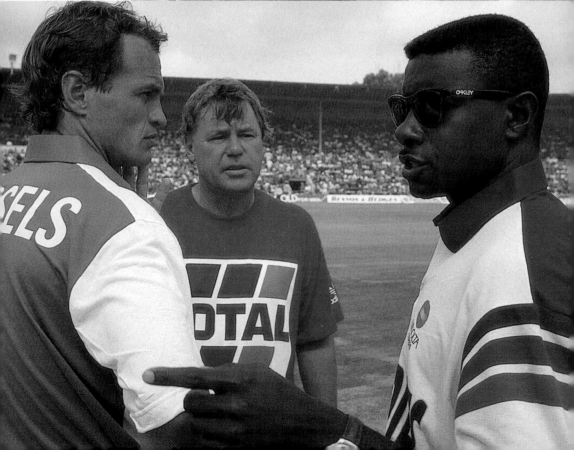

Icing on the cake: It was the first day of real Test cricket played in South Africa since 1970, against India in Durban. Once again, Wessels rose to the occasion and scored a century.

orth a 100-year wait: Eastern Province won the Currie Cup for the first time in 1989. The end of Clive Rice's brave
sistance (*above*) was the vital breakthrough and Wessels was soon holding the trophy (*below right*), although Dr Danie
aven would later scold him for not wearing a shirt.
*elow left*) Concentrate, concentrate… Dave Richardson and Wessels under lights, at work for Eastern Province.

One captain, one team, one country. As readmission took place during an uncertain era of political transition, Wessels
team was elevated as a positive symbol of national unity.

corrects them,' Tshwete said. Introduced by Flip Potgieter, a cricket official in the Eastern Cape, Bacher and Tshwete, hand in hand, would guide cricket to readmission.

Raised near East London, Tshwete was enthusiastic about rugby in his youth but he also inherited a love of cricket from his father for whom he would sometimes walk 10 kilometres to buy a newspaper with the latest Currie Cup scorecards. He played the Englishman's game using the long branch of an aloe tree as a bat, with a pair of trousers pulled over an anthill as stumps.

When white domination sparked an angry flame in his teenage soul, he joined Umkhonto we Sizwe, acting as a commando sabotaging power lines. In 1964, he was arrested and sent to prison on Robben Island. There he was subjected to gross indignities.

Released in 1979 and branded *persona non grata* in 1985, he fled to live in Lusaka but returned from exile two days before the Groote Schuur Accords in May 1990. A member of the ANC's national executive, he was primarily responsible for national organisation but soon assumed the role of powerbroker in a series of unity talks between various sporting bodies, impressing everyone with his open pragmatism and his complete lack of bitterness. This was a man with much to remember, but who chose to look forward.

At every key meeting, at every momentous Press conference, Tshwete and Bacher were invariably to be seen sitting side by side; and finally, in June 1991, 17 months after Gatting had flown home, unity was announced between SACU and the rival SACB.

The United Cricket Board of South Africa (UCB) was founded in a spirit of compromise. The Springbok head, for generations the emblem of the national side, was replaced by a blue and yellow logo incorporating cricketing and African symbols: circles representing the sun and growth, small dots for fertility, chevrons to symbolise uneven or undulating ground from which plants will grow, stumps and a cricket ball. The bokkie was put out to grass.

A month later, the International Cricket Council met at Lord's and officially readmitted South Africa. Bacher, overcome by the moment, was cheered by the very same meeting outside which he had often stood during the dark years of isolation, begging to be heard. By his side sat Geoff Dakin and Krish Mackerdhuj, presidents of SACU and SACB respectively, and... Steve Tshwete.

The four men tucked their knees beneath a table in the Long Room at Lord's and faced the Press. 'This is the happiest day of my cricketing life,' Bacher told the Fleet Street journalists. It was becoming his catchphrase. So many happiest days...

After 21 years outside, South African cricket stepped back into the world. In Port Elizabeth, Wessels had followed the latest developments in the newspapers, scarcely believing it was all true. 'Even before the ICC meeting, I was sure something would go wrong,' he recalls. 'I thought there would be a hitch.'

His instincts were right. Soon after South Africa had been readmitted to the ICC, he was startled by Peter van der Merwe, who bounced up, said that it was fantastic to be back in world cricket but added that he was sorry about the decision.

'What decision?' Wessels asked.

Van der Merwe, who only months before had been beaten in his attempt to oust Wessels as the Eastern Province captain, went on to explain how he had heard that the ICC wanted Wessels to serve out a full ten-year residential qualification, starting from the date he left Australia, before he could play for South Africa. It meant he would not be eligible until April 1996.

Wessels could hardly believe it: 'I was certain that I had qualified by the rules, but I also knew about cricket politics. I started to wonder whether some kind of deal had been done at the ICC with me as the fall-guy. It was stupid.'

After several nervous days, he was eventually put at ease by Bacher and Dakin, who said the ICC had made no such decision and confirmed that he was eligible immediately. From where had Van der Merwe picked up the story? It is not clear.

As convener of the national selection panel and president of the Eastern Province cricket union (which, after unity, became the EP cricket board), he wielded considerable power and influence yet he appeared, at best, unpredictable.

Amid a flurry of telephone calls and faxes, all carrying the crucial ANC approval, South Africa was hurtling into international cricket. At another ICC meeting in Sharjah, United Arab Emirates, on October 23rd, the prodigal sons were placed on the tours schedule and hastily included in the draw for the 1992 World Cup. From Sharjah, a high-powered and excited UCB delegation set off on a whirlwind tour of India, Pakistan, Sri Lanka and Kenya.

In Calcutta primarily to discuss plans for an Indian tour of South Africa in November 1992, the UCB representatives were merrily surprised by the warmth of their reception.

Jagmohan Dalmiya, energetic secretary of the Indian board of control, had a problem. Pakistan had cancelled a short tour because of security fears and India needed a country to play against before leaving for a full tour of Australia. He said he knew it was short notice, but, if it was at all possible, he would like South Africa to come and play three one-day internationals.

'When?'

'Well... next week, actually.'

Bacher was eager to accept. India, after all, had formally proposed South Africa's re-election to the ICC. His only concern was that the UCB should not be seen to rush back into international cricket with unseemly haste. An emergency UCB executive meeting was called for Sunday November 3rd to consider the matter.

The UCB executive, comprising ten representatives from SACU and ten from SACB, was virtually split down the old party lines but not in the manner which might have been expected. SACB members, who had opposed international contact for so many years, were suddenly keen to get on the road again, while many SACU voices felt it would be unwise to leap in without real preparation.

Finally, the invitation was accepted on a 12-8 vote. The UCB office staff were summoned to work at Sunday lunchtime. They had waited 21 years for this moment, now they had to organise a tour in the space of four days. The team was scheduled to leave for India on the Thursday evening. This was lift-off.

What team? Amid rare excitement, the UCB selection panel, comprising three members from SACU, two from SACB and with Van der Merwe retained as convener, had ironically scheduled to gather for a strategy meeting that same Sunday. Now, they were instructed to select a 14-man squad for the three-match tour.

It seemed right to go ahead. The players, including Wessels, felt strongly that any international experience at all would assist their preparations for the World Cup; and the people wanted to take on India. They had waited a long time. Why delay?

Van der Merwe, who had opposed the tour, going so far as to suggest that the side be downgraded to a South African XI, presided over a selection meeting which was forced to base its decisions on the previous season's form. Denied any time to prepare his personal preferences, or to campaign vigorously among other selectors before the meeting, the convener accepted the clear majority opinion that an experienced squad should be chosen...

As the sun sets this dramatic Sunday, Rice is arriving at his Johannesburg home after playing for his club when his son Mark bounds up and tells him that a Mr Van der Merwe has phoned during the afternoon: 'Dad, you're going to be the South African captain.' Sacked 18 months before, Rice has returned . . .

On the road between Kimberley and Bloemfontein, the manager of a Free State district side, Seppi Lusardi, flashes his lights at the car in front, being driven by Allan Donald. Both vehicles pull over. What's the problem? No problem. 'Allan, you're in the side to go to India.' Lusardi has heard it on the radio . . .

In Port Elizabeth, the Wessels family have just arrived home from a barbecue and have not been watching the TV1 news, on which the team was officially named. The telephone rings soon after seven. It is Kepler's father. 'Have you seen the side? You're in. Congratulations . . .'

Clive Rice (capt.), Jimmy Cook, Andrew Hudson, Mandy Yachad, Kepler Wessels, Peter Kirsten, Adrian Kuiper, Brian McMillan, Dave Richardson, Tim Shaw, Clive Eksteen, Richard Snell, Allan Donald and Craig Matthews . . . all around South Africa, 14 men who had grown up with the fact of isolation, were tearfully coming to terms with the news that they would represent their country on an official tour. Suddenly, the famine had ended.

Wessels' international career, seemingly buried when he left Australia and then buried again when he withdrew from the Springbok side at Wanderers, had been dramatically revived. After all the strife and trouble, he would, at long last, play real international cricket for South Africa. From his earliest days practising in the nets at Grey, that was all he had ever wanted.

The squad gathered in Johannesburg amid such excitement and anticipation that the once raging issue of Wessels' eligibility was not even raised. 'Hello, Clive' . . . 'Hello, Jimmy' . . . 'How are you doing, Kepler?' What was past, was mercifully past.

Early evening on November 7th, 1991, the South African squad boarded their charter flight and flew into the sunset. Arriving in Calcutta, they were met on the tarmac by Indian cricket officials, garlanded, daubed with a tilea on the forehead, ushered on to a bus and driven into a land of pure fantasy.

It would normally take no more than 20 minutes to drive from Dumdum airport to the Oberoi hotel in Calcutta. On the morning of November 8th, the trip took just under three hours.

From the boundaries of the airport, the streets were packed with people, ordinary people, shouting, all smiling. SOUTH AFRICA! YOUR COMEBACK A GREAT VICTORY FOR CRICKET, read one printed poster. And they waved, roared. From tenement buildings and shacks, people flocked to stand ten deep on the pavements. Calcutta, the eccentric city of 11 million people that once turned out 80 000 fans at three o'clock in the morning to welcome Pele, the Brazilian soccer hero, had come out to celebrate. Everywhere, people.

Three times the team bus was brought to a halt; three times, Mackerdhuj, Rice and Dakin were ushered out to stand on a prepared platform and address the crowd. Festival. The Cricket Association of Bengal had provided an impromptu, grinning motorcycle escort and distributed UCB paper flags among the crowd. Round every corner, more crowds, more laughing, battered motorcars with beaming faces popped out of all four windows. Happy, happy. Welcome, welcome.

Barriers of khaki-clad policemen stood shoulder-to-shoulder at the entrance to the hotel and enabled the overwhelmed cricketers to scramble from the bus to the foyer. The milling crowd remained outside the Oberoi hotel throughout the South Africans' stay. Each arrival, each departure would be a rousing adventure.

Wessels had sat and watched. He had toured India seven years previously with Australia, but the scale of the reception astounded him: 'I knew how enthusiastic most Indians are about cricket and I was surprised that quite a few of them seemed to remember me from the previous time I was there. It was great, but I felt relaxed the entire week because I knew what to expect most of the time. I knew the stadiums and I knew how it would all feel.'

He was allocated a room with Adrian Kuiper, the big-hitting all-rounder, an apple farmer from Elgin, near Cape Town. 'Sharing a room with Kuips was good for me,' Wessels reflects. 'I know that I sometimes get too tense but he was so naughty and upbeat the whole time that he helped me relax. I really enjoyed it.'

Still quiet and subdued, Wessels took his place in the South African side without fuss, without controversy, without suspicions. He was just another player, exactly what he always wanted. 'I think Kepler and I shared a lot of similar opinions in India,' Kuiper recalls, 'and we talked a lot. He's a much more intense person than I am, so we seemed to complement each other well. He played well, and he really seemed to enjoy the week.'

After a frantic visit to Mother Teresa on Saturday morning and a hasty net practice at Eden Gardens in the afternoon, the team prepared to face an Indian side, captained by Mohammad Azharuddin and supported by at least 92 000 spectators. 'That's the capacity,' an official said, 'but another 10 000 usually get in.'

As many thousands of his bleary-eyed compatriots dragged themselves out of bed at 5 a.m. to watch the live television coverage, Rice led his side out amid a deafening roar which seemed to bounce all around the huge concrete stands. Arriving in the middle, the South African players stood in a loose group, turning, grinning and all thanking the crowd, with their palms placed together and directed upwards in the traditional Indian greeting.

With South Africa sent in to bat, the honour fell to Hudson and Cook to take the first steps into a new era. A country that had forgotten what it felt to be proud, swallowed hard. Inevitably, the nerves frayed. Hudson was dismissed by Kapil Dev for nought in the first over and the team struggled to reach 177 in 47 overs. Only Wessels, who scored 50 batting at No.3, and Kuiper, 43, managed to settle on a pitch which kept very slow and very low.

When India batted, they found Donald bounding in, all raw speed, to seize five wickets for 29 runs but it was not sufficient. Sachin Tendulkar, the 18-year-old prince of Indian batsmen, struck 62 and the home side cruised to victory by three wickets with more than six overs to spare. For South Africans, the match had been a rude awakening to the real world of international cricket.

Rice was not downhearted. Leading a team of débutants with minimum preparation against formidable opposition, he had admirably tried to pool all knowledge and experience, repeatedly consulting with his senior players throughout the game. To the wonder of those who thought the years of provincial rivalry had bred resentment, he worked exceptionally well with Wessels.

'Kepler was extremely good,' Rice recalls. 'His advice and contribution on the field were excellent and I used him quite a bit because I often wanted to know what his thoughts were. Kepler has a good cricket brain and he was an ideal player from a captain's point of view because he is so disciplined and reliable you don't have to worry about him.'

The esteem ran in both directions. Wessels had never played in a side captained by Rice, but he enjoyed it. 'Clive leads from the front and that works because he's very gutsy,' he reflects. 'He is brave and he never gives up, so I liked the mood he set within the side and I felt very comfortable with it.'

There was no time for reflection after the Calcutta defeat, no time for anything. Up at dawn again, the squad flew to Agra for a photo opportunity at the Taj Mahal and on to Gwalior, home town of Madhavrao Scindia, president of the Indian board, where the second one-day international would be played. A sorely required net practice was planned, but it did not take place because the players arrived from Calcutta five hours before their kit. It only turned up after night had fallen. This was India.

Rice began to feel the strain. Was this a package holiday or was it a cricket tour? Looking back, he concludes: 'It was mainly a diplomatic exercise. That was fine. We were there to make friends. I mean, we were doing things like making certain everyone played in one of the first two matches. They were exceptional circumstances.'

This reality was lost on an expectant public back home. Yes, it was fun to be back. No, it was no fun to lose. When South Africa lost the second international, the criticism began. India, sent in, scored 223 in 45 overs. In pursuit, there was only the experienced Wessels, scoring 71 out of a paltry 185 for eight.

In Gwalior, in defeat, controversy boiled over. The touring squad and its officials, unavoidably naive in the street rules of international cricket, had been astounded to find the ball swinging alarmingly after 30 overs of the South African innings in Calcutta. When they looked at the ball, they saw several scraped cuts on one side and a still shiny surface on the other. Was this 'reverse swing', a first glimpse into the underworld of ball-tampering? What was happening?

Bacher, manager of the squad, raised the matter casually and reminded his hosts that this was a goodwill tour. It was after all his role to represent the players, and they were angry. In Gwalior, after the ball had performed strangely again, the Indians decided to take Bacher's words as a profound insult. A private issue became a public incident and Dakin subsequently issued a full apology on behalf of the UCB. Bacher was made to seem unfairly chastened but the South Africans were simply learning the ropes.

The match was followed by an opulent and fine banquet at the Maharajah's palace, where liqueurs were carried around the table on a model railway; and, at midnight, the increasingly exhausted squad flew on to New Delhi. The pressure was growing. The team hovered on the brink of a three-nil humiliation. They needed to win. 'It had all been jolly at the start,' Wessels recalls, 'but the officials were getting a bit snappy. The results suddenly became important.'

The third and final match was to be played under floodlights at the Jawaharlal Nehru stadium in Delhi, the ground where Wessels had scored 107 for Australia in 1984, and, on its third outing, the rusty South African engine finally roared into life.

Such a revival did not seem imminent when India raced to 287 for four from 50 overs, with Ravi Shastri and Sanjay Manjrekar both taking centuries off the South African bowlers, yet, confronted by an immense chase, the touring team grew up.

Rice took control, calculating how many runs would be needed after 10, 20, 30 and 40 overs and writing out the targets on a card which would be given to the openers and handed to incoming batsmen as necessary. The captain conveyed to his team his own belief that, even if India had just scored their highest ever total in a one-day international, victory was still within reach.

The side, finally chosen on merit alone, believed him. Cook and Wessels, a distinguished right-left partnership now installed as openers, launched the innings briskly, reaching 39 in the first 10 overs, just one below their target. Cook was dismissed for 35 but Wessels and Kirsten carried the score to 89 for one at the end of the 20th over, still only one run behind the rate.

After 30 overs, it was 147 for one, three behind the target. The pursuit was progressing at a perfect pace. Wessels was scoring at virtually a run a ball, looking every inch a world class batsman as he moved towards a second century in Delhi.

But, on 90, he was adjudged LBW to a full toss from the left-arm round-the-wicket spinner, Raju, which seemed highly unlikely to hit the stumps. Rice grinned wryly. He had been warned that Indian umpires would sometimes give an outrageous decision if they thought they could bring their side back into the game. Still, Wessels had done his job, facing only 106 balls and guiding South Africa to 183 for two, within reach of an improbable triumph.

Kirsten, in touch, was joined by Kuiper and the pair began an assault on the Indian bowlers, slaying an exhilarating 105 runs from only 12 overs. South Africa won by eight wickets with three overs to spare. The top four had batted magnificently.

Back in the dressing room, the jubilant squad formed a tight circle, their arms wrapped around their team-mates on either side, and shouted *'Bokke!'* in unison as they clenched even tighter. This was the first *voelmekaar,* the first expression of the remarkable team spirit that would serve them so well in the months to come. It was a practice more familiar to the Springbok rugby team, but the cricket side would now adopt it as their own.

As the satisfaction of victory slowly soaked in, several of the senior players lingered in the dressing room that happy night in Delhi, talking, relaxing, planning, anticipating. Rice and Cook of Transvaal, Kuiper of Western Province, Kirsten of Border, Wessels of Eastern Province; now all of South Africa, together, united in a common cause, pulling together, no longer provincial rivals. The World Cup was 15 weeks away. The World Cup...

'We suddenly realised that we had the potential to compete extremely well in international cricket,' Rice recalls. 'With the World Cup coming up, we began to feel we could do quite a job. We knew it was going to be hard but we had a chance. It was exciting. Our strength was obviously the fast bowlers because Donald's sheer pace had terrified most of the Indians. That was a huge boost.'

Wessels, named South Africa's Man of the Series after scores of 50, 71 and 90, felt secure and established. 'We all knew that we were a long way behind,' he reflects. 'I knew it and Clive knew it but we knew what we had to do. There was a good feeling.'

Around South Africa, the experience of watching Currie Cup heroes transported to the world stage had exhilarated new legions of cricket supporters. For five amazing days, a large proportion of the country had lived for the cricket. One country rallying behind one team. It had been an unforgettable week.

The day after victory in Delhi, one of the UCB development scheme training sessions was stopped by rain. More than 25 enthusiastic 15-year-olds from Mamelodi huddled beneath an overhanging roof near their nets at the University of Pretoria, and soon found themselves subject to an impromptu quiz by their coach. A young white boy, who happened to be standing nearby, asked to join in.

'Who is the South African captain in India?' asked coach.

'Clive Rice,' replied the Mamelodi boys in unison.

That, it transpired, was the extent of their knowledge. They were, of course, relatively new to the game of cricket. Soccer had been the passion of their fathers, and grandfathers.

'Who does Zane Moosa play for?' asked coach.

'Mamelodi Sundowns,' the boys replied, swiftly recognising the elusive midfield player of their local soccer team. All except one. The white boy stood silent, his hand held up, oblivious to the correct answer already given. 'India,' he ventured.

One blurred tour had not cured all the old divisions within South African cricket, but it had been a start.

As the team returned to a warm welcome at Jan Smuts airport, Wessels pushed his own trolley through the throng with the Man of the Series trophy perched on his suitcases. Ushered aside for the interview from which his Sunday newspaper column would be written, he was asked what should be done next.

'The most important thing now,' Wessels replied, 'is for the selectors to confirm Clive Rice as captain for the World Cup. That would give a clear direction and it would be right.'

# 11

# Raiders of the World Cup

---

T here is a commotion in front of the Wanderers dressing room. Clive Rice is there, so is Graeme Pollock and Jimmy Cook. They're in deep conversation and they seem agitated, concerned.

Wessels is fielding, watching the group from 70 metres away, stealing a glance between balls, but he can't quite make out what's happening. His Eastern Province side are playing a Currie Cup match against Transvaal, but everyone's mind is on the announcement of a preliminary 20-man South African squad for the World Cup. There are rumours in the air, lifetime ambitions on the line.

'Howzat!'

The fourth Transvaal wicket falls. Rice, the hoary veteran, excuses himself from the group and, already padded up, strides down the steps, out into the arena where he has reigned for more than a decade. As he reaches the pitch, the old warrior seems somehow sad. He looks across to Wessels, fielding at first slip.

'Good luck in Australia.'

'What do you mean?' Wessels asks.

'I'm not going,' Rice replies. 'You're the captain.'

\* \* \* \* \*

It was the greatest honour of his career, yet Wessels was named as the captain of South Africa amid searing controversy. The selectors had dropped Clive Rice and Jimmy Cook from the World Cup squad. It was a decision that amazed, saddened and enraged a large proportion of the public. Selection furores are as old as the game itself, but few had provoked such an impassioned reaction.

As a result, Wessels would lead what many people considered a weakened national side through the first four months of 1992. The World Cup in Australia and New Zealand would be followed by a brief tour to the West Indies. Whatever the results, this first bloom of readmission would unfold as history in the making. If Rice and Cook had been allowed to add their experience and know-how to the young talent, it might have been history for the taking...

He had not believed it. Soon after arriving at the Wanderers that morning, Wessels had been shown a scribbled list of 20 names by Alan Kourie, the Transvaal team manager. Kourie said it was the squad that had been selected. No Rice. No Cook. No Kirsten. Wessels looked, and laughed off the list as a joke.

'Pull the other one, mate.'

When Rice told him the news, his throat turned dry. For two or three overs, his mind raced. There was nothing to say. One part of him was thrilled, another thought it was all wrong. Captain? He knew the idea had been floated in the newspapers but, truly, he had never contemplated leading the side.

The Currie Cup match continued.

That evening, the squad was announced on the TV1 news. Peter van der Merwe, convener of selectors, phoned Wessels early the next morning to offer congratulations. The conversation was brief. The new captain sought no explanation. Thanks.

'I was sure Rice would captain the squad to the World Cup,' Wessels reflects, 'and I was happy with that. I also thought that, after our stand in New Delhi, Cook and myself would open. I didn't think there was any doubt about Kirsten either.

'If I had been the sole selector, I would probably have taken all three of them to the World Cup, but, at that stage, I honestly hadn't doubted that they would be selected.'

Had anyone doubted it?

Rice was still a muscular, reliable and tough all-rounder, the man to bowl the closing overs, the man to batter a brisk 50. He was 42, but he was no fading veteran. His physical condition was that of a 30-year-old, his enthusiasm was that of an 18-year-old. To many, he seemed an automatic choice both as captain and as the pivotal all-rounder in the side.

Cook remained the upright military officer of an opener. A prolific spell with Somerset had given him a global reputation, and also contributed to an alleged slump in Transvaal colours, but the fact remained he had plundered runs against all the world's leading bowlers. He had shown indisputable class.

Kirsten was the wristy, feisty batsman with a point to prove. He had left Western Province to play for Border, newly promoted to the Currie Cup competition, and was still scoring the runs.

Their talent was undeniable, their fitness beyond doubt and their hunger for success was immense after 20 years of isolation. Together, the three men represented a nucleus of class and experience that appeared indispensable to a raw squad thrown in at the deep end of international cricket.

So what happened? Peter van der Merwe happened.

The convener would probably not have named Rice among his Top Ten friends. In fact, they were not friends at all. This could partly be explained by a perceived history of enmity, but it was also an instinctive conflict. The all-rounder's central ethos of being tough and confrontational ran against Van der Merwe's more cultivated and judicious grain. It was a classic personality clash.

When the preliminary squad of 20 was first discussed, Van der Merwe argued that Wessels should replace Rice as captain by drawing a distinction between commercialism and professionalism.

Rice, it was said, was commercial because he was staying in cricket for as long as possible simply to make money. His fishing, his motor racing and the sponsor's cap which he loyally donned for any television interview all showed, they said, that the Transvaal captain had started to exploit the game.

Wessels, the theory ran, was professional because his primary concern still lay on the field and he had been rewarded by success with his Eastern Province side; and he was only 34.

Van der Merwe's broader conviction (and there is nothing to suggest he was not absolutely sincere in his beliefs) was that the World Cup squad must be chosen on the basic criteria of form, fitness and fielding. Sharing the view that the team had appeared too old, too ponderous and too geriatric in India, he carried the banner for youth. 'Only a young squad will survive a tough World Cup programme of eight matches in 18 days,' his chorus chanted.

Did they mean a young squad or a physically fit squad? Were they necessarily the same thing? They seemed to be.

With no reference to class or experience, Cook and Kirsten, let alone Rice, were always going to struggle on this selection scale. Aged 38 and 36 respectively, they were rudely dismissed as 'too old'. During one match, as Kirsten set off to chase a ball to the boundary, Van der

193

Merwe leaned forward and exclaimed: 'Look at him! Look at him!' They were condemned by birth certificate.

This was the convener's publicly stated theory, but a second hypothesis was growing in some quarters: namely, that Cook, Rice and Kirsten, all former Springbok captains in their own right, were dropped because they were seen as possible catalysts for opposition to the new captain. All three dismiss the assertion, stating they would happily have played under Wessels, but it is conceivable that once it was decided that this was to be Kepler's Era and absolute discipline was essential, all potential rivals were eliminated.

This is logical. But utterly unreasonable. In 19 seasons as a first class cricketer, Wessels had done and been through enough to have no need for any ill-conceived protection. He could comfortably look after himself. No, Uncle knew better.

Van der Merwe took his views to his five fellow selectors and canvassed. Tony Pithey, a friend and team-mate from the 1960s, could be relied upon for support but Peter Pollock, the brother of Graeme and a former Springbok, and Lee Irvine, another ex-Bok based in Johannesburg, could hold differing opinions. It soon became clear that the decisive votes would be cast by S.K. Reddy and Rushdie Majiet, the two national selectors nominated to the panel from the former South African Cricket Board.

Reddy had been the SACB convener of selectors and Majiet had been a prominent SACB personality, but, in simple terms, they were both unfamiliar with the mainstream players. Neither was remotely qualified to make decisions that would make or break careers. Power had been thrust into their hands by political necessity, and they soon had cause to be grateful that Van der Merwe gave generously of his time and advice to ensure power was not abused.

The preliminary squad of 20, only selected at all because the Australian organisers wanted to prepare their tournament brochure, was duly announced. No Rice. No Cook. No Kirsten. Captain Kepler and the Kids would take on the world. Van der Merwe's blueprint had prevailed. By five votes to one.

Outrage.

Some sought to minimise the issue, mocking it as a storm in a teacup, but they were drowned in the outcry. What set the situation apart was the unique nature of the 1992 World Cup for South African cricketers. It was not just another tour, as it may have seemed to Englishmen or Australians. This was to be their long-awaited moment of readmission and, in many minds, three men who had sustained the game through isolation were being deprived of a belated chance on the international stage not because they were not talented enough but because of what seemed a petty personality clash.

The extent and fervour of protest was extraordinary: 71 per cent of provincial players told the *Sunday Times* they had no confidence in the selectors... a run-of-the-mill floodlit match drew 12 000 people to the Wanderers when fewer than 5 000 were expected, most of them simply wanting to gather and demonstrate support for Rice and Cook... a petition collected more than 10 000 signatures... the newspapers' letters columns overflowed.

Johannesburg's rage knew no bounds. It was said that Van der Merwe, who acted as Eastern Province cricket board president quite apart from being convener of the selectors, was spearheading a Port Elizabeth-based group in a campaign against Transvaal. That, they spat, was why he pushed Wessels, and axed Rice and Cook. Some officials were adamant this was true: 'Van der Merwe and Dakin (Geoff, the UCB president) have run a campaign to get Eastern Province people into top positions,' a leading administrator maintained. 'They hate Transvaal and they're biased in almost all their decisions. South African cricket has been hijacked by these people.' In Port Elizabeth, such views were dismissed as Johannesburg paranoia prompted by the fact that Transvalers were no longer in control.

So it went. When Van der Merwe sought to deflect criticism by stressing that players not in the 20-man group could yet be called into the final 14-man squad, he succeeded only in encouraging the belief that sustained protest would force Rice, Cook and Kirsten to the World Cup. As the day of decision neared, the controversy took on the status of an election campaign − except, of course, for the fact that only the six selectors would vote.

Rice's fate, however, had been sealed before the poll. If any hope of a recall ever existed, and it may not have, it was removed by his blunt criticism of the selectors. His die was cast and years after the World Cup he would still be expressing forthright views in the media, still erring on the side of saying too much.

In 1971, he had been selected as the bright young hope of the Springbok squad to tour Australia, but that trip was cancelled when demonstrations threatened. The cruel fate of Clive Rice was to miss out on representing his country in official cricket as the curtain of isolation fell and, notwithstanding the diplomatic tour of India in November

1991, to be overlooked when it was raised. The powerful all-rounder would have been an automatic choice in any South African squad selected between 1971 and 1991, but, almost to the day, those were the years of the sporting boycott. He would never play in an official Test match or take part in a World Cup.

Rice reflects: 'If I wasn't playing up to that level, I could have accepted it, but I was. I look back and think I played for all those years supporting South African cricket and then that was the loyalty they showed me. Then, you look at Kepler who went away to Australia and came back, and you see the support he got. And I have to say Kepler got it right. He exploited the situation correctly. I got it wrong. There is no loyalty in sport.'

The pre-poll predictions appeared much brighter for Kirsten. There seemed a growing acceptance that he could, after all, provide crucial experience at the top of the batting order. As the harassed selectors gathered to nibble supper at Van der Merwe's residence in Port Elizabeth before choosing their final squad, Wessels, who had been invited to join the concluding deliberations, was relieved to hear a series of positive references to Kirsten.

Cook, however, remained the marginal seat. His case was still too close to call. As the discussion started, Irvine, who regarded the Transvaal opening batsman as a 'must-go', moved straight to the crux of the argument. He turned to face Wessels.

'Kepler, our first match is going to be against Australia in Sydney,' Irvine said. 'You know it's going to be tough. Who do you want walking out beside you to open the innings?'

'Jimmy Cook,' the captain replied immediately.

In two words, Wessels proved himself big enough to set aside a history of mistrust with Cook, to cast out any thought of revenge for his unease during the Test against the unofficial English tour and to look forward in the best interests of his team. In the tiny-minded world of professional sport, such magnanimity is rare. It's not easy to find a Number 1 trying to look after Number 2.

'I was concerned about a lack of experience,' Wessels says, as a matter of fact. 'So it was good to have Kirsten, but I felt we needed Cook too. They asked what I thought so I told them. I didn't exactly put a gun to their heads because it was basically their job to select the team, but I made my opinions clear.'

His efforts on Cook's behalf were in vain. There was no way back. It was decided that he and Rice would be left behind. Kirsten would be recalled. 'I felt very sorry for Clive and Jimmy,' Wessels concludes. 'I know how they must have felt.'

The drama had finally reached its conclusion. For many, the protest was justified by Kirsten's recall; and when he emerged as the top runscorer in the World Cup group matches, he acknowledged the role played by the campaign in his success. Sadly, not one of the selectors was able to concede publicly the idiocy of omitting Kirsten from the initial 20-man squad.

Van der Merwe was replaced by Peter Pollock as the convener before the next season. Within 18 months of the World Cup, he had withdrawn from all regular involvement in cricket administration, resigning from the Eastern Province cricket board amid a financial crisis prompted by the building of a new stand.

Some have suggested his strategies were vindicated by South Africa's success at the World Cup, but the issue was never a matter of opinion to be proved right or wrong by subsequent results. The criticism was that he had allowed his judgement to be clouded by what appeared to be a personality clash. Only he knows if that was truly the case. The facts of this sad, unnecessary saga stand for themselves.

* * * * *

As the words 'Rice' and 'Cook' melted out of the headlines, Wessels took over the captaincy and the work began. A squad training camp was scheduled in Cape Town. This would be a crucial time. Wessels, in charge and intense, wanted to seize control.

'I was apprehensive,' he recalls. 'It was a real honour to be captain, but I was nervous about taking such an inexperienced side into that competition, especially into the match against Australia at the SCG. That played on my mind. I tried to put aside all these fears and get the squad thinking positively. I didn't particularly want the captaincy. I had never thought about it, but once I had been given it, I had to make the most of it.'

Welcome to Camp Kepler.

It is a world where every minute counts, where jokes are fine but not in the nets, where one man is in charge. He is a man who will let you know what he expects of you, a man whom you will admire for all he has achieved. You may not warm to him and there might be times when you curse him as a moody so-and-so, but he won't worry too much about that so long as you do your job. You will never cry on his shoulder. Don't try. Both shoulders are bone dry. Then, when your limbs ache at the end of the day and you have done everything he asked and you feel you can give no more, you will look up at him and feel an overwhelming sense of . . . respect.

Through two days of running, fielding exercises and military discipline, Wessels put his squad on the rack. He suspected the top South African players had been pampered and spoilt like household kittens during the years of isolation and feared that they would be exposed and devoured in the World Cup jungle. So the sergeant-major clicked his heels and the squaddies fell into line.

Mark Rushmere had seen it all before with Eastern Province, but he did notice some softer touches. Wessels appeared to ease off national squad players in situations when he would once have bitten into a provincial journeyman for slacking.

Even so, cellulite was shaken, eyebrows were raised.

'Is he always like this?' panting players would ask, out of the corners of their mouths, out of earshot.

Rushmere would smile, and start the next lap.

When Wessels saw Brian McMillan, the broad all-rounder, doing what was required, when he watched Richard Snell rolling in off a full run-up with gleaming steel in his eyes, he sensed it was going to work. This team, at this time, would respond. That was a relief. In private moments, he had worried. Would the players accept him? Would they toe his line? They clearly would.

Perhaps the selection row had worked in his favour. Beyond the acrimony and dispute, a generally young and raw squad began to look upon their captain as a steadfast rock. He was offering them guidance, knowledge of Australian conditions and a disciplined hand on the rudder, leading them boldly into unknown territory. Nervous and apprehensive, they were happy to follow.

The captain's initial task of establishing command was hugely assisted by the calm competence of the United Cricket Board office, notably demonstrated by Dr Bacher. The expert MD would telephone Wessels regularly, and with almost grandfatherly concern, taking care to iron out problems as they appeared.

Such administrative support is often unappreciated, but the captain's life becomes impossible without it. Later in 1992, Naas Botha led the Springbok rugby team on tour to France and England and was accompanied by officials of such mind-boggling ineptitude that, at one formal banquet, two of them spent the evening speaking Afrikaans across the female French Minister of Sport. Wessels was lucky. He never found himself in such an invidious position because the soothing Doctor Bacher was always on the end of the line, and also because a well-spoken advocate from Pretoria would soon be appointed as team manager for the World Cup.

It's hard to look past Alan Jordaan. His dark hair is swept into a fastened fringe, his dark eyes threaten. There is a harshly defined conviction in his face. For years, he played a good game as the Northern Transvaal captain. Then he started talking a good game to be elected president of NTCU. His Afrikaans accent was thick and heavy, but the performance was silk-smooth.

One Friday in December 1991, Jordaan was at home. The phone rang. It was Geoff Dakin asking if he would be manager of the World Cup squad. It had been broadly assumed that Bacher would take that post, but the UCB president was searching for an alternative candidate only 48 hours before the appointment was to be made. UCB wars: the president and MD were at loggerheads again. Bacher arrived at the Sunday meeting expecting to be named as manager of the World Cup squad, but he was ambushed when Dakin argued that the MD should not be away from the office for so long. Jordaan was in.

If the manner of his appointment was questionable, Jordaan's success in the role was beyond doubt. He worked effectively with Mike Procter, retained as coach after the tour of India and, most importantly, he clicked with the captain. No tension, no problem. 'Alan has the ability to say the right thing at the right time,' Wessels enthuses. 'The management was one of our saving graces at the World Cup. He was brilliant.'

But Procter and Wessels click? Surely not. While the captain had much in common with Jordaan, he appeared to have nothing in common with the coach. Wessels led a sober and disciplined life. Procter enjoyed a drink and followed the horses. Wessels had always admired the sportsman who worked hard. Procter had been one of the most naturally gifted cricketers of his era.

Cast as opposites, they had clashed on the field during the 1970s: Wessels seeing Procter as a typically aloof English speaker to whom everything had come too easy, from school at Hilton to the Springbok side; Procter regarding Wessels as a tense and defensive Afrikaner from Bloemfontein, the figure of fun with the pudding-bowl fringe. When, match after match, Procter dismissed Wessels with his outswinger, the rivalry grew. Upper lips tightened.

How could these men work together?

'I was apprehensive,' Wessels concedes, 'but we both made an effort to communicate regularly. We knew that we were different as individuals, but it worked well. He has his way of doing things, I have mine, and that was fine. We got along.'

Procter, to his credit, committed himself whole-heartedly to proving wrong the general expectation that coach and captain would collide. He had coached Free State and Natal, and Northamptonshire in England, but his solid reputation had frequently been laced with tales of the high life. In some ways, his relaxed manner made him an easy target for criticism, but he, too, rose to the challenge of the World Cup. 'People had plenty to say about Proccie,' Wessels says, 'but I was there and he did an excellent job.'

Considered as a whole, the management structure handed to Wessels could hardly have been better tailored to his needs. He had Jordaan as manager, a man whom he liked and who liked him, Procter as coach, a man keen to make a success of the position and, finally, there was Adrian Kuiper, a high-spirited Roy of the Rovers, as his vice-captain. There was no obvious opposition within, no bulls. The UCB had created a system where Wessels held power. He would, it was soon clear, dominate. He would have his way.

By the time Zimbabwe had been defeated in Harare, the opening match of the warm-up schedule, played en route to Australia, the new king was seated securely on his throne.

On Friday, February 7th, 1992, Wessels and his team arrived at Perth airport. At the outset, he laid down the law. 'None of you can imagine the size of the task that lies ahead of us,' he told his wide-eyed players, 'but, whatever happens, I want us to stay loyal to each other. Life will not be easy for any of us over the next three weeks, but I don't want to hear anyone complaining or moaning about anyone else. If we can stick together, then we've got a reasonable chance of success.'

Through warm-up matches in Perth and Adelaide, the team started to find some sort of form. The captain, in contrast, was struggling. He had scored only 49 runs in four innings, and was becoming morose. When he was just a player, such dark moods were tolerable. As captain, his depression cast a general pall.

'I started to panic,' Wessels recalls. 'I had taken on this huge task, and I just couldn't score a run. Everything began to get on top of me and I couldn't stop thinking about our first match in Sydney against

Australia. I was scared that we would be thrashed. The whole thing was like a sore in my head.'

He was straining under the burden of captaincy. In India, under Rice, he had been able to concentrate on his batting but now there was no time. He was too busy worrying about everyone else. 'I decided,' he remembers, 'that I simply had to make time.'

An innings of 72 in a practice match win over Pakistan at the Manuka Oval in Canberra restored some confidence, but Wessels soon found something else to worry about, another crisis to which he could fix his frequently tortured intensity. It was not within his nature to sit back and relax. He functioned in adversity.

'More bad weather coming in over Sydney,' twanged the weather forecaster. 'It's going to rain, rain, rain.' Wessels flicked off the television in his hotel room, threw himself back on his bed and sighed. How could he prepare a side to take on Australia when there was no opportunity to practise? How? How? How?

The final warm-up match against a Donald Bradman XI in Bowral was rained off. Warmed-up? Wessels felt stone cold. His frustrated team were reduced to a miserable bus full of frowns driving through grey Sydney suburbs in search of indoor nets. 'We mustn't freeze,' Wessels kept telling his players. But would they?

Back home, expectations soared. World Cup fever spread across millions of faces, most of them white but many black faces too. Messages of goodwill were received from State President F.W. de Klerk and Nelson Mandela. One nation behind one team. 'They are the first completely representative national side,' Bacher declared.

Wednesday, February 26th, 1992 was drawing near: Australia vs South Africa. The hyped-up, hot favourite hosts taking on the new boys, the prodigal uncertainties, before a full house under lights at the Sydney Cricket Ground. *Carpe diem.*

* * * * *

The door of his hotel room, appropriately perched 43 floors above the vanquished, flickering city of Sydney, wouldn't open. It was a moment before midnight. Perhaps not quite everything on this most sublime of occasions would go right for Kepler Wessels.

Then, the lock clicked and the hero of a nation waking up to a forgotten surge of pride on the other side of the world, hurled his kitbag on the floor, ordered a toasted chicken and mayonnaise sandwich from room service, cracked open a chilled bottle of orange juice, sank into the sofa, and beamed.

'I can't believe it,' he said, hours of tension draining from aching limbs. 'I thought about this one match so often but it never worked out quite like this. I don't believe it.'

More than 22 years after departing the international stage following a four-nil Test whitewash against Australia, South Africa had returned by annihilating the defending champions on their home ground. It had been a victory of mythical proportions.

Wessels, still unshowered and wearing his green kit several hours after striking the winning runs, had scored 81 not out and led his team with a calm purpose. 'It was strange,' he said. 'When I was batting, and we were getting closer and closer to the target, I found it hard to concentrate. I kept looking around at that Australian team I know so well and I kept thinking of all the people at home. It was very emotional.'

On the eve of the match, the rain had relented and both the South African and Australian sides were able to practise fielding, side-by-side on the SCG outfield. 'It's nice to see someone copying us,' noted Allan Border, as he watched the opposition move through the same fielding drills as his own team. Wessels had never tried to conceal the fact that he wanted to mould his team in the Australian image.

Tension was everywhere. Australia had lost the opening match of the tournament four days earlier to New Zealand in Auckland and, with the top four countries in the round-robin league advancing to the semi-final stage, they could not afford another defeat at this stage. They needed to defeat South Africa.

Merv Hughes, the folk hero fast bowler, was relaxed enough as he mischievously began to stoke South African anxiety. Both squads had headed for the nets after fielding practice, and Hughes arrived just as Allan Donald was preparing to bowl. The eager South African had placed a marker on the ground where he was aiming to pitch the ball. Hughes, strolling beside the net, took one look and remarked: 'Mate, that's much too full. Put it there, and you're going out the ground.' Hughes grinned. Donald said nothing.

South African nerves were frayed, that tense, touchy Tuesday, but, amid the general pessimism, Wessels played a trump card. He invited Alan Jones, the former Australian rugby coach, to address the squad on the eve of the match. This dapper, waspish and eloquent man was introduced to the players, one by one. Looking at Snell, Jones mused:

'Ah, and I suppose you must be the decadent one.' The squad laughed as one for what seemed the first time in days. It was the sound of breaking ice.

Jones, who had been sympathetic to Wessels during his trials and troubles with the ACB in 1985, spoke about the Australian team in decline, told how they were tired and overplayed, and how cracks had appeared in the squad following the dropping, and then recall, of Geoff Marsh. He provided the classic motivational talk. 'Make tomorrow your day,' he told the South Africans. 'Just fix your mind on getting your job 100 per cent right 100 per cent of the time.'

Snell recalls: 'I went into that room wondering how we could win, and I came out wondering how we could lose.' Others felt the same way. Perhaps the tide had been turned.

On the team bus on the way to the ground, there was an unearthly quiet. Wessels sat near the front and simply listened to the silence. What were they thinking of, these young men being driven to the SCG on this long-awaited day? Of their families at home waking at five in the morning to watch the TV broadcast? Of their friends in such a high state of excitement? Of all those players who had been denied this enchanting experience during isolation?

The Sydney Cricket Ground was deserted when the team arrived just before noon and the players quietly drifted out to inspect the pitch. The feel of what Wessels rates as the best cricket venue in the world visibly began to exhilarate them.

Kuiper gazed at the six modern stands complementing the two green-roofed original constructions, the Members Stand and Ladies Stand, and began to wheel his arms wildly. Donald started his own high-stepping wicket-taking dance for no particular reason. Jonty Rhodes waved to an imaginary, cheering crowd.

After 22 years, it had all come to this. Instinctively, the squad linked arms in a tight circle, a *voelmekaar,* and clinched on the third shout of 'Boks!', just as the victorious team had done in New Delhi. Rare, raw desire lit up every face.

Thirty minutes later, the stadium gates swung open and Sydney poured in: gentle members to their stands, boisterous masses to the open concourses. Within an hour, the SCG was buzzing.

Border and Wessels strode out for the toss amid bedlam. This was no ordinary match and no ordinary day. Twelve years before, the two captains had been working for McConnell Holdings, playing side by side for club, state and, later, country. Today they were rivals at the

World Cup. They had rediscovered each other two weeks before in Adelaide and had talked at length, with Border generously passing on advice about taking on the other countries. The tiffs of 1985 were past. 'Best of luck, mate.' ... Yeah, good luck.

Border won the toss and decided to bat first, only to watch in pain as the pitch gently flattened into the evening. Wessels was not disappointed. He would probably have batted first as well. It was a marginal decision, a good toss to lose.

At 2.28 p.m., the South Africans fanned on to the field to the thumping accompaniment of 'Who'll Rule The World', the tournament's official rock anthem. Even in 29-degree heat, strange shivers shot down the spine of every South African in the crowd.

As the public address announcer read out the team, the beery blokes on Yabba's Hill, once a gentle grassy bank but now buried in concrete and plastic seats following repeated incidents of drunken disorder, responded in their own jocular fashion.

'Kepler Wessels,' boomed the tannoy speakers.

'Couple'a beers, mate!' yelled a group on the Hill.

'Peter Kirsten.'

'Peter who?'

'Hansie Cronje.'

'Nancy who?'

Marsh, opening the innings, took guard. Donald ran in to bowl the first ball of the match. Marsh fended airily, and was caught by Richardson. What a start! The South Africans were jubilant... but umpire Brian Aldridge, from New Zealand, was unmoved. Within seconds, the giant TV screen replay confirmed the truth that Aldridge's mistake had denied a moment of rich drama. Not out.

Maybe unnerved, the bowlers lost control and Australia raced to 35 for nought after seven overs. When Boon crashed Donald for four, Wessels prepared himself to chase 'at least 250', but the compact opener soon became the victim of a schoolboy run-out, and a South African student began to apply the squeeze.

Snell, a 23-year-old who had risen swiftly through the ranks, conceded 10 runs in his first seven overs and applied the brakes. At home, he had grown used to playing while under the pressure of his next exams at Wits University in Johannesburg. Now he was blossoming on tour, applying himself to cricket from dawn till dusk. He bowled in the off-side channel and Wessels' carefully planned field placings held the Australian batsmen in check, under pressure.

Then, McMillan applied aggression. At one stage, he fielded a strong drive off his own bowling and glared down the wicket as Dean Jones, the idol of young Australia, shaped to run. 'Just ****** try it,' the South African shouted. Boom, boom. This wasn't in the script. The new boys were suddenly calling the shots.

Minutes before 4 p.m., the pressure paid big dividends. Kuiper's medium pace dismissed Marsh and Border in successive deliveries and the home team's innings started to tumble through 76 for three, 97 for four, 108 for five, 143 for six, 146 for seven, 156 for eight and then to 161 for nine when Rhodes, leaping to his left, ran out Craig McDermott. The exuberant Natalian was thunderously applauded by exhilarated spectators, this time for real.

Australia's last wicket stand became a target of ridicule on the Hill, with each run scampered by Mike Whitney being greeted by ironic cheers and mock genuflection. 'These guys haven't played for 20 years and they're whipping us,' wailed one inebriate as he slid back to the public bar behind the stand.

The home side ended their innings at 170 for nine, and Border spent the last 15 minutes of the supper interval gazing out at the field from the window of the dressing room, hurling a ball from his right hand into his left palm, over and again. For the veteran of 235 one-day internationals, the match which he had said represented one of his few remaining ambitions was turning sour.

Not only did his bowlers lack fire, his fielders fumbled and bumbled. Into the evening, South Africa's run chase became a steady jog as Wessels took control. He had struggled at first, offering a sharp chance on 23 to Boon, but he settled into a rhythm of careful glances and studied drives. When he pulled Bruce Reid high into the black night sky, the multi-coloured electric scoreboard proclaimed: WESSELS — 2000 RUNS IN ONE-DAY INTERNATIONALS. 'Yeah, and 1 950 of them were for us,' wailed a voice on the Hill.

Andrew Hudson scored 28 of the most significant runs of his entire career. His duck in Calcutta had prompted raging self-doubt, but this wonderful night in Sydney he showed the world, and most importantly himself, that he could play. Heh, I can bat. Look, I'm all right. Confidence flooded the senses. He was eventually undone by Taylor's spin, but the first wicket only brought Kirsten to the crease at 74 for one, and he was soon in full flow.

Cruising along at around the modest required runrate of 3.45 runs per over, Wessels ended the match with a flurry of strokes in the 47th over.

He cut Reid for four, deftly glanced for two, drove for another four and finally pushed the last single, breaking his stride to high-five Kirsten in mid-pitch. The captain, named Man of the Match, had scored 81. Kirsten finished with 49.

Border stepped across to offer his congratulations, and most of the Australian players made a special point of shaking Wessels' hand as they left the field. The South African captain gulped back the emotion. Their reaction meant a lot.

South African flags had suddenly unfurled in all corners of the ground. The 'no-hopers' had won by nine wickets with two overs to spare. Back home, it was mid-morning, but millions had not even thought of work. Tearful eyes gazed into televisions.

The South African dressing room was soon packed with media and well-wishers. At one stage, amidst the elation, it was possible to count no fewer than 13 reporters within two square metres of the besieged captain. Yes, of course, he was thrilled.

At the end of the Press conference, Steve Tshwete appeared at the door behind the captain. Tired and emotional after a momentous evening, the delighted ANC official gripped Wessels by the shoulders and hugged him, first with his head to the right, then to the left, to the right, left, right. The cameras snapped and the photograph, the ultimate image of national reconciliation through sport, would be printed across nine newspaper columns in Johannesburg the next day.

Van Zyl Slabbert, a leading progressive politician, was there among the throng, saying the result would swing 10 per cent of the country to vote YES in the forthcoming referendum on reform. Barry Richards was there, so was David Frost the golfer, and many others, all of whose grandchildren will hear the tale of how...

Back at the team hotel, more than 250 faxes had brought the reception desk to a standstill. The State President had been trying to contact Wessels since the winning run was hit and, the moment he arrived back from the ground, the captain was ushered directly into the manager's office where he took the call. The presidential congratulations were duly offered and the conversation broadcast, in full and as live, on the main national evening news.

Wessels returned to the foyer after speaking to De Klerk, and found himself confronted by Rice, of all people. The all-rounder had been recruited as a commentator by Australia's Channel Nine network. Without envy, he was in raptures.

'Fan-tas-tic, Kepler,' Rice declared.

'Thanks, Clive.'

As the two men debated the evening's events, Rhodes appeared from the opposite end of South African cricket. 'It's the captain, my captain,' he shouted, high-fiving Wessels. The young man was on an unforgettable high. So was South Africa.

Eventually the captain reached his room and slept. February 26th, 1992 was over. A cricketing nation had been born again.

\* \* \* \* \*

Why must every great party be followed by a hangover? The following morning, the South African group flew to Auckland and were brought down to earth by what they regarded as the obstructive behaviour of local organisers. When practice facilities are poor and unavailable when you want them, cricket tours become a hassle.

'The other problem was of our own making,' Wessels remembers. 'We had focused all our preparation, physical and mental, on that first match against Australia. We studied their players and planned our tactics, but there had been no time to prepare anything for the other teams. We were going in blind. Sometimes, we didn't know if an incoming batsman was right or left-handed. It wasn't our fault. Everything was so frantic. There wasn't any time.'

The South Africans arrived to play New Zealand at Eden Park and, batting first, discovered Dipak Patel, a spinner, opening the bowling on a barren pitch of crusty, dusty mud. A spinner? The batsmen had hardly recovered from the shock before Patel had dashed through seven overs at a cost of only 13 runs.

Even though Kirsten struck a defiant 90, a target of 190 did not stretch the well-organised New Zealanders once Mark Greatbatch had erupted in a blaze of strokeplay. The home side cantered to victory with 15 overs to spare. Ouch.

'If we are going to play like that, we might as well go home tonight,' Wessels barked at his players. His side had been utterly outclassed and outplayed. He felt embarrassed. He reflects that he was too harsh on the youngsters. But it hurt.

From the gutter to the sewer. Only two days later, the heroes of Sydney were defeated by Sri Lanka in Wellington. 'We were facing the nightmare scenario,' Wessels remembers.

The captain's meticulously prepared batting strategy had been set aside amid increasing, but uninformed, pressure to hit out in the first 15 overs. Wessels had yielded and agreed to a proposal that Kuiper should be moved up the order to open the innings. It was wrong. There was a whiff of panic in the air.

In the event, Kuiper could not latch on to the irritating Sri Lankan bowlers, swung, missed and was dismissed cheaply. Now what? Order had been lost. Wessels grimly dug in and crawled to 40 in 94 balls, but he was batting far too slowly. Kirsten, of course, led a certain kind of recovery and, with Rhodes, took the total limping to 195. The innings had been a shambles.

Worse followed. Donald seized three early wickets, but then contributed to a farcically undisciplined bowling display. No fewer than 13 wides and four no balls were marked down and yet, even with such charity, it was only Arjuna Ranatunga's innings that took his rank outsiders to victory in the last over. He was so delighted he literally danced off the field with Ramanayake.

South Africa had no excuse for the defeat. If they had batted decently or if they had bowled decently, they would have won. They had done neither. Played three, lost two.

At home, extreme delight turned to extreme criticism. No one knocks their heroes like a disappointed South African sportsfan. Believe it? An overworked fax machine at the team hotel in Wellington after the defeat against Sri Lanka provided the proof.

'YOU'RE A NATIONAL DISGRACE, JOU ****.'
'KEPLER, YOU'RE ******* USELESS.'
'WHY DON'T YOU STAY IN AUSTRALIA, *****?'
'*******! *******! ******* ******!'

The fax number had been published in South African newspapers inviting supporters to send messages of goodwill. Following such a stunning defeat, the public began to fax bile.

'I don't think anyone who saw the pile of faxes that arrived for Kepler would believe it,' Jordaan recalls. 'I went through all of them and I could not understand why people went to so much trouble to be so abusive. Some were absolutely disgusting. In the end, Kepler told me he'd had enough, and I started throwing the negative ones away. He never saw them.'

A large section of the public regarded Wessels as the villain because, egged on by simplistic TV commentators, they believed the team's problems were caused solely by the fact that he preferred to provide a sure-footed start to the innings rather than launch a carefree assault from the first ball.

It didn't seem to matter much that he had played more than 60 one-day internationals in a career speckled with Man of the Series and Man of the Match awards. No matter that, innings after innings, he had played an impeccable anchor role. He didn't know what he was doing, did he? The television pundits, the preening fools with zero experience of international cricket, knew better.

The ignorant abuse from complete strangers hurt. Of course, it did. Wessels, however, was mentally strong enough to retain the strategy which experience told him was right, and he was encouraged by Jordaan's support. In hard times when Wessels seemed to cut a lonely and isolated figure, when even he appeared vulnerable to the erosion of self-doubt, the manager came through.

'Kepler was extremely upset,' Jordaan recalls, 'but I said we should keep to our battle plan. Before the World Cup, we had agreed that our basic target would be 200 runs in 50 overs and then to win the games with our bowling and fielding. We made the calculation on the basis of our strengths and weaknesses. Unless Kuiper came off, we didn't have the batsmen to reach 240 or 250.

'In the games against New Zealand and Sri Lanka, I thought we batted only marginally too slowly but we bowled very badly. Kepler was wondering whether to drop himself down to No.6 or No.7. I told him we'd be foolish to change our strategy. Something near 200 was usually a winning score. We all knew that and we needed him to open and provide a steady start. That was his job.'

Right words at the right time. Wessels listened carefully. He was grateful, and he knew Jordaan was right. The next day, at nets in Christchurch, he started to pick himself and his players off the floor. 'There are five matches left and we will have to win four of them to reach the semi-finals,' he said. 'In form, we can do that, but we must be more disciplined. That includes me.'

After two defeats, the South Africans might have chosen less demanding opponents than the West Indies in Christchurch, but there would be no respite. Again, they knew little about their celebrated opponents. Equally, the West Indians knew little about the gangling fast bowler from Cape Town named Meyrick Pringle.

By the end of March 5th, the West Indies knew all about Meyrick Pringle. He had been left out of the preliminary 20-man group, but forced his way into the World Cup squad on form. On one occasion he had sent the team into fits of laughter when, walking back to his mark, he asked the umpire how many balls were left in the over. 'Three,' came the reply. 'Is that three gone or three to go?' said Pringle. This day in Christchurch, he would prove you don't need a Masters degree to roll over the West Indies and thrill your country.

After South Africa had hit their declared batting target and scored exactly 200, Pringle seized the ball and tore the Caribbean stars apart: Brian Lara, neatly caught at point by Rhodes; Richie Richardson, trapped LBW; Carl Hooper, caught Wessels at slip; Keith Arthurton, also competently held by the skipper.

Pringle, arms and legs whirling with delight like some kind of crazed giraffe, had taken four wickets in the space of 11 balls. The West Indian total was 19 for four. Desmond Haynes, who retired hurt and bravely returned to bat later, and Gus Logie did not lie down but there was no way back into the match. The West Indies were beaten by 64 runs. All hail, Meyrick.

An extraordinary day had demonstrated both the strength and weakness of one-day cricket. Of course, it had been hugely exciting entertainment but it had also proved how the artificial structure of the game was so restrictive that one inspired individual effort would invariably be sufficient to seal victory.

'Anyone can beat anyone in one-day cricket.' The words were spoken by Border after Australia's defeat against South Africa, but they might have been the motto of the tournament. Each team had its plans and tactics, but one devastating spell of bowling or smashing display of batting could upset everything. Most matches defied any sort of meaningful analysis. They just happened. The World Cup was a multi-coloured game of poker. It wasn't chess.

Seasoned internationals, like Border, accepted this, and were consequently cheered by success but hardly dismayed by defeat. Two years later, the Australian captain would be asked for his memories of the World Cup match against South Africa. 'Not much,' he would reply. 'It was just another one-day game.'

If many players took a sanguine and relaxed view, the South African public, eagerly feasting after two starved decades, did not. Every match was 'crucial' and the victory over the West Indies was acclaimed. The fax machine at the hotel suddenly changed its tune, and the congratulations began to flow again.

'KEEP AT IT KEPLER.'

Jordaan read that fax and passed it on. The captain, however, was concerned by some unfinished business with the media. The South African players had been kept regularly informed by the UCB office of what the various reporters on tour were writing, and what the radio and TV commentators were saying at home, and he was livid. Put simply, he blamed them for encouraging the perception of him as the slow-scoring bad guy.

He had wanted to hit back following the Sri Lankan match, but he was experienced enough to know that it's best to keep quiet when things are going badly. He kept his powder dry until the correct moment presented itself, which it did following victory against the West Indians. Then, angrily, he struck.

'You guys just don't understand what's going on,' he told a huddle of South African journalists. 'You expect us to go out there and smack eight runs an over off Ambrose or Walsh. Well it's not like that at this level. The people back home don't understand either. They've got no idea. We're here trying to win a World Cup, and we're tired of being criticised by people who really don't know what they're talking about.'

Jordaan took it upon himself to repair the public relations machine. His first port of call was Wessels' hotel room.

Knock. Knock.

'Kepler, I think you should withdraw what you said about the people at home not understanding,' Jordaan pleaded.

'No, I meant what I said.'

'But, look at it this way, you're talking about everybody. That's not just the people sending faxes. That's my own family and Jonty's family, everyone. It's not right.'

'No. I'm sorry. I meant it. It's true. You know it's true and I'm not going to back down. There's no reason.'

Jordaan, who remembers his captain as being 'very adamant and difficult at the time', nimbly found a path out of the controversy by stressing to an SABC news team that the remarks were general and not intended to offend anyone. The teacup settled.

This episode was exceptional. In general, Wessels took care to maintain cordial relations with the media. He was never going to be a darling because he was not one of those ardently aware sportsmen who cynically make a point of greeting and flattering reporters in order to earn a favourable mention in dispatches, but he understood they had a role to play and a job to do.

Privately, like many prominent sportsmen, he saw most of the media as people who had never played the game at the highest level and who could never understand the pressures. He respected few, and he confided in even fewer. That was his nature.

'People have told me that if I had been more trusting of the journalists, they would have written more positively, but I totally disagree with that,' Wessels states with conviction. 'I think you have got to be honest and straight with them because they have an important role but, beyond that, you should take them pretty much as you find them, as you would anyone else.'

Honest and straight, he was. Readily available, he would give a run-of-the-mill question a run-of-the-mill answer day after day. Peter Robinson, Colin Bryden, Ray Williams and Trevor Chesterfield, all experienced cricket writers, concur: they don't have a problem with Kepler. He was polite, helpful and decent.

'The empty wagon makes the most noise,' the American pioneers used to tell each other. Wessels would have accepted that. He left others to trumpet the banner headlines and manipulate the media. He was content to talk a less spectacular game... 'Obviously we'll be trying to win, but they're a very strong side...'

Their hopes revived by victory over the West Indies, Wessels' side were relieved to be leaving the obstructions and frustrations of New Zealand. Their next destination was Brisbane, the captain's home for seven years, and a match against Pakistan.

Hudson, Cronje and McMillan all batted effectively in hauling the South African innings to a defendable 211 in 50 overs, but this match would earn a prominent and celebrated place in the amorphous history of World Cup cricket because of an incident that took place during the 30th over of the Pakistani pursuit.

Inzamam-ul-Haq was joining Imran Khan in a charge towards the rain-reduced target of 194 in 36 overs when he pushed to the gully area and, with the required runrate soaring towards nine runs an over, set off for a burgled single.

Imran sent him back. Inzamam swivelled in mid-pitch. Rhodes, dashing in from cover point, gathered the ball without breaking his stride and sprinted for the stumps. He would not throw. He was going to back his pace against Inzamam. In a famous instant, Rhodes dived into the stumps with Inzamam five inches short. What a moment! The boyish grin was beamed all around the planet.

The run-out ended what faint hope Pakistan retained once rain had interrupted their pursuit and the ludicrous rules had reduced their innings by 17 overs but the target by only 14 runs. This day, South Africa took advantage and won by 20 runs. Such a transitory injustice was swiftly forgotten amid the excitement surrounding the Metro Goldwyn Mayer run-out by Jon-teeee.

By broad consensus, Rhodes had been lucky to go to the World Cup. His batting average was mediocre, his technique was unorthodox and batsmen of greater ability were left behind. Many of his fellow players had expressed disbelief when the grin-grinning 22-year-old from Natal was named in the squad. It seemed so unfair. What had he ever achieved? A solitary first class century.

His selection, however, was inspired. Brilliantly agile at cover point and infectiously enthusiastic, he was swiftly adored by the crowds and media alike. His fielding galvanised his team-mates, and he improvised neatly and briskly with the bat.

Wessels enjoyed having the grin around. 'Jonty was a positive influence on the team,' the captain notes. 'He and Hansie (Cronje) would field on opposite sides of the wicket and keep everyone on their toes. That enabled me to concentrate on the strategy. Once or twice, he probably went over the top and said the wrong thing at the wrong time but he never meant any harm. That was how he was. It was his sheer tenacity that got him through.'

Even though his name went up in lights, a nagging suspicion lingered among fellow provincial players that Rhodes was all teeth and extravagant grandstanding, that he did not have the talent to feed his image, that he would soon be found out. Even the famous diving run-out was regarded as something out of the shop window. If Inzamam had stretched an extra six inches back into his ground, the fielder would have been rightly criticised for not throwing at the stumps. In sport, the difference between glory and disgrace can be tiny. Inzamam was out, and Rhodes was made.

In subsequent matches, however, the new idol proved doubters wrong, those in the Press box, those in the stands and those in the dressing room. He produced the performances. Who needs the textbook when you've got guts and a temperament like that? Peers ate their words. Rhodes became an instant selection and one of South Africa's most idolised personalities.

This 'Jontymania' stretched far beyond the hearts of panting teenagers. On the back of a squeaky-clean image as a wholesome winner, he became a commercial force, endorsing a brand of trousers, computer games and a campaign to promote a wider understanding of epilepsy, a disease from which he, himself, had suffered.

Fame, happily, did not go to this freckled head. When a high quality car manufacturer invited him to drive one of their luxury sedans soon after the World Cup, Rhodes politely turned them down, explaining that a less glamorous firm had offered him a smaller car when he was nothing more than a young hopeful and that, on balance, he felt he ought to remain loyal to them. He hoped they understood. Fair head in demand, feet firmly on the ground.

God helped.

Some years before, Rhodes was prompted by the pressure of top-class cricket to be 'born again' as a Christian. 'From that moment, religion became the dominant force in my life,' he says.

Through the stresses and trials of the World Cup, several of the South African players had joined Jordaan, the manager, in a prayer group which began to meet on a regular basis. Jordaan, who had been 'born again' in 1987 and had become a lay preacher at a Pentecostal church, provided the impetus for a development which some regarded as sinister, muttering about a Bible-bashing clique, but which was utterly inoffensive and may have been inspired.

Jordaan recalls: 'It all began early in the tour when Kepler spoke to me in a general manner about his faith. We had both made a strong Christian commitment, so we said we would get together and talk about it, and pray. After a while, Andrew (Hudson) and Jonty approached us and said they would like to join. It usually worked that we met before the matches but we didn't pray to win or score runs. We took ourselves to the Lord. We assured Him we were in His hands and we asked that we shouldn't let Him down. Whatever happened on the field, we confirmed we are available to Him. We said that we know when we go out there, we don't go out alone. We always have Him with us.' The effect of the prayers, and the overwhelming faith that supported them, was to relax the players. Wessels enjoyed it. 'I think it was good for Kepler to see other players sharing the same fears and doubts,' Jordaan says.

Victory over Pakistan took South Africa to third in the log, as confidence grew again. The semi-final was not far away. Two more wins from their last three matches would be sufficient to secure a place among the last four. Life was exciting.

Only 3 165 spectators turned up in Canberra to witness South Africa dispatch Zimbabwe with a big brotherly shove. Kirsten, still razzle-dazzling on the international stage, nabbed three wickets as Zimbabwe were bowled out for 163, and then scored an unbeaten 62 in the sure-footed chase. Wessels hit 70, and two more points had been packed away with almost five overs to spare.

Another flight, another hotel, another day to remember. South Africa had not played England (that is official England as opposed to Gooch's England or Gatting's England) for 27 years. History flowed fast (and with ice, thanks) at the Melbourne cricket ground as officials toasted another 'joyful' day. Out on the field, there was yet another 'crucial' match to be won.

On the evidence of six matches, South Africa had been widely branded as better hounds than hares in the belief that they could chase a score, but they struggled to set the pace. England invited them to bat first, expecting the consensus to be proved again.

It wasn't.

After 35 overs, the total was 151 for no wicket. Hudson, who finished with 79, and Wessels had found a prosperous rhythm and the captain continued to thrive briskly until he was dismissed for 85 in the 46th over. The critics held their tongues. He had played an ideal anchor, and the subsequent onslaught bolstered the total to a stately 236 for four in 50 overs.

Alec Stewart and Ian Botham launched the chase but, with the total at 62 without loss, another of the irritating autumn showers which were fast putting a dampener on the tournament blew in to distort the target and the contest. The batsmen finally returned to find they had lost nine overs but their target had been reduced by only 11 runs. When Botham, Smith and Hick departed within the space of eight deliveries, England seemed doomed.

They weren't and, as the South African bowlers strayed, Stewart and Fairbrother launched a heroic fightback that took their team to victory with a ball to spare. England were installed as hot favourites but, six days later, they lost to Zimbabwe. 'Anyone can beat anyone': the words of Allan Border would not go away.

South Africa's task was now simple: they had to defeat India at the Adelaide Oval to win a place in the semi-final. When Wessels was woken by the pitter-patter of falling rain on the window of his hotel room, he sighed. This most consequential of matches would be reduced by more wretched weather to the competitive level of Blind Man's Buff. After some grey hours of skyward glances, the drizzle subsided and the umpires made their calculations.

They would play 30 overs per side.

Ready, steady, smash.

The Indians, already eliminated and demoralised after a hard tour of Australia before the World Cup, were longing for home, but Mohammad Azharuddin responded to the challenge and crashed 78 in 77 balls and when Kapil Dev contributed 42 in 27 balls, it seemed as if the game was running away from South Africa. India ended with an imposing total of 180 for six in 30 overs.

Amid growing tension, Wessels remained the model of cool and calm experience. He decided to drop himself down the order, enabling the wonderfully in-form Kirsten to open the chase with Hudson. This was not an admission of weakness on the captain's part. It was rather a gesture of quality under pressure.

It paid off. Hudson hit 53 and Kirsten struck a fine 83. They had taken their team most of the way but, when Kirsten was finally bowled by Kapil, South Africa still required 24 runs from the last three overs. Everything, all their effort, the whole campaign came down to this last challenge. Win and they would be heroes. Lose and they would be failures. Stand or fall.

Wessels, batting at No.5 in the order, approached the crease and supplied the composure when it was needed most. Manufacturing a run a ball and striking anything remotely off line for four, he piloted the final surge with such authority that, when Cronje pulled the winning boundary, there were still five balls left. Not a one-day player?

Ring the bells.

They would be heroes.

While established teams such as the West Indies and Australia were eliminated, Wessels' young squad had finished third on the log and were advancing confidently on the semi-finals. The captain recalls, 'We'd had some luck, notably in the game against Pakistan, but I felt we had earned our place in the last four.'

Kirsten remembers the atmosphere in the changing room at the Adelaide Oval after victory over India as among the finest feelings of his career. Each player celebrated his own personal achievement but, for this prime batsman, the World Cup had unfolded as at once a glorious vindication and a triumphant healing.

He was vindicated because he had proved to the selectors who left him out of their preliminary squad that, at 36, he was not too old to compete; and he was healed because, after all the years with his nose pushed up against the window of international cricket, he had finally found a way inside and proved that he could score runs against the world's best teams. Plenty of runs.

The revelation of Kirsten had been superlative: an unbeaten 49 against Australia, 90 versus New Zealand, 47 against Sri Lanka, 56 versus the West Indies, a calf injury ruled him out of the game against Pakistan, 62 not out against Zimbabwe, 11 versus England and then the fizzing 83 against the Indians. An aggregate total of 399 runs left him as the leading scorer in the tournament after the group matches. Average: a princely 79.8.

Amid the excitement of success, he did not forget how he had almost been left behind. 'It was obviously a great shock to be left out of the first squad,' Kirsten recalls. 'The turning point for me was in Harare. I had thought it was the support of Kepler and Mike Procter that had got me back into the squad and, before the warm-up match against Zimbabwe, they came and told me that I was the first choice No.3 batsman and that they were backing me. That made a huge difference, and I really just built on that.'

If Kirsten held the batting together, there was no doubt that the primary strength of the squad was the fast bowlers. In Donald, Snell, Pringle and McMillan, Wessels commanded an enviable battery of seam and pace. They were talented. All of them. But, at stages, they also conceded a bewildering rash of wides and no balls. The white ball, the bowlers complained, was hard to control. Procter, the coach, went to work. He took the bowlers to the nets, laid down a towel just outside the line of off-stump and asked them to hit it again and again, but the problem would not go away. The bowlers, notably the increasingly vocal Donald, grew frustrated with Procter; and Procter grew frustrated with the bowlers.

Tempers frayed and some of the bowlers began to complain that Procter was unable to identify technical problems. They said he had been such a natural in his own career that he had never studied the game closely. They said, he's a nice guy, but ... Wessels noted the conflict and backed his coach: 'He was firm with them, and that was right,' he recalls. 'Proccie was doing his job.'

The fast bowlers, almost as cricketing tradition demands, had started to keep to themselves on tour, grumbling about prima donna batsmen, feeling overworked and unappreciated. They were upset when the captain expected them to bowl in the nets for as long as the batsmen wanted. 'Why can't he get local bowlers if he wants to bat all day?' they groaned. 'We're exhausted.'

When, late in the tournament, the captain wanted the team to practise immediately after arriving at a new venue, several of the fast bowlers asked him if they could have a day off.

'Fine,' Wessels replied. As a batsman-captain, he had been gently accused of not understanding the bowlers' problems, but this was not the case. He admired their talent and constantly considered their welfare. Admittedly, he was frequently amused by their simple antics, but the truth was that he cherished them.

Donald was the big gun. 'I got to know him well,' Wessels says, 'and I realised I had to be calm with him. There was no point giving him a kick up the backside. I wanted to keep his confidence high, and that meant telling him he's our number one strike bowler and saying how we relied on him. That was true. When he was firing, the whole team got a lift. On the other hand, if he was struggling, everyone seemed to be on a bit of a down.'

Pringle was the big heart. 'I knew all about Meyrick from Eastern Province and I wasn't worried about him,' Wessels says. 'He is talented and he gives it everything every time he bowls. I have a lot of time for him because he gets the job done.'

Snell was the big brain. 'I think a few people are fooled by Richard,' Wessels says. 'He comes across as being ultra-relaxed but, behind the cool facade, there is a very determined individual. He wants to succeed very badly. I liked him a lot.'

McMillan was the big talent. 'His main quality is that he's a really aggressive cricketer,' the captain says, 'as a bowler and a batsman. I enjoy that. He goes looking for the batsman with bouncers and stuff, and he's got a big heart. Off the field, I used to tease him about moaning but it was just a bit of banter. All the way through the World Cup, he was great.'

There were disappointments as well. Kuiper had arrived at the World Cup touted as an explosive big-hitter second only to Botham. The memory of his century in 49 balls against the English rebels in Bloemfontein was still fresh in the public's mind, but he began to labour under the burden of public expectation.

Hard though he tried, and he tried mightily, the burly apple farmer from Elgin could not find the same form at the World Cup. He emerged as a valuable vice-captain, but the sparkle in his eyes was dulled by his lack of success. When, training at the SCG before the semi-final, he clubbed the ball clean out of the nets with familiar strength and timing, he turned to a group of onlookers and remarked sadly: 'It only happens in practice.'

South Africa's semi-final, it had now become clear, would be against England in Sydney on March 22nd, but first there was a bigger match to be played back home. If that was lost, the South African team might have to be withdrawn from the World Cup.

State President F.W. de Klerk had called a referendum for March 18th, four days before the semi-final. The white, coloured and Indian voters were to be given a simple choice: YES or NO to reform, make or break, adapt or die, move forward or backwards.

'If there is a NO vote,' Dakin, the UCB president, had told journalists in Australia, 'it will be impossible for us to continue within the competition.' Such a result had seemed unlikely when De Klerk announced the referendum to reaffirm his mandate against right wing opposition yet, as the day of decision neared, the arithmetic seemed less encouraging. When, 48 hours before the poll, the *Sunday Times* front page headline declared ON A KNIFE EDGE, the message got through to the increasingly worried cricket team at their hotel in Sydney that nothing could be taken for granted.

Wessels, far from home and nervous, could not have been more forthright in his *Sunday Times* column before the referendum, urging readers 'VOTE YES for a fair and prosperous future.'

They did, in unforeseen numbers. At an emotional time when the country's destiny seemed to lie in the balance, the result from the Port Elizabeth region was the first to be declared on the TV special. The YES campaign was hoping for a 55 per cent win to indicate a positive national trend... 'Port Elizabeth — 74 per cent YES'.

Something startling was happening. When all the results had been gathered, the final YES vote was declared as 68.7 per cent. De Klerk stood on the steps of Tuynhuis and, voice taut with emotion, proclaimed 'the closing of the book on apartheid'. National transformation, it later became clear, would not be so straightforward. Many difficult days lay ahead before a settlement was reached, yet the referendum still stands in history as a major watershed.

Whisper it. How many voters were swayed not by an urge to put right the wrongs of apartheid but by a desire to watch South Africa compete in the World Cup semi-final against England? Probably very few, even in this most exceptional electorate, but the cricket factor was without doubt a major boost to the YES campaign.

The success of Wessels' team at the World Cup had offered an appetising, and irresistible, glimpse of the sort of pleasures and excitement which could be aroused by being part of the world again. For an entire generation, this was a new sensation. Vote NO, and go back to the bad old days of isolation? For every cricket supporter glued to his television, it was unthinkable.

Wessels received the result of the referendum at his Sydney hotel and was soon posing for photographers, showing the thumbs-up sign. Thank goodness. Back to work. A place in the World Cup final against Pakistan (who had chased down a large New Zealand total to win the semi-final in Auckland) was one game away.

One game, one day away.

'We were just trying to keep the momentum going,' Wessels recalls. 'Things seemed to be going our way and some of the guys were starting to think that our name was on it. Sometimes, you just get the feeling that things are meant to be.'

The contrast between the nervous side that arrived at the SCG to play Australia on February 26th and the team that bounded eagerly into the ground for the semi-final on March 22nd was astounding. They had come a long way in little more than three weeks, on and off the field. Then, the Australian crowd had seemed so hostile but, today, the ockers on Yabba's Hill were supporting South Africa. They might well have backed anyone against the genetically hated English, but their enthusiasm was a reflection of how effectively Wessels' side had presented themselves. People liked them.

When dark clouds moved in over the ground shortly before the start, the South African captain left the dressing room to consult the SCG's state of the art meteorological equipment. He had inspected the pitch and wanted to bowl first but, if it was going to rain much later in the evening, then that tactic might be courting disaster.

The ground official studied the high-tech radar readings and told Wessels there would probably be a ten-minute shower much later in the evening, but nothing more. He added it shouldn't affect the playing hours. That was fine. Wessels resolved he would bowl first if he won the toss. He did...

Donald, wide eyes, roars in. Gooch edges. Howzzzzaaaaaaaaat! England are 20 for one, but the TV replay suggests the decision was harsh. Before too long, Botham is bowled by Pringle. Thirty-nine for two and Wessels senses his side are on a roll. Graeme Hick walks nervously to the crease, and Pringle is soon racing in. He bowls, pitched up, cutting back. The ball thuds into pads. Wessels doesn't even bother to appeal. He's racing up the pitch to celebrate. It's a sure-thing LBW. Thirty-nine for three. England are collapsing. Let's go.

Not out.

Wessels looks up, and swears. What? OK, OK, calm down, guys. back to your places. One of those things. Come on. Pringle is still shaking his head as he returns to his mark. His next ball is short of a length, drifting away. Hick edges towards first slip. Wessels steadies. He's got it. He holds the catch. Yes!

'On your way, Hick.'

Not out.

Wessels looks up, and swears again. The umpire is signalling a no ball. So it goes in cricket. Gooch was not out, but he's out. Hick is out twice, but he's still in. Calm down...

The Zimbabwean took handsome advantage of his early fortune, moving on to score 83 in 90 balls. Stewart and Fairbrother also hit hard and effectively before Reeve and Lewis provided carnage in the closing overs. Reeve struck Donald for 15 runs in one over, leaving Wessels standing solemn and silent at slip. England had reached 252 for six in 45 overs when the umpires called a halt because the allotted time for the innings had expired (the games were neatly structured to fit in with Australian television schedules).

South Africa were later accused of deliberately bowling their overs slowly to deny the rampant English batsmen a full quota of 50 overs. 'It wasn't our strategy from the start,' Wessels says, 'but, I admit, when I saw the rule could work in our favour, I didn't do anything to speed up the overrate. We had lost control of the whole situation. They were on their way to 300.'

The mood in the South African dressing room over supper was that the required runrate of 5.62 was steep. They knew they hadn't bowled well, but, hey, this is their World Cup, isn't it? They can do anything. Confidence still blinked bright neon.

Their chase was launched with vigour but Wessels and Kirsten, the two stalwarts, were dismissed before the total had passed 61. Hudson was moving neatly towards a fourth successive fifty, when a cricketing nation turned its heart to Kuiper. He had been promoted to No.4 in the order, and he appeared from the pavilion whirling his bat, striding out. Surely his luck would change. This was the man, and this was his moment. Sport does this sometimes. It sets up an occasion, brings all the ingredients together and sweetly, impeccably, dreams happen.

Kuiper, visored, took guard.

He settled calmly. South Africa urged him to swing hard... Gladstone Small bowls to Kuiper, who launches himself, shoulders, hips, soul, at the ball. Mid-on stares. Four runs.

Next ball. Small bowls. Kuiper pulls. Boundary.

Next ball. Small bowls. Kuiper cuts. Boundary.

Yes! Yes! Yes! An infinite number of South Africans leap up in front of an infinite number of television sets. It is happening. Kuiper is coming right. It's mid-morning from Pietersburg to Cape Town, but few have even thought of work. Portable televisions perch in crowded offices and cheering classrooms as people, some of whom had never previously shown any interest in cricket, arch their backs to get a clear view. That's it! Come on, Kuiper, man.

Silence.

Kuiper is out for 36. Years later, he would reflect on the innings as a door to glory through which he did not step. 'I felt so good. It was all there,' he would rue.

Still there was hope. Like the small brother forever tagging along, the South Africans would not be shaken off the pursuit of victory. Cronje bustled a brisk 26 and Rhodes improvised a swift 43. They always seemed some 20 or so runs off the required rate, but they were never so far off the mark that anyone could say they were out of it. With guts, they were hanging in there. When McMillan and Richardson found each other at the crease, 44 runs were required in five overs.

They needed boundaries, and Richardson provided two of them, one crashed memorably through extra cover. With McMillan scampering invisible singles, some of England's bowlers were starting to wilt. Lewis conceded 15 runs in one over and South Africa seemed to have seized an ominous momentum. Twenty-two were needed off 13 balls.

Suddenly, the evening air seemed to turn cold. Wessels, sitting beside Jordaan on the balcony outside the dressing room, braced. No, this can't be. Not now. He looked up at one of the floodlight pylons, and saw the first signs of driving rain illuminated against the night sky. There was no mistaking it. Here's the promised shower. Both captain and manager immediately understood the consequences.

'We're stuffed,' Jordaan announced.

Out on the field, the England players were reaching out their palms to greet the rain like drought-stricken farmers. Umpire Brian Aldridge was quickly getting wet. He walked over to ask the batsmen and Gooch if they wanted to continue. McMillan could hardly get the words out fast enough. Yes, he certainly did.

The England captain turned to face the umpire: 'Brian, do you believe the conditions are fit for play?'

'No,' Aldridge replied.

'All right, I think we had better go off.'

Allan Lamb, standing behind the umpire, had been frantically signalling at Gooch to leave the field, and he led the pale blue charge to the pavilion. There's no doubt that the English players were relieved to see the rain rescue them from what was becoming a dangerous, probably a 50/50, position.

During the 12-minute downpour, the umpires together with the coaches and managers of both sides, Mickey Stewart and Bob Bennett of England, Procter and Jordaan of South Africa, gathered next to the pitch to discuss the situation, also to be seen to be active by an increasingly restless and frustrated crowd.

There was, however, no dispute. Everyone knew the rules. The rain fell for 12 minutes. That meant two overs would have to be cut from the innings, so there would be one ball left. The target was then reduced by the number of runs England had scored in their two least productive overs. They were both maidens.

Jordaan returned to an emotional dressing room and, again, found the right words at the right time. 'Guys, I'm afraid that's it,' he told the team. 'Those are the rules and we have to accept them. Let's stay calm. Let's behave properly.'

The umpires finally returned to the middle, followed by the players, with McMillan, his thunderous face matching the weather, and Richardson trudging slowly, sadly behind. When they reached the crease, the massive scoreboard confirmed what they had already been warned would be the adjusted match situation:

South Africa require
22 RUNS
from
1 BALL

The crowd groaned as one. The rain rule, devised to promote close finishes, had been emphatically revealed as a nonsense. Lewis cantered in to bowl, McMillan disconsolately patted back a single, and that was that. Amid farce, England had won.

Weather conditions were now perfect. The rain had passed as swiftly as it arrived. It was just after 10 p.m. on a summer evening and a World Cup semi-final was finishing two overs early because of an ill-conceived rule. This wasn't a tragedy. No one died. It was, however, cricket gone wrong, deplorably wrong.

At the end, the South African players cascaded down the steps from their changing room to congratulate and shake hands with the Englishmen as they left the field. When it would have been easy to sulk, they kept their heads high and said thanks for the game. Back inside several minutes later, Kirsten gazed out on the SCG stands and made an inspired suggestion to his team-mates.

'Come on,' he suggested with a grin. 'We're not coming back. Let's do a lap of honour. We deserve it.'

Happy endings. The entire beaming squad, all except McMillan and Richardson who were still taking off their kit, filed back on to the field and started to jog around the boundary. Kuiper had rushed out with a towel wrapped around his waist. All the tension fell away in an instant. It was over, but it had been fun. Hands clap-clapping above their heads, the team thanked the Sydney spectators who, section by section, stood and cheered their appreciation back. Wessels choked up again.

The captain felt no sense of injustice. 'We weren't cheated,' he recalls. 'We gambled on the weather and lost. There was no anger, just a lot of disappointment. Some of the guys were upset. We had come a long way and it was an unsatisfactory way to lose, but the same rules had worked in our favour against Pakistan.' Jordaan looks back and agrees, adding: 'In truth, we didn't play well that night. It would have been worse if we had outplayed England.'

The South African players, tired but happy, were not booked to fly home for another five days and most took advantage by going to watch Pakistan defeat England in the final at Melbourne. In their group match, the Englishmen had bowled Pakistan out for 74, but the match was then washed out and the single point Pakistan received for the no-result draw had been crucial in taking them into the semi-final. Such was the World Cup of 1992.

Bad weather, the indifferent Australian performance and the rules made for television, not the game, had combined to undermine the status of the tournament but South Africa's emergence had been one bright beacon in the gloom.

When the flight home was delayed for three hours, the squad grumbled. When they were informed that Bacher had arranged a parade on an open-top bus through the streets of Johannesburg for the next morning, the groaning grew louder. They simply wanted to go home to their families... 'What's Bacher up to now?' The players had not the slightest inkling of what lay ahead, of how their efforts had captured the imagination of millions, no concept of how South Africans had reacted to seeing their team reach the World Cup semi-final. The weary heroes yawned.

Jan Smuts airport had never known such a scene. Thursday was becoming Friday. It was midnight. The international arrivals hall would usually have been populated by several round-Africa backpackers sleeping on a luxury bench. Not on March 27th. Around 7 000 cheering and chanting supporters had packed themselves into a hall no larger than an average rugby field. Festival, everywhere.

'We want Jonty! We want Jonty!'

When the aircraft touched down on South African soil, several players saw floodlights on the tarmac. 'Is that emergency services? Maybe there's a problem.' There wasn't. It was television cameras, broadcasting The Homecoming live on TV. Gathered before the cameras was a group of the wives and girlfriends, flown to Johannesburg by the UCB and ushered in beside the aircraft.

The heroes were reunited with their loved ones and escorted into the terminal and on to the balcony overlooking the sea of faces. Wessels led the way, and seized the microphone to thank the crowd. The players were introduced to the crowd one by one, each man bathed in cheers.

Homemade banners were unfurled. JONTY WILL YOU MARRY ME?... I LOVE SNELL... KEPLER FOR STATE PRESIDENT... Encore. Encore. Uproar. On past two in the morning. When the players were finally driven to the nearby hotel where they would sleep, Rhodes was almost trampled by a herd of yelping teenagers.

The team's popularity had stretched beyond cricket. They were the image of earnest, hard-working South Africans. Not one of them was a smoker, few guzzled alcohol, they were all brave. Best of all, they had taken on the world and, so the hordes believed, only lost because of unfair rules. They were truly adored.

Next day more than 40 000 people lined the streets of Johannesburg as the squad paraded through ringing cheers and multi-coloured ticker tape to a reception outside the City Hall. It was a day of bright sunshine and broad smiles and just a little madness. One woman, old enough to know better, too happy to care, heaved into a barrier and screamed:

'Jonty! Jonty! Jonty!' She yelled to the world that she had six daughters and the instant celebrity could take his pick.

'We were all amazed by the welcome,' Wessels recalls. 'We had no idea the public reaction would be so great. In some ways, it was all a bit scary but it was a great experience. Once you've had a day like that, no one can take it away from you.'

All night at Jan Smuts, all day in the city, no one had mentioned the names Cook and Rice. 'It's impossible to say if either of them would have made a difference,' Wessels says. 'There were times when we could certainly have used their experience. I'm sure we wouldn't have done any worse with them. Another player we missed was Craig Matthews. He could have been very effective in the conditions. The selectors admitted that later, but we had done well.'

Generous about the faxes, pragmatic about his rivals, proud of his team-mates: all this on the outside. The iron man inside had his own agenda . . . prove the critics wrong. They said he could not bat properly in one-day cricket, they said he was boring, they said he was negative. Even amidst the applause and jubilation, the basic competitor remained fierce, focused, angry.

He returned to Port Elizabeth after the parade on the Friday afternoon. The following Monday he was back in charge of an Eastern Province first team net session, still working because the Benson and Hedges night series final against Western Province was due to be played at the Wanderers stadium just two days later.

St George's Park felt like home again. Life had settled down after the bickering. Wessels had reasserted authority at the start of the 1991/92 season and the team had begun to win again. His own form was outstanding (his first class batting average in the first four months of the season was 132.50). Centuries in both innings of a match against Free State had set his side firmly on track for a third Currie Cup title in four years and, even when he was absent during February and March, his influence remained.

The Castle Cup, as the Currie Cup was known after unity, had been clinched while the captain was in Australia, but he returned to be doubly motivated for the night series final: first, the match offered him an opportunity to mock further those who had tried to oust him as Eastern Province captain by winning yet another trophy; and second, he itched to show the usually hostile Johannesburg crowd, many of whom doubtless had used their fax machines during the World Cup, that he could perform in one-day cricket.

The occasion neatly lined his critics up against the wall. He prepared studiously, and scored 103, leading his side to a dazzling victory before a capacity crowd of 17 500. Western Province had hit an imposing 244 for two in 45 overs, but Wessels had taken his side on an assured chase, which was completed with five balls left. Raising the trophy, he felt vindicated. His critics were stilled. They would shout again, of course. That's cricket. Ups and downs. But, that night, they were delightfully quiet. It was April 1st and there was no doubt who were feeling like fools.

Sitting in the changing room after the match, Wessels found himself confronted by a young boy asking for a piece of his kit 'as a souvenir'. It was a bold request, but the boy received a just-used pair of batting gloves for his trouble.

'Thanks, Kepler. You're the tops,' he said, and left. At the end of another happy night, Wessels smiled again. Outwardly contented, inwardly satisfied. His season, however, was not over. No rest yet. Two days later, he was expected in the Caribbean.

\* \* \* \* \*

'Call for you, Dr Bacher. It's Kepler.'

The buzz of activity in the UCB office has been sustained by the proposal of a visit to the West Indies in April 1991, starting a week after the World Cup. More history to organise. The team captain is on the line. He's concerned.

Clyde Walcott and Steve Camacho, officials of the West Indian Cricket Board, have visited South Africa and proposed a lightning tour consisting of three one-day internationals and a five-day Test in Barbados. That's all. A take-the-money-and-run job.

'Morning, Kepler. What's news?'

The captain explains his anxiety about throwing his team into a test against the West Indies without adequate preparation. He points out that the side won't have played any first class cricket for almost three months before being hurled in against the world's most successful Test side at the Kensington Oval, a ground where the West Indies have not been beaten since 1935.

Bacher understands this and knows that, in cricketing terms, the schedule is formidable, but the first ever tour of the Caribbean by South Africa was going to be of such phenomenal political and diplomatic value that it simply could not be turned down. In a drive to present encouraging images of cricket in the townships and to embrace more old enemies, the cricketing needs would have to be set aside.

'But couldn't we have one or two first class warm-up matches before the Test?' Wessels pleaded hopefully.

'Sorry,' Bacher replied. 'There isn't enough time.'

Fair enough?

On April 4th, a week after their victory parade, the World Cup squad was flying to Jamaica. Although Corrie van Zyl later replaced the injured McMillan, the squad had initially been retained lock, stock and barrel. The decision was hailed as a vote of confidence but, in truth, it represented another set of basic selection principles being casually and expediently discarded.

The panel had not even met to discuss the issue. A series of telephone calls sufficed. There was no debate about whether a squad picked expressly for a one-day tournament could also be regarded as the best available combination for a five-day Test, or whether some players were so exhausted that they needed a rest.

Thus, the South African squad that was joyfully welcomed in Jamaica appeared, in motoring terms, to be running on empty. Their selectors had neglected the chance to make changes and effectively refuel. They looked tired, felt tired, were tired. It was true, of course, that the West Indians had also been at the World Cup and might also have been exhausted but their years of experience had taught them how to pace themselves, settling into a smooth rhythm without burning on all cylinders. The earnest South Africans, by contrast, had charged into each game since readmission with passion and verve, never easing their foot off the accelerator. Now, five months on, they were out of petrol.

This largely explains why South Africa were thrashed in each of the three one-day internationals that opened the tour. Hustled into action 48 hours after arriving, given no time to get used to the conditions, they were hammered by 107 runs in Jamaica, then by ten wickets and seven wickets in Trinidad.

Off the field, however, the tour was a triumph. In Trinidad, the flashpoint of anti-apartheid demonstrations during an England tour six years earlier, the one-time representatives of apartheid received a standing ovation when they first emerged to jog round the ground. Wounds were healed on the cricket field.

The captain found little consolation in the reception. He was more concerned about what appeared to be a dramatic collapse in form. 'We were down,' he recalls, 'and it was becoming difficult to motivate the guys. I tried to keep their focus on the Test.' Several solid days of practice in Bridgetown, Barbados served to steady the team ahead of their seemingly impossible task and, as the match neared, the fates began to smile on the tourists.

The West Indians were confronted by troubles of their own. Richie Richardson, the captain, was struggling to lead the side beyond the era of Viv Richards and Malcolm Marshall. He had been relentlessly booed in Jamaica ('The worst I've ever seen,' says Wessels), and he seemed even less popular in Bridgetown. The island unity, forged by Clive Lloyd during the 1970s, was threatened.

Barbadian cricket supporters were angry following a series of selection decisions which they felt revealed a strong bias against their island. Echoing a 'Transvaal' state of mind, they complained first when Richardson was preferred to Haynes (of Barbados) as the new captain, secondly when Marshall (of Barbados) was omitted from the World Cup, and finally when Anderson Cummins and Carlisle Best were left out of the Test team to play South Africa.

This anger was expressed in a widespread decision to boycott the Test match. As a result, the stands that were usually packed by can-clanking hordes yawned wide, almost empty. The Kensington Oval invariably intimidated the visitors but, this Test, it would be the home side who were unsettled by their surroundings. Over five days, no more than 6 500 people would pay to watch.

Wessels steeled himself again. On the day he became only the thirteenth cricketer to represent two countries in an official Test, he won the toss and followed his own instinct. Procter thought South Africa should bat first. Wessels had looked at the green pitch and wanted to bowl first. So South Africa bowled, but the pressure was again on the captain to justify his decision.

Shortly before tea on this first day, Wessels was standing at slip, hand propping up his chin, and looking across at a scoreboard that read 219 for three. The West Indies were in charge, but within two hours they had collapsed to 262 all out. When they might have rolled over, all his bowlers had stuck at it. Snell seized four for 83, accounting for three of the top four batsmen. 'It was exactly what we needed,' Wessels recalls. 'Test cricket is about applying pressure, and we had done that really well.'

Thirteen without loss overnight, the tourists lost Rushmere early on the second morning, bringing Wessels to the crease with a mission. He had taken upon himself the task of further emboldening his players. 'I wanted to play the West Indians the same way that I did when I was representing Australia: pouncing on anything short, and scoring quickly. If you get tied down by their quicks, you're asking for trouble. I had told the guys in teamtalks that we could get after them but, to be honest, I'm not sure they really believed me. I reckoned I would have to go out there and show them myself.'

Courtney Walsh lopes in to bowl. Short. Wessels shuffles into position and pulls. Boundary. South African players sit up in their seats. The skipper is having a go. During the course of the next 95 minutes, the mood in the tourists' dressing room changed from nervy fear to assertive aggression. Wessels, by reputation the pusher and prodder, ridiculed that image by striking five boundaries and a six in scoring 59 before getting out just after lunch.

He had altered the course of the Test.

'It was one of the finest innings I've ever seen,' says André Bruyns who was commentating for SABC TV. 'Kepler turned the whole psychological attitude of the team around. We lost an early wicket, we'd been stuffed in the one-dayers and morale was low. The players were grumbling about being tired and it looked as though we were in for a hiding. He just took them on.' Wessels' players were in awe. 'It was a top, top, top innings,' Snell recalls.

Hudson, in fine form since the latter half of the World Cup, remained and proceeded to play perhaps the bravest, finest innings of his career. Refusing to be overawed, the personable Natalian was dropped twice, on 22 and 66, but stood firm against whatever the West Indians threw at him. He seemed so calm.

Wessels admired his fellow opener for his technique and his powers of concentration but, above all, for his religious faith. It was surely that quality which enabled him to accept a stunning duck against India in Calcutta and a century in Barbados with the same disarming smile. Hudson prospered into the third day, ending with a memorable 163 in South Africa's total of 345. 'The lead was only 83 runs,' Wessels recalls, 'but it was a crucial advantage.'

Pressure. Pressure. Impose it. Resist it . . .

Donald rumbles in. Initially there is frustration when a ball hits Haynes' off-stump but fails to dislodge the bails. Then there is anger when Lara steps on his wicket and, when both umpires claim they were unsighted, refuses to walk. Finally, there is mirth. The South Africans relish a magnificent afternoon.

They rip through the West Indian batting, again. Donald takes three, and so does Snell. The fielding is electric and the catches stick. High five. High five. By stumps, the 'invincibles' are 184 for seven. The visitors' dressing room is alive because a victory which no one had thought remotely possible at the outset, suddenly seems distinctly probable. It's hard to believe.

The rest day is spent lounging amid the deep blues, lush greens and blinding sunshine of paradise, waiting for tomorrow. It is an atmosphere conducive to innocent dreams. Ten of the touring team are making their Test début. Their inexperience starts to tell amid foolish expectations of a stroll to victory.

One of the XI is not smiling, the one who played 24 Tests for Australia and learnt not to take anything for granted at this level of the game, especially against the West Indies. He knows very well that, even if Richardson's team lead by no more than 101 runs with three wickets in hand, the match is not over.

It wasn't. On the fourth morning, Jimmy Adams, the last recognised West Indian batsman, launched the fight-back in partnership with obstinate tail-enders. Benjamin, Walsh and Patrick Patterson all held their ground for substantial periods while Adams, who finished unbeaten on 79, cajoled the total to 283.

Priceless runs had been conceded in the most frustrating of circumstances and, true to fashion when life was hard, the captain was blamed. Some slammed him for not placing a sweeper on the cover boundary, others said he was too defensive. Maybe the truth lay in between. Maybe the strategy was about right. Maybe it was just one of those days when the ball beats the bat without finding the edge. Such days defy analysis, so hyenas seek a scapegoat.

South Africa were left requiring 201 to win. It still seemed a reasonable target, but the knowledge that it could, maybe should, have been around 150 began to stir some doubts. When Rushmere and Hudson soon departed, the match was slipping away.

Wessels and Kirsten came together on a deteriorating pitch that had begun to keep low and demonstrated their pedigrees as world class batsmen. Into line. Hit the bad ball. Stay positive. Wessels moved to 73. He seemed ready to win the Test on his own. By stumps, they had taken the score to 122 for two.

The captain called a team meeting that evening: 'Some of you may be thinking it's all over because we only need another 79 runs and we've got eight wickets in hand,' he said, 'but there's still a bit to do. You must understand the West Indian psyche. They won't give up until the last run is scored and if they see the slightest chance, they'll get right in there and take it. That's why they've become the strongest team in the world.'

Yeah. Yeah. Yeah. He's got to say that, hasn't he? The South Africans had been complacent once, and almost thrown the advantage away. Jordaan recalls frankly: 'It didn't really matter what Kepler said that night. Some of the guys couldn't help themselves. They looked at the scores and they had to fancy our chances. Looking back, I think it was almost impossible for us not to be a little complacent.'

The next day the team arrived at the ground no more than 79 runs away from a sensational victory, yet much depended on Wessels and Kirsten to sustain their partnership. When, having added just a single to his overnight score, the captain drove at Walsh and was caught by Lara in the slips, the team wobbled.

*Après Kepler, le déluge.*

Cronje lasted 13 balls. Kuiper was caught behind off a near unplayable delivery. Kirsten yielded for 52. Richardson scored two, Snell nought, Pringle four and Donald, the last man out, bowled for a duck. The last eight wickets had tumbled for 26 runs and, before the South Africans knew where they were, the West Indians were linking arms and setting off on a joyous lap of honour.

'It was a shattering experience,' Wessels remembers. The South African dressing room was silent. It felt as if four days of honest application, concentration, hard work and success had been thrown away in 90 mad minutes on the fifth morning.

That wasn't the whole story, of course. Ambrose and Walsh had both bowled, unchanged, with an overwhelming blend of speed, bounce and accuracy to steal the 52-run victory. Ambrose ended with four victims and Walsh with six for 34. In lambasting their team, some South Africans forgot to praise the bowlers.

Wessels admits to being bitterly disappointed because a rare opportunity had been missed, but he wasn't angry. 'Ambrose and Walsh were almost unplayable that morning,' he recalls. 'The point about Ambrose at his best is that he bowls wicket-taking balls, and he gives you nothing to hit. Some people said we were not positive enough and that we patted back half-volleys. That was nonsense. On that day, the West Indians were just too good, but we were a young side and I knew we had learnt a valuable lesson.'

The team had suffered a wound which would only be properly healed at the Sydney Cricket Ground almost two years later. Yet the oldest player in the team is able to provide some perspective on a bemusing morning. Peter Kirsten reflects: 'It was almost as though someone somewhere was saying, "Hold on a moment, you're going too fast. Let's have a bit of reality here." Everything had happened so quickly for us. It just wasn't meant to be so easy.'

Soon after the South Africans flew home, the West Indian Cricket Board of Control was able to announce that they had made a financial profit on a home tour for the first time in 15 years. The gate receipts may have been low in Barbados but BP South Africa, as sponsors, had paid all the touring team's expenses. On their return to Test cricket, South Africa were good box office.

Wessels arrived home in Port Elizabeth, exhausted. Only three months had passed since the selection row before the World Cup, but they had unfolded as three of the most dramatic and momentous months in all the 102-year history of South African cricket; and, at the heart of the action, the captain had sweated, plotted, prayed, coaxed, and batted his guts out.

He had taken a team of débutants to the World Cup semi-final and to the fringe of triumph in Barbados, from relative obscurity to the hearts of the nation. Long after the critics and their groans about slow scoring are forgotten, Wessels will be remembered as the man who successfully led South Africa in from the cold.

# 12

## Unity in Cricket, Healing the Land

It is just after two o'clock on another Tuesday afternoon outside the café where the wind swirls dust up into your face and where, at this time every week, the players stand and wait.

The Mamelodi under-16 cricket side, the only regular XI in the mighty township near Pretoria, are waiting for the bus that will drive them away from their ramshackle city to practise in perfect turf nets at the University of Pretoria...

They had been introduced to the game in 1987 by a dedicated lady primary schoolteacher, but all their coaching was halted in 1990 amid the protests against the English rebel tour. The scheme was not revived in Mamelodi until September 14th, 1991.

Hap-happy day. Tshepo Mokoena, bowling in the Tukkies nets for the first time, bounded in, hit the seam and cut the ball away from the right-hander. There was no edge, no wicket, but the boys whooped in admiration. They knew cricket. Through the long months without coaching, they had practised relentlessly in the streets, and now they were back, yearning for the learning.

Within three months they had progressed to a level where they could form a team and compete against most established white schools in Pretoria. One clean, dry afternoon, they lost by 30 runs to Afrikaans Hoër Seunsskool but there were side-effects far beyond the result. When the Affies teacher welcomed Mokoena by shaking his hand, he had done so in the African shake-clasp-shake style. Mokoena beamed, and his team felt accepted, maybe even healed.

Through the matches that followed, the Mamelodi team thrived. It is unlikely that any of them will grow up to represent Northern Transvaal, let alone South Africa, yet that was never the point of teaching them the game. This development scheme, like all the others presided over by the UCB around the country, was sport for sport's sake. No more, no less. It represented a concerted effort to broaden cricket's base, to put something into deprived lives and then to bring South Africans together through the game. It was not, as it has sometimes been portrayed, a hectic search to find a black fast bowler who will play for South Africa.

Judged on this criterion of breaking down barriers, expanding the cricketing population and healing the land, the UCB development programme succeeded over and over again ...

This Tuesday afternoon, however, the Mamelodi team is being driven to nets and Ephraim Mokonyama, a talented all-rounder who walked two kilometres to watch South Africa's World Cup matches on television at a friend's house, sits in the passenger seat, eyes glazed, dreaming. Approaching the Watermeyer Street on-ramp to the N4, the bus passes Wessels Street on the right.

'Wessels Street ... Kepler Wessels Street,' murmurs Mokonyama absent-mindedly, seeing the sign. 'He's a good player, eh? And he's a good captain as well. He's from PE, eh?'

At nets later that afternoon, Nicholas Maphopha was bounding in off his full run-up, with suncream daubed across his nose like Allan Donald. During fielding practice, Moses Matome was diving to stop a ball on the boundary, scrambling to his feet and hurling in a perfect low trajectory throw above the stumps. 'Jonty! Jonty!' he screams in delight. 'I'm our Jonty!' Batting, Mokoena rocks back on his heels, dabs a dainty late-cut down to the boundary at third man and declares: 'Kirsten. Just like Kirsten.'

All this may be too sugar-sweet for the hard-bitten cynics to accept. But it all happened. Boys who, hitherto, had no good reason to identify with any of their white compatriots (but many causes to resent them) suddenly found common ground. The plain fact is that the performance of the South African team, both at the World Cup and in the West Indies, had a massive impact on the development programme, firing enthusiasm and prompting many thousands of small incidents which, combined, helped to build the new nation.

When white parents watched their sons play against a township team, or when black boys played fixtures at white schools, or when white cricketers became heroes in the townships, the rusty cogs of reconciliation were grinding into action. If peace and justice beyond apartheid are to be earned as much by uniting the hearts and minds of a once bitterly divided people as by the signing of lauded documents, then history will judge that the country's cricketers played a major role.

Wessels' team had become a symbol of national unity, and, in recognition of their responsibilities, the players agreed to donate a percentage of their earnings to the development fund. 'We were all aware of the importance of development,' Wessels says emphatically. 'It was the future of the game, and quite a few of the players were involved in the coaching.' He himself had not participated in Eastern Province's development schemes on a regular basis, but he did contribute to raising the profile of sport in the townships through boxing (see chapter 13).

Bacher's commitment to development remained deep and conjunctive to the soul of the entire project. 'South African cricket stands on the brink of the greatest period in its history,' he wrote. 'It will triumph, I know, because unity and a resolve to take cricket to all the people in this country has brought a strength and sense of purpose that none of us have ever witnessed before.'

Into this exhilarating, emotional and historic mood stepped Mohammad Azharuddin and his talented squad. India's visit to South Africa in 1992/93 was dubbed the Friendship Tour and it would keep a promise made by the UCB when the Indians formally proposed South Africa's readmission to the ICC. 'You'll be the first team to tour the new South Africa,' Bacher said. So they were.

They appeared a strong side. Sachin Tendulkar, Ravi Shastri, Sanjay Manjrekar and Azharuddin headlined the batting. The usual array of spinners and seamer Manoj Prabhakar would bowl, and then there was the legendary all-rounder Kapil Dev. The UCB's marketing machine moved into gear. Hype, hype, hooray.

Never mind the facts. India had been thumped by four Tests to nil the previous year in Australia, seeming vulnerable to fast bowling. They had proved woeful tourists in recent times, winning a single Test match beyond their own shores since 1986 and, overall, they had won only six out of 65 Tests in the last decade. When they were held to a drawn Test by Zimbabwe on the way to South Africa, the publicity slogan became a desperate 'Don't underestimate them'.

As the tour turned out, underestimation would have been some feat. With the exception of one dazzling Kapil innings, India proved as thrilling and exciting as one of those roly-poly American boxers who habitually arrive in South Africa, promise much, hardly throw a punch and quietly slump to the canvas. Their visit would unfold not as a fanfare for the new era, more of a lullaby.

The South African squad, none the less, prepared as carefully as ever. Peter Pollock had replaced Peter van der Merwe as convener of selectors and the accusations that the panel was somehow against Transvaal players largely subsided. 'I like Peter Pollock very much,' Wessels says.

'He isn't influenced by anyone and he does the job as he sees it. That's excellent.' Some pointed out that Pollock had stayed away from top-class cricket for almost two decades before becoming a selector in 1991, but, as such, he found himself appropriately detached when he became convener.

With Wessels on the field, Procter in the nets, Pollock as convener, Bacher organising the office, and Krish Mackerdhuj as the president, the UCB hierarchy in 1992/93 proved itself as modern and efficient as any in the world. There was no stuffy pecking order, no bickering, no waffling, no long lunches: just a clear direction, a passionate unity of purpose and a shared zeal.

It worked. The UCB even devised a format for paying the national team that generally satisfied the players. Before the series against India began, it was agreed that all squad members would be contracted for six months and paid a monthly retainer which ranged from R3 000 for players on the top tier to R2 000 for those on the lowest tier. A three-tier structure had been established with the players ranked according to experience. They also received a match fee of R6 000 per Test and R2 000 per one-day international, plus an equal share of prize money and commercial revenue.

The contracts were later extended from six months to a full year, and adjusted to weight the retainer and reduce the match fee. By 1993/94, star players on the top tier were receiving R10 500 per month, those on the second tier R9 000 per month, and junior players on the lowest tier were paid R7 500 per month. Match payments were set at R3 000 per Test and R1 000 for a one-day international, all of which meant that the leading South African players were receiving something in the region of R175 000 per year.

Added to a provincial contract, revised because of absence, worth, say, R30 000 per season and an equipment sponsorship of, say, R15 000, it becomes clear that the players had started to share in the financial rewards of readmission. These figures were comparable with those set down in other top cricket nations.

When a marketing consultant, Keith Griffiths, was appointed to handle the squad's commercial affairs, the idea was received in some minds that the cricketers were enjoying a bonanza. They were not. The time demands of international cricket, which took players away from home for months on end, were such that it was impossible to pursue another career. Through isolation, most South African cricketers had been semi-professional but, for most of the national side, the game was now their sole source of income.

'It was hard for some of the guys,' Wessels reflects. 'They had to reorganise their lives to a degree, so it was important that we established the system of a properly contracted squad.' And most of the players were satisfied. Why not? They were earning almost as much as the country's leading rugby players.

The Indian squad, meanwhile, were being seduced by the famed hospitality that South Africa extends to visiting teams. The most useful word in the vocabulary of any serious touring squad in South Africa is 'No' as in 'No thank you. We're busy'. Azharuddin's team usually said 'Yes'. In the first week of their tour, they attended the UCB welcome banquet, were presented to Nelson Mandela, visited a farm outside Lenasia where Mahatma Gandhi once lived, launched a card promotion, and had supper with Nicky Oppenheimer.

A child of the mining dynasty, Oppenheimer had built his own cricket ground in Midrand, north of Johannesburg and, by making a substantial contribution to the development fund, had purchased the honour of staging the opening match of each incoming international tour: a one-day fixture between the touring side and his very own team of provincial players.

The match was conceived in the tradition of the Duchess of Norfolk's XI game at Arundel which generally launches an Australian tour of England. But there was a difference. The Duchess of Norfolk didn't actually play herself. Oppenheimer did, and he rose to the occasion, striking a couple of boundaries against the Indians.

After the bonhomie in Midrand, the serious cricket began and the jokes stopped. So did the entertainment. Through a slow victory over a Bowl XI in Springs and a pedestrian three-day game against a President's XI at Centurion Park, Verwoerdburg, the tourists barely raised an eyebrow among the scattered spectators.

Brett Schultz, a 22-year-old fast bowler from Port Elizabeth, seized the vacant headlines and 'arrived' at Centurion Park when he produced enough bounce and pace to take five Indian wickets for 35 runs. A week later, the fair left-arm-over paceman was named in the South African side for the first Test at Kingsmead.

' From our point of view, the central conflict was between our bowlers and their batsmen,' Wessels recalls. 'On that basis, I felt fairly confident. If we could produce wickets with a bit of life, I reckoned we would have the beating of India.'

The first day of official Test cricket in South Africa for 22 years dawned still and quiet. Graceful Kingsmead waited. It was on this turf that Graeme Pollock struck 274 against the Australians in 1969/70, building the legend that would sustain the game during the dark days of isolation. Now the torch would be ignited again, and held high. The new era began on Friday 13th, 1993.

Durban had been awarded the first Test because the UCB hoped the local Indian population would respond to the presence of their mother country's team and generate a memorable atmosphere but, whether it was the high ticket prices or the unpopularity of five-day cricket, there were barely 6 000 people in the ground on the first morning. History was made with a murmur rather than a roar.

Wessels, of course, was more preoccupied with the contest. He had arrived at Kingsmead soon after nine in the morning, alone, the model of meticulous preparation and absolute concentration, to look over the pitch and ensure it was what he wanted. He was glad to see enough grass to provide a lively reception for the Indian batsmen. That was fine. Now he had to win the toss.

'Heads!'

Azharuddin, the only Muslim in a team of Hindus and a captain in need of success to secure his position, peered at the coin as it tumbled to the turf. It was heads. He grinned, with obvious relief, and indicated that his side would bowl first.

'Kepler, you must be disappointed to lose the toss,' asked Trevor Quirk, the SABC's anchorman with the captains before the game. Wessels, hands clenched behind his back, replied that it was a pity, but his side would make the best of it. His words hardly leapt with joy. They marched. His mind was racing elsewhere. Blast. It was a bad toss to lose.

Hudson would open the innings with Cook, who had bravely won back his place in the side by scoring a huge volume of runs. Making his official Test début at the ripe age of 39, the Transvaal opener prepared to face the first ball from Kapil Dev. Disaster. He pushed forward, edged towards third slip and Tendulkar swooped to seize the catch. Nought for one. Wessels strode into a crisis...

Awkward conditions, a legendary bowler in full flow: 'this is the sort of situation where, again and again, Wessels has shown the temperament and the mental toughness to succeed. Kapil bowls, it's overpitched and wide, Wessels rocks back and cuts it neatly to the third man boundary. Four for one. All right...

As the first day ran its course, Wessels emerged as the only batsman with the technique and application to survive. Soon after tea, South Africa were struggling at 194 for five, but the captain was still at the crease, proving his class.

His innings was not decorated with 24-carat gold drives past cover, nor with diamond-encrusted cuts glittering to the boundary. It was forged in iron and steel, in resolve and concentration. It was, in fact, sheer Kepler, sheer courage. He did not bat with the style of a Gower or a Richards, and he didn't bathe in the praise usually showered on the game's great talents, yet his innings was no less valuable or admirable for that.

The essence of Wessels' quality as a batsman at Kingsmead, in fact throughout his career, was, first, his ability to concentrate and ultimately prevail in a crisis and, secondly, a technique that was so carefully planned, devised and trained that it turned the art of batting into the science of gathering runs.

He explains his powers of concentration with a shrug: 'It's a question of self-discipline and not letting your mind wander. That comes from your basic approach to the game. People say I don't smile enough. Maybe it's difficult to smile and concentrate.'

His batting stance is not pretty but the stooped shoulders, the twitching toes, the short backlift and the prodding around the front pad are each a consequence of his evolving technique. He has adjusted and honed, forever working to minimise the risk of getting out. Tony Greig is one of those who believe Wessels has over-complicated what was once a free-flowing natural talent.

'I don't accept that,' Wessels says. 'I think my batting has improved as I've got older and that's because I have never stopped working at it, changing things to improve. People say I'm complex, but I think I have become more straightforward. My aim is always to be consistent. That's why I've spent so much time working out which are my "get-out" shots and stopped playing them.'

The lofted drive has gone. The head-high hook has gone. The airy waft down the leg-side has gone. The whirl of the bat outside off-stump has gone. In comes discipline, the Big D. His favourite scoring shots are relentlessly, impeccably executed: the square cut which is almost a chop, and the short-arm pull which is whipped off his hip. Solid, fruitful and reliable. These strokes were not born in the genes. They were developed in the nets.

There are some who believe he has taken the maxim of 'playing within your limitations' too far. They cite innings when he has cut loose in flamboyant fashion, such as his first innings in the Test against the West Indies, and they conclude that he has effectively imprisoned his talent in too many precautions. 'If I threw caution to the wind each time, I might come off once in every ten innings,' Wessels replies. 'That's not enough. I want to be more consistent than that, so I have to be more careful. That doesn't mean blocking everything. You judge each ball on its merits and be patient. If it is a good ball, you block it. If it's a bad ball, you hit it. Then, with luck, I'll come off six times out of ten.'

In the first Test against India at Kingsmead, with his team-mates falling around him, Wessels put this strategy into action. On a perilous first day, he scored 118 runs in 332 minutes of unbroken concentration. He faced 264 balls, 18 of which were 'bad' enough to be punished and dispatched to the boundary. Such controlled aggression ensured that his score was more than half the total throughout the day. The captain played the situation perfectly. If ever his status as a Test batsman is questioned, let the detractor watch the video tape of this day's play. Wessels was out shortly before the close, which South Africa reached at 215 for seven. (He had incidentally become the first man to score a Test century for two countries, though the fact hardly registered with him at the time.)

On the second morning the home side scrambled to 254 all out before the fast bowlers, Schultz and Donald, were finally let loose on the Indian batsmen. Their opening burst left the tourists 38 for four, and Wessels wishing he had won the toss.

The collapse was sustained with the assistance of an umpire sitting in the stand. In the stand? This was the latest innovation that South Africa had given to cricket: a third official watching television replays of run-outs and stumpings in the stand who, if called upon by one of the umpires on the field, could deliver his verdict via a row of lights in the grandstand.

Some players, including Wessels, would initially question the system, but Bacher pushed it through, arguing that 'if technology can help us get the decision right, we would be stupid not to use it. The game must develop.' Within 18 months, the third umpire was being used in internationals all around the world.

At Kingsmead, Tendulkar became its first victim, sent on his way by a flashing green light after Rhodes had pounced, but India would not roll over. Praveen Amre, on his début, led the long crawl back and they were finally dismissed for 277. With Schultz injured and inactive, South Africa had let their advantage slide away and the Test seemed neatly poised after three days.

It was neatly ruined when the fourth day was washed out by rain, leaving South Africa to make use of the final day as batting practice. Cook emerged from his golden duck trauma to hit a steady 43, but the words of an Englishman, Trevor Bailey, echoed round the empty grandstands: 'Cricket is a situation game,' he noted. 'When the situation is dead, the game is dead.'

Wessels, however, was satisfied. His team had played tough in a feeling-out process. 'We had obviously come a long way since the Test in Barbados. The guys had confidence in themselves and we were learning fast. People were quick to forget that the Indians were much more experienced than us in five-day cricket.'

The circus moved on to Johannesburg and a Wanderers stadium which had been transformed. The old scaffolding bullring, built in 1955, had been ripped down at the Golf Course end for the Centenary Stand and then at the Corlett Drive end to build the Unity Stand, a R23-million project that was part of the ambitious stand-building programme set in motion all around the country following readmission. South African cricket was on the move. The evidence was there in bricks and mortar.

As crowds flocked to the refurbished arena, they were treated to four days of magnificent, intriguing Test cricket and a bitterly disappointing fifth day that prompted debate about Wessels' ability as a Test captain. Welcome to Wanderers...

Day One: Bang! Prabhakar captures three wickets within the space of six balls, Rhodes on nought is dropped at slip, then Wessels is out. South Africa are caught cold at 26 for four. All-action Rhodes tries a single but seems to come short. Steve Bucknor, the neutral umpire from the West Indies, rules not out and declines to call for the third umpire. He opposes the innovation, says he can do without it. TV viewers watch Rhodes run out by a foot. Rhodes survives with Cronje and then McMillan. The middle order have stood their ground. South Africa reach the close at 226 for seven.

Day Two: Craig Matthews batters 31 but Pringle is hit on the eye socket and retires hurt. McMillan holds the fort, finally last man out, well caught at fine leg two runs short of the century he deserved. South Africa are all out 292. India collapse again, five of their top seven don't even sniff double figures. Reduced to 128 for six by stumps, Tendulkar carries their hopes.

Day Three: Happy times are here again. The Saturday of the Wanderers Test brings a near-capacity crowd to the revamped stands and Nelson Mandela, the ANC president, to visit both teams during tea. On the field, Tendulkar, 19 years old, moves to his fourth Test century, at times so slowly that he scores only 14 runs in two hours before lunch, at other times in a blaze of strokes. India are finally all out for 227. South Africa return to the crease and dawdle, reaching only 75 for one in 39 overs before the close. Why the slow batting? Still, they lead by 140. It's promising.

Day Four: India apply the brakes. When South Africa should be looking for quick runs, Anil Kumble, the elegant, bespectacled leg-spinner, pushes the ball through with astounding accuracy and takes six wickets for 53 runs in 47 overs. Held in check, the home side takes 80 overs to score 173 runs before a declaration is made at 252 for nine. It's too slow. Hudson, Kirsten and Richardson have all scored runs but no one has taken charge. India, set 314 to win, must survive the fifth day to earn a draw.

Day Five: There is a spring in the step of spectators walking the four kilometres to the ground from where they were able to park their cars. What a prospect! All three results are possible. It's a Monday, but it feels like a Saturday. Such expectation, but there is only sad anti-climax. India bat appallingly slowly for the first session and, even when four wickets fall after lunch, South Africa are unable to push for victory. The Test is finally called off with an hour left and India at 141 for four. Neither side had shown the courage to go out and win the Test, both were terrified of falling behind in the four-match series... dead end.

Why play if you don't try to win? The same question would be asked later in the series. It was a fair question.

The mood of the post-Test Press conference was hostile. In the dock, Azharuddin appeared dozy and frankly uninterested while Wessels was defensive, claiming that the loss of Pringle to injury had been a blow, that he could not have attacked any harder with only three tired bowlers at his disposal. Heads shook. André Bruyns left the media centre with Alan Jordaan.

'That was probably the worst captaincy I've ever seen,' said Bruyns, who had been commentating on the match.

'It's very difficult,' Jordaan answered. 'No one can talk to Kepler, not even Proccie.'

The criticism of the captain mounted over the following days. It was said that (i) he dictated tactics because there was no one strong enough to argue with him, (ii) he made no effort to win the Test when Donald took the second new ball because he called in only two slips, even though India had no chance of winning, (iii) he stopped attacking because the bowlers were 'tired' — what sort of bowler is 'tired' when there is a Test to be won?, (iv) he had failed in his basic obligation to entertain a large crowd.

Around the stands, in the Press box, on television, Wessels was condemned as being thoroughly negative, but it's worth pointing out that this opinion was not shared in the dressing room. Kirsten, the vice-captain, understood his captain's position and Cronje, the emerging crown prince, accepted the strategy: 'Kepler hates to lose and I agree,' he reflects. 'We were a young side and we didn't know how good we were, so it was much better to play safe. It's easy to attack when you've got the players, but once the more experienced guys had been left out, I think Kepler felt there was a lot riding on him. So he decided to play it safe. With such a young side, you can't really blame him for being conservative.'

Wessels dismissed most of the critics as people who had no experience or understanding of Test cricket. He thought they wanted him to take risks in the second match of the first home series for 22 seasons, and he brushed them aside. Why should he listen? He had played in his 27th Test at Wanderers. What had the critics ever done? He believed he was right. That was all.

'There were two points,' he recalls. 'The first was that our chances of bowling India out with three tired bowlers were small and I was not going to grind the guys down so early in the series. The second was that the Indians were not really attacking us. They were playing like a boxer who runs around the ring, waiting for us to do something rash. I was wary of the sucker punch and, that fifth day at Wanderers, someone like Kapil could have come in and turned the whole game on its head. We had to be careful. It would have been a disaster to go one-nil down in the series.

'With all that in mind, I was not going to lead some kind of death or glory cavalry charge which just might have let them back into the game. Test cricket is about taking your chances, but it is also about being patient enough to wait for them.'

Hindsight suggests Wessels' strategy was right. Given the task of leading this hugely inexperienced side into the harsh world of Test cricket, he decided to play a steady game and to err on the side of caution. Anything else would have been suicidal. At times, he was inflexible. At times, he was too vigilant. But, in Wessels, South Africa found a captain who offered strong leadership when it was most needed, in the nervy dawn of readmission. He laid down the strategy, withstood the fickle pressure, and ultimately led them to astounding success. South Africa was lucky.

Importantly for Wessels, the convener of selectors recognised his approach and provided total support: 'People don't understand Kepler,' Peter Pollock suggests. 'Since I began working with him, I have been particularly impressed by the sheer amount of homework he puts in before each match. I have not met anybody in cricket who spends as much time studying the game, so when he does something, you know he has thought about it very carefully. When you add that to his leadership ability and the fact that he has the conviction to stick with decisions, you end up with a formidable cricketer. He has been criticised, but unjustly. I was part of the decision to appoint him as the captain to lead us through readmission and, more and more, I am convinced that we were right. I think cricket could do with more people like Kepler Wessels.'

After the Wanderers Test, the Indian tour was hurled into a frenetic series of seven one-day internationals. The holiday month of December would become a vibrant kaleidoscope of runs, wickets and action before capacity crowds nationwide.

\* \* \* \* \*

'My ball.'

'My ball.'

The sickening thud of skull on skull rings around Newlands. During fielding practice before the opening one-day international between South Africa and India, Wessels and Fanie de Villiers have moved to catch the same high ball, four eyes looking skywards, and they collide. There is blood on the turf. De Villiers' eyebrow is hanging loose. Wessels, gashed, looks across at the scoreboard and sees it moving from left to right . . . call an ambulance. At the hospital, the doctor took one look at the cricketers and instantly assumed they had been in a car accident.

Thirty-five stitches were sewn in the wound above Wessels' eye and he was strongly advised not to play the next day. OK, Kirsten would captain the side... At 2.15 p.m. on Monday, December 7th 1992, Wessels led his side out at Newlands. He had woken that morning to find his left eye completely closed by the swelling, but it had opened by lunchtime, so he decided to play. He thought his team needed him. He felt dizzy in the field while India were restricted to only 183, but he cleared his head sufficiently to compile 43 in another sure and steady march to victory.

His reaction to injury, his sheer bravery in adversity was admired by his players. He was leading by example, and he was being followed. Whatever was said by those on the periphery, Kepler was still king inside the dressing room. Just 48 hours later in Port Elizabeth, the crown very nearly slipped.

Relations between the teams had been cordial, at least as cordial as they usually are between two international sides of the modern era (the days of beers in the opposition's dressing room have largely passed and a pattern of sporadic individual friendships bobbing in a sea of monosyllabic grunts and macho glares has emerged), but sparks of tension began to fly when several Indian players raised the ostensibly marginal issue of Kirsten backing up too far at the non-striker's end before the ball was bowled.

At Newlands, Kapil had removed the bails with the experienced South African out of his ground, but did not appeal. That had been a clear warning. Even the headlines screamed: KIRSTEN WARNED BY INDIANS. Fair enough. He shouldn't steal ground. No problem.

When the tourists continued to struggle in the second one-day international at St George's Park, bundled out for a wretched 143, they became needled and volatile. They dismissed Hudson early, but Wessels and Kirsten settled and started to establish the rhythm for what seemed a reasonably straightforward chase. Wessels was facing Kapil, the score was 20 for one, the crowd was merrily relaxed. All was well. Kirsten was at the non-striker's end...

Kapil moves in. Kirsten starts to back up, dragging his bat to the crease... forward... forward... beyond the crease. In an instant, Kapil whips off the bails.

'Howzat!'

'Do you want me to give him out?' the umpire asks.

'Tell him to **** ***,' Kapil replies.

The solitary finger is raised.

Kirsten stands and protests. What is going on? Kapil, tiger eyes burning bright, raises three fingers.

'I warned you three times! Three times!' he says.

Tempers boil over. Wessels walks down the pitch. **** ******. Kirsten finally heads back towards the pavilion, but a thunderous roll of discontent is brewing around the ground. Matters threaten to get out of hand. Back in the players' area, non-playing members of the Indian squad are quarrelling with South African players. We warned you ... that's an absolute disgrace.

Wessels is seething. Only three days after being concussed at Newlands, he's losing his mind. He has never seen anything like it and he thinks Kapil is completely out of order. The stadium has sprung to life as the bowler returns to his mark and the batsman settles. One ball is blocked, a second ball is blocked. Kapil is being booed. Wessels pushes the next delivery gently into the leg side and sets off for the single. As he turns to see whether a second run is on, he swings his bat round in an arc, and the side of the blade crashes into Kapil's shins. Kapil winces. *****. ******* ...

The South African captain was eventually out for 30, but Dave Callaghan and Cronje took the side to victory. The result, however, had been overshadowed by the incident. Did he or didn't he? Cyril Mitchley, one of South Africa's finest umpires, found himself at the centre of the storm. What had he seen? What was he going to write in his report? What would happen? Mitchley, typically, had taken the bull by the horns and had already spoken to Kapil on the field immediately after the incident.

'Did he hit you intentionally?' Mitchley had asked.

'I'm not sure,' Kapil replied.

'Thank you very much.'

That was that. Mitchley reported that the case was unproven, but Clive Lloyd, the ICC's match referee, then announced he would stage his own inquiry and asked to see the SABC video tape of the incident. Amazingly, the SABC replied they were sorry, but none of their cameras had managed to film the fracas. When Lloyd called a full disciplinary hearing at the UCB offices, the rumours began to run loose. That afternoon *The Star* newspaper in Johannesburg led their sports pages with a story speculating that, if found guilty, Wessels could be forced to step down as captain.

His future seemed to hang on the suggestion that any contact between his bat and the bowler's colourfully bruised shins had been unintentional. Lloyd summoned Kapil to the inquiry.

'Do you think he meant to hit you?'

'I can't be sure,' Kapil replied.

Wessels, sitting in the same room with his eye still swollen from the collision at Newlands, was in the clear, and Lloyd declared at a tense Press conference that Kirsten would be fined R1 000 for 'remonstrating and using offensive language'. In a thinly disguised warning to the South African captain, the West Indian added: 'If the conduct alleged did take place it would be reprehensible and would warrant extreme censure.' His job had been on the line.

The furore blew out as quickly as it had blown in, but the practice of crashing your bat into the bowler's shins when seeming to turn for a second run is known to most first class batsmen. It is also broadly accepted among leading players that, even allowing for warnings, it is not legitimate practice to run out opposition batsmen backing up. Under the circumstances that hot night in Port Elizabeth, it seemed in everyone's interest that the whole episode be consigned to the dark corners of history.

So it was. In a position to cause havoc, Kapil had acted with wisdom. Perhaps one old professional, understanding the pressures, had saved the bacon of another old pro; in a rough sort of way, a kind of justice was done. On reflection, Wessels regrets the furore. He saw red. That was wrong, but that was all.

As far as his own players were concerned, he had been absolutely right. Cronje regarded Wessels' reaction to the run-out as the ultimate example of a captain standing by one of his players. For his part, Kirsten looks back and says: 'I did raise my eyebrows a bit. I thought to myself, well, that is one man I will always take to war.'

The one-day series developed into a triumphant march around the country for the home side. There was a hiccup at Centurion Park when opener Woorkeri Raman, named after the tiny village in southern India where he was born, scored a century as the tourists chased down 215 to win, but South Africa reasserted their command with victories in the fourth match at the Wanderers and, 48 hours later, at Springbok Park, Bloemfontein.

Four-one. The team's success at the World Cup was joyfully confirmed. Kepler, Jonty, Hansie *et al.* could do no wrong. The captain's strategy was working well. All four victories had been secured when South Africa batted second. They were still happier chasing a target than setting one, but there was no harm in that. This was the way they were going to win one-day matches against India: restrict them to a sub-200 total with their aggressive bowling and outstanding fielding, leaving the steady batsmen to chisel away calmly at the runs.

Wessels, the steadiest of the steady, played a crucial role within this strategy. Ideally, he would bat through the innings and effectively 'drive' the chase, taking the first corners smoothly to avoid any early accidents, easing on the accelerator and gradually upping the tempo. Steady, steady as a rock. At Wanderers, his side was set to chase 161 and Wessels put the innings on the road with a top-scoring 45. In Bloemfontein, the target was 207 and the captain took the wheel again, contributing a sober 55 to a state-of-the-art limited overs opening stand of 135 with Hudson.

His value to the side as an in-form, utterly reliable anchor was beyond dispute. The chorus of critics was quiet. Almost. 'Yah,' they muttered, 'but Wessels can't set a target...'

Welcome to Kingsmead. India win the toss, and South Africa are to bat first. Wessels strides out, in form and in his element. He strokes a sprightly 78 in difficult conditions, still firmly in control, driving his side to a total of 216. That is a target the Indians never threaten to reach once Fanie de Villiers holds on to a magnificent outfield catch to dismiss Azharuddin.

From the chorus of critics? There is no sound. Even when the tourists won the last match of the series in East London, reaching a target of 203, the home captain had scored a blameless 57.

'Wessels can't play one-day cricket' — that had been the cry of the sheepish masses, but only the utterly stupid were repeating it after the series against India. He had scored 342 runs in seven innings, including three half-centuries, with an average of 48.85. The Man of the Series award was heading to his crowded mantelpiece at home. He had performed magnificently.

So, indeed, had his team, winning by five matches to two. The garden of South African cricket seemed in bloom: Callaghan had made his début in the national side, after a remarkable recovery from cancer; Cronje's nagging medium pace seemed to have solved the problem of finding a fifth bowler; and the fast bowlers had finally shown the discipline to match their talent.

As 1992 came to an end, South Africa turned joyfully towards its cricketers. The Springbok rugby team had lost four out of five Test matches, the nation's athletes had been humbled at the Olympic Games in Barcelona, the soccer side had struggled, but the continuing success of Wessels' side shone in the gloom.

'It was good,' he recalls.

Full stop.

Just as he had been largely unmoved by criticism, Wessels did not let the praise go to his head. One-day heroics were fine, but it was the Test series that mattered most. The third Test would be played in Port Elizabeth where St George's Park looked in superb condition with an elegant stand built at the Duckpond end. It had cost R25 million and almost bankrupted the Eastern Province cricket board but, none the less, it looked great.

Wessels, at home and at ease, won the toss and followed his instinct. Nine times out of ten, he would have batted first at St George's Park but, this time, he opted to field. His strategy was simple: strike hard and fast at the Indian batting, secure a first innings lead, apply the pressure, bowl them out again and knock off the runs. 'In the first two Test matches,' he recalls, 'we had got them into trouble but never managed to pin them down. They kept wriggling off the hook. So I was determined to land an early punch in Port Elizabeth, and the obvious way of doing that was by letting our fast bowlers get at them.'

The South African team showed two changes from the Wanderers Test, with a spinner, Omar Henry, replacing the highly unfortunate Cook, and Schultz returning to oust Pringle. The captain asked for a performance of blistering aggression. No holding back.

Wheel out the big gun.

Allan Donald, broad, fair and 26 years old, measures out his run-up at the ground where, six years before, he had made his début for South Africa against the Australian rebels. Those days, he was gawky, raw and giggled at, just another dim Dutchman from the Free State. A story did the rounds that OFS cricket union officials had once put him on a flight from Bloemfontein to East London and asked the stewards if they would please make sure he didn't get off the plane when it stopped to take on passengers in Port Elizabeth. This was not true, but still the people sniggered.

Respect arrived when he started to shatter stumps, catapult the bails and tickle breastbones on a regular basis. His reputation spread when he joined Warwickshire and tore through batting orders on the English county circuit, and he began to mature into a world-class bowler when he came under the instruction and guidance of Bob Woolmer, the former England batsman who had long passed his winters in Cape Town and subsequently became the Warwickshire coach. When things were going wrong, whatever the time, wherever he was, Donald would simply get on the telephone to Woolmer.

He was dubbed 'the fastest white bowler in the world', but this odious title was used far more enthusiastically abroad than in South Africa. For Free State and then for Warwickshire, 12 months a year, he ran in and won matches. Quite apart from developing a rare accent which seemed to blend Birmingham with Bloemfontein, he grew in confidence and stature to such an extent that, by the time South Africa was readmitted to international cricket, he was nearing his prime. Donald was the big threat, all the rage.

When he shook, rattled and rolled the Indians as the new dawn broke in Calcutta, he glimpsed superstar status, but his inability to control the white ball contributed to a frustrating World Cup and he had appeared tired in the West Indies. His shoulders started to slump, his hands protested on his hips. Too much cricket? Was he being burnt out on the county circuit?

The home series against India seemed a perfect stage to blast away the doubts. Roll it on. Rev it up. And yet, he took one wicket for 69 in the first Test at Kingsmead and rarely threatened to take more. Peter Pollock, the convener of selectors and former Springbok fast bowler, was joining a debate in the media about Donald's 'lack of rhythm'. There was a marginal improvement in the second Test and during the one-day series, but still no devastating streaks of what the Afrikaans newspapers called 'white lightning'. Amid the bravado and swagger, creeping self-doubt was evident.

So once again, it is Donald from the Duckpond end. The slips crouch, the crowd hushes. Let the Test begin. He high-steps in, bowls, fast but wide outside the off-stump, the Indian batsman offers no stroke, Richardson collects, no run. Second ball, the same. Over after over, the same. Wessels, at first slip, is becoming agitated. The captain has placed his neck on the line by putting India in to bat and his celebrated fast bowlers are wasting the new ball. He frowns. Donald sighs.

'OK, Allan. Thanks. Take a rest.'

Donald slopes to third man, it's 25 for none and the Indians thrive until lunch. Over his salad, Wessels considers his options. There aren't any. He calls up Donald for a second spell, hoping the big gun is loaded this time. Boom, boom, boom, boom. India collapse to 98 for four. Donald's fuse is alight. Azharuddin and Kapil earn some respite, but the innings is in free fall when Prabhakar falls to a disputed catch by McMillan. By the close, India are stunned at 186 for eight. The captain's decision to field first has paid off handsomely. Thank goodness. Thank Donald. When the innings ends at 212 the next day, he has taken five for 55.

Wessels had the pressure. Now, a forceful batting performance was required to consolidate a platform for victory. Head down, chin in, concentrate. The captain takes guard calmly, but is soon bowled by Prabhakar's yorker without scoring...

In need, South Africa was well served by another earnest son of the Orange Free State. The vast plains which once sprouted only maize and rugby players had started to yield a bountiful harvest of fine young cricketers. Johan Volsteedt and Wessels had sown the seeds of development at Grey College almost two decades before and, in 1992/93, the high energy provincial side brought home two of the three domestic trophies. The happy, successful captain of the Free State team was Hansie Cronje.

Tall and dark, he had been bred in the purest pedigree: Grey, Orange Free State and South Africa. To the manner born. Thrown into the provincial side in his teens, he was notoriously conned into a suicidal declaration in a Currie Cup match versus Transvaal, but he learned fast, worked hard and was soon leading his growing team to massively satisfying victories at the Wanderers.

Taken on the first tour of India as an 'observer', Cronje was drafted into the World Cup squad on the crest of the form, fitness and fielding regime, and never looked back. Dynamic and alert, one quality he never seemed to lack was confidence. His antics may have been a front for the usual self-doubt suffered by every sportsman, but at times the young Free Stater strutted and preened.

Such cockiness was not altogether a bad quality in a young cricketer eager and unafraid to take on the world and, in the Test against India at St George's Park, Cronje swiftly grew up as an international batsman, putting his head down and playing an innings of immense patience. While Hudson departed for 52 and Kirsten fell victim to an umpiring error for nought, the bold, determined young batsman stood firm at the crease and, with the reliable McMillan, nurtured South Africa to 162 for three by the close.

McMillan, Rhodes and Richardson fell in quick succession on the third morning, but still Cronje remained at his post, defending sternly, dispatching the bad ball, taking care and moving securely towards his maiden Test century. 'People had told me a century in Test cricket was a totally different feeling to any other century,' Cronje recalls. 'I never believed them because, you know, I always thought a hundred is a hundred. But when I got to 92, I knew they were right. Luckily, I got two bad balls from Kumble and I was able to get my hundred quickly. It was incredible.'

Henry and Craig Matthews provided support down the order as Cronje guided the innings towards respectability. After almost nine hours at the crease, he was the last man out, swinging wearily at Kumble. He had scored a career-building 135 out of the total 275. South Africa's innings lead was 63 runs. Wessels was satisfied. No more than that. There was still work to be done.

With 90 minutes remaining for play in the third evening, the captain led his team on to the field once again, lobbed the new ball to Donald and asked him to get out there and win the Test. That he did. The batting princes of India, idolised by millions around the subcontinent, were dramatically routed. Raman played on, Manjrekar was bowled, Tendulkar and Azharuddin were caught behind, Amre was caught off the leading edge, and Shastri gloved a catch down the leg-side. All in a blur of home town delirium.

The tourists had subsided to 31 for six, with Donald at the apex of the whirlwind. 'Allan basically won the Test match for us,' Wessels recalls. 'It was a golden period of play for all of us. We caught everything and that was that.'

Kapil arrived at the disaster scene and struck out. For the titanic all-rounder, it would be quick death or glory. By stumps, he had reached a hard-hit 33, out of 71 for six, and he continued his assault into the fourth morning, at one stage cracking Matthews for four, six, four in successive deliveries. Finishing with 129 from 177 balls, Kapil enabled his country to reach 215.

India had fallen to Donald. With seven for 84 in the second innings, his match analysis of 12 for 139 left no one in any doubt that, at his best, he was almost irresistible. The fast bowler, himself, was quick to praise the man who claimed nine catches in the Test, equalling the South African record. Richardson, the wicketkeeper, had given yet another quiet, able performance.

South Africa required only 153 to win with almost a day and a half to play. Mindful of the collapse in Bridgetown, Barbados, the situation needed one of the experienced players to take command and march the troops efficiently to their objective. As the first Test victory in 22 years beckoned, Wessels moved to the fore and played an appropriately impeccable innings.

Determined to finish the Test within four days, the captain set about the Indian bowlers with a chain of neat drives and pulls. Hudson and

Cronje played the minor roles, scoring 32 and 16 not out respectively, but it was Wessels who finished the match with style, rushing to an unbeaten 95 in 167 balls, out of a total 155 for one. He pulled the winning runs past mid-wicket and walked off the field wreathed in smiles. 'Thanks for the game.'

He arrived back in the pavilion to discover the home dressing room had once again been turned into a backslappers' convention. It irritated him that hangers-on would crawl out of the woodwork when things went well and steal the players' moment. 'Yeah, thanks.' He showered, changed and celebrated quietly.

As the fourth and final Test in Cape Town approached, Wessels imagined the Indians would adopt a more aggressive strategy to try and salvage a drawn series. All summer they had sat back, waiting for the South Africans to make a mistake but now they would have to come forward and throw a few punches of their own.

They didn't. The tourists were lost in an indefensible mist of lethargy and, with South Africa understandably content to sit on a one-nil lead (it was their first series in two decades), the Test at Newlands unfolded as an unmitigated disaster. The captains said the pitch was too slow, but their combined lack of ambition was the chief reason for five days of stultifying boredom.

South Africa, who made their intentions clear at the outset by picking six specialist batsmen, won the toss and batted for the first two days before declaring at 360 for nine. Daryll Cullinan made 46 on his long-awaited Test début, Rhodes scored 86 (and would finish top of his team's batting averages for the series on 45.83), and McMillan amassed 52 in just under four hours. Aside from these contributions, nothing. No passion, no verve.

On the third day, the dreary Indians proved what many of the yawning spectators would probably not have believed possible: that it was indeed possible to bat with even less ambition. They raced to 161 for five in no fewer than 97 overs. The Test stirred briefly from its coma on the fourth day when Tendulkar and Kapil struck out but, when their last four wickets fell for a single run, India were 276 all out. All of this had been far too exciting, and the South African batsmen restored the more gentle pace of the match, moving to 48 for two in 33 overs before the close.

Indian hopes flickered briefly on the fifth day, but Cullinan and Rhodes settled, remained and scored the odd run as the Test match petered out in the draw which had seemed inevitable ever since the first day.

A total of 795 runs had been scored in 433.4 overs at a rate of 1.83 runs per over. At a time when bold attempts were being made to promote five-day cricket, the match was condemned all around the cricket world. It was, however, also true that the onus had been on the Indians, as the side trailing in the series, to play aggressive cricket. Instead they performed with the bare minimum of pride and passion, almost giving an impression that they didn't care. If they had been a rebel side, they would have been scoffed at by the South African public as a waste of time and money.

Wessels was also lambasted because his team had scored at no more than 1.75 runs per over. Critics maintained the Indians were so shell-shocked after the defeat in Port Elizabeth that he should have gone for the jugular at Newlands, instead of sitting back and defending the one-nil lead. Against this line of questioning at the post-match Press conference, he allowed himself to be riled and the series ended on a sour and dispiriting note.

The captain was bewildered by the media reaction. He returned to his hotel room and reflected how he had been appointed to lead this wholly inexperienced side into Test cricket, how he had worked harder than ever, how he had worked out a strategy where they could defeat vastly more experienced opponents and how, in fact, they had won the series by one Test to nil... and how the media and others were still complaining. What did they want?

'People seemed to think one-nil wasn't enough,' he reflects. 'I didn't say anything at the time because it would only have made things worse but I think the problem was that the only Test series most South Africans had spoken about for the last 20 years was the four-nil thrashing of Australia in 1969/70, and that was all they had to base their judgement on. It was almost as if they thought we should win every series 4-0. They simply could not understand that modern Test cricket is tough and competitive. The fact was that we did tremendously well to win the series. There was so much moaning at the end, you would have thought we had lost.'

He accepts the Newlands Test went sadly wrong, but points out that his team could never get in a position to attack. 'The pitch was terrible,' he adds. 'Some of the experts said the great batsmen could have scored more quickly on it. That was top stuff. We would have liked to bat more fluently, but we certainly weren't going to take any risks. At the end of the day, we won the series against a major Test team, and I was delighted with that.'

The Indians left for home with little fanfare. Aside from a sporadic Kapil-blitz, they had, not for the first time in history, proved poor tourists. Geoff Boycott, the former England batsman who was in South Africa to commentate on the series, described them as probably the worst Test team he had ever seen.

That verdict unjustly diminished the achievement of Wessels' side. Moreover, it wasn't true because Azharuddin's squad returned home and promptly won all three Tests against England. Perhaps they were the second worst team Boycott had ever seen.

* * * * *

Until the mid-1970s, a spectator needed to have more than the right ticket to sit in the best seats at a major cricket stadium in South Africa. He also needed to have a white skin. Blacks, coloureds and Indians were sent to their own section of the ground.

At the Wanderers, the so-called 'non-whites' sat on that part of the scaffolding bowl which stretched from the scoreboard towards Corlett Drive. At Newlands, they sat under the Planes. A surprising number of these designated second-class citizens did come to watch the matches (and, understandably, to support whichever touring side was playing against South Africa), but non-white involvement in the flagship sports, cricket and rugby, was minimal. Political reality suppressed any innocent sporting inclination.

WHITES ONLY — SLEGS BLANKES. That was the law...

It is February 1993. The South African cricket captain, an Afrikaner born and bred in Bloemfontein, sits in the home changing room at Centurion Park in Verwoerdburg, a new town named after the architect of apartheid, and reflects on the day's events: 'It felt as though we were playing in Karachi or Lahore,' he says, then he shakes his head and smiles. 'It's incredible.'

Life had changed. The United Cricket Board had arranged a triangular one-day series to follow the Indian tour, with Pakistan and the West Indies flying in to play South Africa. Diplomacy was still directing UCB invitations. Almost 18 months after readmission, the team was still playing only non-white nations. It had wisely been decided that old wounds would be healed before the traditional ties with Australia, England and New Zealand were renewed.

As a result, a series which produced much fine cricket was primarily remarkable for the scenes in the grandstands. Cricket in South Africa a white man's sport? Never again. Pakistan, the world champions, filled stadiums around the country, drawing enthusiastic crowds of all races, together, at last, and the West Indians galvanised interest in cricket around the townships.

Some of the South African players became exasperated by the level of shouting and flag-waving support enjoyed by the visiting countries, but there was no need to take offence. These were times of transition. The point was that, even if they were waving green flags for Pakistan, a new constituency of cricket supporter was appearing in their thousands. Given time, they would wave the right flag. Reconciliation wouldn't happen overnight, but at least it had started.

Wessels surveyed the changing scenery with interest, but his prime responsibility remained on the field. The two strongest teams in the world had arrived to challenge his young, learning team. 'It would have been hard to arrange a more difficult schedule than the one we faced after readmission,' he recalls. 'We were sent to India at four days' notice, we were hurled into the World Cup, we took on the West Indies in the Caribbean with no warm-up matches. India at home offered a little respite, but then we were in against the top two teams in the world. It wasn't easy.

'I told Ali (Bacher) that we would have to play very well each day if we were to reach the final of the triangular series and I suggested we should rather have one of them and a weaker team, perhaps Sri Lanka, but it was out of our control. We had to get on with it and accept the flak if things went wrong.'

Expertly hyped by the UCB as a head-to-head shoot-out between the fastest bowlers in the world − Curtly Ambrose, Courtney Walsh, Patrick Patterson and Ian Bishop of the West Indies, versus Waqar Younis and Wasim Akram of Pakistan, against the local lads, Donald, Pringle and De Villiers, the format of the Total Power triangular series involved the teams playing each other three times in a round robin section with the top two in the log then contesting a final.

South Africa was joining Australia with their snouts deep in the trough of one-day cricket, scheduling as many one-day internationals as possible (as many as 15 per season), to make as much money as possible. England, by contrast, would play two or three in a home summer. It remains to be seen whether the golden goose will lay, and lay − or whether it will eventually collapse, exhausted.

Wessels saw his side produce a strange contrast during the early games of the series. Twice they bowled and fielded superbly to beat the West Indies, and twice they collapsed from winning positions to lose against the Pakistanis.

The collapses ultimately cost them a place in the final. Set to chase 208 for six against Pakistan at Kingsmead, Hudson and Wessels constructed an opening stand of 101 and South Africa seemed to be cantering to victory at 159 for one. Then the pressure-panic syndrome took its toll as Waqar returned to the attack and ripped through the batting order, seizing five for 25, as the home side collapsed to 198 all out. Not for the first time in his career, Waqar had proved infinitely more devastating with an older, worn ball than he had with the new ball earlier in the same innings. It was strange.

Six days later at Buffalo Park in East London, Javed Miandad cracked a century as Pakistan, again batting first, reached 214 in 50 overs. Chasing down a target reduced by rain to 172 in 31 overs, Cronje, Wessels and Rhodes all batted efficiently, driving the team to 148 for three in 24 overs. All they needed was five an over off the last seven with wickets in hand. Surely, this time, they would finish the job. No. Wasim, the left-arm-over quick bowler, captured four wickets in 13 balls and South Africa performed their imitation of dominoes again. Pressure-panic. All out 162.

As Oscar Wilde might have said, to collapse once against the Pakistanis is unfortunate, but to collapse twice is plain careless. A bemused nation wanted to know why. 'Experience. That was the main reason,' says Wessels. 'It was a worry that our batting was so brittle and liable to collapse, but there was no technical problem. We had to learn to cope with the pressure, and that would only come with experience. Waqar surprised our guys in Durban because they hadn't seen 100 mph deliveries which swing late and fast. I could live with that, but the East London defeat was really disappointing because we had that game all sewn up.'

'How to play Waqar' became the topic of conversation in top boardrooms and playgrounds around the country. Some said you must play a yard out of your crease to reduce the swing, others said it was better to stand outside leg-stump and play with the bat and pad tightly together; still others said play only in an arc between mid-off and mid-wicket, resisting temptation to cover drive or cut. Wessels had advised his batsmen to take a shorter backlift and play the ball as late as possible. Ultimately, each individual batsman would have to decide for himself.

Despite these two disappointments, South Africa sustained their challenge in the series by prevailing over the West Indies. They bowled out Richie Richardson's team for 149 at St George's Park in Port Elizabeth and, when Kirsten and Rhodes guided the side out of trouble at 33 for three to victory by six wickets with two overs to spare, the nation was dancing again.

Wessels' side then produced its outstanding performance of the series against the West Indians at Newlands on February 17th. It was a collective cameo of courage, another red letter day for this team which did not know when it was beaten, which refused to give up and which was growing in the image of its captain.

Sent in to bat, the South Africans struggled on a green pitch and relied on Cullinan's 40 in 56 balls to reach 140 for nine in 50 overs. As the inherently laid-back Cape Town crowd anticipated a Caribbean cakewalk to victory, Wessels gathered his team. If he has nothing to say, this captain will say nothing. He will not jabber but, this day at Newlands, he had something to say.

'The people out there, they think we've got no chance of winning this,' he cajoled, 'but, on this pitch, I know we can. Let's keep everything tight, try to encourage each other the whole time, bowl straight and, well, I think we might surprise ourselves...' The team sprinted on to the field and famously defended their low score.

Cullinan, playing his first one-day international, recalls: 'There was this fantastic sense of purpose. It was a real vibe. The guys were all pulling for each other and we made things go our way. Kepler stood there, controlling it all. It was a wonderful effort by the whole team, and a really wonderful day.'

Rhodes (who else?) lit the fire, running out Desmond Haynes from backward point, and Cronje, emerging as a talented all-rounder in one-day cricket, sustained the pressure: running out Brian Lara, having Gus Logie caught at mid-wicket, running out Junior Murray, trapping Carl Hooper LBW and excitedly getting Walsh caught behind by Richardson. Yo, Hansie! High five. Low five.

Ambrose and Patterson carved out a last-wicket stand but, when Ambrose was adjudged LBW to Pringle, the West Indians were all out for 136 and South Africa had triumphed by four runs. Sitting in the Members' Stand, the State President was thrilled. He leapt to his feet when victory was secured, stood with his fists in the air and a hint of moisture around his eyes, and was soon heading to the dressing room to congratulate the team.

There he found bedlam. Cronje, named Man of the Match after making 31 and taking three for 27, was exhilarated beyond control, again the beaming prankster. As De Klerk moved to shake his hand, the young Free Stater wrapped one arm around the State President's neck and, with his other arm, started to tilt a bottle of champagne above the VIP head. Embarrassment threatened.

'No, Hansie, stop!' yelled Wessels above the din. 'You can't do that. It's the Prez. Stop it!'

Alert to the situation, Procter removed his hat and held it between the neck of the bottle and the head of state. Then Cronje took the bottle away and beamed. What a day.

The physical and emotional energy spent that day at Newlands effectively exhausted the South African team. As they had tired at the end of their first season back in international cricket, so the demands of the 1992/93 schedule took their toll. Batsmen found it harder to concentrate, bowlers battled to hold their line and even the fielding sagged. The batteries were flat.

So the triangular series, and the season, ended with emphatic defeats against Pakistan in Verwoerdburg and then against the West Indies in Bloemfontein, where a Brian Lara century entertained a crowd that included several hundred boys from Grey College. The two touring sides were left to contest the final, which the West Indies won before another full house at the Wanderers.

Wessels was disappointed and tired. He had scored only 166 runs in six innings during the triangular series but his average of 27.66 was still the highest in the South African side. His team had bowled and fielded well, but the batsmen had struggled to withstand their first prolonged exposure to world-class fast bowlers such as Ambrose and Waqar. Experience, alone, would heal.

The captain was also concerned that his team, still charging into each match like the first schoolboy into the tuckshop, should learn to pace themselves. The West Indians, for example, were on their way home from a full tour of Australia, yet they had seemed so fresh and keen in South Africa.

'They were an example to us,' Wessels recalls. 'The key to surviving the heavy schedule of a modern international cricketer is to settle into a rhythm and to stay calm. The West Indians go all out to win Test series, but they have a relaxed attitude to one-day matches. As long as they win more than they lose, they're happy, so they're not thrown off course by a couple of one-day defeats. They know that Test cricket is their main priority.

'For us, everything was so exciting and new. The spectators and media regarded every match as a make-or-break situation, but as time passes we will learn not to take the one-dayers so seriously. No one else does. Of course, we'll want to win, but we won't plunge into a state of national crisis if we lose a few. That sort of high pressure and intensity caused us to tire quickly. Our highs were too high and our lows were too low. With a level-headed approach to one-day cricket, we'll conserve energy better.'

The quiet fade-out apart, Wessels' squad finished the season comfortably in credit. They had won their first full Test series, competed gallantly against the West Indies and Pakistan and, above all, they had continued to learn and improve.

Wessels had been central to this achievement. Vintcent van der Bijl, the former Springbok, wrote to the captain soon after the triangular series. 'One of the most difficult things in South Africa, I think, is, in spite of the criticism, to go ahead on a chosen path with full and positive commitment,' he wrote. 'You have done that and therefore have captured the respect of the people.'

The letter provided a neat epitaph to a momentous season. He had been asked to lead South Africa back into world cricket and, no matter how incessantly the critics carped, the results were in the book. Wessels was doing the job. With distinction.

*   *   *   *   *

The cricket season never ends in Mamelodi. The grass may turn brown and crisp in the cold winds of a highveld winter, but the coaching continues. The under-16 side were asked if they wanted to rest from April until September. No, they didn't. As Tshepo Mokoena eagerly pointed out, they would be able to catch up on the established school sides if they practised through the winter. 'Especially the good players,' he continued, sternly. 'I mean the ones who want to play cricket as their career.'

That was their goal: to go to schools like Pretoria Boys' High with their graceful buildings and resplendent grounds, and win. The enthusiastic fledglings had competed against the pristine boys with the latest kit but they had not won. Yet. For all of the team, none the less,

1992/93 had been the best season of their lives. They had played 23 matches and trained at the University nets twice a week. Twice they had seen the South African team in action.

First, they were given free tickets to watch the third day of the Wanderers Test against India and sat among 300 other youngsters from the townships. No one abused them, no one shouted at them, but, best of all, no one seemed to notice them. Then they paid R20 each to watch the one-day international against India at Centurion Park. It was a lot of money, but it was worth it. Again, they were happy to feel accepted in a world from which they had once been excluded, to sit wherever they wanted. The following weekend, the cry of 'I'll be Kapil' joined 'I'll be Donald' at the Tukkies nets.

All season, they too had played hard and learned hard. From the most celebrated team in the land to just another bunch of kids dreaming, it had been a happy time of progress.

# 13

## Mere Flesh and Bones

He is an ordinary man with an extraordinary resolve.

The alarm stirs at six o'clock in the morning, and, while the ordinary man may seek stolen moments of slumber, the extraordinary resolve leaps into action. Ever since boyhood, rising at dawn has been the general rule. So it is this day at home in Walmer, a calm and genial suburb of green avenues in Port Elizabeth.

Just another day.

Out of bed, into a tracksuit. Wessels' wardrobe marks out his career in sportswear. There are bright yellow tracksuits from the Australian days, a range of dark green creations variously worn by South African teams and the evolving cherry red fashions of the Eastern Province squad. Pressed and washed, they hang side by side, like the grey suits of a chartered accountant.

There is a rustle of activity in rooms along the corridor, and the dawn chorus breaks out. Have you got your homework, combed your hair, brushed your teeth, got your lunch?

Sally Wessels organises Riki, aged eight, and Rebecca, going on six, into the day. Breakfast is eaten.

'All right, mate, are you ready?' asks Dad.

Riki, wearing the grey and light blue blazer of Grey junior school, casually and comfortably replies that he is. The father-son relationship is clearly more easygoing Brisbane than starch-collar Bloemfontein. There is discipline, but the affection is candid and clearly stated... 'So, what you got on today, mate?'

The boy is as keen, bright and enthusiastic as any father could want his son to be. He follows the cricket eagerly, knows the nicknames of the Eastern Province players and relishes summer days spent sitting with his friends on the boundary at St George's Park, just as his father used to sit near the touchline at the Free State rugby stadium. Only the fringe is different.

Sport, inevitably, is the spice of Riki's life. He is gifted, whether playing cricket at Grey or walloping forehands around the tennis court behind the family house. Dad looks on, encourages and helps, but rarely coaches and never, never pushes. If Riki wants to do this, he can do it. It's his decision.

The presence of his son strips away the frowning reserve that Wessels generally shows the world. The gladiator's face softens and the eyes relax. 'All right, mate?' Four years ago, there had been a nightmarish day when he was anything but all right. Kepler had been playing cricket in a Currie Cup match at St George's Park, and Riki was spending the afternoon at a friend's house when he fell off a gate, landing heavily on his elbow. He was rushed to hospital, and Kepler dashed to his bedside after close of play.

Open surgery saved the joint and Riki made a full recovery, but Wessels had been shaken by the sight of his son in such agony. The hard man had shed quiet, private tears.

'Mate, are you ready? Come on.'

At last, he's ready. Father and son drive off together, as they do every morning, past the numbered avenues of Walmer, through Port Elizabeth and on towards Grey. Named after the same gentleman as Grey College, Bloemfontein, but otherwise unrelated, Grey has long been recognised as one of the Eastern Cape's finest schools. Stately white buildings overlook the main cricket ground, named the Pollock Oval, after Graeme, a celebrated old boy.

The car turns up the tree-lined avenue towards the school and comes to a halt, but Riki doesn't get out. What's the problem? He explains that he has seen a teacher arriving whom he is quite keen to avoid this particular morning. Dad laughs. Come on, get out. OK, OK. See you later, mate. Have a good day.

It's just after seven o'clock when Wessels' routine takes him to the Body Concept gym, another outlet for the South African trend of exercising in high-tech rooms with mirrors. Luxurious health and racquet clubs have sprung up in major cities, surrounded by immense car parks that fill each early morning and each early evening. Body Concept provides a similar service and has offered a special group membership to the Eastern Province cricket squad.

The captain walks in, eliciting a cheery greeting from the staff and furtive glances from other customers at various stages of their work-out.

Everyone knows him, most of them see him every day, a few talk to him... Good game yesterday. He will smile and he'll say thanks, but he won't stand around and chat.

At the gym, Wessels pulls on his public persona for the first time in the day. A furrow deepens across his brow, his eyes focus keenly and he looks solemn, even grumpy. Occasionally, he *is* solemn and grumpy, but most of the time he is simply absorbed in whatever he has to do. Ali Bacher has observed that 'Kepler goes into a kind of trance'. That's it. It's absolute concentration.

So he concentrates on his sit-ups and his press-ups, a daily dose of the drug to which, he says, he is addicted. 'I've always been a fanatic about exercise,' he admits. 'It began at Stellenbosch and, when I was around 20, it became a daily work-out. I haven't let up since, not even for a week. I would tell myself that if I didn't train hard, I wouldn't play well. It always gives me a lift. I think I use it to get over things. It's a kind of escape, but I'm concerned that it has become a problem. I think I've become addicted to it. I find it difficult not to train every day. If for some reason I can't get to a gym, I start to get withdrawal symptoms by about five in the evening. It's bad.'

Wessels' obsession with training has already caused problems, most notably when he was struck down not long after the end of the 1992/93 season. One quiet, autumn afternoon, without warning, he collapsed. His appendix had exploded. He was carried into hospital on the shoulder of a doctor, rushed in for an emergency operation and told to rest for a month. Within two weeks, he was back in the gym, preparing for the tour of Sri Lanka.

'The doctor was pretty severe on me,' Wessels recalls. 'He said that I was burning myself out and that I should take a rest. I had been swallowing anti-inflammatory tablets for two years to get by with my knee problems. That had made me sick. But what can I do? I know the doctor is right, but I can't take a break. He said it's a combination of the mental and physical pressure that takes its toll. As long as I can get through the next couple of seasons before I retire from cricket, I'll be all right. Then I'll take it easy for the rest of my life.'

By 7.45 a.m., as usual, Wessels arrives behind his desk in office number 1113 on the eleventh floor of the tower block at the University of Port Elizabeth. To his left and right, there are magnificent panoramic views of the Indian Ocean. On the wall behind him, there is a collection of team photographs: the Australians in England, 1985; the unofficial Australians, 1986/87; Eastern Province, 1988/89 Currie Cup champions.

His parking berth at UPE is numbered and reserved, and his future as a senior public relations officer seems equally secure. A post was created for him when he arrived in 1986, and, despite the time-consuming demands of cricket, he has proved a valuable asset, whether fund-raising or flying the flag at schools in the Transvaal and Natal, his areas of responsibility. At umpteen meetings, he has persuaded talented schoolboys to consider UPE.

Jan Roos, chief director of Liaison Services, heads Wessels' department. 'Kepler is a very promotable person,' says Roos. 'It showed great foresight of Kotie Grové to get him here in the first place and, although cricket takes up a great deal of his time at the moment, I'm sure he will continue to make a major contribution to the university after he retires from sport.

'There was one day when I went to Pretoria Boys' High School with him, and the impression he made on the boys was unbelievable. When he sits on the platform wearing a UPE blazer, he really is a great representative for us. Our policy is not to lure students to Port Elizabeth. We simply try to sell the product, and when we put Kepler on stage, we've virtually sold our varsity.'

Wessels has been well treated by UPE. Despite the demands of cricket, the university has continued to be utterly supportive and understanding. Roos concludes succinctly: 'We value him very highly because he's such a decent person. I mean, that's important to me. If he's not sitting in his office by eight o'clock on a cold Monday morning, I know he's not just lying in bed.'

As the morning runs its course, cricket is never far away. The South African captain keeps in regular telephone contact with Bacher, the UCB managing director, and also with Peter Pollock, the convener of national selectors. There is always something pending to discuss: arrangements for an upcoming training camp, who's in form, who isn't. Fellow players often phone, reporting on injuries, asking advice on career options or just for a chat. The telephone rings incessantly. Brrrr-brrrr. It's his anthem.

This day, after lunch (one toasted cheese and tomato sandwich at the UPE canteen), Wessels leaves his office to attend a meeting in the early afternoon. Beyond his primary responsibility to the university, he has further business concerns. Cricket has provided him with a high standard of living, but wealth has raised questions of investment. Where? When? How? He has heard stories of prominent sportsmen, idolised on the field, who have been conned into losing their money in the belief that they are equally invincible off the field. Down that road, legends have wandered.

Wessels is, in his own words, 'para-paranoid' about the risk: 'A lot of people come to me with business proposals and I look at all of them, but it's in my nature to be cautious.' He has suffered no financial disasters, although he almost bought a piece of land in Australia that turned out to be a swamp, and he resists regular temptation to dabble in shares. He doesn't trust them.

In early 1991, however, he was persuaded to invest in something which is both a passion and a business. Pindile Gaika, a former South African boxing champion working at UPE, succeeded in turning the cautious head by explaining how he was running a stable of amateur boxers in New Brighton, a township outside Port Elizabeth.

'We need help.'

'OK, I'll get involved.'

Boxing had always excited his enthusiasm. He had incorporated the basic drills into his training since the early days at the Ferreiras' gym in Pretoria, and subsequently at the Railway Institute gym when he lived in Brisbane, and he was even excited by the largely insidious world of professional boxing, rarely missing a fight on television, enjoying the theatre of match-making. The sport was full of brave, down-to-earth people, his type of people; and he would relax more comfortably among boxing folk than anywhere else, smiling, chewing the fat. If cricket was work, boxing was play.

So Gaika took Wessels deep into the township and showed him a world where eager young boys learn to box with milk cartons pulled over their fists, instead of gloves. The Eastern Cape had long been established as a hotbed of boxing, where big township bouts attract vast crowds, and large bets, in rundown arenas. Gaika spoke of the potential imprisoned within the squalor, of talent, enthusiasm and what could be. The gym was intact, but it lacked almost everything except fighters. The visitor was intrigued.

In the months that followed, Wessels arranged sponsors to pay the bills and secured a grant from local government to buy brand new equipment. He began to visit the gym regularly, usually twice a week, keeping an eye on the progress, identifying ability, building up a stable of 30 amateur fighters and as many as seven professionals. Within weeks, he and Gaika were mapping out the careers of young boxers, arranging multi-fight bills for them in New Brighton. He enjoyed it hugely, working with the sponge and water as a cornerman for the fighters, urging them on. Head down, chin in. The old maxim worked in the ring too.

Wessels became a familiar figure in the dusty streets around the gym, driving on his own without fear, and his contribution in New Brighton was rewarded by a touching allegiance.

In 1991, Wessels agreed to take part in an exhibition bout as part of Dave Richardson's benefit box-and-dine function. He has rarely been able to decline such invitations over the years, once getting himself pummelled by Hector Thompson, a former Commonwealth champion, at a Brisbane shopping centre, but his opponent over three rounds this time was to be Anton Ferreira, his old team-mate from Pretoria and a capable amateur heavyweight of days gone by.

'We were ready to go into the indoor hall at St George's Park, when I heard the singing start,' Ferreira recalls. 'They were harmonising like a choir. Then I saw them, all these smiling black faces on the balcony, singing in support of Kepler.'

No one at the New Brighton gym had wanted to miss the sight of Wessels in the ring, so they packed into six minibuses and drove to the hall where the bout was taking place. As he climbed between the ropes, they began to chant and sing, beautifully. The generally stoic features cracked with pleasure. Wessels smiled.

It had been a rare evening. Time moved on. An increasingly familiar pattern was emerging among development programmes in South African sport: when the initial gloss wears off, problems mount and exasperation sets in. The adventure of advancing sport in deprived townships rarely unfolds as the join-the-dots philanthropy that, in the first burst of enthusiasm, some anticipate. It swiftly becomes a trial of patience, persistence and resolve.

As the gym grew, the frustration grew. Wessels was bitterly disappointed when young fighters whom he had developed decided to leave the gym and sign for a local black promoter. However hard he tried, however great the new opportunities he offered, Wessels was still a white man. Whether it was some kind of underlying distrust, a residue of apartheid, that swayed the young fighters to 'go back to their own' or not, there was no loyalty in the investment. The old divisions were still too wide, too sore.

Wessels temporarily backed off, and when political unrest spread through the townships he was forced to stop visiting the gym altogether. He was white. They were black. At that time, there were no shades of grey. In years to come, he would once again be an active promoter in

Eastern Cape boxing, arranging tournaments and showing an impressive depth of understanding and knowledge, but he would steer clear of managing the fighters.

He also turned to a wider involvement in boxing, a handshake association with Thinus Strydom of World Sport Promotions. A slick operator in a hard-hearted world, Strydom courted Wessels to help publicise and promote his fights and fighters. It helped, needless to say, that Wessels was frequently hired by the SABC, and then by M-Net, as an expert commentator on television.

One hot day in Nelspruit, a fighter called Ginger Tshabalala defeated an overseas import to sustain his progress. Ginger was on Strydom's books, Wessels was providing the expert comments on the SABC TV coverage. This was not unethical. To Strydom, it was neat business. To Wessels, it was a hobby. 'I get a lot of pleasure out of boxing,' he says. 'I might become more involved.'

By half past three in the afternoon, his meetings are over for the day and Wessels' attention returns to the prime business of his life. It's almost time for cricket practice.

In his 26th season on the treadmill of professional cricket, it would not be surprising to find some traces of weariness in his approach to yet another training session with the Eastern Province squad. If such tiredness exists, however, it is buried far beneath the concrete slabs of his routine.

He drives into St George's Park and goes to work. He rarely goes to play. There is a set procedure, a monorail of habit, and he follows it: oversee preparation of the pitch for the next fixture, check any news in the office, get out to the nets, warm up, have a throw, maybe a net, practise slip-catching, always keep an eye on the other players, sort out problems, drive home.

Idealists will point to a lack of joy and innovation in the entire process, yet Wessels has found success in this routine based on good habits and discipline. Professional sport, he seems to have realised long ago, must always be work, not play.

So he strides out to inspect the pitch, watched only by the yawning grandstands. All is quiet. The St George's Park groundsman, alone, follows and the discussion ensues: maybe cut a bit more here and water a bit there. Wessels looks, prods and bounces a ball. In times spent at Bloemfontein, Stellenbosch, Pretoria, Hove, Brisbane and now Port Elizabeth, he has seen a few pitches before. He knows what he wants, he asks for it and he gets it.

Around the EPCB office and at the nets, as the players start to arrive, he exerts a silent, secure sense of authority. Everyone, from the ground staff to the vice-captain, seems aware that Kepler is here and Kepler is in charge. There is no screaming or shouting, just the occasional bark, and as he strolls around, head bowed deep in thought, he carries an aura of control.

It is virtually impossible to imagine anyone standing up to him, arguing the odds on some issue, holding their ground and still being able to go home and enjoy their supper. They may groan behind his back, but very rarely to his face.

The players gather around the nets and start to warm up. Some days they run round the park, others they'll dash down and back up the heart-breaking Brickmakers' Hill, outside the ground. Once upon a time, Wessels would lead the youngsters up the climb but no more. He has conceded that much to age, and his worn-out knees: 'But I'll still match anyone in the gym,' he adds.

At the nets, Wessels is content to let the coach organise who bowls where and who bats when. His style of captaincy is quiet and understated. There is no waving of arms, no grand displays, but he never stops watching, glancing from the corner of his eye, checking who is performing and who is slacking, constantly scribbling mental notes. He is the all-seeing eye.

Over the years, he has also learnt to set time aside for his own practice so, with Dave Callaghan today, he steps aside for some throwing practice. It's a drill he finds more efficient and useful than batting in the nets, more professional.

The two men, both all padded up, stand ten metres apart and Callaghan, taking balls from a bucket of 20, starts to throw short-pitched deliveries at Wessels, who either strokes securely into the off-side off the back foot or pulls. Over and again: the same ball and the same group of strokes. Until the bucket is empty. Then they change and Wessels throws short at Callaghan. The second rotation is full-pitched deliveries driven through cover or whipped off the toes. The third and final rotation is a mixed bag.

This method of training follows the same principles as a top golfer grooving one stroke at a time, and it is everything Wessels expects of a practice: it has a clear purpose, it is thorough and there is no wasted time. The unspoken advantage over normal nets is that you don't have to rely on unpredictable fast bowlers to bowl properly. It works. 'Thanks, Callaghers.'

Wessels joins in the out-fielding practice with the rest of the squad, still saying little, still watching. There is some mild banter. He smiles a little, jokes a bit but this is not the general pattern. It's still work. At the end, with no selection meetings to attend, he says goodbye to everyone and no one, hurls his coffin of kit into the boot and points his car for home.

The house is alive with children, and homework, and laughter, and television, and the evening meal in the oven.

'How was your day?'

'Fine.'

The pressures, and sometimes the problems, generally stay at St George's Park, but not always. 'It is something I have to work on,' Wessels says. 'I can get grumpy if things are not going well but I try not to get snappy with the kids and take it out on them. When I get stressed, I get tired and ratty. I can feel it coming on and I try to deal with it. That doesn't mean I actually can deal with it. The kids are good though. They usually understand.

'I have grown to accept that I am an intense sort of person. That's the way I am. I take things seriously, and I do get upset if things go wrong. I get quiet and very morose. Usually, I get tired and just want to sleep. I have found that there's not much in life that can't be healed by a decent night's sleep.

'In general, I think professional sportsmen are difficult to live with because the ups and downs are so huge and the pressure is always there. Everything is so public. If you make a mistake, the whole world knows about it. It knocks you back.'

A substantial number of top sportsmen have sought the help of a specialist sports psychologist to level out the highs and lows of their daily existence, to establish some kind of balance and stability in their roller-coaster lives. Wessels has not.

'That type of thing certainly does help some guys,' he says, 'and, if it suits them, that's fine, but I feel the only thing that will put me right is a better performance. If I'm out cheaply, the best cure is to get out there and score a hundred, and that will be something I must do for myself. Whatever anyone says, no one else can do it for me. I've got to sort it out for myself.'

Tonight, however, there are no problems. Riki is sitting at the table, writing out sentences for his homework and Rebecca lays herself out comfortably on her father's lap.

'So what did you do at school?'

'Painting.'

'Painting what?'

'Painting pictures, Daddy. What else?'

Laughter. Loafing with his daughter on his lap, Wessels is unrecognisable from the frowning captain at first slip, but public images rarely reflect private natures. Beyond the fact that he may score too slowly in the first 15 overs, beyond the fact that he may be too conservative, he remains a husband who loves his wife and a father who loves his children. Occasionally, when the criticism is at its greatest, that's a point worth making.

Riki is rushing through his homework because the Australian rugby league is on television at six. It's Wessels' only 'must-see' programme of the week. The Brisbane Broncos are his team. When he left Australia in 1986, he took with him more than a suitcase full of cricketing knowledge and experience. Seven years on, he remains more Australian than the ACB might ever imagine.

Visits to see Sally's parents in Woy Woy, a small town north of Sydney, have sustained regular contact, but there remains much in his approach to life and in the things which give him the most pleasure that is quintessentially Australian: the outdoor life, the down-to-earth style, the rough humour, the sport, the freedom, the sun, the opportunity, the struggle, the guts.

These influences have been thickly streaked through his basic Afrikaner background to produce a contrasting nature. One moment he can seem as open and up-front as an Australian, the next closed and suspicious like an Afrikaner. He wants his children to speak more Afrikaans, yet they are as relaxed and easygoing as any sun-kissed youngster playing in the sand on a Sydney beach.

The contrasts work well. There is no conflict. Sally, more than anyone, has sewn the seams. She has committed herself to South Africa, learning Afrikaans, yet she retains the Sydneysider's knack of being able to look on the bright side. Enthusiastic and bright, she tends to provide the ideal balance to her husband's more sober approach. Day after day, the family unit prospers.

Dinner is usually eaten at home. Wessels doesn't much enjoy going out in the evening, except to the cinema, preferring to eat and get to bed, often before half-past nine. He has tended to steer clear of parties, disliking the scatterbrained small talk of social events. He would simply rather stay at home.

'There was one time when Kepler came to dinner at our house,' recalls Kotie Grové, 'and, as soon as he arrived, he told us that he was going to leave at half-past ten. He didn't want to be rude, but that was it. So he came in and we talked and ate, and everything was fine. Then, at half-past ten, he got up and left. I know some people might have taken offence at that, but we didn't. That's how he is. He wanted to get a decent night's sleep. That was fine.'

Such an attitude has not always been accepted by team-mates. Wessels will invariably join his side when they go out to celebrate a victory, and he'll enjoy himself, but he won't stay until two in the morning just to keep people happy. The ravers may scoff, but he has never been one of the boys. Around the circuit, the word has spread that he doesn't have hundreds of friends.

The word is true. Wessels does not have hundreds of friends. In fact, he neither seeks nor needs hundreds of mates. Wherever he has lived, he has made a handful of close friends, and they have been lifelong friends. That's enough.

It's often said that the human condition is so insecure that almost everyone requires regular reassurance that they are OK and that people like them if they are to function properly, but Wessels is one of the few who seems so secure in his routine that he seeks no external approval. Perhaps necessity has taught him to rely on himself: as an Afrikaner in the English game, then a South African in Australia and finally an Australian in South Africa, he has had to stand alone. Now, he stands alone, in comfort.

Wessels' mental strength is astounding. He genuinely has no need to be bolstered by praise and he is unswayed by criticism. He relies on himself, and Sally. No one else.

'I've always been happy on my own,' he says. 'I have never felt that I need a big circle of friends. I reckon it's much better to have just a handful of people who you know you can rely on than a whole mass of people hanging around. I know I'm reluctant to open up to people, and that's probably because I've been let down in the past, but I just don't need to have people around. Even when things go wrong, I prefer to keep my emotions to myself.'

So the tag of 'introvert', a euphemism for boring, has been hung around his neck, but this is not accurate. As Grové confirms, you could put Wessels among a group of five strangers and he would sit quietly and say scarcely a word. With people he is unsure of, if he has nothing to say, he will say nothing, but, with people he trusts, he is tremendous, animated company.

His family has remained important throughout, and he is glad his parents and sister Marietta also live in Port Elizabeth. 'It's good to know they are close,' he says. His brother, Wessel, is still in Pretoria but the bond remains strong. 'Kepler asked me to drive with him on a business trip to Nelspruit recently,' Wessel recalls, 'and we talked for about seven hours. I think his family has always been very important to him.'

So, into the evening, he speaks to Sally, maybe watches some sport on TV (he follows rugby and boxing closely) or reads another popular novel, until he heads for his bed.

Before he sleeps, he prays.

Every day.

He prays.

To him, it matters more than anything else.

Back at the Gabba in November 1982, Wessels had surprised the hard-bitten cricket writers of Australia by telling them that he attributed all the glory of scoring 162 on his Test début 'to God'. Long before the practice became fashionable, he was prepared to stand up and proclaim his faith in public.

His father recalls that, while the entire family attended the Dutch Reformed church every Sunday, 'Kepler always took that extra bit of trouble.' Into his youth and the generally secular world of cricket, he sustained a close relationship with God.

However, strengthened by Sally's own conviction, his arena for worship moved from the strict procedures of the NG Kerk to the more relaxed mood of a Pentecostal church in Brisbane. Settled in Port Elizabeth, the Wessels family became members of the Harvest Christian Centre, a fully charismatic place of worship where outward signs of adoration are actively encouraged.

Since international readmission, Wessels has been part of a movement within South African cricket in which leading figures have put their Christian faith on public display: Alan Jordaan, the team manager, is a lay preacher; Peter Pollock, latterly the convener of selectors, had declared his faith for many years; Andrew Hudson, Jonty Rhodes and Wessels joined in prayer meetings at the World Cup and subsequently attended various Christian rallies; Hansie Cronje fell to his knees in the middle of the St George's Park pitch after reaching his first Test century against India.

Such widespread proclamations delighted many Christians and, in their minds, raised the status of the game to something rather more important than the result of the next Test.

It would, however, be foolish to pretend that others did not voice concern. The combined effect of all these individual acts of faith prompted the suspicion that cricket was being unintentionally used to promote one religious group above others. When posters were displayed in Johannesburg advertising an address by 'Evangelist and World Cup manager Alan Jordaan', a group of officials saw the sport moving into territory where it does not belong.

Wessels sees nothing sinister, nothing wrong. 'It's not vital to exhibit your faith,' he says calmly and thoughtfully, 'but you should never deny it and never be ashamed of it. Religion is basically private but, if someone asks me about it, I will tell them. I'm not scared to stand up for Christ.

'And I don't want to create the impression that religion is especially important for my cricket. It is the most important thing in every aspect of my life. The point is that I have faith that, in the long run, things will work out right; and I never feel alone. I count myself lucky because I've always had this faith.

'I have always been able to talk to God whenever I want. Quite often, I will pray during a match, not to win, just to do my best but my relationship is such that I don't have to show everyone I'm praying. At times like that, He helps me stay balanced. Whether things are going right or wrong on the field, I feel that He makes sure I don't get too carried away.'

A cynic might wonder whether this Wessels who claims such a close relationship with God could possibly be the same Wessels who swears at opposition batsmen from first slip, who won't walk unless he's given out and who plays so tough. By proclaiming himself a Christian, doesn't he open himself up to public scrutiny? Is he satisfied that his deeds have matched his faith?

'Nobody is strong enough to live up to their ideals,' he replies. 'In cricket, you have to play the game tough. You've got to go in hard, and I do swear at people. It happens. It happens more than it should but there are many temptations to sin. Being a Christian means you make a bold attempt to resist.'

During 1993, Wessels and several other cricketers raised more eyebrows when they became publicly associated with Ray McCauley, a reformed bodybuilder turned preacher at the Rhema church in

Johannesburg. Critics see McCauley in the mould of popular American preachers driving around town in a Mercedes Benz. Wessels sees him as a clear thinker and an inspired guide.

'As far as I'm concerned, Kepler Wessels is a fine individual and an excellent role model for young people,' McCauley stated near the 18th green at Royal St George's golf club in Sandwich, England. He was taking time to watch the 1993 British Open and support Wayne Westner, another of his well-known sporting friends.

Some of those more used to the traditional form of worship have frowned on Wessels because of his association with McCauley, yet he has carefully thought through his religion. He attends Bible classes with Sally in Port Elizabeth, and discusses religious issues at home as other couples might discuss the weather. Wessels is blessed with a vivid and living conviction, not a blind faith.

He continues: 'People shouldn't argue about the differences between traditional and charismatic churches. It's more important that their faith in God is strong. Once they have that, they should choose whichever church they feel comfortable with.'

His faith is strong. Amid all the turmoil of his life in cricket, that much has been secure. He doesn't try to force it down anyone's throat, but he is not afraid to say that his faith in God has helped him through the difficult times.

Finally, at the end of this average day, Wessels switches out the light and gently falls asleep. He says he needs seven or eight hours of sleep each night and, sometimes, he dreams.

'It's usually one of two dreams,' he concludes. 'Either it's my turn to bat and I'm stuck in the dressing room because I can't get my pads on, or it's me fielding in the slips when someone gets a big nick and the ball whacks me in the chest.'

But the dreams don't bother him. He has never had difficulty strapping on his pads, nor has he been struck in the chest. He has faced greater problems than dreams, and conquered them.

And so he sleeps.

Soundly. Always.

ll right, mate, best of luck.' Riki Wessels braces himself for his first day at Grey Junior School in January 1992. His
ther buttons his blazer while his sister, Rebecca, poses for the camera.

All smiles, at home: Kepler and Sally Wessels *(above)*. All scowls, at work: Wessels and Mike Procter *(below)*. Differ natures and different views sometimes came between captain and coach.

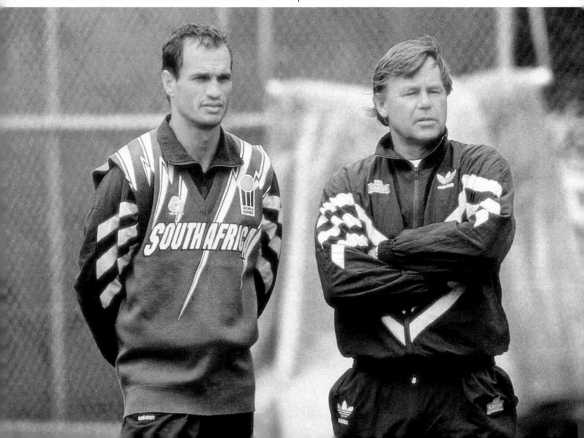

'He was such a positive influence on the side that he made himself indispensable' – Wessels on Jonty Rhodes, the all-
action, grinning symbol of the South African side after readmission.

History in Sydney (*above, left to right*): Craig Matthews, Fanie de Villiers and Allan Donald lined up in the South African pace attack for the second Test, while Shane Warne (*below*) carried Australia's hopes.

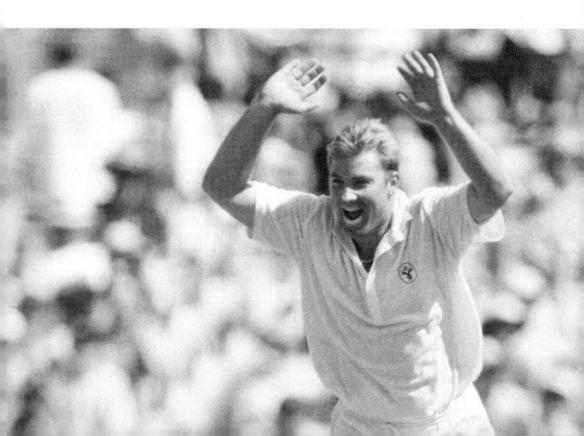

History in Sydney: Australia needed 117 to win, but De Villiers took six for 43 in the second innings and the home side were 111 all out. *Above,* he traps Tim May LBW for 0. *Below,* some of the South Africans celebrate: *left to right,* Brian McMillan, Daryll Cullinan, Dave Richardson, Hansie Cronje, Andrew Hudson, Craig Matthews and Gary Kirsten. 'It was a great day,' Wessels recalls.

Though injured, Wessels had played a full role in planning the rout with vice-captain Hansie Cronje in the second Test against Australia, and the captain rushed on to the field at the end. Amid delirium, South Africa had won.

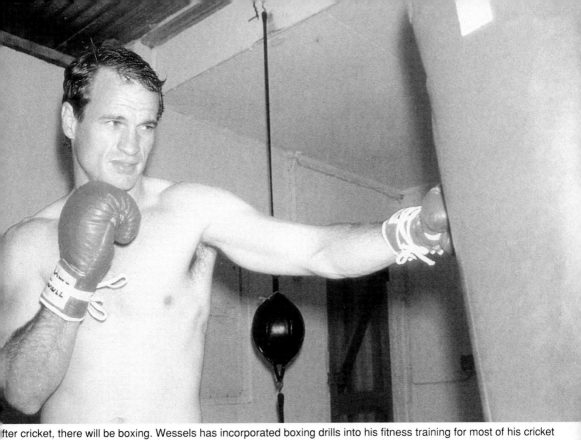

fter cricket, there will be boxing. Wessels has incorporated boxing drills into his fitness training for most of his cricket areer (*above*), and is now a TV commentator (*below*).

*overleaf*) The Winner's Smile: by February 1994, Wessels had led a young and inexperienced South African side into 10 ests, winning three times and losing once. Long after contemporary criticism has been swept aside, the facts will testify his achievement.

# 14

## One Captain, One Way

A slight, track-suited figure paces up and down outside the Sandton Holiday Inn. It is just another cricketer waiting outside another out-of-town hotel. He glances at his watch. It's getting past ten. The convener should be here by now. No sign. Other guests pass by and double-take.

'Isn't that...?'

'Yes, I think it is.'

At last a car pulls up and carries the South African cricket captain away to a meeting with the national selectors. It is late March, usually the end of the season. Not in 1993. They will choose a squad to tour Sri Lanka in August and September. Season without end. On and on.

As usual, Kepler Wessels takes his own ideas to the meeting. He sits, listens, puts forward his views and then lets the selectors get on with making the decisions. He has his say, but no more than that. He does his job, they do theirs...

The results of their debate were announced immediately after the night series final at Kingsmead the following Wednesday. Peter Pollock, the convener of selectors, strolled into the Press box and read out the names of the 15 men 'to represent South Africa'.

KEPLER WESSELS, CAPTAIN... HANSIE CRONJE, VICE-CAPTAIN (as he utters the words vice-captain, the room murmurs — it's bad news for Peter Kirsten, vice-captain against India)... JIMMY COOK (the Transvaler has played himself back into the team)... DARYLL CULLINAN (the batting prince)... FANIE DE VIL-LIERS... (a wiry fast bowler from Pretoria)... CLIVE EKSTEEN (a fast-improving Transvaal spinner)... ANDREW HUDSON (still a pillar in the batting)... BRIAN McMILLAN (the only all-rounder — it's alphabetical order and Kirsten is gone)... STEVE PALFRA-MAN... (a self-assured wicketkeeper from Border)... JONTY RHODES (the action man)... DAVE RICHARDSON (the No.1

wicketkeeper)... BRETT SCHULTZ... (the left-arm-over fast bowler)... RICHARD SNELL (the seaming talent)... PAT SYMCOX (the
in-form Natal spinner).

That's it.

'Any questions?'

There are none. Almost two years after readmission, the squad is
settling. Most of the players pick themselves...

Through April, May, June and July, Wessels maintained his fitness,
kept in contact with his players by phone and arranged nets at St
George's Park for the Eastern Province players on their way to Sri
Lanka, laying on spin bowlers to help hone the batsmen for the
particular challenge which lay ahead.

He had toured Sri Lanka before, with Australia in 1983, and his
memories were still vivid of the grinding cricket and the 'best
firecrackers in the world'. He had enjoyed it, but was fully aware that
the home team had improved immeasurably in ten years. Recent Test
victories over England and New Zealand, and a close match with
Australia were evidence of their strength at home.

As part of his preparation for the tour, he telephoned some of his
Australian friends to ask their advice. Both Dean Jones and Allan
Border gave him the same message: Don't get upset by the umpires.
'Chopper, there's nothing you can do about it,' Jones said. 'Just accept
them.' The UCB later requested neutral umpires for the Test matches
and Brian Aldridge, of New Zealand, was appointed to stand.
Ironically, he would prove a much less reliable official than the
surprisingly capable local men.

Through two sweat-soaked days spent training en route in Singapore,
Wessels emphasised to his players the importance of not being rattled by
the conditions. 'You might not like the food, you may not like the hotel
and we know it's going to be hot, but we are here to win the series,' he
said. 'That's our job. Moaning isn't going to help anyone. We must stay
positive.'

As ever, the captain had fastened on a clear strategy, set solid in his
mind as the best way of defeating Sri Lanka and he was absolutely
determined that it would be pursued. Others had doubts, but he would
not be swayed. One captain, one way. Wessels was in control, just as he
had been ever since readmission. He was going to lead, others would
follow. There would be no fudging, no buck-passing, no muddle. There
was absolute clarity.

'Everyone was worrying about our spinners and how we would bat against spin,' he recalls, 'but I thought it would be foolish to go there and take them on at their own game. Our strength was still our fast bowlers and I knew from 1983 that, while their pitches are suited to spin, they're often underprepared. I thought our quicks could get something out of them. So that was my plan. Hit them with the fast bowlers, bouncers, real pace, the lot. I wanted us to play to our strengths, not theirs.'

The criticism of this strategy began before a single ball had been bowled. One journalist, discreetly encouraged from within the squad, wrote: 'Despite strong evidence to the contrary, Wessels is adamant that, although the wickets will be prepared with no grass and no pace, his quick men, led by Allan Donald, will still take wickets'... damn Kepler, he's so stubborn...

Most of the mumbling was doused on the very first day of the opening match against a Board President's XI in Galle. Schultz, all pace and raging aggression, took four for 18 and genuinely scared the batsmen. Wessels was triumphant. The home side was rattled out for 90. Schultz took seven wickets in the match and, well supported by the accurate Eksteen, carried the team to victory early on the third morning, by an innings and 13 runs.

The second three-day match, played against another Board XI in Kurunegala, an hour's drive through the mountains from the team hotel, unfolded as a satisfactory draw with all the batsmen scoring runs and De Villiers' five for 68 providing further evidence of the fast bowlers' role. Wessels was evidently winning the argument over tactics and yet, for the first time since taking over as captain, he could detect some grumbling in the ranks. He set it aside. Keep on the job. Stay focused. Concentrate.

'It was only an instinct,' he recalls. 'The spirit in the side was still good. We had the ghetto-blaster playing stuff like UB40 in the dressing room and it was fine. I just had this feeling that a few guys were muttering in the corners.'

When the first one-day international was abandoned as a draw after four interruptions for rain, Wessels turned his attention to the first of the three Tests, to be played at the Tyronne Fernando stadium in Moratuwa, a nondescript suburb 15 kilometres down the coast from the island's capital, Colombo.

He looked at the pitch, by reputation a spinners' dream, and saw no grass, only baked mud. Determined to take six specialist batsmen into the opening Test, he was confronted with a choice between a second spinner or a third fast bowler. For once, his resolve yielded to the general hue and cry. McMillan was left out, both Symcox and Eksteen would make their Test débuts. The Sri Lankans won the toss and decided to bat.

'Within two overs, I knew we had made a mistake,' Wessels recalls ruefully. 'The quicks were doing the job. We should have picked McMillan. It was my fault. I blamed myself.'

Donald, firing on all cylinders, and Schultz, wreaking havoc by pushing the rising ball across the right-hander, were astutely used in short spells to protect them from the oppressive heat, and they bit hard into the batting line-up, reducing Sri Lanka to 168 for five. At that stage, Wessels supped frustration. He knew that a third fast bowler might have buckled the innings, but the big guns were tired and he had no more bullets to fire.

Cronje, pressed into service as a purveyor of wobbling medium pace, ably sustained some pressure by bowling 19 overs for only 18 runs but the spinners both disappointed, enabling Ruwan Kalpage and Hashan Tillekeratne to prosper into the evening. By stumps, the Sri Lankans had reached 241 for five. Wessels left the field, showered and immediately returned to his hotel room. He had wasted a chance to take control. Now the match would be a struggle.

Schultz and Donald, refreshed by sleep, resumed their assault the next morning and Sri Lanka were bowled out for 331. Donald took five for 69 and Schultz, on his 23rd birthday, four for 75. In sedate reply, Wessels and Hudson eased the score to 81 without loss by the close and, after the rest day, to 104 during the third morning but the captain's dismissal for 47 triggered a collapse. Cronje was bowled by Muttiah Muralitharan, and eight wickets tumbled for only 88 runs. But for Cullinan's bright 33 and Symcox's cracked 48, South Africa would not have reached 267.

Into the fourth day, the South African attack was dominated by the venerable giants of Sri Lankan cricket. Aravinda de Silva and Arjuna Ranatunga batted with splendour, at one stage adding 50 runs in six and a half overs. Ranatunga, who had made his début against Australia and Wessels a decade earlier, hit a stellar 131 enabling him to declare the innings closed at 300 for six with a lead of 339 and leave enough time to dismiss the tourists.

Amid the firecrackers, the oppressive heat, the pressure and the heaving bedlam, some of the South African players had lost their cool.

They had allowed themselves to be upset because Ranatunga was adjudged not out when he seemed to have been caught and bowled by Cronje, and discipline was lost when first Symcox, then Rhodes struck the batsmen with errant throws. Both maintained the contact was unintentional but the match referee, John Reid, the former New Zealand player, issued an unofficial conduct warning to the South African team. Wessels felt this was undeserved.

The tourists' situation deteriorated further when Hudson and Cronje were both dismissed in the 11 overs that Sri Lanka bowled before the close. At 26 for two, with still a full day to survive on a slow-turning pitch, catastrophe was looming. Wessels was not optimistic. 'It wasn't looking too bright,' he recalls. 'I reckoned Daryll (Cullinan) and I would have to bat through until lunch if we were going to have much chance. It was going to be hard. Their tails were up.'

In only the ninth over of the morning, the captain swept at Muralitharan, the off-spinner, and was caught on the leg-side. He trod slowly back to the pavilion. Cullinan and Cook both staved off the bowlers for two hours but, when Richardson departed swiftly and unhappily after another doubtful umpiring decision, defeat loomed large and sad with the score 138 for six.

Sound of trumpets! Rhodes came riding to the rescue. He began nervously against the spinners but soon settled into a pattern of survival, thrusting his front pad at all manner of deliveries sent buzzing and fizzing through the sapping heat towards him. The boy-next-door idol stood firm for his country. He was ably supported at the opposite end by Symcox, who battled for 21 overs, and then by Eksteen who batted with monumental patience, amassing a total of four runs in the 92 minutes he spent protecting the thin white line. He was unbeaten when the draw was secured.

Rhodes had reached his maiden Test century with a four and a six, and, suspended in a state of delirium afterwards, spoke of his 101 not out as 'the greatest innings of my career'. He had earned the glory, but maybe the greatest satisfaction in the latest South African fightback lay in the fact that, once again, someone had stood tall and hung tough in a crisis. Another day, it may have been Rhodes who got the rough decision and Richardson who got the century. The point was that, with each passing series, the team and its nation of supporters were growing more confident that, whenever disaster loomed, someone would stand firm.

This was a battling side. At Moratuwa, they had got out of jail. Team spirit had prevailed again but, through the pair of one-day internationals which followed, this one quality, valued so highly by Wessels, would be threatened.

The two matches, played within the space of four days, both took place at the Khetterama stadium and they could hardly have produced more contrasting results. On the Tuesday, McMillan returned to action and inspired South Africa to win by 124 runs, their largest margin of victory in a one-day game since readmission. Two days later, set 199 to win, the touring side crumbled to 77 for seven, then 103 for nine before being bowled out for 154. The sudden slump in fortunes provoked a public row between Wessels and Procter over the team's batting strategy in one-day matches. This simmered for weeks and will be discussed at length later in this chapter, as part of the never-ending debate surrounding the captain's suitability to one-day cricket.

Of greater immediate concern to the captain was a campaign of whispering being conducted behind his back. Kepler this, Kepler that. Since readmission, the great strength of the team had been its unbridled unity and its high-fiving harmony...

The South African team has been named for the second Test, and, again, Jimmy Cook has been dropped. Once lauded as the finest opening batsman in the world, he is becoming frustrated. In for the tour to India, out for the World Cup, in for two Tests at home against India, out for the rest of the season, in for the first Test in Sri Lanka, out again: what might have been a glorious, glowing conclusion to a distinguished career was unfolding as a sad letdown. The fact was that he could not hold his place in the side, and the warm rays of readmission seemed to be passing him by.

Who was there to blame?

The captain, perhaps: Wessels, the man who played 24 Tests for Australia while Cook stayed home and taught at Fairways Primary School and who then returned to be given the fatted calf of leading the national team to the World Cup.

This day in Sri Lanka, Cook has found an audience of eager journalists to regale. 'I couldn't believe Kepler after we lost that night match in Colombo,' he says. 'I mean we had been thrashed and he didn't have a word to say. He didn't have anything to tell the team. It was typical. That's when a captain should get the guys round...'

Over and again, Wessels had asked his players to discuss any problem with him, face to face. Cook never mentioned his complaint to the captain, preferring the company of journalists. Whether he was right or wrong, his conduct was not direct. Nothing could have irritated Wessels more intensely. If anyone had a problem, then he wanted to know so he could sort it out. He loathed anyone who spoke behind his back, could not abide two-faced team-mates.

* * * * *

But was Cook right?

Was Wessels too much of an introvert, at times a grumpy and detached introvert, to be an effective leader? Was he capable of motivating the team? Could he communicate? Was it time for Cronje, the appointed heir, to take over the side?

Innumerable discussions around South Africa, and a few within his own team, began to examine Wessels' performance as captain, not so much as a tactician (although that was also criticised) but as a leader of men. The pot had been effectively stirred. Wessels hears out the grievances and responds, one by one:

*Grievance 1:* His teamtalks are inadequate. Cook's anxiety in Colombo reiterated the sentiments expressed by Rod McCurdy in 1991: 'Kepler's not a good talker. He never makes the sort of speech that makes you want to run out and rip the stadium down.'

Wessels: 'There was no point saying anything that night in Colombo. We had lost a one-day match and it was pretty obvious why. It's much better just to leave things after a disaster like that, and then to discuss the game the next day when people have calmed down and the dust has settled.

'Unlike rugby, cricket is not a sport where the captain must whip his team into frenzy. You don't want your players bursting any veins. I see the teamtalk as more of an outline of our aims. It's almost a discussion within the side. I encourage other guys to put forward their views. As a rule, I don't shout.

'I try to take a calmer, more considered approach in motivating the team. The first step is to let every player know precisely what I'm expecting from them. I do that on a one-to-one basis, and I reckon I have done that successively within the squad. Players have often come to speak to me privately, and that's fine.

'The second step is to keep watching them to see how they're going. I know them all fairly well. I make it my business to know them. Often I just look at them to know what's going through their mind. I know when they're scheming and when they're pulling my leg. I know their mentality. I can see. Some hide it better than others. Jonty I can pick better. Hudson I can see straight away. It took me a while to work out Snell's mentality, but I got him. Donald took me a while before I learned how to handle him.

'All of these guys are top players. You can't just shout at them. You must treat them like individuals and you have to respect them. I mean, I won't just tell Donald to run some shuttles. I will ask him what he feels he needs to do for his fitness. Most of the time, each player will know what he requires. My responsibility is to make sure that our goals are clearly defined and that the whole squad works professionally towards them.'

*Grievance 2:* He is grumpy and detached. Some national team players spoke of their frustration at being unable to get close to Wessels, to understand him as a person. At various stages, players have been disconcerted when, for example, they pass the captain in the corridor and he scarcely acknowledges their presence.

Wessels: 'I never mean to be rude. There are times when there is something on my mind and, to be honest, I wouldn't notice who passed me in the corridor. And I know that I'm not an easygoing type. That's my nature. It's really not necessary for everyone to be best buddies but I do want players to tell me if they have a problem, and then I'll do everything I can to help them sort it out. I'll always listen.

'You know, my job is to captain a cricket team and I have done that to the best of my ability. I wasn't appointed to crack jokes and make people laugh. If doing the things I believe are right for the team makes me unpopular, so be it. I can live with that. Just because one or two of the players don't like something we do, and go away moaning about it to outsiders, doesn't mean it was wrong.

'I also think there should be some tension in the relationship between captain and players. I have to stand apart because it's me who must impose the discipline. I want them to listen when I speak to them. You've got to have that.'

*Grievance 3:* He sulks at first slip when things go wrong in the field. The pose is familiar: one hand folded across his chest, the other propping up his chin, and a frown across his face. Such a sight is particularly familiar to fast bowlers who have been clubbed to the boundary and to fielders who have dropped a catch. Some people, notably those watching, feel he could be more supportive. The bowlers, themselves, are less adamant.

Wessels: 'I'm not specifically doing anything. I'm too busy thinking about the bowlers and setting the field to think about my arms. There again, if someone has messed up, it's right that they should know I'm not happy. The whole body language thing has become a bit of a joke. Some of the Western Province guys have started taking me off, and even the Eastern Province players laugh about it. I don't mind that at all.

'On the other hand, I think it is possible for a captain to talk too much on the field. You have to communicate with bowlers, and I do, but most of the guys know what they have to do. I reckon they would get irritated if I kept telling them.'

People must reach their own conclusions, but it is surely worth pointing out that since Wessels returned to South Africa in 1986, he has captained Eastern Province to unprecedented success and South Africa to the World Cup semi-final and series victories over India and, eventually, Sri Lanka. Look at the record! It's in the book, and it's really not so bad for a man who was supposedly incapable of communicating with his players.

Two men have played alongside Wessels at both provincial and national level, and thus should be better qualified than most to unravel the enigma that Wessels, as a captain, seems to present.

Dave Richardson, the wicketkeeper, has stood beside Wessels, at slip, through thousands of overs, through setbacks and triumphs, through hundreds of matches since April 1986. 'It is strange but even though I have stood next to him for so long, I haven't really got to know Kepler as a person,' he says. 'I don't know. We're only cricketing friends. We haven't become personal friends. Sometimes I think he's distrustful. It takes a lot to make him feel confident with you, or that you're not against him. He's a difficult person to understand, but once he has confidence in you then he values that very much. He will be very loyal, through thick and thin.'

The concept of a softness beneath the tough exterior is supported by Dave Callaghan. Over the years, Callaghan has taken the route to compatibility with Wessels first used by Barlow at Stellenbosch and subsequently by many Australians: tease him, wind him up, laugh, don't cower and always, always be loyal.

'The key to getting on with Kepler is never to grumble behind his back,' Callaghan says. 'He hates that more than anything else. If you have a problem, you must go straight to him. If he sees you being up-front and working hard, then he'll support you and he'll be incredibly loyal, but you have to prove yourself.

'Of course, I know he can seem difficult. There was one time I remember when Eastern Province were on tour in Holland. I wanted to play in one particular match, so my wife and I drove through the night from Rochdale in northern England to get there on the morning of the game. It rained the whole way and it was still raining when we arrived at the hotel. The guys were having breakfast, so we went in to see them, and Kepler hardly looked up to greet us.

'He was frustrated because it had rained for most of the tour and another game was at risk. He didn't mean it personally. He just takes cricket seriously and it's because he takes it so seriously, even if that means sometimes getting intense about things, that he has been so successful. It's very difficult to argue with what he has achieved in the game. People forget that.'

There are different types of captain. Morné du Plessis, the Springbok rugby captain, for example, may have had the personality to put his arm around a player and gently coax the best out of him, but that was never Wessels' style. He led by setting a disciplined example and challenging his players to follow him. Neither method is 'better' than the other. Neither is 'right'. Both have worked at different times, and both have been criticised.

Finally, the opposition to Wessels' captaincy should not be exaggerated. The grumbling of a few players — McCurdy at Eastern Province, Cook with the national side, how many more? — should not be allowed to distort the reality. In general, his teams have been successful and happy.

That's the fact.

* * * * *

There are four Test cricket venues within the city of Colombo, two of which are to be found less than 500 metres apart on the Maitland Avenue. The Colombo Cricket Club was founded first but for the sole use of European settlers and, as recently as 1958, the CCC did not admit natives. The natives, therefore, wandered down the road and launched their own Sinhalese Sports Club, a modest venue with a pavilion and just one permanent stand.

Both had been full in March 1993 when Sri Lanka beat England in a Test match at the SSC. Five months later, Wessels led his side out at the same ground for the second Test. South Africa made two changes from the first Test match, Cook and Eksteen being replaced by McMillan and Snell because Wessels was determined that all four of his fast bowlers should be unleashed upon the Sri Lankans. That was his strategy for the series and he would not change course.

Three and a half days of clinical, robust cricket gloriously justified his resolve. South Africa stormed to the largest Test win in all their history and Sri Lanka suffered their heaviest defeat. It was all over by lunch on the fourth day.

Sri Lanka had won the toss and, to Wessels' delight, decided to bat first on another hard, bare pitch. They were all but ruined by this self-inflicted collision with the fast bowlers on the first day. A shower of catches were held in the slip cordon. Schultz took five for 48, McMillan and Donald took two each and Snell snared the other. The home side were all out for 169.

Mercilessly drilling home the advantage, Hudson and Wessels put together an opening stand of 137 and, with the captain moving on to score 92 before falling, again, to Muralitharan, South Africa reached 280 for two by stumps on the second day. Progress had been slow but sure. A middle order collapse to 333 for six on the third morning was put right by Cronje's mature century. Still aged only 23, the vice-captain batted for nearly seven hours to score 122. He had previously struggled on tour yet, at the crucial moment, he had shown a resolve reminiscent of his captain.

After Symcox and Snell indulged in some late fireworks, the touring team were finally dismissed for 495. In control. There was still time to bowl 20 overs at Sri Lanka on the third evening and by stumps, the home side had staggered to 49 for four. That was just about that. The straight-armed pace of Donald, the bounce of Schultz and the movement of Snell had proved altogether too much. Rout, rout, rout. Sri Lanka were all out for 119.

With match analysis of nine for 106, the beaming Schultz was named Man of the Match. South Africa had won by an innings and 208 runs. Even the sharpest critic conceded that, far from home, it had been an exceptional all round team performance. When South Africa last won a Test on foreign soil, defeating England in 1965, only four of Wessels' side had been born.

'We blitzed them,' he recalls. 'I was pleased because we had produced some really hard, uncompromising cricket. Our quicks were fired up and there was a fair amount of sledging going on. It was good. Sri Lanka had begun the series thinking they'd win, but I don't think they knew what had hit them.'

The third and last Test was scheduled for the P. Saravanamuttu Oval, tucked away in the back and beyond of Colombo. The history of the ground bore more witness to the island's divided past. As the settlers played at the CCC and the natives at SSC, eager cricketers from the minority Tamil group were forced to form their own club, the Tamil Union, at this neat white-washed Oval.

Sri Lanka's present was racked by painful divisions as well. President Premadasa had been assassinated by a suicide bomber in Colombo on May 1st, and the sad, vicious ongoing conflict between the Sinhalese majority and the Tamil Tigers continued to simmer in the north and eastern sections of the island.

The South African cricketers had seen no hint of civil war, and most of them had lacked the initiative to leave their hotel and discover a country of stunning beauty. Some muttered about spending long periods in the same hotel, of being bored and hot, of having nowhere to go and nothing to do, yet they never saw the bejewelled palaces, the gigantic statues of Buddha, the huge tea plantations, the magnificent beaches or the wildlife parks. They winced at curry served hot, very hot, fiery or explosive and found the beer watery and thin. Few tasted the cool, clear water which can be found by hacking the top off a 'thambli', a king coconut.

Several months earlier, an England cricketer, Philip Tufnell, had been criticised for remarking midway through the tour of India: 'Done the poverty, done the elephant, might as well go home.' With some exceptions, notably De Villiers, South Africa's finest took only a marginally more sophisticated approach. Their response would be that they were there to win cricket matches and not see the sights, but it seems a pity if the two have become so incompatible. Once upon a time, touring was the exciting perk in a cricketer's life, a prized opportunity to discover new places and new people, but in the modern era, touring has too often become a dull cycle of hotels with hamburger room service and in-house video, of visits to buy portable CD players in duty-free shops.

Their minds safely on the cricket, the touring team arrived at the Saravanamuttu Oval with the iron-clad aim of defending their lead in the series. As Azharuddin and India would have been able to confirm, the final Test of a series in which any team captained by Wessels is leading one-nil is unlikely to see a dash for glory and two-nil. The South African captain will play it safe, lock up the Test match, throw the key into the nearest river and solidly store away another series triumph to his credit.

With an unchanged side from the second Test, Wessels won the toss but faced a dilemma. In an effort to blunt his fast bowlers, the pitch had been flooded the previous day, dried out and shaved of grass. 'My instinct was to bat first and dominate with a large first innings,' he remembers. 'On the other hand, I reckoned the pitch would still do a bit and that we could rattle them out for around 180. In the end, I decided to bat because I didn't want to risk them getting the big score on the board, but perhaps I should have taken the risk and bowled first.'

In awkward batting conditions, Wessels' side seemed on the brink of deep trouble at 128 for five. The captain had been bowled by Liyanage for 22, Hudson and Cronje were also dismissed in their 20s, Rhodes was stumped by yards and McMillan was given out caught off the pad, another victim for the umpires.

On this occasion, Cullinan instigated the revival. Together with Richardson, he calmly supervised the team to 231 for five by stumps on the first day. The following morning, their match-saving partnership was extended to 122 runs before the brave Richardson was dismissed for 62. With Symcox's breezy 30, South Africa eased towards respectability and finished 316 all out.

To widespread delight, Cullinan had held the innings steadily together and reached his maiden Test century. The thoughtful young batsman had released himself from more of the onerous expectations which had washed over him ever since the day he became the youngest South African to score a first class century. Aged 16 years and 304 days old, he had broken Graeme Pollock's record.

Through the following seasons at Western Province, Cullinan had offered sweet glimpses of an opulent talent, enough to maintain his rich promise but not consistently enough to pacify the critics. As the years passed, the doubts escalated, both without and within. He became introspective and somewhat withdrawn. Heavy-handed officials in Cape Town ignorantly labelled him a trouble-maker when, one day, he was asked his opinion in a team meeting and he replied that the captain and coach should both resign. 'Thanks, Daryll.' He was no ordinary cricketer to whom ordinary rules applied. Western Province could not understand that, and they lost him. In 1991, a veteran in terms of experience at 24, he joined Transvaal.

Amid the fuss surrounding the omission of Cook and Rice from the World Cup squad, Cullinan's name was hardly mentioned, but the fact that he had been preceded on to the international stage by younger, less talented men had frustrated him.

He hurled himself into a physical fitness regime and began to give his ambition a more steely edge. He was finally, many said belatedly, picked in the national side for the fourth Test against India and he did enough in the triangular series that followed to book his place on the winter tour to Sri Lanka.

Scores of 33, 46 and 52 in the first two Test matches would have satisfied some but, standing at second slip after dropping two catches in the space of 15 minutes during the second Test, Cullinan was seized by a dread fear. 'I have rarely felt so miserable on the field,' he recalls. 'I had this vision of me being an ordinary Test player with an average of around 30. I want to be better than that, and the third Test seemed a chance to make a start.'

His century was patient, lasting almost six hours, but it was embellished by 17 boundaries, the finest of which were stroked off the back foot past frozen fielders at cover point. The sheer relief of reaching his century prompted him to offer an easy return catch, but his innings of 102 in Colombo marked another step on the long road to the realisation of his huge potential.

Wessels saw Cullinan's emergence as the solution to a long-standing problem: 'People had said that we needed a strokemaker in the top order, someone who could really take on the bowlers,' he recalls, 'and that was possibly true. Daryll had shown that he had the potential to fill that important role.'

Sri Lanka's innings in reply to 316 bore the hallmarks of a team who had had the stuffing knocked out of them. After losing two early wickets, and then a third to some more brilliant fielding by Rhodes at cover, they seemed unable, or unwilling, to fight for the victory which would level the series. Aravinda de Silva and Arjuna Ranatunga contented themselves with survival.

Jayasuriya's extrovert 65 on the fourth morning prompted a declaration at 296 for nine, but the match headed for a draw when, after a minor collapse, Cronje and Rhodes dragged the score to 159 for four by the close. The fifth day promised little, and little was lost when heavy overnight rain ruled out any prospect of play. The series was over. South Africa had won.

'We are aiming to become the best side in the world in two years and we have the team to achieve it,' Procter declared at the final Press conference of the tour. 'At present, we probably rank fourth behind the West Indies, Pakistan and Australia.'

Bushy-tailed confidence was everywhere. Schultz had finished with 20 wickets in the series, taken much of the glory and emerged as the perfect foil to Donald, even though his immediate future was to be blighted by injury. Most of the batsmen had scored runs and even if Wessels the batsman had been blunted by slow pitches suited to a stronger backlift than his, Wessels the captain felt generally encouraged as the tour of Australia loomed.

'No one was going overboard,' the captain recalls, 'because we had only just scraped out of the first Test with a draw, and things could have been difficult if we had lost there, but we had played a fair amount of tough cricket. That was good.'

None the less, there had been talk of divisions in the camp. The bout was billed as Coach Procter versus Captain Wessels. The issue was the team's batting strategy in one-day cricket. Procter favoured an aggressive approach from the start, Wessels argued for a solid base laying the platform before a later assault.

Vivid images were drawn of the coach, who had been such a tenacious player himself, finally breaking his silence and speaking up against the conservative tactics of his captain. The media moved in to devour what seemed a plausible conflict.

Ignition had occurred soon after South Africa collapsed and lost the third one-day international in Colombo. Wessels, upset by the defeat, had dropped his guard during the Press conference and told the journalists: 'If we set ourselves and get off to a good start, we are bombarded from everywhere because we are not scoring quickly enough. Then, if we play shots and lose wickets, that is also wrong. We're either going to play good, constructive cricket or we're going to have a bash in the first 15 overs, like Proccie wants, and lose a lot of wickets like tonight.'

With finely-tuned news sense, one of the journalists turned off his tape recorder, strolled briskly back to the South African dressing room and played the tape to Procter. The coach was shocked by Wessels' comment and he felt obliged to defend himself. In the heat of the moment, the battlelines were drawn.

A series of articles threatened the equilibrium of the side and, sensing trouble, Bacher convened a meeting at the UCB offices between Procter, Wessels, Peter Pollock and himself soon after the squad returned from Sri Lanka. Following the obligatory 'full and frank discussion', some sort of muddled, face-saving compromise was established and the storm blew itself out. At a subsequent meeting in Durban, it was resolved that all personal differences within the squad would, in future, be resolved in private.

Procter seemed bemused by the furore: 'It was all blown up out of proportion,' he said afterwards. 'There really wasn't such a big difference between us.' Wessels also regrets the public nature of the row, conceding that he 'shouldn't have mentioned Proccie at the Press conference'. Fair enough. Life went on.

The issue, however, would not go away.

It had become one of the unthinking refrains of South African sport, repeated so relentlessly that mere jaundiced opinion becomes accepted as more confirmed fact. Just as 'Naas Botha kicks too much on the rugby field', so 'Wessels bats too slowly to be effective in limited overs cricket'... et cetera... et cetera.

The myth is hard to expose. Joe Sportsfan, and even Johan Sportsfan, has little time between his beer and his braai to bother with the facts. Ever since he can remember, everyone has said that Kepler bats too slowly. From the highbrow hecklers seeing the world from the balcony of their luxurious pavilion at the Inanda Club to the glassy-eyed teeny tots, motherless on shandy, staggering around Castle Corner during a night match, all agree.

But what are the facts?

Throughout his career, Wessels has consistently scored runs in all forms of cricket. He has sustained a distinguished first class average around 50 for some years, and his limited over mark hovers in the region of 43. Both are exceptional, but the latter average tells half the story. In one-day cricket, it is not simply how many runs you score, but how quickly you score them.

Wessels' career strike rate (i.e. number of runs scored per hundred balls faced) is 59.56. Desmond Haynes, the globally admired West Indian opener, has an all-time scoring rate of 61.32. It could be argued that both play an anchor role for their national side, playing cautiously to guard against an early collapse and laying a platform for an assault later in the innings.

There have been poor innings when both Wessels and Haynes have batted too slowly, sometimes much too slowly, but there have also been days when they have scored more quickly. The fact is that the batting average and the scoring rate do not lie. Overall, both men have played the anchor role admirably over the years, but how often is Haynes mocked and lambasted as being too slow?

'Most of the criticism leaves me cold,' Wessels responds. 'My role as an opening batsman in one-day cricket is to get the innings off to a good start. As a rule, I aim to get 50 off between 80 and 90 deliveries. Sometimes I haven't kept up to that rate but I don't think people understand how important it is to get a steady start in one-day cricket. You must have wickets in hand when you chase runs later in the innings. That's crucial. It's better to be 100 for one after 30 overs, than 150 for seven.

'The other factor that isn't widely acknowledged is that most international teams have worked out one-day cricket. Field placings are more efficient, bowlers are more disciplined and fielding has improved dramatically: all of which means that a score of 200 in 50 overs has become the bench-mark. The pitch conditions can change that, but 200 is generally about par for the side batting first.'

As an opening batsman within this context, he feels that he's doing a reasonable job. He continues: 'The strength of the South African side lies in our bowling and fielding, so the batsmen have set themselves to reach that 200-point by running well throughout, and keeping wickets in hand for the last 15 overs. Very roughly, if you score three an over for the first 20, four an over for the next 15 and six an over for the last 15, you get 210.'

That's the case for the defence. Yet the melody lingers on. A critic argues: 'The problem with Kepler's approach is that, if he is to succeed, he must bat the whole way through. It's a gamble. If he bats for, say, 30 overs and then gets out, the youngsters must come in under huge pressure and slog like hell.'

Another adds: 'Kepler can be a fine player in one-day cricket and, when he's in form, he can be very effective because he scores off virtually every ball and hits boundaries, but his weakness is that he decides on a plan and then allows himself to be locked into it. Targets through an innings are fine but they don't take account of variables like the weather and the standard of the bowling. As a result, neither does Kepler's strategy. If he was more flexible, he would avoid the occasional disaster that we've seen.'

A third points out: 'The crucial time in one-day innings is the first 15 overs when the rules force four men to field within 30 metres of the bat. That is when the batsmen should be hitting over the top. Instead, we've got Kepler prodding around.'

Wessels does not accept the logic of the first: yes, it is better if he can bat through but, if he is out, the pace should not change. Someone else will adopt the anchor role. 'You can't have everyone blazing away at the same time,' he says. He essentially agrees with the point of the second critic but adds that he hopes he is flexible in his approach. To the third, he responds: 'Please go out and show me how to hit Ambrose over the top.'

There were other critics who needed no reply. Robin Jackman, the former England player turned South African tour guide, was giving expert commentary for the SABC during the second one-day match in Colombo, setting a familiar scene. He niggled at Wessels, among others, for batting too slowly on their way to 222 for seven from 50 overs, maintaining they needed 250. When Sri Lanka were bowled out for 98, the commentator sagely told the watching nation: 'Now we will never know if 222 was enough.'

Beyond such nonsense, Peter Pollock concludes: 'After the disagreements in Sri Lanka, we had a meeting where our whole one-day strategy was discussed and everyone expressed their views. At one point, Kepler said: "Hold on. You know I've played a bit of one-day cricket, in fact about 90 one-day internationals. I'm not saying I'm right, but at least I should know what I'm talking about." I was glad he said that. People are quick to condemn him, but they forget he has more experience than most. You know, he might just have got it right all along.'

Six weeks after arriving home from Sri Lanka, Wessels would be on the road again, leading South Africa to a one-day tournament in India and onwards to a three-Test tour of Australia.

Onwards, ever onwards.

A young team lined up behind one captain, one way.

# 15

## Guts and Glory in Sydney

I f Charles Dickens, Herman Charles Bosman, Wilbur Smith or any other celebrated storyteller had been asked to conjure up an ideal concluding chapter to the Kepler Wessels saga, they would surely have settled for him leading South Africa on a tour of Australia: representing the land of his birth in the country that gave him the biggest break of his cricketing life, effectively dotting the 'i's and crossing the 't's of a unique career.

So it happened.

In November 1993, Wessels led his team into the same Sydney airport where, almost 15 years before, he had first arrived as an audacious 21-year-old. He walked calmly, with the confidence of an established and respected Test captain, finally at peace with his turbulent past. The wheel had come full circle.

He was excited by the prospect of taking on Australia, but much of the pressure, and the scowling despair, which had marked his early years as South African captain was gone. He was relaxed, at ease and transmitting the assured air of an Olympic marathon runner who is within sight of the stadium: he's weary because it has been a gruelling race, but he's happy because the home straight beckons. His 36th birthday had passed, and his battered body was starting to plead with his brain. 'Please, not too much more.'

The end was in sight, and by November 1993 Wessels was freely contemplating the dread word of professional sport ... retirement. For him, however, it held no fears. He had achieved his ambitions and the fact that he had never particularly enjoyed the limelight meant that he would not miss the attention and adulation. He was, in fact, emerging as a rare phenomenon, the top sportsman who is fulfilled, content to leave centre stage and looking forward to life beyond.

When the time comes to shuffle aside, so be it. No problem. No crisis. No breakdown. Whatever the fates, or selectors, decide, he will accept.

Until that moment, however, it would be full steam ahead, 120 per cent effort, raw courage and careful planning.

Destination Australia.

The easiest way for South Africans to reach the land of aggressive cricketers with thick moustaches and foul mouths is to take a direct flight from Johannesburg. The United Cricket Board, however, sent Wessels' squad on a rather more demanding route, via a tournament of one-day matches to mark the 60th birthday celebrations of the Cricket Association of Bengal. Hello, India.

'We knew at the time that three weeks in Indian conditions would be the worst possible preparation for a tour of Australia,' Wessels recalls, 'and that's how it turned out. We were making life difficult for ourselves. Of course, there were diplomatic and political reasons for going to India, but that didn't make our task any easier, and we knew that it was us, the players, who were going to be blamed if things went badly, not the officials who agreed to the arrangements. Anyway, there was no point complaining.'

The South African squad arrived in Bangalore to find the Hero Cup in a state of confusion-going-on-crisis. Pakistan had withdrawn from the tournament at the last moment, citing security risks and casting into doubt their ability to co-host the 1996 World Cup with India and Sri Lanka, and the television coverage was threatened by a travesty of internal political wrangling and squabbling which was ultimately only resolved by the Supreme Court.

They also found unceasing rain. When two days of training and the first match against Zimbabwe were washed out, the 1992 edition of Wessels would have been growing tense and irritable, but the 1993 model wasn't. This was India. What could he do...

Next stop, the West Indies in Bombay. More rain. The tournament organisers are fretting. 'Yes, the field has been drenched by a thunderstorm,' they say, 'but there's a large crowd in and it's drying quickly, so please won't you go out and play?' The umpires lead the players squelching on to the field.

Batting first in oppressively humid conditions, South Africa reach 180 for five in 40 overs thanks to a pedigree 70 by Daryll Cullinan, who then collapses with heat exhaustion. The West Indies manage only 139 in reply as they succumb not to a devastating spell of bowling but to a devastating burst of fielding. It's the winning grin again. 'Jon-tee! Jon-tee!', the crowd are chanting. The totem of teenage South Africa is now a hero in India.

Five times the ball has flown into his airspace, five times he has taken off and grasped it. He takes your breath away, and his five catches in one match establish a new world record for an outfielder in international one-day cricket...

Rhodes is brilliant, but the best fielder in the world? There's also Mark Waugh. What about the greatest South African fielder ever? He might be among the best within 30 metres of the wicket, now that he has started to hit the stumps more often, but his throwing from the deep doesn't yet overwhelm those who saw Colin Bland patrol a boundary. Beyond any question, he is a massively popular role model for young South Africans, whose appeal stretches far beyond cricket. A winner in Bombay, Wessels stands in awe of Rhodes: 'It was one of the best individual displays of fielding I've ever seen.'

All aboard for Guwahati, a town that is surely loved by those who live there but which, to the modern international cricketer, represents India at its most notorious. Wessels, on his third visit to the subcontinent, looked around at the squalor, the heat and the dirt, and moved into his Indian survival mode:

* Never drink anything out of an unsealed bottle.

* Never put ice in your drink.

* Never eat snacks at cocktail parties.

* Choose a basic meal at the hotel restaurant and, if it doesn't make you ill, stick to it.

* Never eat outside the hotel.

'There's no problem with the major hotels in the big cities,' says Wessels, 'but you have to be careful in smaller places.' On a strict diet of omelette, after omelette, after omelette, he led his side to a comfortable and impressive victory over the Sri Lankans in Guwahati, scoring 50 in the process.

With two wins and a rain-draw in three matches, South Africa had already secured their place in the semi-finals, so the general lack of urgency shown in an unsatisfactory defeat against India in Chandigarh was not altogether unexpected. A shower of no balls and wides helped India set a target of 230 which the touring team never threatened to reach. At least Krish Mackerdhuj, the UCB president, emerged victorious in Chandigarh, winning his struggle with gatemen who persistently refused him entry to the ground.

Wessels' team had finished on top of the round robin section and their reward was a semi-final against India in Calcutta on an electrifying night at Eden Gardens, the first floodlit match ever played at the huge concrete bowl. (Students of trivia will note the occasion completed a notable quartet for Wessels: he had previously taken part in inaugural floodlit fixtures at the Melbourne Cricket Ground, the Sydney Cricket Ground and Newlands.)

That night, the South African fielding might also have been measured in amps and watts. Twice, Cullinan swooped on a single and rattled the stumps with batsmen stranded, reducing India to 18 for three. 'They're not just good fielders, they're brilliant,' gushed Geoffrey Boycott in the television commentary box. Sparked by Rhodes and Cronje, drilled by Wessels and Procter, the touring squad laid claim to be the best fielding side in the world. In many ways, the all-action, diving, chasing displays in the field were simply an extension of the team spirit, doing it for the guys, not letting anyone down. The sight of Rhodes, for example, flinging himself around the field with grotesquely grazed elbows inspired more sedate gents to new levels of athleticism. All in it together. 'Come on guys, keep it tight.' Walk in. From long-off to fine leg, the vibe was almost always simmering.

Mohammad Azharuddin and Praveen Amre pulled the Indian total to 195 in 50 overs, but it appeared inadequate until a handful of ordinary umpiring decisions — Wessels and Cullinan were gunned down LBW — brought India back into the game. Richardson and McMillan set the pursuit back on track with admirable vigour, but the match was tossed away by two crazy run-outs as the pressure mounted in the closing stages. 'It's not so bad if you take a risk and you're run out by a direct hit,' Wessels reflects, 'but I was disappointed when we lost wickets because of stupid misunderstandings with guys stuck at the same end. There's no excuse for that.'

India celebrated victory in awe-inspiring style as thousands of rolled-up newspapers were set alight and waved as torches among the 90 000 crowd. Azharuddin's side went on to beat the West Indies in the Hero Cup final before another delirious mass of spectators at the same stadium three days later.

Meanwhile, Wessels and his team sweated through three days of fitness training in Calcutta before finally flying south for the main event: the first tour of Australia by a South African side since 1963. In an ideal world, the squad would have arrived in Sydney prepared, fit, fresh and eager, but, after three tough weeks in India, they were tired, suffering chronic sore throats and chest pains, and regularly hurtling to the lavatory.

Most of the squad had caught a bug, something akin to the debilitating Delhi-belly, and Wessels' sanguine acceptance of the demanding schedule was being dangerously stretched. He was becoming exasperated. 'We were battling even to put a side in the field,' he says. 'It was always going to be a tough tour and now it was getting off to a bad start. It was very hard.'

It soon got harder... from Port Elizabeth came the news that Brett Schultz, the most effective strike bowler against Sri Lanka, would not, as anticipated, be able to join the tour. His recovery from arthroscopic surgery on his knee was painfully slow. 'That was bad,' Wessels recalls. 'Brett not only gives our attack some variety, but he also seems to get Allan Donald going. I had wanted to get them both blasting away at the Australians.'

And harder... with the sick list longer than the fit list, South Africa lost their first two matches in Australia: a one-day thrash against a Prime Minister's XI in Canberra, by four runs, and then a four-day fixture against Victoria in Melbourne.

'Pretty ordinary, mate.' That swiftly became the consensus public opinion of the South African touring squad. Australia, at large, was not impressed. This nation in adolescence, young, brash, emerging, and often critical of anything from anywhere else, was not at all impressed. 'Yeah, pretty ordinary, mate.'

In absolute contrast, the home heroes were hailed. KILLER SPINNERS screamed one of the newspapers in this country where calm understatement is almost unknown. Shane Warne and Tim May, the spin bowlers who had destroyed England and bamboozled New Zealand, were now going to rout South Africa. There it was in print.

Wessels was absolutely unconcerned. He turned on the television, sat back and simply laughed at the bravado, because he had seen it all before — from the other side of the fence. 'The Australians have this sort of media campaign they put together to try and psyche out the touring side. They build up their own players so much that if you believed everything you saw and read you'd think they were invincible. Unless you're careful, you can get in such a panic about them that you're virtually beaten before a ball is bowled. There's usually a lot of hot air blowing around before a Test series in Australia.'

Of course, Warne was a threat. The South African captain knew that. But he was not going to revise his entire strategy because of a pudgy 24-

year-old blond with an earring who had proved himself able to find more turn and bounce in a cricket pitch than anyone else had in two decades. Respected judges were describing the hotshot leg-spinner as the most devastating bowler in the world. To Australians, many of whom were absorbed by a kind of pubescent republicanism, he was simply a . . . well, a prince.

Wessels recalls: 'We studied video tapes of Shane Warne, and we tried to isolate the threat he posed. He gets a lot of spin on his stock leg-spinner and the other problem is the flipper which is a ball that sort of hurries on to you. You've got to pick it as it comes out of his hand, or else you're in trouble. We discussed all this, but we didn't go on and on about him at every meeting. I mean, we didn't want to sound like an Australian newspaper. As far as they were concerned, the series was a foregone conclusion. That was fine. They motivated our guys brilliantly.'

Into the second week of December, the Indian illness began to clear up, at last, but the opening rounds of the World Series (the relentless triangular one-day tournament which annually fills the coffers of the Australian Cricket Board) against the hosts and New Zealand was imminent and the captain knew his side was not ready. He was concerned because Hudson and Cullinan, two of his frontline batsmen, had been unable to play since Calcutta, and then alarmed when Brian McMillan injured a knee at the MCG and was ruled out for three weeks. Gary Kirsten, half-brother of Peter, was flown out as a replacement, another left-hander to counter the leg-spinner.

Never mind. The show must go on. Dressed to thrill in green kit with golden streaks of lightning crackling across the shoulder, Wessels led his side out at the Melbourne Cricket Ground to open the series against the Australian invincibles.

Pretty ordinary, mate?

Australia 189 all out. South Africa 190 for three. As the good citizens of Melbourne streamed home from the monumental Great South stand, the sound of eggs smattering on red faces rang around the stadium. Ordinary? Rhodes had dazzled, running out David Boon and Steve Waugh with direct hits as the home side collapsed from 106 for one. Ordinary? Cronje struck an impressive unbeaten 91 and Wessels hit 70, at one stage raising the morale of his team, yet again, by stepping down the pitch to drive Warne over mid-on. One bounce into the fence. Four runs. Ordinary? The hero spinner was countered and struck for 43 runs in 10 overs.

The Channel Nine television commentators, the self-appointed cheerleaders of Australian cricket, attempted to console the nation in the wake of this stunning defeat: 'A one-day win doesn't make a summer,' they wailed, working hard to make a drama out of a crisis. (It was, in fact, their job to make a drama out of anything, to turn a gentle game into a kind of Wrestlemania. The tour would give South Africans their first exposure to the scripted and aggressive commentary style of Bill Lawry and Tony Greig, via live coverage of the series broadcast through the night on M-Net.)

When their next match against New Zealand was rained off in Adelaide, the South Africans were suddenly sitting pretty at the top of the World Series log. Their city-hopping schedule of flight, practice, hotel, match, flight, practice, etc. brought back happy memories of the World Cup, and all seemed well.

For a few days, they were up. Soon they were down. Again.

Australia 172 for nine. South Africa 69 all out. The Sydney Cricket Ground was crammed to capacity, but the pitch was green and wild, like the Wanderers used to be. The Australians had recovered from 96 for six, but the touring side had found no way back after Cronje and Wessels were dismissed. Yes, their batting was fragile, but the pitch was awful. 'Someone should get a kick up the arse for this,' Allan Border remarked afterwards, and the crowd deserved a refund. Cricket as Russian roulette was no fun.

South Africa 147. New Zealand 148 for six. The batsmen had never got off the ground in Hobart against nagging, bits-and-pieces bowlers and the Kiwis won with five overs to spare. Bad memories of the World Cup... 'It was exactly the same as our game against them in Auckland,' Wessels recalls. 'We were down.'

Up and down. When you're up, you're one of the best teams in the world, the hotel fax machine whirls in a reel of praise and you feel great. When you're down, you're just a bunch of turkeys who shouldn't be there in the first place. Ups and downs. When you win, you're up. When you lose, you're down. Simple as that. It makes no difference how well you played. Conditions, opposition and umpires are all peripheral. Some days, you may play well and lose, other days you may play badly and win. The margins between winning and losing may be infinitesimal. It doesn't matter. Don't waste my time. Did you win or did you lose? That's all South Africa wants to know. It is unfair. But that's sport. Win or lose. Up and down. Accept it. Or go play netball with the girls.

Netball has never been an option for Wessels, but there have been times when he has not reacted well to the downs. When life was hard during the World Cup, he had set new standards of being grumpy and dismal. The responsibility of being both captain and the main batsman had weighed heavily on his shoulders, but time had moved on and he had become clearly more relaxed. Defeat in Hobart carried him not into despair but into philosophy.

'International cricket is a tough world,' he mused. 'There's a lot of pressure around and, to a certain extent, only the fittest survive. I mean, I think we're seeing on this tour that some guys have the personality and the attitude which thrives, but others are going to fall by the way. Look at Jonty. There's no way that he is the most naturally gifted batsman in South Africa, but he's strong and he's tenacious and he keeps producing the goods and he's going to carry on succeeding at Test level because of all that. In this world, 80 per cent of the battle is won in the mind.'

Wessels identified as his responsibility the task of ensuring that as many of the young South African players as possible learned to be mentally resilient and to cope with the pressures. He would do this, he determined, not by sitting them in a corner and talking 'at' them (as opposed to 'to' them), but simply by showing the way. It was up to them to follow his example.

Kepler in charge. Still one captain, one way.

It had become increasingly clear over the two years since readmission that Wessels' brand of strong, disciplined captaincy effectively made redundant the post of team coach. Mike Procter remained on the payroll, but his contribution had steadily diminished to a point where his main responsibilities in Australia were to deal with the media and oversee practice. It soon became obvious that Procter, a decent and likeable man with a contribution to make, had been placed in a virtually impossible position.

There seemed very little for him to do, so he did very little and became progressively resented by a number of players who felt he was unable to offer them any useful advice. There were a handful of exceptions, but Procter became 'a nice guy, but...'

What was an awkward situation became even more strained when the relationship between captain and coach deteriorated after their public row in Sri Lanka over the one-day batting strategy. Wessels, who had backed his coach up until that point, felt undermined and alienated. He had tried to get along with Procter since the World Cup, but that was it... Let him go and do what he likes. It really doesn't matter. We'll get on with the job... Through India and on to Australia, the frost had set in between captain and coach. They scarcely tolerated each other's presence. Discussions were terse, contact was minimal and trust was non-existent.

Wessels blamed Procter, and Procter blamed Wessels, but the breakdown was not necessarily anyone's fault. Perhaps a captain as firm and strong as Wessels simply didn't need a coach. A competent, well-organised team manager would have sufficed. Robbie Muzzell was trying to fill that role on tour in Australia.

'I think the whole idea of having coaches has been overdone,' Wessels reflects. 'It has become something of a fad, but cricket is not a sport like rugby or soccer where a coach on the touchline can lay down the tactics. In cricket, that is the captain's job. He is in charge. Sometimes a weak and inexperienced captain can be dominated by the coach, but in teams where the captain is strong, I don't think there's any point having a coach hanging around as well.

'The other point is that cricket is such a diverse game that there are very few coaches who can give technical guidance to both the bowlers and the batsmen. It's better to call in experts as and when they are needed. That way, players can get help from people they particularly trust. Allan Donald, for example, finds Bob Woolmer helpful, so he phones him when he has a problem.'

This was a view shared by a clear majority of players in the South African side and, as a result, the reservations about Procter's role never became a source of conflict within the squad. There were no rival camps because the players remained absolutely united in the challenge ahead. Two one-day defeats may have knocked morale, but there was still a job to be done. The first Test in Melbourne was little more than a week away. Head down, chin in.

A four-day match against Queensland in Brisbane represented the squad's only chance of restoring confidence before the Test and Wessels' appeal for an improved performance was answered by Cronje and Cullinan who both scored centuries on the first day's play at the Gabba, and then by De Villiers and Donald, who helped to bundle out the state side for only 183. Wessels seemed relaxed at his former home ground, wreathed in good-to-see-you-again-Chopper grins as he caught up with old team-mates like Greg Ritchie and Jeff Thomson, and Trevor Hohns, who had become an Australian selector.

Meanwhile, the South African dressing room had already begun rocking to a chorus that would undermine the tour. The players were convinced that Australian umpires were biased. From the very first match, crucial decisions seemed to have gone against them at crucial times. In the Queensland match, this discontent boiled over into a confrontation between the national captains.

Border had been bowling to Wessels on the third day when he was convinced his former team-mate had nicked a drive and was caught behind by Ian Healy, the Australian wicketkeeper and the captain of Queensland. Howzat? Not out, said the umpire. Wessels leaned on his bat and stood his ground. Seven years in Australia had taught him to accept the umpire's decision right or wrong.

He was not going to walk. No one walks in Australian cricket. Border knows that, Healy knows that and Wessels knows that. But the Queensland players started to perform. ****** ***** ********! At the end of the over, Border hurled the ball to Healy, narrowly missing Wessels. The South African captain smiled. He had seen Border upset before, and he was amused.

'You're a lucky ******,' said Healy, as he changed ends.

'Yeah,' Wessels replied, 'and I reckon that makes the score about 10-2 in your favour.'

'No, Chopper, it's only 4-2,' Healy said, grinning.

The following morning, as South Africa searched for wickets to force a victory, De Villiers grew progressively frustrated when appeal after appeal was turned down. Walking off the field at the lunch break, he began to let off steam, shouting out loud that the Australian umpires were 'just a bunch of cheats'.

Border had been standing just outside the Queensland dressing room when he was stirred by De Villiers' outburst. 'Heh, who do you think you're talking to? You've got no right to talk like that,' snapped Border indignantly. 'You're a guest in this country.'

As De Villiers answered back, Wessels emerged from the South African dressing room where he had been receiving treatment for his injured right knee and eagerly entered the fray.

'Hold on a minute. Who do you think you are to be shouting at one of my players? You mind your own business.'

'No, you keep your mouth shut,' Border barked.

Wessels was trying to stay calm. 'Look, Allan, we've made a real effort to play this series in a good spirit, but you're going way over the top out there. If you want to play it tough and dirty, then we can as well. It's not a problem for us.'

'Well, go ahead, Chopper.'

'Fine, we will.'

'Go ahead.'

'We will.'

The cussing, fretting captains returned to their respective changing rooms and Queensland held out for the draw but Wessels had been encouraged by his team's performance. 'It was much better,' he recalls, 'but the first Test was still coming too soon for us.' McMillan was definitely not going to play at the MCG and Rhodes, who injured his left hand fielding in Sydney, was doubtful. There seemed no end to the South Africans' misfortune.

There wasn't.

With the Test due to start on Boxing Day, the tourists booked a last training session at the MCG on Christmas morning to complete their preparations. They were being written off by their hosts, as usual, but Wessels sensed a keen resolve within the squad. Players were looking forward to the contest. So was he.

The captain's right knee had swollen towards the end of the Queensland match, forcing him to miss the last day's play, but he was not unduly concerned. So he took his place in the line for some fielding practice at the MCG. The training drills were familiar but, as he sprinted in to gather a ball, Wessels lost his footing on a worn outfield which had been trampled out of condition during recent pop concerts and fell heavily on his leg. His right knee buckled.

'I knew straightaway that it was serious,' he recalls, 'but I tried not to show it. I didn't want the other guys to see what was going on because they had enough to worry about, and I didn't want the Press to know anything either, so I just sort of limped back to the changing room and told everyone I was fine.'

In fact, the pain was excruciating. In similar circumstances, the vast majority of players would have withdrawn from the Test and resigned themselves to a quiet month of convalescence. Not Wessels. He would not even contemplate the idea of standing aside. There was no debate. He was going to play. The only issue was what sort of treatment would ease the pain. After joining the rest of the squad for lunch, he spent the rest of Christmas Day with physiotherapists and doctors, who applied ice, massaged the damaged joint with ultrasound equipment and began shooting electric currents into the knee. His relentless quest for relief ended at 11 o'clock that night, but still the knee was aching.

Wessels had tolerated the injury for 15 years, ever since the day he tore knee ligaments while playing squash during his National Service. A blundering South African Defence Force doctor had operated on him and succeeded only in causing more damage to a knee that became more

305

worn as the years passed. In April 1993, he underwent a fifth operation to clear the joint and ease the grinding of bone on bone, but discomfort had returned in Sri Lanka.

He simply accepted the pain as part of his life, just another obstacle to be overcome. After a long innings or at the end of an arduous day in the field, his limp would be pronounced and he would invariably be found sitting in the dressing room with an icepack on the knee. Painkiller injections and anti-inflammatories carried him for several years, but they seemed to have little effect now. The knee joint was battered and worn. Yes, it was sore, but... 'No, really, it's fine.'

Boxing Day 1993, should have been a momentous occasion in Melbourne with 80 000 spectators at the MCG to watch the first day of Australia's first home Test against South Africa for three decades. Instead, it rained. The wettest Christmas weather in the state of Victoria for 60 years would ruin the Test.

Border, speaking amicably to Wessels again after their row in Brisbane, won the toss and decided to bat when play finally started after tea on the first day. The stadium was grey, damp and sad, but Donald rose to the big occasion again, and produced his best form of the tour when it really mattered, rattling Mark Taylor and Michael Slater, the openers, as the home side scrambled to 71 for two by the close. Wessels had taken his place in the field and been enormously encouraged by the bowlers' success.

When the second day was entirely washed out by the rain, the captain took the opportunity to visit a knee specialist well known in Australian cricket. He was becoming concerned. In the past, treatment had eased the pain, but this time it seemed to be having scarcely any effect. It was serious. He sensed it was becoming a major problem.

The X-rays confirmed his fears. The cartilage of the knee joint had been worn away, and the grinding of bone on bone had left two rough surfaces grating against each other. The specialist advocated an immediate operation to clear the joint and smooth the chiselled bones. At least, that would ease the pain.

'No thanks.' Wessels was convinced that an operation at this stage would effectively finish his career. He would rather guts it out and simply see how far he could go. The specialist replied that was fine, but the pain would be virtually intolerable. Wessels said he knew that already... 'No, really, it's fine.'

When only two hours' play was possible on the third day, the Test was hurtling into the history books as one of the most pitiful anticlimaxes in memory. Former players had gathered, festival had been planned, but there was only rain. Officials shook their heads and watched the anticipated gate revenue drip away.

Taylor, who had been lucky to survive a confident appeal for LBW off the second ball of the match, reached his century just before lunch on the fourth day. He had spent more than eight hours at the crease and almost 14 hours sitting in the dressing room waiting for the rain to stop. He was finally out for 170 after tea, and Border declared the innings closed at 342 for seven. Donald had taken one for 108, but his analysis would have better reflected his performance if two slip catches had been held.

Hudson provided South Africa with a steady and assured start, but he had opened with Gary Kirsten. Wessels had fielded throughout the Australian innings until lunch on the fourth day and, with a draw seeming inevitable, was persuaded to give his knee a rest. He said he would bat at number six in the order, if necessary.

That did not seem likely when Hudson and Cronje thrived into the fifth morning, taking the score to 159 for one. Then Hudson was struck high on the arm by Warne's errant shy at the stumps and, to the amazement of his captain, the opening batsman decided to retire hurt. He was within sight of scoring a hundred against Australia and he was walking off the field with a bruise.

In the circumstances, many captains would not have worried. The Test match was dead and drawn, after all. Wessels, however, was upset and bitterly disappointed. He wanted his team to be tough, play hard, never give up and always fight. It annoyed him intensely that an established batsman should give away the chance of scoring a Test century. Such behaviour ran contrary to his entire ethos.

He reacted by going to strap on his pads, complete with the extra padding around the right knee. He would not scream or shout. He would not make a performance. He would simply get out there and show his players what sort of fortitude was required to succeed in Test cricket. Yet again. He would show the way, and it was for the players to decide whether or not they were going to follow. Some would, others wouldn't. Some had what it takes, others didn't.

'I was a frontline batsman,' the captain recalls, 'and I wanted to show the guys that I would do my job. It was important to make that clear. I don't like to see guys baling out.'

Angry and resolved, he strode out to bat and remained at the crease for three hours, resisting the spin of Warne and the second new ball from McDermott. The Australians were not holding back. It was still a

Test match. Wessels was simply making a point to his team. He would not fail. Together with Rhodes, he added 103 runs and guided the innings to 258 for three when the match was finally called off as a draw. Those who knew the extent of his injuries were amazed by the captain's innings of 63 not out. 'It was incredible,' Ali Bacher says. 'I have never seen a more courageous cricketer.' He had shown exemplary guts.

Almost two hours after the Test ended as a draw, Wessels and Cronje made their way across to the Australian dressing room, one hobbling and the other striding, and there they sat drinking Victorian Bitter with Border and Boon, talking and laughing like rival players of days gone by. By the time they emerged, the South African bus had left the ground. 'No problem, Chopper,' said Border. 'We'll give you a lift back to your hotel.' So they did. Thanks very much... OK, mate, see you in Sydney.

The second Test was to start 48 hours later at the Sydney Cricket Ground, and the South Africans flew north in high spirits. The fact that, despite the rain, they had competed so strongly in Melbourne had restored their morale and confidence. Despite what the newspapers said, the Test had proved that (i) the Australians were not unbeatable; and (ii) the South Africans were something more formidable than 'pretty ordinary'.

* * * * *

The pitch is white, powdery and rough. Wessels is not surprised. He had expected as much. Australia are desperate to win and they have prepared, perhaps even doctored, a pitch that will turn square from the first day... At your pleasure, Shane Warne.

Wessels can see the odds are stacked against his side, but he is invigorated by the prospect of a struggle. His knee still aches and grinds, but he is going to play. He wants to be there. Rhodes is still suffering from a painful broken hand, but he is also going to play. He wants to be there as well. McMillan undergoes a fitness Test on his injured knee and withdraws. Fine. This Test match will be fought in the trenches. Infantrymen only.

Warne is everywhere. On television, in the newspapers, on everyone's lips. All are agreed: this is going to be his Test. The South African squad has been impressed by his immense ability, but they are not thrilled by his occasional over-exuberance on the field. When you have bowled a delivery which pitches nine inches outside leg-stump and turns to flick off-stump, is it really necessary to fire a volley of obscenities at the batsman as he heads back to the pavilion? In contrast, away from the field Australia's hero is a charming good guy, chatting to South African fans, organising match tickets for them, chewing the fat.

As the South Africans gather for their teamtalk on the eve of the Test, Wessels is resolved to stress the positive. He guides his team through the Australian players, outlining where to bowl at the batsmen, suggesting how to play the bowlers. He speaks freely. He's in his element, thoroughly prepared, as usual.

'OK, guys, I know we've been through this before, but we've got to control their batsmen. They mustn't get away from us because I don't think this is going to be a high-scoring Test. If we look at the openers, Mark Taylor is probably their top Test player. We should look to get him caught behind early on. That will be our best chance. Michael Slater can be dangerous if he hangs around because he likes to attack, so I want us to bowl short and over off-stump at him. We must get him on the back foot fending.

'David Boon is strong on the on-side, so we should bowl at him in the off-side channel and maybe we can try to nip one back at him because he likes to cut hard. The Waugh brothers are completely different. Mark is strong on the leg-side, but he does tend to hit in the air when he cuts, so we'll have two gullies for him. Steve is very strong on the off-side, but I think he's a bit gun-shy, so the quick bowlers can give him a working over . . .'

The players listen. That's what they're paid for, and Wessels expects them to remember what he has said. Mark Waugh is strong on the on-side, Steve is strong on the off-side. He doesn't want his bowlers carelessly feeding anyone's strengths. Studious preparation has always been one of the strengths of his captaincy, even if it's largely unrecognised beyond his own dressing room.

As the team meeting moved on someone mentioned sledging, the predominantly Australian strategy of trying to unsettle opposition batsmen by swearing at them incessantly. It was a sensitive topic and one which Wessels was eager to confront because several of the younger players, most notably Rhodes and Cullinan, had already been subjected to appalling verbal abuse by Border's team.

Such tactics had long been used in South African cricket, but not to the same degree as in Australia, where there seemed to be no limits to the vulgarity. 'Now let his nightmare continue,' a chorus of fielders would scream at out-of-form batsmen on their way to the crease. Other less sophisticated remarks are, obviously, unfit for print; suffice it to say that they were trawled from the darkest and dingiest depths of the English language.

'You've got a choice,' the captain told his players. 'Give it straight back to them or say nothing, but you have to make your decision beforehand and stick to it. That way, you stay in control and they won't rattle you. Personally, I say nothing until I've got a few runs, then I give them a real go back.'

Wessels knew what he was talking about. He himself had been ruthlessly schooled in the subject of sledging during seven seasons with Queensland and Australia, emerging as a formidable sledger in his own right. He agreed with the standard disclaimer of Australian cricketers questioned on the issue: 'What's said on the field stays on the field. We all have a beer afterwards.'

This is inadequate. The notion of a brotherhood of cricketers who accept sledging as part of the game, and the implication that outsiders should not interfere, is as much errant nonsense as the suggestion that punching is admissible on the rugby field (though not on the street) because most players join in.

Sledging, like punching, is wrong. No debate. But it will only be halted when the ICC match referees are instructed to impose instant and heavy fines on guilty players. Until that time, most international cricket involving Australians will continue to be played in an atmosphere so offensive and coarse that it is more suited to the roughest bar in downtown Sydney.

The teamtalk concluded, Wessels walked back to his hotel room and found another handful of faxes wedged beneath the door. He read the first one and smiled. It was from Louis Schuller, his former team-mate from Queensland days: 'Show them you've still got what it takes, Chopper. Duck and weave, guts it out.' That was his kind of language. As the captain finally climbed into bed, his right knee twinged with pain. He ignored it. And slept.

More than 32 000 people had clicked through the turnstiles at the Sydney Cricket Ground by the time Wessels and Border walked out to toss up on the opening day of the second Test. The South African called correctly and opted to bat first, reasoning that even if the pitch did turn from the outset it would have deteriorated even more for the team batting last. As Gary Kirsten and Cronje settled after the early loss of Hudson, the decision was looking good. When they had taken the total to 91 for one by mid-afternoon, it was looking inspired. The touring side appeared in control.

Then Cronje was superbly caught in the gully by Mark Waugh, Australia's 'finest fielder in the world', and Border whistled in the direction of the blond leg-spinner fielding at fine leg. 'Now it's the fella you've all been waiting to see,' boomed the public address system. Warne jogged into the limelight, took the ball in his hand and shot the South Africans out of the sky.

Cullinan was bowled by the flipper. Rhodes was LBW to a ball that hurried on, Kirsten was stumped for 67, Richardson was caught at slip, and Wessels played a dipping full toss back to the bowler. When Matthews and Symcox were dispatched soon after tea, Warne had taken seven consecutive wickets. He had single-handedly dismantled South Africa from 91 for two to 152 for nine, and inscribed another golden page in his legend. Blue eyes burning, rosy face alight with delight, he appeared every inch the most exciting thing to happen in world cricket for more than a decade.

AND THE CROWD'S GONE MAD read one banner amid euphoria at the SCG. AND HE'S A VICTORIAN read another. After each over, Warne had been thunderously cheered as he trundled down to field in front of Yabba's Hill, the bare-chested, breast-beating, big beer-swilling, wisecracking epicentre of Australian manhood.

The South Africans sat in their dressing room after stumps, silenced and stunned by the spinner. Defiant De Villiers had struck out at the end of the innings and Donald had produced a fine lifter to dismiss Taylor at the start of Australia's reply, but the Kepler Wessels textbook of playing Test cricket suggested there's rarely a way back for any team who are bowled out for 169 on the first day.

That evening Wessels joined his wife for dinner and ran into two more former team-mates. 'Some days are diamonds, some days are stones,' said a voice. It wasn't John Denver. It was Greg Ritchie. 'And, Chopper, you just had one big stone.'

It was hard to argue, but Wessels tried. 'I wouldn't take too much for granted yet,' he replied. 'That pitch is a shocker and it's going to get worse. If we hang in there and set you guys about 150 to win on the last day, you never know...'

Greg Chappell was listening and, when he agreed with Wessels' point, the South African captain took heart. If we can just hang in there and set them 150 to win... At the end of a truly dismal day, he sensed a glimmer of hope. It was something.

The second day would be a day of restraining the Australians, of ensuring they didn't score too quickly, of keeping it tight, of hanging in there, hanging tough. Before breakfast, Wessels drew out some field placings, forever modifying — an extra slip here, a wide mid-off for him — and committed them all to memory. If he was going to go down, he would go down planning.

He set the strategy and he was nobly served by his players. Symcox was a smoker and drinker who had seemed unlikely to fit into such a fresh-faced, disciplined team, and yet he had, and the tall off-spinner rose to the challenge of following Warne by sending down 34 overs for only 56 runs. De Villiers bowled hard and straight, and Donald always threatened. All of which meant that while Border and Slater added 104 runs for the fourth wicket, they did so in fully 60 overs. The brakes were on.

Minutes before Australia reached stumps at only 200 for five, Wessels had reason to be satisfied with every aspect of his team's performance except one: three catches had been put down in the slip cordon. That irritated him, so, with only a few overs remaining, he once again took the responsibility on his own shoulders and, moving the luckless Cullinan to first slip, placed himself at second slip where most of the chances had been flying.

Almost immediately, Healy pushed at De Villiers' outswinger and the ball flew hard and fast, short of Wessels. He dived forward but succeeded only in splitting the webbing between the fourth and fifth fingers of his left hand. As the blood began to flow, he left the field and was swiftly swathed in bandages.

'I would get an X-ray of that,' suggested Ali Bacher in the dressing room later. 'It doesn't look too good.'

'No, it's just a cut,' Wessels replied. 'I'm fine.'

Next morning the captain woke with a monumental headache and a hand which had swollen alarmingly. He was rushed to St Vincent's hospital for an X-ray which duly revealed a major compound fracture of the hand. The doctor was astounded at the cricketer who thought it was 'only a cut' and instructed nurses to put the patient on an antibiotic drip as a precaution against infection. The fractured bone was exposed, the wound was a centimetre deep.

Off the drip and into a taxi, Wessels was driven directly to the SCG where Peter Pollock, the convener of selectors, Muzzell and Procter had already assembled to discuss their captain's situation. Wessels was upset. Everything was happening so fast, and it was all moving in the wrong direction. He felt as if he was sliding down a slippery slope to an inevitable conclusion. For a few more seconds, he wriggled on the line and held his ground.

'I don't want to leave the tour,' he told the three officials facing him. 'I don't think it's necessary. My knee is fine and the doctor says my hand will be right in three weeks, so that means I will be ready for the third Test in Adelaide.'

The discussion continued until Pollock finally laid down the facts of the matter to the inestimably brave man who was standing in front of him with a bandaged hand and strapped knee proclaiming that he felt fine. 'Now listen, Kepler,' the convener began. 'We're going to need you for the home series in February and March, and I think it's in everyone's interest that you go home after this Test, rest your knee and get yourself back to full match fitness.'

Fair enough. The fish was reeled in. For the third time in his career, Wessels swallowed the bitter pill of having to leave a tour early because of injury. He loathed it. 'I was quite angry at the time because I really wanted to stay,' he recalls. 'But Peter (Pollock) was right. I realised that later.'

It was further decided that Peter Kirsten, the 38-year-old veteran who had been widely written off the previous season, would be summoned as a replacement. He had hammered a career best 271 in the Castle Cup and was promptly resurrected as a Test batsman. An old truth had been underlined again: in sport, only fools say never.

Wessels left the officials, fetched his kit and headed off to the SCG nets to confirm that his various ailments would not prevent him batting in the second innings. He wore a glove that was cut and resewn to accommodate a splint on his injured finger and proceeded to strike the ball well enough to persuade any doubters. He was in agony, but he kept that detail to himself.

Fielding, however, was impossible and, with Australia ready to resume their innings, he gave Cronje, the young vice-captain who would now have to guide the side, a brief summary of tactics: frustrate them, keep it tight. As his players trooped on to the field, Wessels perched on the table in the front section of the dressing room and sighed. It had been a rough morning and he was on his way home. Still, there was a Test to be won.

With the captain watching each ball and sending advice out to Cronje at every break in play, South Africa maintained their steady line and dismissed Australia for 292, Donald and De Villiers both finishing with four wickets and great credit. Faced by a deficit of 123 runs, Wessels calculated his side would need to score something like 260 to 270 in the second innings to have a chance.

Hudson again fell early, but Gary Kirsten and Cronje salvaged admirably until the former was bowled by McDermott. At 75 for two with 41 minutes remaining on the third evening, a moment of truth had arrived. Wessels was not found wanting. He promoted himself to No.4 in the order and walked out to face the music, resolved that his side would not lose another wicket that evening.

Alan Lee, writing in *The Times*, described the captain's 'last, departing gesture of selfless courage', and Muzzell recalls that 'he must have been in unbelievable pain, but he didn't show anyone. Kepler simply proved that he is a man with unlimited guts.' The cricketing world looked on in awe, admiration and respect.

Early in the innings, Wessels rocked back on his heels to cut McDermott past point but, as ball hit wood, a bolt of agony shot up through his arm and he dropped the bat. It was bad. Fair enough. He would not cut at McDermott. When Warne was brought into the attack, he simply tried to get forward and play the spin with soft hands. Delivery by delivery, he and Cronje survived.

Heroically, they reached the close at 94 for two. Cronje was unbeaten on 37, Wessels was unbowed on seven. Up in the Press box Australian reporters were recalling tales of the young batsman who was hit in the ribs by Andy Roberts during World Series Cricket but went on to make a half-century, and of the Australian opener whose elbow was struck by Courtney Walsh but who stood up to score 98, of a cricketer who simply didn't know when to quit.

Neither Cronje nor Wessels lasted long on the fourth morning, but they had set the tone which others duly joined to create a chorus of resistance. The captain was annoyed to have been bowled by Warne's fifth ball of the day, but he had scored 18 (and no one could know how valuable his runs would prove). When Cullinan fell to yet another of Warne's flippers, South Africa had lurched to 110 for five, still 13 runs behind Australia. Wessels' side was facing overwhelming defeat, probably inside four days.

When the situation cried out for a big heart, Rhodes arrived at the crease and played an innings of massive significance. At the start he appeared no more likely to survive against Warne's wiles than a circus clown has of walking along a tightrope, but the most popular sportsman in South Africa prospered through more than three hours of resourceful scrapping on a dusty pitch.

He added 72 with Richardson for the sixth wicket, stood firm as four wickets tumbled in quick succession and finally inspired an invaluable tenth wicket partnership with Donald that contributed 36 runs to the cause. When South Africa were ultimately dismissed for a fighting 239, Rhodes remained unbeaten on 76, the personification of valour. Border recognised the stature of the innings and he strode across to shake Rhodes warmly by the hand as the players left the field, briefly setting aside the fact that his own leg-spinner had taken 12 for 28, the best match figures in a Sydney Test for a hundred years.

Australia required 117 runs to win.

Wessels had sat and watched. He would have given anything, certainly his left hand or right knee, for another 30 runs, but he knew there was still a chance. Amid the bustle between innings, the captain ran through the tactics with Cronje: start with Donald and De Villiers, get them to bowl straight, we can't afford to give any runs away, keep them focused, best of luck.

De Villiers accounted for Slater in only the second over, and Donald should have seized a return catch from Boon soon afterwards but put it down. The dressing room sighed. If this miracle is going to happen, the catches need to be held. As Boon and Taylor squeezed out the runs, Australia eased to 51 for one.

Then, towards the end of another sweltering day, De Villiers dug deep and found something extra. Boon was caught by Kirsten, May was trapped LBW and, amid leaping fielders, Taylor was caught by Richardson. Three wickets had fallen within the space of five balls and, all of a sudden, South Africa were back in the Test. Over and again through four exhausting days, they had clawed their way back from the brink of disaster and now with the final straight in sight they were still snapping at Australia's heels.

Border entered the fray, fretful and stern-faced, and he guided his side to 63 for four by the close. The odds were still in the Australians' favour, but not overwhelmingly so. When one of the Channel Nine experts rated South Africa's chances as being 'less than zero', he seemed to be tempting fate.

January 6th dawned warm and cloudless in Sydney, and almost 16 000 people headed to the SCG for the fifth day of what had been an enthralling Test. The morning papers unanimously looked forward to an Australian victory, though most added that nothing could be taken for granted on such an awkward pitch. Australia required 54 runs; South Africa needed six wickets. Simple.

The South African squad arrived at the ground and were led through their usual fielding drills by Wessels, Procter and Cronje. The captain recalls an ideal state of mind among the squad: there was nothing to lose, enough chance of success to motivate and every kind of glory to be gained. The Australians, in contrast, appeared nervous, with everything to lose, little to gain...

Let's give it a go! The mood in the South African dressing room is upbeat and positive. Wessels calls his squad together for a brief discussion. He has something to say: 'I just want to tell you what the Australians are thinking about right now,' he says. 'They can't get their minds off Headingley in 1981 when they were set 130 to beat England and they were bowled out for 111, and they're also remembering the Test at Edgbaston three weeks later when they were set 151 to win and they messed it up again. They don't like chasing small targets and they're not good at it. I'm telling you guys that you have more chance of going out and winning this Test than any of you believe.'

Then Cronje, growing with the responsibility of leadership in the field, urges the players to be positive in their approach. He has discussed bowling strategies and field placings at length with Wessels, and he feels prepared. It is going to be a big day for the 24-year-old, still the youngest player in the squad, but it is not in his nature to shrink from the big challenge.

'Only six balls. That's all it takes.' De Villiers, sincere and straight, has hit upon the motto of the morning. He repeats it over and again. Team-mates laugh. Pollock, the convener, surveys the dressing room scene and wonders at the vibe: 'The guys actually believed they were going to win,' he would reflect later.

Wessels, more nervous than usual even though he is condemned to sit and watch, is looking for Donald. 'OK. Now listen, Allan,' he says. 'I want you to try something. I know Allan Border pretty well and I reckon you can get him early on if you can slide a couple of outswingers across him and then nip one back. It's a hunch I've had all morning. Just go and give it a try.'

Sometimes you tell a bowler to do something, he messes it up and no one says anything, but sometimes you tell him and he gets it absolutely right... Donald waits at the end of his run-up, Border takes his guard. It's the first over of a tense day.

The first ball is fast, ducking away, Border leaves it. After almost 16 years in the Australian side, ten as captain, he has seen this sort of situation before. He was at Headingley in 1981, and at Edgbaston three weeks later. Now, elevated to the status of adored national hero and playing what is touted as the last home series of his superlative career, he's there again. The second ball is fast, ducking away, Border leaves it. Frowning, compact, tense, the hero of all Australia fends anxiously at the next ball. Donald glares at him down the pitch. The tension crackles.

Soon Donald is bounding in again. He pitches just outside the line of off-stump, Border offers no stroke, but this ball doesn't duck away. It nips back and strikes the top of the off-stump. He's out! Bowled! Border looks down at his broken wicket, aghast. Donald charges down the pitch in fist-wheeling delight. No one can quite believe it. What a start! When the fast bowler returns to his mark, he lifts his eyes and searches for Wessels in the dressing room some 70 metres away to his left. In an instant, their eyes meet. Donald shows the thumbs-up and Wessels smiles. It had worked. The hunch. Thanks, skipper.

The loss of Border's wicket seems to knock the stuffing out of the spectators, out of the Australian batsmen, even out of the Channel Nine commentary team. The standard-bearer has fallen and his wide-eyed comrades suddenly take fright.

For two freakish, inexplicable, historic and quite stunning hours on the fifth morning, the mighty Australian batsmen appear as tentative as schoolboys, while the 'pretty ordinary' South African bowlers seem unplayable and irresistible.

Crash! Mark Waugh falls LBW to Donald's rocket yorker. Bang! Healy inside edges De Villiers on to his stumps. Wallop! Cronje chases a ball into the off-side, gathers, turns and throws down the wicket at the bowler's end to run out Warne. Back in the dressing room, Wessels can hardly contain himself. He's sitting beside Dave Callaghan and Errol Stewart, all smiles. Yes! Incredible! Australia have cascaded to 75 for eight. Now, let's go!

Out on the field Cronje is performing magnificently, keeping the players on the boil, clapping, goading, repeatedly coaxing the bowlers. Keep it tight, keep it straight. Come on, guys. After each wicket, he is the first to congratulate the bowler. He's doing all this because he's excited, and because his dream is happening. He's setting the vibe of high energy, high excitement and high fives, and the other players join in.

Australia are gone. Or are they? McDermott becomes the first Australian batsman to set about his task without fear. He clobbers Donald for successive boundaries, then he clouts De Villiers to the fence. What was all the fuss about? The game which seemed so hard a moment ago suddenly looks so easy. Damien Martyn stands firm at the other end as Australia edge closer and closer.

Past 80, into the 90s, past 100. The total is 110 for eight. McDermott has scored 29 in a 35-run ninth wicket stand with Martyn. Only seven more runs are needed, but Cronje is calm, still clapping and goading. Keep going, guys. There is now no room for error. In the pavilion, Wessels' smile turns to a stare. It has been so good, but perhaps his team's heroics won't be enough.

Out of the blue, Martyn loses patience and drives loosely at Donald. The ball loops to Hudson at cover and the ninth wicket has gone down. Hope springs eternal. Glenn McGrath, the last man, heads out towards the middle with, still, seven runs needed. Five days of intense struggle have ebbed and flowed to this final scene.

McGrath, tall and gangling, is no batsman, but he manages to survive three deliveries from Donald and then scrambles a single to retain the strike. De Villiers takes the ball and prepares to bowl his 12th over of the morning. Cronje is talking to him, again. Keep it quick and straight. Amid astonishing tension around the ground, McGrath copes with two deliveries, then faces the third.

De Villiers bowls on the spot and full. McGrath prods forward and spoons the ball back to the bowler. A catch! He's got it! Yes! McGrath stands still at the crease, head bowed, a distraught figure momentarily lost in a sea of South African bedlam... Victory was theirs. Victory by only five runs in one of the greatest Tests ever played. Historic, joyful, magical victory.

Legs apart, arms braced at right angles, fists clenched, De Villiers stood astride the pitch, a veritable cricketing Atlas. He was the totem of the triumph, and this was the greatest moment in a career that had virtually fizzled out two years before because his back ached and because he had been bored by cricket in isolation. Readmission renewed his enthusiasm and relentless accuracy carried him into South Africa's one-day team. He was not, however, rated as a Test match bowler. 'I'll never say I represented my country until I've played in a Test,' he pledged. He was selected for the first Test match in Melbourne, and retained his place ahead of Snell for Sydney.

De Villiers' performance at the SCG, claiming six for 43 in the second innings, and match figures of 10 for 123, earned him not only the Man of the Match award but also widespread popularity back home. '*Vinnige Fanie*' became the craze, newly installed beside 'Jon-teee' in the nation's affections. A gentle man, he accepted it all with equanimity. He had returned to visit his new-born baby in Pretoria between the Indian and

Australian legs of the tour. Almost 30 years old, he seemed to know how to keep transient idolatry in perspective.

At the clinching moment of triumph, Wessels had found himself almost gasping for air. He was overwhelmed, and impulsively led the non-playing members of the squad charging out of the pavilion on to the field to celebrate with the team. He was searching for Cronje amid this small group of blissful South Africans on a Sydney field, and, within moments, the vice-captain had seized the captain around the waist and was bear-hugging him off the turf.

Pollock, Mackerdhuj and Bacher arrived in the dressing room, tearful and proud. 'That was the greatest performance by any South African team ever,' Bacher announced. So, in the exact same room where they had marked their return to international cricket with a World Cup victory over Australia, this happy band of men celebrated their re-emergence as a force in the Test arena.

At home, Test triumph had the effect of a Reactivan injection on a population racked by nerves and political uncertainty. HOWZAT? AWESOME, screamed *The Star*'s front page, and Radio 702 broadcast the result as its lead story all morning. Hundreds of thousands had sat from 2 a.m. to watch the live TV coverage, and others gathered happily around televisions to enjoy a full replay at 7 a.m. Chests puffed out right across the country, young and old, white and black, and once again a bleary-eyed army of sportsfans was trudging late to the office. However, whatever cricket cost the nation in lost productivity, it more than made up in the restoration of national morale.

The word on everyone's lips was . . . guts. The team had been depleted by injuries, dropped catches, been routed by Warne, widely written off, and yet had still battled back to win.

When De Villiers told a Channel Nine interviewer in his hard, wooden, uncompromising and proud Afrikaans accent: 'You know, South Africans, we never give up', he appeared to hit the nation's nerve. He's right, eh? We've got huge problems, but we never give up. That is why, whatever the future holds, we're going to be OK, because we never give up. In such a way, victory on the cricket field affirmed the central faith of the people, nothing less.

'So, Kepler, the team showed fantastic guts out there today.' The captain is being interviewed on M-Net television.

'Yes, I thought Hansie and the guys did a tremendous job, and we're all very proud,' Wessels replies.

'But the guts, Kepler. It comes from you, doesn't it? You led the side by example, batting with a broken hand and a swollen knee, and the guys followed. It comes from you.'

Wessels smiles self-consciously. He sometimes seems quite as uncomfortable with praise as he is with criticism. He doesn't play for the limelight, he plays to prove himself.

'Well, we all do our best,' he says.

'Thanks, Kepler. And congratulations...'

The interviewer was right. South Africa's guts-laden triumph was as much the product of Wessels' leadership as anything else. A group of talented young players, much like sapling trees, had been matured over two seasons on the frame of their captain's courageous example. At the SCG they stood brave and bold, every inch the team constructed in the image of Kepler Wessels.

One team's delight was another team's misery. One man's ideal send-off was another man's gut-wrenching disappointment. If Wessels had left the SCG on a high, what appeared to be Border's final Test in Sydney had petered out in a depressing low. The previous season his side had lost by one run to the West Indies. 'It would be nice to win one of the close ones,' he said afterwards.

Wessels and Border, still 'Chopper' and 'A.B.', had travelled a long road to this dizzy day, and winner gently commiserated with loser amid the post-Test hubbub. 'This is a stupid game, Chopper,' said Border sadly. 'We're supposed to be the batsmen, but we can't get a run and a guy like Craig McDermott gets 29.' Wessels sort of grinned. 'Ah, well,' said Border, 'I suppose life goes on.'

Returning to the South African dressing room, Wessels decided his departure would be short and sweet. It was difficult to leave. In fact, he hated it. But he packed his kit and said goodbye to the players. They presented him with a massive Get Well Soon card which they had all signed and written messages in. And that was that. The door shut. All of a sudden, the leader was gone. He was immediately and profoundly missed, his influence, his standards, his guidance, his knowledge... but the tour would go on.

Cronje took over as captain, becoming the second youngest man ever to lead the South African cricket side. He was only 24, but he projected such an assured image, every inch the crown prince, that, high on victory, some observers began to wonder if this was not the right moment for him to take over permanently.

Blind critics of Wessels had maliciously hijacked events in Sydney to claim that victory had only been achieved because he was off the field and because Cronje's 'bright' captaincy had brought a new, positive energy into the team. This view was promoted on M-Net by Clive Rice and Rod McCurdy, neither a member of the Wessels fan club, both apparently bitter and wounded by past battles.

It was nonsense, mean-spirited nonsense. The fact was that Wessels had remained centrally in control of tactics throughout the Test. What Cronje had done, and done well, was to keep the players going through the final morning. That was all. 'It would be stupid for anyone to say Kepler was not involved,' reflects Muzzell, who was at the SCG, rather than in the M-Net studio.

None the less, Wessels did sense after the Test that his era may have come to its natural conclusion. He told journalists that he would happily play under Cronje and would accept whatever the selectors decided. He added that he had achieved all his ambitions in cricket, and felt entirely satisfied.

Beyond the sour antagonism of the M-Net panel, South African cricket was fortunate that the transition of captaincy from Wessels to Cronje, whenever it was going to take place — after the Sydney Test or after the home series versus Australia, or even after the tour to England later in 1994 — would be virtually seamless.

The two men were close friends, with a similar temperament, an equally serious approach to the game and a shared background in Bloemfontein where, almost 30 years previously, Cronje's mother had coached Wessels at tennis. When Cronje was learning to play cricket at Grey College, Wessels was the role model. 'I still remember when Kepler scored 162 on his Test début for Australia,' Cronje recalls. 'The school first XI watched his innings on a video tape.'

Following international readmission, Wessels became Cronje's role model once again. The were virtually inseparable at the World Cup, getting up early to jog each morning. Then in the West Indies, when Wessels cut his hair short, so did Cronje. It was Tweedledum and Tweedledee to such an extent that other players began to resent Cronje as a nodding puppy on the captain's lap.

Cronje, however, did not lack desire. Early in 1993, he was eagerly enquiring when Wessels was planning to retire and he rarely made any secret of his ambition to be the captain. To this end, he would have been right in thinking that the way to learn as much as possible as quickly as possible would be to follow Wessels like the proverbial shadow. That, he unquestionably did.

Since leaving Grey, he had taken giant steps comfortably in his stride, moving into the Free State side and on to the national team with hardly a hiccup but taking over as South African captain midway through a tour of Australia brought immense pressure on young shoulders far too soon. To his credit, Cronje would later prove man enough to admit as much in the media. His time would come.

Just 48 hours after the Sydney Test, and Wessels' departure, South Africa suffered one-day defeats against New Zealand and then Australia in Brisbane which appeared to rule them out of the World Series finals. Yet the team fought back magnificently the following weekend in Perth, beating both rivals by large margins and battling into the three-leg final against the hosts.

Once again, critics of Wessels tried to turn the team's form into a vehicle for beating their hobby horse. They claimed the fact that South Africa had scored well over 200 represented a brand new aggressive batting strategy when, in reality, it was simply born of necessity because the team's overall runrate needed to be raised if they were to survive in the competition. Amid the general euphoria, the injured captain was shamefully criticised. 'Who needs Wessels?' the fools cried. 'We're better off without him.'

Cronje's side produced another excellent performance to win the first leg of the final at the MCG, but were then outplayed in the second and deciding legs on successive hectic nights in Sydney. Border was cheered to the rafters as he raised the World Series Cup, but the young South African captain cut a lonely figure in defeat and under pressure.

When South Africa lost the third Test in Adelaide, losing their last seven wickets in two hours on the final day and leaving the series drawn at 1-1, it had become abundantly clear to everyone that Cronje was still too young to take over as captain. Quite apart from some doubtful tactical and selection decisions, his own batting form had deteriorated alarmingly under the burden of leadership. 'Come back, Kepler!' the fools cried. 'We need you!'

Wessels surveyed the fickle public outcry with despair. It was all so unnecessary. He did not see any rivalry between Cronje and himself, and he had spoken to the acting captain several times on the telephone, during the third Test in Adelaide, offering advice whenever it was asked and giving support at all times. He was still supporting the team, still backing the guys.

Many people in his position might have felt ambivalent about the result of the third Test because the facts were that if South Africa had won, he might well have been deemed surplus to future requirements, but Wessels, let the record show, was in no doubt.

He was not at all concerned about his future — something that he regarded as the selectors' business, not his — and he wanted the side that he had built to win. There was no one more enraged by the bemusing series of appalling umpiring decisions which sealed South Africa's fate in the second innings at Adelaide.

'It was a disgrace,' Wessels recalls, 'but it had been going on throughout the entire tour. Whenever the Australians needed a big decision, they seemed to get one. It was great in the days when I was playing for Australia, but it wasn't so much fun being on the other side. In the third Test, there were a couple of LBW decisions that looked absolutely ridiculous on television.

'To be fair, I don't think any of the Australian umpires are malicious. I'm sure they're not deliberately cheating, but I think it's true that they are placed under such great pressure by the bowlers and fielders, and the atmosphere around the ground, that there are times when they crack and up goes the finger. This sort of problem will hopefully be solved by the introduction of neutral umpires.'

When the South African squad returned home to an enthusiastic welcome at Jan Smuts airport, Wessels was there to join his team on the balcony above the cheering crowds. When the UCB invited him to fly up from Port Elizabeth for the occasion, he had hesitated, not wanting anyone to think he was muscling in on the limelight, but he was finally persuaded and he enjoyed the occasion.

Standing in the hall waiting for the flight to arrive, he had been besieged by hundreds of supporters and autograph hunters, none of whom were muttering about slow runrates or conservative tactics. No, the wind had changed. He was now cast as a 'Captain Courageous without whom we are lost'. All hail and glory. Within a fortnight he had duly been reinstated as captain for the home series against Australia.

It is perhaps an indictment on South African cricket at large that it only learned to fully appreciate Kepler Wessels' value when he was not in the side; but, better then than not at all.

At least, after Australia, no one was in doubt.

# 16

## So What?

Whthe it's all over, when your name disappears from the scoreboard and the last spectators drift away, when no one stops and stares in the street, when you have to find a real job, when you have to pay for your ticket at the gate, when the world seems to be passing you by and forgetting who you were, it can be hard.

You played first class cricket, day in, day out, for almost 20 years. You played with all your heart, gave everything, battled and battled again, never gave up, invariably prevailed and, at the end of it all, finished with an average above 50.

Sometimes the people stood and cheered. Sometimes, the very next day, they stood and jeered. Season after season, you played at the top of your game, all around the planet, ever in the spotlight, every move discussed, dissected, judged. You lived under relentless pressure and you kept going, batting, winning.

Many people admired you. That was fine, reassuring. 'Thanks a lot.' But others criticised you with such malice that you learnt to avoid the television and newspapers. Why? For what? You burgled no bank and murdered nobody. But that was sport.

Now it's over. Your 40th birthday still looms ahead, but it feels as though you're almost dead. You sit quietly, amid the faded cuttings and fractured memories, and it's hard. It's hard not to look back, reflect, and ask yourself: 'So what?'

\* \* \* \* \*

'So a lot,' Kepler Wessels replies firmly. 'So I was given a talent and I went out and made the most of it. So I earned a good standard of living for my family. And so I've still got almost half my life left to go and be successful at something else.'

324

He continues: 'I know many sportsmen have found retirement a very difficult time. But when it's my turn, I really don't think I'll miss cricket. It was just something I could do well, so I went out and did it. I was very dedicated, but it wasn't the be-all and end-all of my life. I definitely won't miss the attention because I never enjoyed that. In fact, it'll be a pleasure to be able to walk around without people demanding your time.

'And there's so much still to do, at the University (of Port Elizabeth), as a boxing promoter in PE and other things. I am actually looking forward to moving on. I'm sure I won't be one of those cricketers who can't leave the game alone, and who go around tormenting younger players with stories of 'When I...' I don't really see myself as a coach or anything, maybe later on at school level, but not any higher. I've had enough.'

But doesn't the South African captain wonder, or worry, how he will be recalled in years to come, what people will say once the waves of contemporary envy have washed away?

'Cricket historians will look at the statistics,' he says, 'and that's fair. At the end of the day, the record book speaks for itself. More generally, it's not something I've really thought too much about. I think it's largely a personal thing. I won't mind if people say Kepler Wessels was boring and uninteresting. That's of no concern to me. As long as I can retire and say that I could not have done any better, then I'll be satisfied.

'I know the people who like me will say I was good, but I hope that those people who don't particularly like me will say: "We didn't like him, he had no personality and is the opposite of what we like, but we've got to give him credit for being a good player." All said and done, I'll be happy with that.'

History may, in fact, be very much kinder.

Once the vitriol of his rivals has subsided, Wessels will be remembered as the man who led South African cricket through the most exciting phase of its history, through two dazzling years when international contact was restored after two decades of isolation, and when the game was transformed from a hobby for the white elite into something approaching a truly national sport.

His achievement will be set down in stone: he took a young side with much potential but zero experience and moulded them into a courageous, professional unit which was capable of defeating any team in the world and which, more importantly, earned the adoration of South Africans. Every age, every race cheered.

Jonty Rhodes, Allan Donald and Hansie Cronje may have been the stars, but Wessels was the leader and the inspiration. Without his wise guidance, South African cricket would have stumbled back into the international arena in the same bungling way as the rugby team, soccer side and Olympic athletes: underachieving, losing and mumbling excuses about 'the learning curve'.

Wessels was the difference between cricket and the rest. It may take some time for that stark reality to permeate the contemporary trivia of runrates in the first 15 overs, but future generations will see the truth. 'They only put flowers on your grave.' It's sad. It's fact.

It is equally certain that Wessels will not be included in any coffee table volume commemorating the 50 finest batsmen of all time. Graeme Pollock, Gary Sobers, Barry Richards, Clive Lloyd, Viv Richards, David Gower, Greg Chappell... these were cricketers who thrilled a crowd in a way that Wessels never could.

That was not his style, that was not the central nature of his ability. He was a grafter, a model of concentration who always made up in consistency what he lacked in flair. In human terms, he was no less admirable for that, and an average of above 50 is evidence enough of a most distinguished international batsman.

There are two other adjectives that will float nearby when his name is mentioned in cricketing circles...

'Gutsy': Innings after innings, almost without exception, he was physically and mentally brave beyond words. 'All through my career, I have tried to beat the odds rather than let the odds beat me,' he reflects. 'A long time ago, I read in some book that people either become stronger or weaker when they're put under pressure. I always wanted to be someone who gets stronger.'

'Mercenary': He has played for six provincial sides and two countries, but never moved anywhere because of money. He joined Free State out of school, Western Province out of university and Northern Transvaal out of the army. He represented Sussex because of Mike Buss, and Queensland because of Greg Chappell. He played for Australia because South Africa was isolated and then for South Africa because the Australians forced him out. He joined two rebel squads because there was nothing else to do, and he signed to play for Eastern Province because of the challenge.

Mercenary? The facts simply don't fit. 'In an ideal world, I would have liked to play for one state and one country through my entire career,' he says, 'but I was born in a less than ideal world where my home country was isolated. It was changing circumstances that forced me to move around so much. That was all.

'As things have turned out, I think I've been fortunate to have represented both Australia and South Africa. Having said that, I've made a lot of my own luck because I've been prepared to have a go at something rather than just sit back and accept it. Of course, I've made plenty of mistakes and done things that were wrong, but I think that's much better than doing nothing at all.'

* * * * *

It was Kepler Wessels' fate not only to play international cricket in an era when the game was ravaged by storms but also to find himself, more often than not, in the midst of these upheavals: the expulsion of South Africa from the Test arena, the introduction of the one-day game, the Kerry Packer revolution, the rebel tours to South Africa, the age of short-pitched bowling.

During this period, what started out as the gentle game of the Empire, a loved haven of good manners and decency, became more violent, aggressive and more marketable. Where once the sport had seemed to speak with a calm, clipped Home Counties accent, it began to scream and shout in a Channel Nine drawl.

In many respects, Wessels was a product of this tempestuous evolution. He was tough, resilient, brave. He played the game hard and rough, played it as a professional and he played it, more often than not, with a dour frown of concentration rather than a smile of carefree amusement spread across his face.

All this said, he never ceased respecting the game and its civil traditions. When an opposing batsman reached his century, he applauded. If the other side had spent the entire day in the field, he usually made his way across to their dressing room for a beer later in the evening. He may not have always walked until the umpire actually gave him out, but he never cheated either.

Cricket was played long before Wessels emerged, and it will played long after he has retired, but the greatness of the game is the sum total of the men who play it, and he will rest assured that he played his part in sustaining an estimable inheritance. Far beyond the runs, the victories, the crises, beyond even the joyful emergence of a new South African team after readmission, that is surely significant.

He didn't play the game slyly or cynically, he didn't play it boorishly. He played it straight from the heart.

Straight from the heart.

# KEPLER WESSELS' CRICKET CAREER

Compiled by Andrew Samson

# Test Career: Match by match
## For Australia

| Test No. | Season | Against | Venue | How out | Scores | Cts | Result |
|---|---|---|---|---|---|---|---|
| 1 | 1982/83 | England | Brisbane | b Willis<br>b Hemmings | 162<br>46 | 2 | Won |
| 2 | 1982/83 | England | Adelaide | c Taylor b Botham<br>c Taylor b Botham | 44<br>1 | 3 | Won |
| 3 | 1982/83 | England | Melbourne | b Willis<br>b Cowans | 47<br>14 | 2 | Lost |
| 4 | 1982/83 | England | Sydney | c Willis b Botham<br>lbw b Botham | 19<br>53 | 1 | Drawn |
| 5 | 1982/83 | Sri Lanka | Kandy | c Dias b DS de Silva | 141 | | Won |
| 6 | 1983/84 | Pakistan | Perth | c Wasim Bari b Azeem | 12 | | Won |
| 7 | 1983/84 | Pakistan | Brisbane | c Omar b Azeem | 35 | 1 | Drawn |
| 8 | 1983/84 | Pakistan | Adelaide | c Zaheer b Qadir<br>c Wasim Bari b Sarfraz | 179<br>2 | 1 | Drawn |
| 9 | 1983/84 | Pakistan | Melbourne | c Wasim Bari b Azeem | 11 | | Drawn |
| 10 | 1983/84 | Pakistan | Sydney | c Wasim Bari b Azeem<br>not out | 3<br>14 | | Won |
| 11 | 1983/84 | West Indies | Georgetown | c Lloyd b Garner<br>c Lloyd b Daniel | 4<br>20 | 1 | Drawn |
| 12 | 1983/84 | West Indies | Port-of-Spain | c Gomes b Garner<br>lbw b Garner | 4<br>4 | 1 | Drawn |
| 13 | 1984/85 | West Indies | Perth | c Holding b Garner<br>c Lloyd b Garner | 13<br>0 | | Lost |
| 14 | 1984/85 | West Indies | Brisbane | b Garner<br>c Gomes b Walsh | 0<br>61 | | Lost |
| 15 | 1984/85 | West Indies | Adelaide | b Marshall<br>c Dujon b Harper | 98<br>70 | | Lost |
| 16 | 1984/85 | West Indies | Melbourne | c Dujon b Marshall<br>b Garner | 90<br>0 | | Drawn |
| 17 | 1984/85 | West Indies | Sydney | b Holding | 173 | 3 | Won |
| 18 | 1985 | England | Leeds | c Botham b Emburey<br>b Emburey | 36<br>64 | | Lost |
| 19 | 1985 | England | Lord's | lbw b Botham<br>run out | 11<br>28 | 2 | Won |
| 20 | 1985 | England | Nottingham | c Downton b Emburey | 33 | 1 | Drawn |
| 21 | 1985 | England | Manchester | c Botham b Emburey<br>c and b Emburey | 34<br>50 | | Drawn |
| 22 | 1985 | England | Birmingham | c Downton b Ellison<br>c Downton b Ellison | 83<br>10 | | Lost |
| 23 | 1985 | England | The Oval | b Emburey<br>c Downton b Botham | 12<br>7 | | Lost |
| 24 | 1985/86 | New Zealand | Brisbane | lbw b Hadlee<br>c Brown b Chatfield | 70<br>3 | | Lost |

# Test Career: Match by match
## For South Africa

| Test No. | Season | Against | Venue | How out | Scores | Cts | Result |
|---|---|---|---|---|---|---|---|
| 1 | 1991/92 | West Indies | Bridgetown | c Adams b Ambrose<br>c Lara b Walsh | 59<br>74 | 1 | Lost |
| 2 | 1992/93 | India | Durban | c Azharuddin b Kumble<br>c More b Srinath | 118<br>32 | | Drawn |
| 3 | 1992/93 | India | Johannesburg | c Azharuddin b Srinath<br>run out | 5<br>11 | 3 | Drawn |
| 4 | 1992/93 | India | Port Elizabeth | b Prabhakar<br>not out | 0<br>95 | 1 | Won |
| 5 | 1992/93 | India | Cape Town | b Prabhakar<br>c and b Srinath | 0<br>34 | 1 | Drawn |
| 6 | 1993/94 | Sri Lanka | Moratuwa | c Tillakaratne b Muralitharan<br>c Wickramasinghe b Muralitharan | 47<br>16 | 1 | Drawn |
| 7 | 1993/94 | Sri Lanka | Colombo<br>(Sinhalese Sports Club) | c Dassanayake b Muralitharan | 92 | | Won |
| 8 | 1993/94 | Sri Lanka | Colombo (P Sara-<br>vanamuttu Stadium) | b Liyanage<br>c Mahanama b Hathurusingha | 26<br>7 | | Drawn |
| 9 | 1993/94 | Australia | Melbourne | not out | 63 | | Drawn |
| 10 | 1993/94 | Australia | Sydney | c and b Warne<br>b Warne | 3<br>18 | | Won |

# Test Matches
## For Australia

| Season | Against | Venue | Tests | Inns | NO | Runs | HS | Ave | 100 | 50 | Cts |
|---|---|---|---|---|---|---|---|---|---|---|---|
| 1982/83 | England | Australia | 4 | 8 | 0 | 386 | 162 | 48.25 | 1 | 1 | 8 |
| 1982/83 | Sri Lanka | Sri Lanka | 1 | 1 | 0 | 141 | 141 | 141.00 | 1 | 0 | 0 |
| 1983/84 | Pakistan | Australia | 5 | 7 | 1 | 256 | 179 | 42.67 | 1 | 0 | 2 |
| 1983/84 | West Indies | West Indies | 2 | 4 | 0 | 32 | 20 | 8.00 | 0 | 0 | 2 |
| 1984/85 | West Indies | Australia | 5 | 9 | 0 | 505 | 173 | 56.11 | 1 | 4 | 3 |
| 1985 | England | England | 6 | 11 | 0 | 368 | 83 | 33.45 | 0 | 3 | 3 |
| 1985/86 | New Zealand | Australia | 1 | 2 | 0 | 73 | 70 | 36.50 | 0 | 1 | 0 |
| Total | | | 24 | 42 | 1 | 1 761 | 179 | 42.95 | 4 | 9 | 18 |

**Highest Score:** 179 v Pakistan (Adelaide) 1983/84

**Bowling:** 90 balls, 42 runs, 0 wickets

## For South Africa

| Season | Against | Venue | Tests | Inns | NO | Runs | HS | Ave | 100 | 50 | Cts |
|---|---|---|---|---|---|---|---|---|---|---|---|
| 1991/92 | West Indies | West Indies | 1 | 2 | 0 | 133 | 74 | 66.50 | 0 | 2 | 1 |
| 1992/93 | India | South Africa | 4 | 8 | 1 | 295 | 118 | 42.14 | 1 | 1 | 5 |
| 1993/94 | Sri Lanka | Sri Lanka | 3 | 5 | 0 | 188 | 92 | 37.60 | 0 | 1 | 1 |
| 1993/94 | Australia | Australia | 2 | 3 | 1 | 84 | 63* | 42.00 | 0 | 1 | 0 |
| Total | | | 10 | 18 | 2 | 700 | 118 | 43.75 | 1 | 5 | 7 |

**Highest Score:** 118 v India (Durban) 1992/93

| All Test matches | | | 34 | 60 | 3 | 2 461 | 179 | 43.18 | 5 | 14 | 25 |

# First Class Record, Season by Season

| Season | Venue | For | M | Inns | NO | Runs | HS | Ave | 100 | 50 | Cts |
|---|---|---|---|---|---|---|---|---|---|---|---|
| 1973/74 | South Africa | Orange Free State | 2 | 3 | 0 | 109 | 66 | 36.33 | 0 | 1 | 0 |
| 1974/75 | South Africa | Orange Free State | 5 | 9 | 3 | 327 | 86* | 54.50 | 0 | 2 | 3 |
| 1975/76 | South Africa | Orange Free State/President's XI | 6 | 11 | 2 | 448 | 88* | 49.78 | 0 | 4 | 4 |
| 1976 | England | Sussex | 2 | 4 | 1 | 181 | 60 | 60.33 | 0 | 2 | 0 |
| 1976/77 | South Africa | Western Province | 8 | 15 | 1 | 511 | 136 | 36.50 | 1 | 2 | 8 |
| 1977 | England | Sussex | 11 | 17 | 3 | 663 | 138* | 47.36 | 2 | 4 | 2 |
| 1977/78 | South Africa | Northern Transvaal | 6 | 10 | 1 | 363 | 146 | 40.33 | 1 | 1 | 4 |
| 1978 | England | Sussex | 4 | 8 | 0 | 123 | 29 | 15.38 | 0 | 0 | 6 |
| 1979 | England | Sussex | 21 | 36 | 2 | 1 800 | 187 | 52.94 | 6 | 11 | 21 |
| 1979/80 | Australia | Queensland | 10 | 18 | 1 | 623 | 93 | 36.65 | 0 | 6 | 2 |
| 1980 | England | Sussex | 15 | 29 | 5 | 1 562 | 254 | 65.08 | 2 | 11 | 13 |
| 1980/81 | Australia | Queensland | 10 | 17 | 1 | 814 | 160 | 50.88 | 2 | 3 | 8 |
| 1981/82 | Australia | Queensland | 11 | 18 | 0 | 1 094 | 220 | 60.78 | 5 | 3 | 6 |
| 1982/83 | Australia | Queensland/Australia | 12 | 23 | 0 | 1 325 | 249 | 57.61 | 5 | 3 | 14 |
| 1982/83 | Sri Lanka | Australia | 2 | 3 | 0 | 199 | 141 | 66.33 | 1 | 0 | 1 |
| 1983/84 | Australia | Queensland/Australia | 10 | 16 | 1 | 733 | 179 | 48.87 | 3 | 2 | 6 |
| 1983/84 | West Indies | Australia | 4 | 7 | 1 | 333 | 126* | 55.50 | 1 | 2 | 3 |
| 1984/85 | Australia | Queensland/Australia | 11 | 19 | 0 | 1 020 | 173 | 53.68 | 3 | 6 | 4 |
| 1985 | England | Australia | 16 | 26 | 1 | 905 | 156 | 36.20 | 1 | 8 | 9 |
| 1985/86 | Australia | Queensland/Australia | 13 | 22 | 1 | 1 030 | 167 | 49.05 | 3 | 4 | 13 |
| 1986/87 | South Africa | Eastern Province/Australian XI | 12 | 20 | 2 | 1 160 | 137 | 64.44 | 5 | 4 | 14 |
| 1987/88 | South Africa | Eastern Province | 8 | 12 | 1 | 504 | 130 | 45.82 | 2 | 1 | 8 |
| 1988/89 | South Africa | Eastern Province | 10 | 15 | 1 | 806 | 146 | 57.57 | 2 | 5 | 12 |
| 1989/90 | South Africa | Eastern Province | 11 | 21 | 3 | 610 | 182 | 33.89 | 1 | 2 | 14 |
| 1990/91 | South Africa | Eastern Province | 11 | 21 | 2 | 871 | 197 | 45.84 | 2 | 5 | 11 |
| 1991/92 | South Africa | Eastern Province | 5 | 8 | 2 | 795 | 212 | 132.50 | 4 | 2 | 7 |
| 1991/92 | West Indies | South Africa | 1 | 2 | 0 | 133 | 74 | 66.50 | 0 | 2 | 1 |
| 1992/93 | South Africa | Eastern Province/South Africa | 10 | 17 | 2 | 832 | 118 | 55.47 | 2 | 6 | 11 |
| 1993/94 | Sri Lanka | South Africa | 5 | 8 | 0 | 298 | 92 | 37.25 | 0 | 2 | 2 |
| 1993/94 | South Africa | Eastern Province | 2 | 2 | 0 | 99 | 58 | 49.50 | 0 | 1 | 2 |
| 1993/94 | Australia | South Africa | 4 | 7 | 1 | 164 | 63* | 27.33 | 0 | 1 | 1 |
| **Total** | | | 258 | 444 | 38 | 20 435 | 254 | 50.33 | 54 | 106 | 210 |

**Highest Score:**　254 Sussex v Middlesex (Hove) 1980

**Bowling:**　1 374 balls, 549 runs, 12 wickets, Ave 45.75
BB 2-25 Queensland v New South Wales (Sydney) 1985/86

# First Class Record, Team by Team

**Teams played for**

## South African Teams

|  | Seasons | M | Inns | NO | Runs | HS | Ave | 100 | 50 | Cts |
|---|---|---|---|---|---|---|---|---|---|---|
| South Africa | 1991/92 — 1993/94 | 15 | 27 | 2 | 893 | 118 | 35.72 | 1 | 6 | 10 |
| Orange Free State | 1973/74 — 1975/76 | 12 | 21 | 4 | 777 | 86* | 45.71 | 0 | 6 | 6 |
| Western Province | 1976/77 | 8 | 15 | 1 | 511 | 136 | 36.50 | 1 | 2 | 8 |
| Northern Transvaal | 1977/78 | 6 | 10 | 1 | 363 | 146 | 40.33 | 1 | 1 | 4 |
| Eastern Province | 1986/87 — 1993/94 | 58 | 97 | 11 | 4 838 | 212 | 56.26 | 14 | 24 | 69 |
| President's XI | 1975/76 | 1 | 2 | 1 | 107 | 88* | 107.00 | 0 | 1 | 1 |

## English Teams

|  | Seasons | M | Inns | NO | Runs | HS | Ave | 100 | 50 | Cts |
|---|---|---|---|---|---|---|---|---|---|---|
| Sussex | 1976 — 1980 | 53 | 94 | 11 | 4 329 | 254 | 52.16 | 10 | 28 | 42 |

## Australian Teams

|  | Seasons | M | Inns | NO | Runs | HS | Ave | 100 | 50 | Cts |
|---|---|---|---|---|---|---|---|---|---|---|
| Queensland | 1979/80 — 1985/86 | 63 | 109 | 3 | 5 492 | 249 | 51.81 | 18 | 22 | 40 |
| Australia | 1982/83 — 1985/86 | 36 | 60 | 3 | 2 584 | 179 | 45.33 | 6 | 15 | 26 |
| Australian XI (in SA) | 1986/87 | 6 | 9 | 1 | 541 | 137 | 67.63 | 3 | 1 | 4 |

# First Class Record, Ground by Ground

## English Grounds

| | M | Inns | NO | Runs | HS | Ave | 100 | 50 | Cts |
|---|---|---|---|---|---|---|---|---|---|
| Birmingham | 1 | 2 | 0 | 93 | 83 | 46.50 | 0 | 1 | 0 |
| Eastbourne | 3 | 5 | 1 | 547 | 197* | 136.75 | 3 | 1 | 0 |
| Hove | 21 | 37 | 6 | 2 002 | 254 | 64.58 | 4 | 15 | 11 |
| Leeds | 1 | 2 | 0 | 100 | 64 | 50.00 | 0 | 1 | 0 |
| Lord's | 5 | 8 | 0 | 256 | 60 | 32.00 | 0 | 3 | 4 |
| Manchester | 1 | 2 | 0 | 84 | 50 | 42.00 | 0 | 1 | 0 |
| Nottingham | 2 | 3 | 0 | 140 | 100 | 46.67 | 1 | 0 | 2 |
| The Oval | 3 | 5 | 0 | 53 | 19 | 10.60 | 0 | 0 | 2 |

## Australian Grounds

| | M | Inns | NO | Runs | HS | Ave | 100 | 50 | Cts |
|---|---|---|---|---|---|---|---|---|---|
| Adelaide | 7 | 14 | 1 | 693 | 179 | 53.31 | 2 | 4 | 6 |
| Brisbane | 37 | 63 | 1 | 2 929 | 168 | 47.24 | 9 | 13 | 28 |
| Melbourne | 7 | 12 | 1 | 315 | 90 | 28.64 | 0 | 2 | 4 |
| Perth | 9 | 15 | 0 | 594 | 128 | 39.60 | 2 | 3 | 3 |
| Sydney | 10 | 17 | 1 | 948 | 173 | 59.25 | 3 | 3 | 8 |

## South African Grounds

| | M | Inns | NO | Runs | HS | Ave | 100 | 50 | Cts |
|---|---|---|---|---|---|---|---|---|---|
| Bloemfontein (Ramblers) | 7 | 12 | 2 | 487 | 78 | 48.70 | 0 | 4 | 4 |
| Bloemfontein (Springbok Park) | 3 | 6 | 0 | 158 | 56 | 26.33 | 0 | 2 | 2 |
| Bloemfontein (University Oval) | 2 | 3 | 0 | 273 | 130 | 91.00 | 2 | 0 | 1 |
| Cape Town | 10 | 18 | 0 | 850 | 146 | 47.22 | 3 | 2 | 6 |
| Durban | 6 | 10 | 0 | 418 | 118 | 41.80 | 1 | 2 | 4 |
| East London (Buffalo Park) | 3 | 5 | 1 | 292 | 146 | 73.00 | 1 | 1 | 3 |
| East London (Jan Smuts) | 4 | 6 | 2 | 272 | 137 | 68.00 | 1 | 2 | 5 |
| Johannesburg | 9 | 16 | 0 | 329 | 60 | 20.56 | 0 | 2 | 12 |
| Kimberley | 4 | 7 | 1 | 313 | 74* | 52.17 | 0 | 3 | 3 |
| Port Elizabeth | 33 | 54 | 8 | 2 829 | 197 | 61.50 | 10 | 12 | 43 |
| Pietermaritzburg (Jan Smuts) | 2 | 3 | 0 | 65 | 34 | 21.67 | 0 | 0 | 2 |
| Pretoria | 4 | 7 | 2 | 230 | 86* | 46.00 | 0 | 1 | 3 |
| Verwoerdburg | 2 | 4 | 2 | 79 | 29 | 39.50 | 0 | 0 | 2 |

## First Class Record, Competition by Competition

|  | M | Inns | NO | Runs | HS | Ave | 100 | 50 | Cts |
|---|---|---|---|---|---|---|---|---|---|
| Tests | 34 | 60 | 3 | 2 461 | 179 | 43.18 | 5 | 14 | 25 |
| Currie/Castle Cup ('A Section') | 57 | 96 | 9 | 4 125 | 197 | 47.41 | 12 | 18 | 64 |
| Castle Bowl ('B Section') | 18 | 31 | 5 | 1 140 | 146 | 43.85 | 1 | 7 | 10 |
| All Currie Cup/Castle Cup | 75 | 127 | 14 | 5 265 | 197 | 46.59 | 13 | 25 | 74 |
| County Championship | 47 | 85 | 9 | 3 943 | 254 | 51.88 | 9 | 25 | 37 |
| Sheffield Shield | 53 | 91 | 3 | 4 779 | 249 | 54.31 | 15 | 19 | 36 |
| Unofficial Tests | 5 | 9 | 1 | 330 | 135 | 41.25 | 2 | 0 | 3 |
| Other First Class | 44 | 72 | 8 | 3 657 | 212 | 57.14 | 10 | 23 | 35 |

## First Class Record, as Captain and as Player

|  | M | Inns | NO | Runs | HS | Ave | 100 | 50 | Cts |
|---|---|---|---|---|---|---|---|---|---|
| **As Captain** | 80 | 135 | 13 | 6 446 | 212 | 52.84 | 18 | 31 | 81 |
| **As Player** | 178 | 309 | 25 | 13 989 | 254 | 49.26 | 36 | 75 | 129 |
| **World Series 'Super Tests' 1978/79** (these matches were not first class) | 4 | 88 | 1 | 291 | 126 | 41.57 | 1 | 0 | 5 |

# First class Hundreds

| Season | | For | Against | Venue |
|---|---|---|---|---|
| 1976/77 | 136 | Western Province | Rhodesia | Cape Town |
| 1977 | 109* | Sussex | Cambridge University | Cambridge |
| | 138* | Sussex | Kent | Tunbridge Wells |
| 1977/78 | 146 | Northern Transvaal | Western Province B | Cape Town |
| 1979 | 113 | Sussex | Derbyshire | Hove |
| | 100 | Sussex | Nottinghamshire | Nottingham |
| | 136 | Sussex | Surrey | Hove |
| | 101 | Sussex | Glamorgan | Eastbourne |
| | 187 | Sussex | Kent | Eastbourne |
| | 146 | Sussex | Somerset | Hove |
| 1980 | 197* | Sussex | Nottinghamshire | Eastbourne |
| | 254 | Sussex | Middlesex | Hove |
| 1980/81 | 134 | Queensland | Victoria | Brisbane |
| | 160 | Queensland | New South Wales | Sydney |
| 1981/82 | 168 | Queensland | Victoria | Brisbane |
| | 103 | Queensland | New South Wales | Newcastle |
| | 106 | Queensland | New South Wales | Brisbane |
| | 173 | Queensland | Victoria | Geelong |
| | 220 | Queensland | Tasmania | Devonport |
| 1982/83 | 103 | Queensland | England XI | Brisbane |
| | 162 | Australia | England | Brisbane |
| | 128 | Queensland | Western Australia | Perth |
| | 129 | Queensland | New Zealand XI | Bundaberg |
| | 249 | Queensland | Victoria | St Kilda |
| | 141 | Australia | Sri Lanka | Kandy |
| 1983/84 | 127 | Queensland | Pakistan XI | Brisbane |
| | 104 | Queensland | South Australia | Brisbane |

# First Class Hundreds (continued)

| Season | | For | Against | Venue |
|---|---|---|---|---|
| 1983/84 (continued) | 179 | Australia | Pakistan | Adelaide |
| | 126 retd hurt | Australia | Leeward Islands | Basseterre |
| 1984/85 | 144 | Queensland | South Australia | Brisbane |
| | 137 | Queensland | Western Australia | Perth |
| | 173 | Australia | West Indies | Sydney |
| 1985 | 156 | Australia | Somerset | Taunton |
| 1985/86 | 107 | Queensland | South Australia | Adelaide |
| | 167 | Queensland | Tasmania | Brisbane |
| | 166 | Queensland | New South Wales | Sydney |
| 1986/87 | 133 | Eastern Province | Orange Free State | Port Elizabeth |
| | 137 | Australia XI | Border | East London (Jan Smuts) |
| | 135 | Australia XI | South Africa | Port Elizabeth |
| | 105* | | | |
| | 129 | Eastern Province | Western Province | Port Elizabeth |
| 1987/88 | 101 | Eastern Province | Orange Free State | Bloemfontein (University Oval) |
| | 130 | | | |
| 1988/89 | 146 | Eastern Province | Border | East London (Buffalo Park) |
| | 108 | Eastern Province | Western Province | Cape Town |
| 1989/90 | 182 | Eastern Province | Northern Transvaal | Port Elizabeth |
| 1990/91 | 197 | Eastern Province | Northern Transvaal | Port Elizabeth |
| | 107 | Eastern Province | Western Province | Port Elizabeth |
| 1991/92 | 168 | Eastern Province | Boland | Worcester |
| | 212 | Eastern Province | Griqualand West | Cradock |
| | 115 | Eastern Province | Orange Free State | Port Elizabeth |
| | 147* | | | |
| 1992/93 | 108 | Eastern Province | Natal | Port Elizabeth |
| | 118 | South Africa | India | Durban |

# Limited Overs Internationals

## For Australia

| Season | Competition/Opponents | Venue | M | Inns | NO | Runs | HS | Ave | 100 | 50 | Cts |
|---|---|---|---|---|---|---|---|---|---|---|---|
| 1982/83 | B & H World Series Cup | Australia | 8 | 8 | 1 | 249 | 79 | 35.57 | 0 | 3 | 3 |
| 1982/83 | Sri Lanka | Sri Lanka | 3 | 3 | 0 | 88 | 43 | 29.33 | 0 | 0 | 0 |
| 1983 | World Cup | England | 3 | 3 | 0 | 92 | 76 | 30.67 | 0 | 1 | 1 |
| 1983/84 | B & H World Series Cup | Australia | 13 | 13 | 1 | 495 | 92 | 41.25 | 0 | 6 | 7 |
| 1983/84 | West Indies | West Indies | 2 | 2 | 0 | 111 | 67 | 55.50 | 0 | 1 | 0 |
| 1984/85 | India | India | 5 | 4 | 1 | 196 | 107 | 65.33 | 1 | 0 | 0 |
| 1984/85 | B & H World Series Cup | Australia | 13 | 11 | 0 | 312 | 82 | 28.36 | 0 | 2 | 7 |
| 1984/85 | World Championship of Cricket | Australia | 3 | 3 | 0 | 55 | 39 | 18.33 | 0 | 0 | 0 |
| 1984/85 | Rothmans Cup | Sharjah | 2 | 2 | 0 | 46 | 30 | 23.00 | 0 | 0 | 1 |
| 1985 | England | England | 2 | 2 | 0 | 96 | 57 | 48.00 | 0 | 1 | 0 |
| **Total** | | | 54 | 51 | 3 | 1 740 | 107 | 36.25 | 1 | 14 | 19 |

**Highest Score:** 107 v India (Delhi) 1984/85

**Bowling:** 737 balls, 655 runs, 18 wickets, Ave 36.39, RpO 5.33 BB2-16 v Sri Lanka (Adelaide) 1984/85

## For South Africa

| Season | Competition/Opponents | Venue | M | Inns | NO | Runs | HS | Ave | 100 | 50 | Cts |
|---|---|---|---|---|---|---|---|---|---|---|---|
| 1991/92 | India | India | 3 | 3 | 0 | 211 | 90 | 70.33 | 0 | 3 | 0 |
| 1991/92 | World Cup | Aus/NZ | 9 | 9 | 2 | 313 | 85 | 44.71 | 0 | 3 | 7 |
| 1991/92 | West Indies | West Indies | 3 | 3 | 0 | 54 | 45 | 18.00 | 0 | 0 | 4 |
| 1992/93 | India | South Africa | 7 | 7 | 0 | 342 | 78 | 48.86 | 0 | 3 | 1 |
| 1992/93 | Total Triangular Series | South Africa | 6 | 6 | 0 | 166 | 49 | 27.67 | 0 | 0 | 5 |
| 1993/94 | Sri Lanka | Sri Lanka | 3 | 3 | 1 | 48 | 28 | 16.00 | 0 | 0 | 0 |
| 1993/94 | Hero Cup | India | 5 | 5 | 1 | 72 | 53 | 18.00 | 0 | 1 | 1 |
| 1993/94 | B & H World Series Cup | Australia | 3 | 3 | 0 | 104 | 70 | 34.67 | 0 | 1 | 1 |
| **Total** | | | 39 | 39 | 3 | 1 310 | 90 | 36.39 | 0 | 11 | 19 |

**Highest Score:** 90 v India (Delhi) 1991/92

**Bowling:** 12 balls, 11 runs, 0 wickets, RpO 5.50

## All Limited Overs Internationals

| | M | Inns | NO | Runs | HS | Ave | 100 | 50 | Cts |
|---|---|---|---|---|---|---|---|---|---|
| | 93 | 90 | 6 | 3 050 | 107 | 36.31 | 1 | 25 | 38 |

**Bowling:** 749 balls, 666 runs, 18 wickets, Ave 37.00, RpO 5.34, BB2-16 v Sri Lanka (Adelaide) 1984/85

# Limited Overs Record in South Africa

## Gillette Cup/Datsun Shield/Nissan Shield/Total Power Series

| Season | For | M | Inns | NO | Runs | HS | Ave | 100 | 50 | Cts |
|---|---|---|---|---|---|---|---|---|---|---|
| 1974/75 | Orange Free State | 1 | 1 | 0 | 15 | 15 | 15.00 | 0 | 0 | 0 |
| 1975/76 | Orange Free State | 1 | 1 | 0 | 38 | 38 | 38.00 | 0 | 0 | 0 |
| 1976/77 | Western Province | 2 | 2 | 0 | 71 | 41 | 35.50 | 0 | 0 | 0 |
| 1977/78 | Northern Transvaal | 1 | 1 | 0 | 5 | 5 | 5.00 | 0 | 0 | 0 |
| 1986/87 | Eastern Province | 6 | 6 | 0 | 243 | 55 | 40.50 | 0 | 1 | 5 |
| 1987/88 | Eastern Province | 6 | 6 | 0 | 252 | 98 | 42.00 | 0 | 2 | 6 |
| 1988/89 | Eastern Province | 4 | 4 | 0 | 82 | 49 | 20.50 | 0 | 0 | 1 |
| 1989/90 | Eastern Province | 8 | 8 | 2 | 345 | 101* | 57.50 | 1 | 2 | 3 |
| 1990/91 | Eastern Province | 7 | 7 | 0 | 411 | 146 | 58.71 | 2 | 1 | 5 |
| 1991/92 | Eastern Province | 6 | 6 | 0 | 135 | 57 | 22.50 | 0 | 1 | 3 |
| 1992/93 | Eastern Province | 5 | 5 | 2 | 326 | 127* | 108.67 | 2 | 0 | 1 |
| **Total** | | 47 | 47 | 4 | 1 923 | 146 | 44.72 | 5 | 7 | 24 |

**Highest Score:** 146 Eastern Province v Border (Port Elizabeth) 1990/91

**Bowling:** 169 balls, 145 runs, 5 wickets, Ave 29.00, RpO 5.15, BB 3-27 EP v Southern Cape (Oudtshoorn) 1989/90

## Benson & Hedges Night Series

| Season | For | M | Inns | NO | Runs | HS | Ave | 100 | 50 | Cts |
|---|---|---|---|---|---|---|---|---|---|---|
| 1986/87 | Eastern Province | 5 | 5 | 0 | 208 | 87 | 41.60 | 0 | 2 | 7 |
| 1987/88 | Eastern Province | 9 | 9 | 1 | 256 | 81* | 32.00 | 0 | 2 | 5 |
| 1988/89 | Eastern Province | 6 | 6 | 0 | 167 | 69 | 27.83 | 0 | 1 | 2 |
| 1989/90 | Eastern Province | 10 | 10 | 1 | 485 | 100* | 53.89 | 1 | 4 | 4 |
| 1990/91 | Eastern Province | 10 | 10 | 1 | 478 | 109* | 53.11 | 1 | 4 | 2 |
| 1991/92 | Eastern Province | 5 | 5 | 1 | 294 | 103 | 73.50 | 1 | 1 | 4 |
| 1992/93 | Eastern Province | 10 | 10 | 3 | 513 | 122* | 73.29 | 1 | 4 | 4 |
| 1993/94 | Eastern Province | 2 | 2 | 0 | 68 | 47 | 34.00 | 0 | 0 | 0 |
| **Total** | | 57 | 57 | 7 | 2 469 | 122* | 49.38 | 4 | 18 | 28 |

**Highest Score:** 122* Eastern Province v Transvaal (Johannesburg) 1992/93

**Bowling:** 79 balls, 69 runs, 2 wickets, Ave 34.50, RpO 5.24, BB 2-40 EP v Natal (Pietermaritzburg) 1986/87

## Unofficial Limited Overs Internationals

| Season | For | M | Inns | NO | Runs | HS | Ave | 100 | 50 | Cts |
|---|---|---|---|---|---|---|---|---|---|---|
| 1986/87 | Australian XI v South Africa | 8 | 8 | 1 | 326 | 122 | 46.57 | 1 | 1 | 1 |

**Highest Score:** 122 (Port Elizabeth)

**Bowling:** 96 balls, 84 runs, 2 wickets, Ave 42.00, RpO 5.25, BB 2-32 (Verwoerdburg)

# Limited Overs Record in England

## Gillette Cup

|  | M | Inns | NO | Runs | HS | Ave | 100 | 50 | Cts |
|---|---|---|---|---|---|---|---|---|---|
| Total | 5 | 5 | 0 | 106 | 43 | 21.20 | 0 | 0 | 5 |

## Benson & Hedges Cup

|  | M | Inns | NO | Runs | HS | Ave | 100 | 50 | Cts |
|---|---|---|---|---|---|---|---|---|---|
| Total | 13 | 13 | 1 | 593 | 106 | 49.42 | 2 | 4 | 6 |

## John Player Sunday League

|  | M | Inns | NO | Runs | HS | Ave | 100 | 50 | Cts |
|---|---|---|---|---|---|---|---|---|---|
| Total | 22 | 22 | 0 | 712 | 88 | 32.36 | 0 | 6 | 5 |

# Overall Record as Captain

## First Class

|  |  | Played | Won | Lost | Drawn |
|---|---|---|---|---|---|
| South Africa | Tests | 10 | 3 | 1 | 6 |
|  | Other FC | 4 | 1 | 1 | 2 |
|  | Total | 14 | 4 | 2 | 8 |
| Eastern Province |  | 58 | 21 | 10 | 27 |
| Queensland |  | 8 | 1 | 0 | 7 |
| Total |  | 80 | 26 | 12 | 42 |

## Limited Overs Internationals

|  | Played | Won | Lost | No Result |
|---|---|---|---|---|
| South Africa | 36 | 16 | 18 | 2 |

# Index

Cowley, Gavin 144
Craven, Dr Danie 7, 31, 159
Croft, Colin 49, 125
Cronje, Ewie 13
Cronje, Hansie 19, 204, 212, 213, 216,
    222, 232, 242, 244, 247-249, 252-254,
    258-260, 274, 277, 280, 281, 283, 287,
    289, 290, 298, 301, 303, 307, 308, 310,
    311, 313-322, 325
Cullinan, Daryll 254, 259, 277, 280, 281,
    289, 290, 296, 298, 300, 303, 309, 311,
    312, 314
Cummins, Anderson 229
Curren, Kevin 32

Dakin, Geoff 146, 165, 167, 168, 174,
    182, 185, 187, 195, 199, 219
Dalmiya, Jagmohan 183
Daniel, Wayne 34, 47, 58, 59, 91
Davie, Michael 45
Davis, Ian 45
Davis, Winston 91
De Freitas, Phil 168, 169
De Klerk, F.W. 177, 201, 206, 219, 259,
    260
De Mel, Asantha 83
Denning, Lorraine 55, 69
Denning, Ron 55, 69
De Silva, Aravinda 280, 290
Dev, Kapil 186, 216, 236, 239, 244, 246-
    248, 251, 253, 254, 256, 262
De Villiers, Dawie 56
De Villiers, Fanie 245, 249, 257, 277, 279,
    288, 303, 304, 311-313, 315-319
Dexter, Ted 34
Dilley, Graham 169
D'Oliveira, Basil 27
Donald, Allan 133, 184, 186, 189, 202-
    204, 208, 217, 218, 220, 231, 232, 235,
    241, 244, 250, 251, 253, 257, 262, 279,
    280, 284, 287, 291, 299, 303, 306, 307,
    311-313, 315-318, 325
Drummond, Rob 29
Dujon, Jeff 91, 96, 97, 99
Du Plessis, Carel 126, 129
Du Plessis, Morné 31, 286
Du Toit, Jackie 10

Dymock, Geoff 68
Dyson, John 71-73, 97, 105, 132, 134, 138

Edmonds, Phil 25
Eksteen, Clive 156, 158, 184, 277, 279-
    281, 287
Elizabeth II 113
Emburey, John 116, 169, 175

Fairbrother, Neil 215, 221
Faulkner, Peter 139
Ferreira, Anton 33, 37, 55, 267, 268
Foster, Neil 169
Fotheringham, Henry 28, 132, 155, 158
Foulkes, Ivor 14
Fowler, Graeme 72
Francis, Bruce 41, 105, 119, 131
Fraser, Malcolm 77, 78, 101
Frost, David 206

Gaika, Pindile 267
Gandhi, Mahatma 238
Garner, Joel 46, 49, 91, 93, 96-99, 106
Gatting, Mike 59, 167-169, 175, 177, 181,
    215
Gavaskar, Sunil 179
Gerber, Danie 129
Gilmour, Gary 25, 26
Gomes, Larry 91, 96, 99
Gooch, Graham 112, 116, 124, 215, 220-
    223
Gower, David 72, 73, 113, 115, 116, 240,
    326
Graveney, David 169
Greatbatch, Mark 207
Greenidge, Gordon 91, 93
Greig, Tony 33-36, 39, 41, 43, 47, 48, 50,
    56, 62, 79, 89, 109, 240, 301
Grey, Sir George 16
Griffith, Charlie 96
Griffiths, Keith 237
Groome, Jerry 56
Grové, Kotie 144-147, 150-152, 159-161,
    165, 266, 273

Hadlee, Sir Richard 109, 117, 118, 179
Hall, Wes 96, 179

Raman, Woorkeri 248, 253
Ramsamy, Sam 127, 178
Rana, Shakoor 168
Ranatunga, Arjuna 83, 208, 280, 290
Randall, Derek 72
Reddy, S.K. 194
Reeve, Dermot 221
Reid, Bruce 205, 206
Reid, John 281
Reid, Terry 148
Rhodes, Jonty 203, 205, 208, 210-214,
   222, 225, 226, 235, 241, 242, 248, 252,
   254, 258, 259, 274, 277, 281, 284, 290,
   296-298, 300, 302, 305, 308, 309, 311,
   314, 315, 325
Rice, Clive 28, 29, 33, 48-50, 55, 129, 132,
   137-139, 143, 150, 151, 154-158, 172-
   176, 184-197, 201, 206, 207, 226, 290,
   321
Rice, Mark 184
Richards, Barry 27, 33, 48, 50, 70, 125,
   137, 206, 240, 326
Richards, David 69, 107, 113, 122
Richards, Vivian 51, 89, 99, 100, 229, 326
Richardson, David 133, 147, 153-155,
   184, 204, 222-224, 232, 243, 251-253,
   268, 277, 281, 285, 289, 298, 311, 314,
   315
Richardson, Richie 91, 210, 229, 231, 259
Ritchie, Greg 68, 303, 311
Rixon, Steve 136, 139
Roberts, Andy 46, 49, 314
Robins, Derrick 28
Robinson, Peter 212
Robinson, Tim 115, 169
Roos, Jan 266
Rowe, Lawrence 125
Rudman, Cyril 11
Rule, Kevin 158
Rushmere, Colin 146, 150, 162
Rushmere, Mark 148, 152, 153, 155, 156,
   162, 163, 173, 198, 229, 231

Schmidt, Uli 129
Schuller, Louis 64, 310
Schultz Brett 160, 238, 241, 250, 278-280,
   287, 291, 299

Schultz, Neil 148
Scindia, Madhavrao 187
Shakespeare, William 113
Shastri, Ravi 188, 236, 253
Shaw, Tim 153, 155-158, 184
Slabbert, Van Zyl 206
Slater, Michael 306, 309, 312, 315
Small, Gladstone 222
Smith, Chris 23, 33
Smith, Robin 33, 172, 215
Smith, Steve 132, 138, 141
Smith, Wilbur 295
Snell, Richard 184, 198, 202-204, 217,
   218, 225, 230-232, 278, 284, 287, 318
Sobers, Sir Gary 179, 326
Stephenson, Franklyn 125
Stewart, Alec 215, 221
Stewart, Errol 317
Stewart, Mickey 223
Stewart, Reg 7
Strydom, Thinus 269
Sturgess, Eric 11
Sullivan, Phil 41
Swart, Peter 30
Sylvester, Lou 10
Symcox, Pat 278, 280, 281, 287, 289, 311,
   312

Tavare, Chris 72
Taylor, Bob 72, 74
Taylor, Lynton 41
Taylor, Mark 306, 307, 309, 311, 315
Taylor, Mick 134
Taylor, Peter 205
Tendulkar, Sachin 186, 236, 239, 241,
   243, 253, 254
Teresa, Mother 186
Thomas, Greg 153, 155, 157, 158, 160,
   169
Thompson, Hector 268
Thomson, Jeff 45, 69, 72, 75, 76, 83, 90,
   91, 121, 303
Tillekeratne, Hashan 280
Titmus, Fred 22
Trimble, Glen 120
Trist, David 147, 150
Tshabalala, Ginger 269

Tshwete, Steve 180, 181, 206
Tufnell, Philip 288

Underwood, Derek 25, 35, 49, 124
Ul-Haq, Inzamam 212, 213

Van der Bijl, Vintcent 27, 28, 30, 33, 59, 261
Van der Merwe, Peter 146, 162, 163, 166, 174-176, 182-184, 192-197, 236
Van Zyl, Corrie 133, 228
Veenstra, Ross 160
Venter, Mark 158
Viljoen, Gerrit 170
Vlok, Adriaan 170, 171
Volsteedt, A.K. 2, 7, 15
Volsteedt, Johan 2, 9, 13-17, 19, 22, 44, 175, 252
Vorster, John 27

Walcott, Sir Clyde 179, 227
Walsh, Courtney 97, 98, 211, 230-232, 257, 259, 314
Warne, Shane 299, 300, 307, 308, 311, 312, 314, 317
Watson, Arthur 68
Watson, Kenny 148
Waugh, Mark 121, 297, 309, 311, 317
Waugh, Steve 300, 309

Wellham, Dirk 109-111, 121
Wessels, Marguerite 3, 4, 8, 17, 32, 33, 44, 100, 274
Wessels, Marietta 2, 3, 4, 274
Wessels, Rebecca 263, 271, 272
Wessels, Riki 122, 124, 146, 263, 264, 271, 272
Wessels (Denning), Sally 54-58, 60, 63, 65, 69, 70, 72, 74, 100, 120, 122, 123, 124, 145, 165, 176, 263, 272-274, 276
Wessels, Tewie 3, 4, 6-9, 11, 31, 33, 39, 44, 184, 274
Wessels, Wessel 4, 6, 7, 9, 17, 18, 176, 274
Westner, Wayne 276
Whitney, Mike 205
Wilde, Oscar 258
Williams, Ray 212
Willis, Bob 72, 76
Wilson, A.A. 75
Wood, Graeme 71, 72, 94, 98, 109-111
Woolmer, Bob 250, 303
Worrell, Frank 91

Yachad, Mandy 184
Yallop, Graham 52, 87, 95, 105, 129, 132, 140
Yardley, Bruce 72, 74
Younis, Waqar 257, 258, 260